THE VIRTUAL CLASSROOM
Learning Without Limits
via Computer Networks

HUMAN/COMPUTER INTERACTION
A Series of Monographs, Edited Volumes, and Texts

Series Editor
Ben Shneiderman

THE VIRTUAL CLASSROOM
Learning Without Limits
via Computer Networks

Starr Roxanne Hiltz

ABLEX PUBLISHING CORPORATION
Norwood, New Jersey

Second Printing 1995

Printed in the United States of America.

Library of Congress Cataloging-in-Publication Data

Hiltz, Starr Roxanne.
  The virtual classroom : Learning without limits via computer
networks / Starr Roxanne Hiltz.
    p. cm. – (Human/computer interaction)
  Includes bibliographical references (p.   ) and index.
  ISBN 0-89391-928-4 (cl); 1-56750-055-2 (ppb)
  1. Distance education–United States–Computer-assisted
instruction. 2. University extension–United States–Data
processing. I. Title. II. Series: Human/computer interaction
(Norwood, N.J.).
  LC5803.C65H55   1993
  371.3'34–dc20   93-13573
                                                             CIP

Ablex Publishing Corporation
355 Chestnut St.
Norwood, NJ 07648

DEDICATION

In memory of my dear friends and colleagues, who cared passionately about teaching, and who are greatly missed:

Robert Wharton, 1926–1985

Rhoda Golden Freeman, 1927–1986

Glenn Halvorson, 1935–1987

Miriam Mills, 1938–1992

Sylvia Kendrick ("Kendy") MacColl Rudy, 1940–1993

CONTENTS

PART IV: VIRTUAL CLASSROOMS AND
VIRTUAL UNIVERSITIES:
PRESENT AND FUTURE

APPENDICES

LIST OF TABLES

PREFACE AND ACKNOWLEDGMENTS

> It was the best of times, it was the worst of times, it was the age of wisdom, it was the age of foolishness . . . it was the spring of hope, it was the winter of despair, we had everything before us, we had nothing before us . . .
>
> Charles Dickens, *A Tale of Two Cities*

There is no longer any question that computers will increasingly pervade our everyday lives. They have moved out of the office and into our homes, and even our appliances, and some of our bodies. In my neighborhood, five year olds play with "Speak and Spells" and other computerized toys. Ten year olds are not only addicted to computer games, but many have their own personal computers. Adults find speech synthesis chips talking to them from their microwave ovens or automobiles, telling them how their dinner is doing or reminding them to buckle their seat belts. Communicating microprocessors are being implanted into human bodies to monitor and alter physiological states (Haggerty, 1981) or to help people to see, hear, or walk.

Yet many of the problems of contemporary society may be traced to technological innovations. The greenhouse effect, acid rain, polluted oceans, and "nuclear winter" would not threaten our future if we had not made the technological innovations which may bring them about.

Will the powerful new technological invention, "the personal computer," bring about "the best of times" or "the worst of times" when it is translated into *social inventions*? (actual systems applied to social processes; Whyte, 1980). Or does the computer's role in the emergence of a new "spring of hope" or "winter of despair" for postindustrial society depend upon the social context in which a system is implemented, and on the social choices that will be made for how to use computers in our everyday lives? I tend to be hopeful that computers can help us to understand and deal with the many problems facing human societies on this planet. One of the specific computer applications inspiring a new "spring of hope" for the future of human societies is the use of computer networks to extend educational opportunities and communications opportunities for people of all ages to learn about and discuss a variety of subjects and issues. "The Virtual Classroom"™ is my name for the social invention of building and operating computer-mediated communication systems to support dispersed communities of active learners, and I feel optimistic about its future in offering a new option for lifelong learning.

Many people who would like to attend college are unable to do so because they haven't the time or means to get to traditional classrooms on a traditional schedule. The person with a career outside the home, the person caring for small children, the disabled person – all of these individuals may find themselves shut out from furthering their education.

Other students find the traditional classroom boring or ineffective for them. For instance, they might like to play a more active role in discussions and projects applying the skills and ideas covered in the courses. They might want more control over, not only the pace at which material is covered, but also what topics are included in a course, and the relative amount of time they spend on them.

Many teachers are also sometimes frustrated by the limitations of teaching within the fixed bounds of a physical classroom and/or laboratory, and within the time limitations of set class periods and office hours. Especially on college campuses that have large classes and diverse students, most of whom are commuters busy juggling a schedule of work, classes, and perhaps family obligations, professors have trouble "reaching" the individual student. Seldom do the students come to office hours for individual attention, especially if they are commuters. Most teachers chose their occupation because they want to make a positive difference in their students' lives. They want to light the proverbial lamps to guide students along the path to knowledge, to "turn them on" to an academic subject area. All too often, when exam scores and course evaluation questionnaires are examined, the teacher feels like a failure. Rather than being perceived as a captain on an exciting voyage of discovery, the teacher is perceived as a drill sergeant putting the students through a series of irrelevant and unpleasant obstacles on their way to the college degree which the students feel they need in order to get a good job in the "real world." The teacher–student relationship is too often an adversarial struggle over grades and excuses for undone assignments, rather than a relationship based on mutual respect and caring.

Teachers "burn out," students "drop out" or "stop out." Both think, there has GOT to be a better way.

The Virtual Classroom™, an innovative program originating at the New Jersey Institute of Technology, brings the university into the homes and work places of students through the use of computers. Specially designed computer software electronically links the Virtual Classroom student to his or her professors and classmates. Using a microcomputer, a telephone, and a device called a modem, the student attends lectures, takes tests, receives feedback from professors, participates in discussions, and undertakes team projects with fellow students, and more. One obvious advantage is that the student need not adhere to a rigid schedule of class meetings. A not-so-obvious difference is that the computer-mediated environment can more easily support a collaborative learning process than can the traditional classroom: a process in which the students and the instructor(s) are actively involved in creating and carrying out learning activities, together.

The quantitative data in this book are based primarily on the full-scale field trials of Virtual Classroom software carried out using a prototype constructed on EIES (the Electronic Information Exchange System)™ during 1986–1987. However, the quantitative examples and conclusions are drawn from a decade of experiences. Before this formal field trial, we experimented with the use of computer conferences and messages to enhance the delivery of college-level courses, but "mixed" it with 25% to 75% of the usual face-to-face classes. Subsequently (1987–1992), we have been implementing the Virtual Classroom within much more "portable" computer environments, which are available for lease to other educational institutions. The Virtual Classroom on EIES 2™, works with UNIX-based operating systems, including machines manufactured by Hewlett Packard, DEC, and SUN. We also continued systematic exploration of the use of Virtual Classroom in combinations with other delivery modes . We have trademarked and copyrighted all our software, names, and publications to protect them from being claimed by others. In particular, the terms *EIES*, *TEIES*, *Personal TEIES*, and *Virtual Classroom* are registered trademarks of New Jersey Institute of Technology.

Much of this book is drawn from formal research reports and technical reports on the software produced at NJIT. Readers who want more details about the software and evaluation research may order the following reports from the Computerized Conferencing and Communications Center, NJIT, Newark, NJ, 07102:

Starr Roxanne Hiltz, *The Virtual Classroom: Building the Foundations*. Research Report 24, CCCC at NJIT, September 1986 ($10).

Starr Roxanne Hiltz, *Learning in a Virtual Classroom*, Research Report 25, CCCC at NJIT, 1988. ($15).

Starr Roxanne Hiltz, *Teaching in a Virtual Classroom*, Research Report 26, CCCC at NJIT, 1988 ($10).

Detailed specifications for the software appear separately:

Starr Roxanne Hiltz, *Branching Activities in Conferences: A Manual and Functional Specifications*. Technical Report 86-1, CCCC at NJIT, 1986 (Revised 1987) ($5).

B.J. Gleason, *Instructional Management Tools on EIES*. Technical Report 87-12, CCCC at NJIT, 1987. ($5).

John Foster, *Final Design Specifications for Personal TEIES 2.0: Text and Graphics Composition System and Personal Communications Manager*. Technical Report 87-15.2, CCCC at NJIT, 1987. ($5).

User Manual for Personal TEIES. ($15).

EIES 2 Users Guide. ($15).

However, the above research and technical reports are difficult to obtain and tedious to read. This book is aimed, first of all, at teachers and students who think that they might be interested in using this technology in their courses. Secondly, I hope to reach both scholars and the "general public" interested in the issues of future possible impacts of computers on society. Finally, the book should be of interest to scholars interested in new communication technologies and in issues of evaluation research related to computer, communication, and pedagogical innovations.

*****

My role as Principal Investigator for this project was something like that of an orchestra conductor. I had a vision of what the final product should be like. To achieve it, however, required the skill, hard work, and the cooperation of hundreds of people. The project described here is the evolving creation of many people working together. If I am the conductor, then four people can be said to have played key parts as "section leaders:" Ellen Lieberman-Schreihofer, Assistant Project Director for Research and Administration; John Foster, Assistant Project Director for Software Development; Steve Ehrmann, The Annenberg/CPB Project Officer, who has always been available for good and timely advice; and Ron Rice, who served as Chairperson of the Evaluation Panel and as a careful and helpful reviewer of this manuscript.

Murray Turoff consulted on software design and managed the systems analysts: Bob Czech, John Foster, Irina Galperin, B.J. Gleason, Tod Gordon, Heidi Harting, Tanmay Kumar, Kenneth Liang, Sal Johar, Steve

Muccione, Kenneth Ng, Srinivas Reddy, and James Whitescarver. Among those who contributed research and administrative support were Bob Arms, Judith Ennis, Kenneth Johnson, Tanmay Kumar, B.V. Sudarashan, Cindy Thomas, and Eivind Kristiansen. George Baldwin volunteered his help in conducting intensive interviews with a small number of students. The offices of the Registrar and Public Relations at NJIT and Upsala College were particularly cooperative in contributing their time to the project. Kent Norman made many excellent suggestions on improving this manuscript.

Faculty members who developed and offered online courses or portions of courses and who endured the extensive demands of the evaluation procedures included Lincoln Brown, Roseann Dios, B.J. Gleason, Glenn Halvorson, Linda Harasim, Enrico Hsu, Robert Meinke, Sylvia K. Rudy, and Mary Swigonski. The full Advisory Board is listed in the Appendix, including identification of those who took on the arduous duty of serving on the Evaluation Panel; they have made many valuable suggestions which helped a great deal in setting the priorities for the project.

Among those who have contributed funds, equipment or other resources are the Annenberg/CPB Project of the Corporation for Public Broadcasting, the New Jersey Department of Higher Education, the New Jersey Governor's Commission on Telematics, IBM, Hewlett Packard, Apple Computer, NJIT, and Upsala College.

[Addendum, June 1993]

The cooperation of the participating students is also fundamental, and I am grateful to each one who has filled out questionnaires, sent a bug report, or shared an idea for improvement in procedures.

Finally, I would like to thank my husband and collaborator, Murray Turoff, for his constant assistance and support throughout this project, including his contributions to the final chapter of this book.

* * * * *

As this book goes to press, a new major grant has been received from the Alfred P. Sloan Foundation to support further research and development on the Virtual Classroom in conjunction with video to deliver distance courses. An entire Bachelor of Arts in Information Systems will be designed and offered via this media mix by NJIT.

PART *I*

FOUNDATIONS

The great end of education is, to discipline rather than to furnish the mind; to train it to the use of its own powers, rather than fill it with the accumulations of others.

—Tryon Edwards (1809–1894)

CHAPTER 1

VIRTUAL ARCHITECTURE/
REAL LEARNING

This is my letter to the World
That never wrote to me . . .

Emily Dickinson

A Virtual Classroom [TM] is a teaching and learning environment located within a computer-mediated communication system. Rather than being built of bricks and boards, it consists of a set of group communication and work "spaces" and facilities, which are constructed in software. Some of these communication structures resemble facilities or procedures used in traditional classrooms. Others support forms of interaction that would be difficult or impossible in the "face-to-face" environment. All are accessed, not by traveling to a university, but by typing and reading from a personal computer which connects by telephone to a mini or a mainframe computer operating the Virtual Classroom software. Participation is *asynchronous*; that is, the Virtual Classroom participants dial in at any time around the clock, and from any location in the world accessible by a reliable telephone system. Emily Dickinson would have loved the Virtual Classroom: it brings "letters" from all over the world!

Colleges and universities in the United States face tremendous challenges in the 1990s. The majority of students will not be 18–21-year-olds who can afford to devote their full time to living on a campus and taking courses. The majority will have families and jobs, and will be either commuters or distance education students. The need to provide access to higher education for working adults is also widely recognized in Europe, where institutions such as the British and Danish Open Universities have provided opportunities for tens of thousands of distance learners.

3

Computer-mediated communication systems (CMCS), especially when enhanced to create what we refer to as a Virtual Classroom[™] can make significant improvements in both access to and the quality of education. Currently over 80 programs worldwide are known to be offering courses partially or completely via computer-mediated communication (Wells, 1990; see Harasim, 1990, and Mason & Kaye, 1989, for short descriptions of many of these programs). Even simple electronic mail can improve access to the professor for students, when used as an adjunct to either traditional face-to-face courses, or distance education courses delivered primarily via one-way media such as video (e.g., see Welsch, 1982). Many universities have experimented with the use of CMCS in the teaching-learning process (e.g., Davie & Palmer, 1984; Haile & Richards, 1984; Harasim, 1986, 1987, 1989, 1990; Mason & Kaye, 1989; McCreary & Van Duren, 1987; Paulsen & Rekkedal, 1990). The Virtual Classroom project differs in two respects: software and evaluation.

Several software innovations were designed and implemented which are specifically aimed at enhancing the standard functions provided by CMCS's in order to support a group-oriented educational process for an online community of learners. The software supports a variety of group process arrangements which are similar to those found in other computer conferencing systems, plus several designed to meet the unique needs of this application.

Secondly, a comprehensive conceptual framework and set of evaluation tools were designed and applied in order to assess the effects of the software as it was used in college-level courses. The theoretical framework will be presented in subsequent chapters. This chapter provides a brief overview of the nature of the Virtual Classroom, which will be described in more detail in Chapter 3. It then describes the goals of the project, and gives a brief overview of the evaluation research. Part II of the book looks at the Virtual Classroom from the point of view of the teacher, drawing on course reports and observations captured from online interactions. Part III returns to the evaluation issue, describing the methods and findings in detail.

A BRIEF TOUR OF THE VIRTUAL CLASSROOM

The Virtual Classroom is one of those things that is best experienced, like a sunset or a swim in ocean waves, in order to fully understand it. It is difficult to describe it in words, because it is a complex set of ever-shifting states, rather than something you can capture with a still photograph. The subjective expectations and perspectives brought to it by the participants do as much to shape what happens in the Virtual Classroom as does the technology. This first chapter will present a subjective description of the Virtual Classroom. Later, we will turn to more objective descriptions and statistical analyses.

The term *virtual* is used in computer science to refer to something whose existence is simulated with software rather than actually existing in hardware or some other physical form. For example, the operating system creates a *virtual machine* for a user, which appears to understand commands in human-compatible language, whereas in reality the machine "understands" only machine language. *Virtual machines* and *virtual memory* create a resource which is much more powerful, and easier for humans to use, than the "real" physical resources.

One way to understand the Virtual Classroom is to follow an architectural analogy. Think of all the different kinds of learning tools and spaces and ritualized forms of interaction that take place within a traditional classroom, and within an entire college campus or high school. All of these things exist within a Virtual Classroom, too, except that all of the activities and interactions are mediated by computer software, rather than by face-to-face interaction.

The Virtual Classroom was first a gleam in its creator's eye during a postgraduate seminar on the Sociology of Architecture, led by Professor Suzanne Keller at Princeton University in 1977. The final assignment was to design "an ideal classroom" for the 21st century. First I sat down and started sketching a set of interconnected physical spaces for different forms of interaction among people and knowledge resources. In this imagined learning environment there was a multimedia lecture hall, where the Professor pronounces words of Truth and Knowledge, and the students try to absorb this and take notes. In a sumptuously furnished circular "conversation pit" with leather couches and marble coffee tables, the Professor as Discussion Leader and Socrates would conduct seminar-type sessions, moderating discussions and presentations in which the majority of the talking was done by the students. There was also a "learning resources" area, with reference materials, computer hardware and software, and perhaps laboratory equipment, where individuals and small groups of students might do research and prepare their assignments. There were obvious problems. How could you create a comfortable, upholstered discussion space for say, 30 people, without having to put in microphones so that participants could be heard across the huge circle without shouting? How could you possibly provide an adequate amount of computer and other resources, so that they would always be available to students for use in assignments, whenever they wanted them, without the endowment of a Princeton or Harvard?

Suddenly it came to me. A teaching and learning environment did not have to be built of bricks and boards. It could be constructed in software.

It could be Virtual! In an era when many teachers and students have their own microcomputers, it was no longer necessary for them to travel to a classroom . . . the classroom could come to them, over their telephone lines and through their computer.

In order to be considered a Virtual Classroom, a computer system must support all or most of the types of communication and learning activities available in the "traditional" (physical) classroom and campus. There should be an interaction space like a classroom, where the "teacher" or others may "lecture" and where group discussions may take place; a communication structure like "office hours," where student and teacher may communicate privately; the ability to administer, collect, and grade tests or assignments; and the ability to divide a larger class into smaller working or peer groups for collaborative assignments. Ideally, there should also be the equivalent of a "blackboard," where diagrams or equations may be posted for discussion or note taking, and where class participants may add to or erase parts of the evolving diagrams. However, whenever one tries to emulate and support noncomputerized processes within a software environment, fundamental changes occur in both the processes and the outcomes. Some things are lost and some are gained.

One difference between the two learning environments is that, in the *Traditional Classroom* (TC), most interaction takes place by speaking and listening, though it may be supplemented by writing and reading from a blackboard or from "handouts." In the *Virtual Classroom* (VC), interaction currently takes place almost entirely by typing and reading from a computer terminal (though it includes the use of print materials such as textbooks, and may be supplemented by an occasional face-to-face meeting or telephone call, or perhaps videotapes). Multimedia computer networks already exist, for use on a "local area network," and will be part of future systems for remote learning .

Because it is located within a Computer-Mediated Communication (CMC) system, interaction among teacher and students in the Virtual Classroom is also primarily asynchronous, with the computer storing waiting communications for each participant. This means that the members of the class typically are not present at the same time or at the same place. They may be, by chance or by plan, but typically, they are spread out in both space and time. The Virtual Class is a "rolling present" that goes on around the clock, 7 days a week. Each student types and reads at the pace and time that is most convenient. Typically, they won't get a response to questions right away, but rather, the next time they sign online, someone will have responded.

This different rhythm of interaction takes some time to get used to. However, asynchronicity, which may at first seem to be a disadvantage, is the single most important factor in creating a collaborative teaching and learning environment. It means that every participant may contribute at the times, places, and pace that is most convenient for him or her. The fact that one of the group members can only take part after the kids are asleep at night, for instance, or that some of the members take two to three times longer than others to be able to read and respond to material, does not determine the ability of others to work at the time and pace that best suits them.

Some things that are simple in the TC, like smiling at or hugging a student, are greatly diminished in the virtual environment. Words and symbols for SMILE :-) and < <HUGS> >just don't feel the same, for instance! On the other hand, some kinds of interaction and learning suddenly become possible and "natural" in the VC. For example, simulations and role-playing exercises can move faster and allow more variations than traditional "laboratory" exercises. Exhibit 1-1 is a scenario for a "typical" (hypothetical composite) student session in the Virtual Classroom.

Using the analogy of software structures to emulate interactional forms in the traditional classroom gives the unfortunate impression that the VC can never be more than a second-best simulation of a TC. On the contrary, a collaborative learning environment that is computer mediated can support some types of activities that are difficult or impossible to conduct in face-to-face environments, particularly if there is a large class. Discussion and communication about the course becomes a continuous activity, rather than being limited to a short scheduled time once or twice a week. Whenever a student has an idea or question, it can be communicated, while it is fresh.

Both face-to-face and CMC as modes of communication have strengths and shortcomings (see Hiltz, 1986a). The relative effectiveness of a VC is contingent, not only on hardware and software capabilities, but also on the teacher conducting the course in a manner that fits the characteristics of the medium, the nature of the course materials, and the characteristics of the students. Learning outcomes in the VC depend on whether or not teachers and students take advantage of its potential to support an active learning process that incorporates extensive interaction among students and between instructor and students (Hiltz, 1986b). A successful outcome also requires adequate access to the necessary equipment (PCs and modems).

This book describes a prototype Virtual Classroom that was constructed at New Jersey Institute of Technology and evaluated, based on use, in over 50 sections of courses. Major funding was provided by the Annenberg/CPB Project of the Corporation for Public Broadcasting. CPB is probably best known as the folks who brought you "Sesame Street." The Annenberg/CPB project is aimed at exploring how new computer and

---

EXHIBIT 1-1
JENNY'S SESSION

Perhaps a scenario is the next best thing to "being there" for understanding what a Virtual Classroom system is like. Picture a snowy Saturday afternoon in early December. Jenny Smith pours herself a mug of coffee, turns down the volume on "Twisted Sister" slightly, and decides to "go to class." She powers up her Personal Computer, presses the key for auto-dial, and she's there.

The first thing Jenny does is check her waiting messages. Her professor has graded the FORTRAN assignment she turned in online two days ago and commented on it ("A careless error in line 34, Jenny. Also take a look at Bob's assignment for a somewhat more elegant solution. Grade: 85"). Then she checks the gradebook to see what her average now is: 88, she's going to have to do a really solid A on the final exam to get an A in the course. Then Jenny joins the class conference. She picks out the "activity branch," where assignments are deposited. There's a special program that allows you to look at the other students' assignments only after yours is completed, too. She finds Bob's program and lists it. Hmmm . . . yes, that was a better way to handle that part of the problem.

Last night, she read the assigned textbook chapter for the last unit of the course. She notes the last "electure" is in the class conference, and downloads it to her PC. (An *electure*, or Electronic Lecture, is a lecture-type presentation in written form. This one, she notes, has some graphical material containing flow charts, as well as text.) Later, she will print it and read it carefully, using a highlighter to mark the parts she will want to review before the final.

An informal "one-liner" appears on her screen: "Hi, Jen – Wanna chat?" (Her account is set to allow others to interrupt with "real time" messages).

"Hi, Sam – not unless you provide a virtual fireplace and some marshmallows," she types back.

Jenny spends about 20 minutes reading the latest comments by other students in the debate about artificial intelligence. (Is it possible? What is it? Is it good or bad?) She adds a comment of her own, then decides to check into the "cafe" before leaving, where there is a discussion going on about surrogate motherhood. That's not part of the course, but sort of an "extracurricular activity," like going to the school pub, that students and professors from many courses can join. Later tonight, when she has studied the lecture, she will sign on again and take the weekly quiz. Jenny works full time, and tries to do most of her work for the course on the weekends.

---

telecommunications technology might do the same things for college students that Sesame Street did for toddlers: increase access to learning opportunities, make it more "fun" to learn, and thus, improve both the speed and quality of learning.

Two basic research questions guided the project:

1. Is the Virtual Classroom a viable option for educational delivery? That is, are outcomes, on the whole, at least as good as outcomes from face-to-face, traditional college courses? Viability or "goodness" of outcomes includes student learning, subjective satisfaction of the students, and demands on and rewards to the instructors.
2. What variables are associated with especially good and especially poor outcomes in this new teaching and learning environment? (In other words, what mistakes did we make that others should try to avoid?)

GOALS AND MEANS

The formal goals of the Virtual Classroom are to improve both access to and the effectiveness of postsecondary education. These goals are obviously linked: if you don't "attend class," you probably won't learn much. The goals are also linked through a pedagogical approach ideally suited to VC: collaborative learning. Collaborative learning means that both teachers and students are active participants in the shared task of seeking to understand and apply the concepts and techniques that characterize the subject area. Groups sized from two to the whole class work together or co-labor to master the subject matter and teach it to one another. The VC's round-the-clock access to a common communication and work space is crucial for facilitating group or collaborative projects. Collaborative learning is in turn linked to the second means or process that is intended to increase motivation and to improve both short-term mastery and long-term retention: fun. The constantly unfolding online dialogues, feedback from the instructor, and interpersonal dramas are sometimes exhilarating, often disappointing, totally unpredictable, and a constant challenge for both teacher and student. In short–fun–if you have a sense of adventure.

Some students and instructors are much happier with predictability and familiarity than with adventure. They probably will like the TC, with its predictable hours of attendance and familiar, ritualized routines, better than the VC. Collaborative learning may seem unfair as well as somewhat repulsive to some. They won't have fun. They won't feel challenged and motivated. They won't work harder at teaching and learning. And, they will probably learn less than they would have in the familiar lecture hall. All of which is to say, this new mode of teaching and learning is not for everyone. As will be detailed in later chapters, no instructor should dive into offering a completely online course without some prior experience and practice, observing other online courses and starting out with an experienced instructor by his or her electronic side, observing and giving advice for the first few sessions.

Improving Access

Steve Ehrmann is the project officer at Annenberg/CPB who helped to build a coherent vision and evaluation plan for the VC. As he points out (Ehrmann, 1988, p. 2):

> Access is a problem for virtually all students. The most severe access problems are faced by people who, for reasons of location, job, handicap, economic or cultural or linguistic disadvantage, age, or other factors cannot enroll in a degree program. But access problems also impede students who are enrolled. Part-time or full-time jobs may make it difficult to attend the particular classes these students most need. They may have time for study, but not when other students are available for a study group. Sometimes the instructional resources they find may be suitable for the average learner, but not for their exceptionally high abilities or their unusually weak preparation.

Access in this broad sense may be improved by the Virtual Classroom in the following ways:

Location.   Students may take any course from any instructor from any institution in the world which is offering courses in this mode. Thus, they are not limited to courses and degree programs offered in their geographic locality.

One course in the Virtual Classroom environment was offered by "Connect-Ed,"™ a completely online master's program in communication. It was taught by instructors in Tokyo, Japan, and Cape Cod, Massachusetts. The participating students logged on from North and South America, Asia and Europe. Though most classes are not this geographically dispersed, a worldwide university is a real possibility in this environment.

Flexible Time.   Students may participate at any time of the day or night that they have the time and the inclination. Opportunities for feedback from the instructor and interaction with other students are not limited to a few fixed times per week.

No Travel.   Students for whom travel is difficult may work from the relative comfort and convenience of their homes. This might include the handicapped, the aged, or those who must be at home as much as possible to care for children or other dependents. Alternatively, they can work while traveling, using a portable PC.

Overhead (Wasted Time). For nonresident students, the time normally spent commuting to and from campus (and finding a parking space) can instead be devoted to coursework. Even for resident students , "wasted" time moving among classrooms is eliminated.

Shared Work Space. The technology makes it easy to exchange information that is difficult to share or disseminate in the traditional classroom. For example, a computer program, as well as the output from a run, may be passed back and forth among students or between student and instructor, for discussion of problems or bugs. Students may be given the privilege of looking at the drafts or completed assignments of other students, in order to comment, compare, or offer constructive criticism.

Participation Opportunity. CMC also allows all students an equal opportunity to ask questions and make comments, even if they have difficulty in putting their ideas into words quickly. They may take as long as they need to formulate their questions and contributions.

However, it must also be recognized that, at least when used as the sole means of educational delivery, access may be limited in the following ways:

Limited Offerings. Currently, only a few institutions offer a few courses online. If a student wishes to complete an entire degree program online, the choice of courses is severely limited at present.

Equipment Requirements. Students who do not have a microcomputer and a modem at home or at work will have to travel to use the necessary equipment, and will be disadvantaged relative to those who do have the equipment which makes access convenient. This is likely to be related to socioeconomic status, since the poor are not likely to own microcomputers, modems, etc., or to have jobs which provide them with such equipment.
However, lack of equipment need not be related to ability to pay. For instance, NJIT provides a microcomputer to all freshmen and transfers who register, which is theirs to use for the years that they are a student. Since the cost is "built into" the tuition, it is state subsidized, and anyone in financial need may receive assistance, which in effect pays for his or her use of the computer as an educational tool.

Delayed Feedback. In the face-to-face classroom, as soon as a question is asked, the answer may be received. In this asynchronous medium, it may be hours or as long as a day until an answer is received. Moreover, the teacher might be more likely not to answer at all, or to send a "group answer" to several related messages, which does not deal adequately with each one.

Immediate feedback is possible with this medium, if the participants are online at the same time. Students working together may arrange to be online at the same time, so that they can pass drafts back and forth and engage in near-instantaneous exchanges of remarks. Students may also work side by side in a laboratory setting, talking about and pointing to things on their screens. However, these are the exception. Most of the time, communication will be asynchronous, with answers to questions delayed.

Textual Skills. Students with poor reading and writing skills may have their effective access lessened, since the communication in currently implemented systems is based on writing (typing) and reading.

Technical Skills. Lack of skill using a microcomputer, and software bugs or hardware "crashes," might severely hamper timely exchange of communication.

Improving Effectiveness

Effectiveness is defined in terms of the extent to which a course achieves a set of learning goals for the learner. Exactly what constitutes a *quality* education, and how you measure effectiveness, are subjects of much controversy. Do they mean short-term mastery and the ability to circle the correct answers on an objective test? That's certainly the easiest to measure. Or do they mean primarily the acquisition of "higher-level" skills and conceptual frameworks that will be applied over a the long term, after the course is over? How effectiveness was measured for this project is described in the next chapter. However, no matter how one defines and measures educational effectiveness, it can be improved in the following ways by the VC, as compared to the TC:

Facilitation of collaborative or group learning in a peer-support and exchange environment. Since students may "work together" asynchronously, they can do joint projects or collaborate in other ways even though their schedules make it difficult to work at the same time.

More "active" learning than in the traditional classroom. The computer forces responses and attention from the participants. They cannot just sit there passively and "tune out"; they must keep doing things in order to move through the materials and activities of the course. The active participation of each student may be "forced" by the software used, which may, for instance, require each student to enter answers to a question or assignment before moving on to another activity.

Facilitation of *self-pacing*, that is, learning at a rate adjusted by the receiver rather than by the sender. The student controls the pace; he or she may read as slowly or as quickly as is comfortable, may answer immediately or take a long time to think over a question or assignment before submitting a response. "Remedial" or "enrichment" modules or activities may be provided for those who need more background or are capable of proceeding further than the average members of the class, and the "average student" may choose not to receive these optional materials.

An example of self-pacing was noted during the pilot phase of this project. Students whose native language was not English spent more time online than those whose language was English. Having taken longer to read and reread materials, however, their level of contribution was equal to that of students for whom English was the native language.

The *use of other computer resources* (such as running a FORTRAN or Pascal program, simulations, or statistical analysis routines) may be "built into" the Virtual Classroom. Thus, students who could not afford to buy all this software themselves may have shared access to computer-based tools useful in their coursework. More importantly, as noted above, teacher and learner may look at one another's input or output from software embedded in a CMC. For example, they may exchange LOTUS™ spreadsheets and programs, or exchange code and outputs for Pascal programs.

Complete notes are an automatic byproduct of the process. These are searchable and manipulatable in various ways. Thus, the student does not have to choose between active participation and having a record of the class, as he or she often must do in a face-to-face lecture/discussion.

There are also several limitations and characteristics of the medium that may lead to less effectiveness. These include:

Absence of audiovisual media.   Some subjects such as art or a foreign language or music absolutely require audio and/or visual components. Though multimedia systems may provide them in the future, the current implementation of the VC for distance learning over ordinary telephone lines include only relatively simple graphics and the possibility of using audiotapes or videotapes to supplement the textual communication. For some students and teachers, the text-based medium may seem to lack stimulation, and the one-way delivery of taped material may also seem more boring than the rich interchange of face-to-face interaction.

Potential information overload. If a large number of students are generating material to share with others, students will need to learn to skim and index materials or they may become overwhelmed with the amount of material made available to them.

Requires motivation/ regular participation. Because the members of the class do not meet at one specific time, each student must make his or her own schedule for regular participation on a daily basis. Procrastination is easy—you just don't turn on the computer to see what's there and respond. Unless participants have the self-discipline to set aside regular times to take part, they will fall behind and become passive "lurkers" rather than responsible members of a learning community.

The factors potentially related to educational access and quality in the Virtual Classroom are summarized in Exhibit 1-2. Because moving learning from a traditional, physical classroom to a Virtual Classroom makes possible all of the possible gains and losses in both access and quality of education described above, it was necessary to carefully evaluate the technology in a set of field trials, in order to answer our research questions about the viability of this new mode of learning.

EXHIBIT 1-2
Potential Advantages and Disadvantages of the Virtual Classroom

FACTORS RELATED TO EDUCATIONAL ACCESS

Advantages	Disadvantages
Location (where you are)	Limited offerings
Flexible time	Equipment requirements
No travel	Delayed feedback
Less wasted "overhead"	Textual skills required
Shared work space	Technical skills required
Participation opportunity	

FACTORS RELATED TO EDUCATIONAL EFFECTIVENESS

Advantages	Disadvantages
Collaborative learning opportunities	Absence of audio-visual media
More active learning	Requires motivation / regular participation
Availability of other computer resources	Potential "information overload"
Complete notes	

EVALUATION

Evaluation of this project was both *formative* and *summative*. As a formative evaluation, observational- and questionnaire-based data were used to obtain feedback on specific subsystems and features designed to support the educational process, in order to improve the functionality and ease of use of the final software designs. As a summative evaluation, the goals are to explore the following questions:

1. What are the most effective teaching and learning processes in the Virtual Classroom (VC)? How do differences in process relate to differences in outcome, in online vs. traditional classrooms (TC)? For example, do students take a more active role online? Do they communicate less or more with other students? Included will be measures of amount and type of activity level by students and faculty.

2. What are the advantages and disadvantages of this mode of delivery for attaining specific educational goals, as compared to traditional classes? How do these vary with characteristics of the subject matter, teaching or presentational techniques, student characteristics, and access to and type of equipment used?

3. Are the overall outcomes for VC and TC essentially exchangeable, or is one mode clearly superior to the other? Are the two modes so different that it is not possible to say one is better than the other, just that they are very different? For example, when differences in student ability or motivation are taken into account, are outcomes such as exam scores essentially comparable? How do outcome measures for classes using single modes of student-teacher interaction (e.g., face-to-face or online) compare to "mixed modes" courses using a combination of delivery media? Is this related to differences in types of subject matter or student characteristics?

4. Given the above findings, what implementation techniques and what applications are recommended for future use of this technology?

Note that the first two goals listed have to do with what would statistically be termed *within group* variance, as compared to *between group* variance. That is, we expect a wide range of variability in observed and self-reported outcomes for students in the Virtual Classroom setting. In terms of priorities, we were most interested in describing and/or explaining the variables which seem to be associated with especially good and especially poor outcomes in this new teaching and learning environment.

The third goal is to identify the "average" outcomes for three modes of course delivery (VC, TC, and mixed) and to determine if there are any significant differences among them. The last, perhaps most important, evaluation goal is to thoroughly document and report what went on in this experiment, so that others can learn from the case history.

In order to explore the evaluation questions, it was necessary to observe a variety of courses, students, and implementation environments. The experimentation and evaluation took place in three phases:

1. Pilot studies. In the early 1980s, we offered several continuing or professional education courses totally online, and experimented with "mixed modes" classes that met face to face for a reduced number of hours and conducted some of the course work online. This gave us the experience to be able to conceptualize the kinds of software enhancements and evaluation questions that would be important to pursue.
2. After the prototype of our enhanced Virtual Classroom environment was constructed, a quasi-experimental design used "matched" sections of courses which had the same teacher, texts, mid-term, and final exams, in order to assess how the educational delivery medium affects educational process and outcomes. In addition, the same evaluation instruments were applied to a wide variety of courses offered partially or completely via CMC at five different institutions, in order to increase the generalizability of results. The courses included in this phase of the study were offered during the 1986–1987 year. The methods and findings of this extensive evaluation effort will be described in the beginning of Part III of this book.
3. Subsequently, we recreated those Virtual Classroom software features that proved most valuable within a new software environment which could be disseminated to other institutions, and engaged in more intensive evaluation efforts in a small number of courses, including five semesters of a Computers and Society course, five semesters of experimentation with a management course (described in Part III), and a writing course (also described briefly in Part III of this book).

This book chronicles an initial experiment with a limited number of subjects. Thus, we do not expect to be able to provide definitive answers to the evaluation questions. The evaluation research was exploratory, aimed at identifying the most important variables associated with differences in course outcomes, particularly the interaction among student characteristics, teacher behavior, and mode of delivery. Further research with a larger number of students, with a wider range of courses and software variations, and with variations in the extent and strategy for employing the Virtual Classroom approach in courses, will be necessary to establish more precise estimates of "causes" and "effects" in this new educational environment.

SUMMARY

Is it possible to create a viable alternative to the traditional college campus constructed in software rather than concrete? "Tools for the Enhancement and Evaluation of a Virtual Classroom" is the official name of the project chronicled in the book. In this chapter we have briefly described what a Virtual Classroom is like, in general terms. We have detailed the objectives of the experiment; increasing both access to and the quality of education. Potential advantages and disadvantages of the Virtual Classroom in relation to educational access and quality are summarized in Exhibit 1-2. In the remaining chapters in this introductory section, we will examine the pedagogical and research foundations for the project and describe the software environment in much more detail.

A Virtual Classroom uses software to construct a learning environment in which students and teachers can exchange ideas and information and work together on projects, around the clock, from anywhere in the world. The objective of the project was not just to simulate the communications processes that occur in traditional classrooms, but to improve them by creating more convenient access to educational activities, and more enjoy-

EXHIBIT 1-3
The VC and the TC: Some Contrasts

TC	VC
Speaking and listening: One person at a time. Mostly, the teacher talks and the students (may) listen.	Typing and reading: Multilogues in which students actively participate as co-learners.
Entire class must move at the same speed	Self-pacing
Set time and place	Anytime, anyplace
Socializing inappropriate	Socializing mixed with "serious" exchanges
Mostly individual assignments	Mostly group exercises and assignments
Students must take notes	Complete transcript automatically saved and reviewable
Computer resources generally not available to each student in the classroom.	Computer resources an integral part of the facility

able and engrossing learning experiences, which will in turn lead to "better learning." The major contrasts between the traditional and Virtual Classroom are summarized in Exhibit 1–3.

This book describes the evolution of the Virtual Classroom from an idea to a reality. A primary emphasis will be on evaluation tools and procedures, which will enable us to assess the extent to which the objectives of this new use of computers were attained. Extensive descriptions will be provided of the software and of the collaborative learning processes that can be supported by software. Pitfalls and problems as well as advantages and successful uses of the technology will be described. Finally, the book will look forward from these initial experiments to the possibilities for use of this technology to expand educational opportunities in the 21st century.

CHAPTER 2

EDUCATION, INNOVATION, AND TECHNOLOGY

> What is really important in education is . . . that the mind is matured, that energy is aroused.
>
> Soren Kierkegaard, *Either/Or*

During the Sputnik era, the shortcomings of the American educational system were summed up by the question, "Why can't Johnny read?" Despite decades of experimentation and hand-wringing, chances are that 18-year-old Ivan can now read and write in two or three languages, and 18-year-old Johnny is enrolled in remedial English in college.

Any brief overview of pedagogical theory and of research on technological innovations in education is necessarily biased. This chapter excludes all of the literature that does not seem directly important to and necessary for understanding the premises of the Virtual Classroom experiment. The speculations about Ivan and Johnny relate to the premise that crucial to making a difference is a technology that enables teachers to creatively engage their students in an intrinsically rewarding and motivating experience, and that supports the use of peer pressure and the family's encouragement to build and reinforce the motivation to work hard at learning.

This chapter summarizes the extensive literature on (a) the effects of medium of communication on learning, (b) educational innovations in general, and (c) the instructional uses of computers in particular. In addition, there are many publications in the area of computer-mediated communication, and a few on the use of computer-mediated communication to support educational delivery. Each of these areas of previous research has relevance for predicting problems, opportunities, and effects in implementing a "Virtual Classroom."

COMMUNICATION MEDIUM AND
EDUCATIONAL OUTCOMES

Previous studies of courses delivered by television or other noncomputer media tend to indicate "no difference" in basic outcomes. For instance, Schramm (1977, p. 28; emphasis in original) states that

> Overall, there is no basis in the research for saying that students learn more or less from television than from classroom teaching. This does not mean that under some conditions of teaching some students do not learn more of a certain subject matter or skills from one medium or channel of teaching than from the other. But the results of the broad comparisons say that there is, in general, *no significant difference.*

Each medium of communication has its advantages and disadvantages. Outcomes seem to be related more to the particular implementation of an educational use of a medium than to intrinsic characteristics of a medium. Implementations that capitalize on the strengths of a medium, and that circumvent or adjust for its limitations, can be expected to be successful in terms of outcomes, while other implementations will be relative failures. Certainly, we know that some courses offered in the traditional classroom are more successful than others, and that this can be related to variations in the teaching skill and style of the instructor. Thus, it is not that "media do not make a difference," but that other factors may be more important than or interact with communication medium in affecting educational outcomes for students. A primary goal in studying a new medium of communication for educational delivery must be the identification of effective and ineffective ways of using it. Clark and Salomon (1986, p. 10) summarize this lesson on past research on the instructional impact of new media as follows:

> Even in the few cases where dramatic changes in achievement or ability were found to result from the introduction of a medium such as television . . . it was not the medium per se which caused the change but rather the curricular reform which its introduction enabled.

The curricular reforms the Virtual Classroom approach may enable are greater utilization of active learning (with its accompaniments, self-pacing, and frequent feedback), and of group or collaborative learning.

THE COMPUTER AND ACTIVE LEARNING

Development of the computer as an aid in the educational process has thus far focused on Computer-Assisted Instruction (CAI). In CAI, the student is communicating with a program in the computer which may provide tutorial, drill and practice, or simulation and modeling exercises. Whenever the computer is used for educational delivery, whether in CAI or in the Virtual Classroom, the student is forced to actively participate, rather than passively listen (or doodle or sleep or stare out the window). Typically, after every screen of information, the student must react and provide some input in order to continue. At the very least, the student must press the carriage return key, which demands watchful attention. More generally, cognitive processing is required in order for the student to make an appropriate response to the material presented: a menu choice, or a numeric, text, or graphical input. An immediate response to the student's entry is made by a computer program. In the VC, this is sometimes the case: for instance, if the student answers a quiz constructed from objective questions, a computer program can grade that quiz and give immediate feedback. However, a CAI program can only process simple inputs and provide preprogrammed responses to expected inputs. No existing CAI program can "grade" an essay response for originality, correctness, and writing style (though, in the not too distant future, we will see programs that can).

At least for certain types of students and instructional goals, computer-assisted instruction (CAI) can be more effective than traditional methods alone. In their comprehensive review of CAI, Chambers and Sprecher (1980) conclude that it has many advantages when used in an *adjunct* or supplementary mode within a regular classroom, with class discussion following. Learners are forced to be actively involved in the learning process, and each may proceed at his or her own pace. Feedback tailored to each individual student provides the kind of reinforcement that will aid learning. However, when used as the sole or *primary* mode of instruction for distance learning, it appears to be effective only if there is also *significant* communication between teacher and student: "Primary CAI, and distance learning in general, may achieve results similar to those for adjunct CAI as long as there is sufficient human interaction accompanying the use of the CAI materials" (Chambers & Sprecher, 1980, p. 336). This interaction can be provided by CMC as well as face to face; a subsequent chapter will describe a very successful combination of a PC-based game and the Virtual Classroom.

Bork (1981) has been prominent among those who have emphasized the possible use of the computer as a "responsive learning environment." Creating an "active learning situation" (Bork, 1985) is the prime consideration in computer applications to education, from this point of view. The drill-and-practice CAI approach has been a limiting and negative influence upon developing the educational potentials of the personal computer. Too often, people using computers tend to simply transpose books and lectures, and so they miss the component of *active* learning which is so crucial for realizing the potential benefits (Bork, 1985).

In the VC, in contrast to CAI, most entries by students are of the essay-type variety. The student may spend minutes to days composing and editing the text, which might vary from a one-line question or comment to a long paper of 100 or more pages. Then other humans – other students as well as the instructor – read what has been contributed.

Part of the motivation for a student's contributions is to see how many other students are stimulated to take the time to respond, with a comment or question. The responses are time-delayed, but they are individually created by other human beings. They may be "nasty" or critical, not just neutral or full of praise. (Peers are that way: unlike Moms, they don't always think everything you do is wonderful!) In fact, in order to learn, it is necessary to receive "constructive criticism" as well as praise; to learn to debate as well as to agree. VC instructors often explicitly develop assignments early on in a course which require students to critically analyze on another's contributions, and to explicitly state their points of agreement and disagreement. Part of the addictive quality of the VC is the unpredictability of responses. Having made an entry, responses from others may or may not occur; and they may occur in a matter of minutes, the next day, and sometimes, even weeks later (when somebody is reviewing "old" dialogue and observes some new relevance or importance in a previous comment).

What occurs in CAI is a very narrow range of machine-generated responses to a narrow range of predicted or expected possible inputs. What occurs in the VC is a constant social process of validation. It is a computer-mediated version of what Charles Horton Cooley (1902, 1927) called "The Looking Glass Self." The quality and importance of one's ideas are socially affirmed or rejected. Participants form opinions of the validity and importance of their ideas based on the responses of others. The student (or teacher) enters a written presentation of self: of ideas or information about the topic at hand. The other participants provide the verdict about whether they find the contributions relevant, stimulating, or worthy of note. They reflect back their perceptions of the value of the contribution, when and if they choose to comment. In addition, since the computer-mediated conversations generally flow into a PC located at home, they may be shared with family members or roommates, and further discussed. This social process of developing shared understanding through interaction is the "natural" way for people to learn.

INSTRUCTIONAL STRATEGIES: THE CONCEPT OF
COLLABORATIVE LEARNING

CMC is particularly suited to the implementation of collaborative learning strategies or approaches. Literally, *to collaborate* means to work together (co-labor). *Collaborative learning* means that both teachers and learners are active participants in the learning process; knowledge is not something that is "delivered" to students, but rather something that emerges from active dialogue among those who seek to understand and apply concepts and techniques. In the collaborative learning model,

> Education does not consist merely of "pouring" facts from the teacher to the students as though they were glasses to be filled with some form of intellectual orange juice. Knowledge is an interactive process, not an accumulation of Trivial Pursuit answers; education at its best develops the students' abilities to learn for themselves . . . Another way to say this is that collaboration results in a level of knowledge within the group that is greater than the sum of the knowledge of the individual participants. Collaborative activities lead to emergent knowledge, which is the result of interaction between (not summation of) the understandings of those who contribute to its formation. (Whipple, 1987, p. 5)

Johnson and Johnson (1975) use the term *goal structure* to refer to the pedagogical strategy or structuring of relationships among students that is used in a course. We are reserving the term *goals* to refer to the desired outcomes, and in the quotations below, have changed their term *goal* to *strategy*.

> Instruction can be defined as the process of arranging the learning situation in such a way that student learning is facilitated . . . Our theory of instruction states that successful instruction depends upon the following components:
>
> 1. Specifying desired outcomes for the students and setting appropriate instructional goals.
>
> 2. Implementing the appropriate strategy: cooperative, competitive, or individualistic.
>
> 3. Assembling the instructional materials and resources needed to facilitate the desired learning.
>
> 4. Creating an instructional climate that facilitates the type of interaction among students and between students and teacher needed to achieve the instructional goals. (Johnson & Johnson, 1975, p. 3)
>
> A [strategy] specifies the type of interdependence existing among students. It specifies the ways in which students will relate to each other and to the

teacher in the accomplishment of instructional goals. There are three types of [strategies]: cooperative, competitive, and individualistic. . . . A cooperative goal structure exists when students perceive that can obtain their goal if, and only if, the other students with whom they are linked can obtain their goal. . . . A competitive goal structure exists when students perceive that they can obtain their goal if, and only if, the other students with whom they are linked fail to obtain their goal. . . . An individualistic goal structure exists when the achievement of the goal by one student is unrelated to the achievement of the goal by other students. . . . Usually there is no student interaction in an individualistic situation, since each student seeks the outcome that is best for himself regardless of whether or not other students achieve their goals. (p. 7)

Most distance learning has taken place using an individualistic or self-study strategy. With a totally individualistic learning strategy, CMC might speed up and increase feedback between the individual student and the teacher, but other students would not be involved in interactions related to the course material. A competitive strategy might be implemented using CMC to help to provide motivation and a reference group for students, so that they could see how they were doing in comparison to other members of the class. However, computer-mediated communication is especially well suited to collaborative or cooperative learning strategies. This is the pedagogical approach the instructors in this project tried to incorporate into their online classes, at least to some degree. One can also use mixed strategies; for instance, there might be two or more groups, each of which collaborates internally but also competes with other groups in the class.

As an example of collaborative learning strategies applied in the VC, most courses included one or more "seminar" type segments in which the students became the teachers. Individual or small groups of students were responsible for reading material not assigned to the rest of the class, preparing a written summary for the class of the most important ideas in the material, and leading a discussion on the topic or material for which they were responsible.

Seminar format is generally restricted to small classes of very advanced students in the face-to-face situation, because it is too time consuming to have more than about 15 students doing major presentations. Secondly, less advanced students may feel very embarrassed and do not present material well in an oral report to their peers, and are even worse at trying to play the role of teacher in conducting a discussion. In the written mode, students can take as long as they need to polish their presentations, and the quality of their work and ideas is what comes through, not their public speaking skills. Other students can read material in a much shorter time than it would take to sit through oral presentations. If the material is poorly presented, members of the "audience" may hit the "break" key, whereas etiquette dictates that they must sit and suffer through a poor student presentation in the face-to-face situation. Finally, it is easier for students to "play the role" of teacher in this medium, which is more egalitarian than face to face communication. Seminar-style presentations and discussions are thus an example of a collaborative learning activity, which is often difficult in the traditional classroom, but which tends to work very well in the Virtual Classroom environment, even with fairly large classes of undergraduates.

Other examples of collaborative learning strategies in the VC include:

- Debates, used in Computers and Society, Anthropology, and several courses offered by Connect-Ed,™ an online masters program for which a degree is awarded by the New School.
- Joint or group projects such as programming teams in Computer Science.
- Simulation and role-playing exercises, used in Management and French.
- Sharing of solutions to homework problems and/or answers to review question for exams, used in Statistics and Anthropology.
- Exchange of, and comments on, draft essays or research plans, used in a writing course and in a graduate research course. The classes were divided into small writing groups or research teams for this purpose.

Collaborative or group learning has been given many labels in the educational literature, including "cooperative learning, collective learning, study circles, team learning" (Bouton & Garth, 1983, p. 2) and "peer-group learning" or "syndicates" (Collier, 1980). The various forms include a process of group conversation and activity guided by a faculty member who structures tasks and activities and offers expertise. Its basic premise is that learning involves the "active construction" of knowledge by putting new ideas into words and receiving the reactions of others to these formulations:

> Students cannot simply assimilate knowledge as it is presented. To understand what is being said, students must make sense of it or put it all together in a way that is personally meaningful. . . . It is as if one were to teach a child to talk by having the child listen in silence to others for the first two or three years of life; only at the end of the period would we allow the child to speak. In reality, the child learns in a continuous process of putting words together and trying them out on others, getting their reactions, and revising speech accordingly. . . . An optimum context for learning provides learners with

frequent opportunities to create thoughts, to share thoughts with others, and to hear others' reactions. This is not possible in the traditional classroom. (Bouton & Garth, 1983, pp. 76–77)

Collier (1980) summarizes many reports of an increased involvement of students in their courses as a result of group learning structures, including better class attendance (Field, 1973), greater expenditure of time on the work outside of class (Collier, 1966; Rudduck, 1978), greater satisfaction with the course (Beach, 1974; Goldschmid & Goldschmid, 1976), and an increased wish to pursue subsequent studies on the topic (Beach, 1974). Collier also notes that, although most reports show "no difference" between courses based on small-group discussion and courses based on lectures and other more traditional modes of instruction (e.g., Costin, 1972), there are some documented cases in which knowledge gained by students was greater in the small-group setting (e.g., Blunt & Blizzard, 1973; Erskine & Tomkin, 1963; Clement, 1971). Finally, there are many reports that group learning enhances "higher order" intellectual skills, such as the application of learned principles in fresh situations, critical thinking, and the synthesis of diverse materials (Clement, 1971; Costin, 1972; Rudduck, 1978; Abercrombie, 1979).

STUDIES OF TEACHING INNOVATIONS

A number of other teaching innovations to encourage "active learning," "self-pacing," and/or "immediate feedback," involving either teaching techniques or technological devices, have been described in the literature. Many of these innovations have been reported as pedagogical successes, but they have not been diffused widely because of the demands made on faculty. For instance, Tarter (1977) describes his use of "group incentive techniques," which divided a class into study groups and based part of the students' grades on the daily quiz averages for the whole group. Though successful in terms of increasing student motivation and performance, the technique was abandoned after 5 years because it was too labor intensive to prepare and grade daily exams.

The "PSI" or Personalized System of Instruction (Keller & Sherman, 1974) emphasizes self-pacing, the use of written materials, tutorial assistance for learning from student peers, and "mastery learning." (Students must score 90% or better on a test unit before moving on to another unit.) Malec (1982) reports that the advantages are that students learn more and like the method; the major disadvantage is that the method requires a great deal of precourse preparation and a fairly elaborate administrative apparatus. Malec confirms that, after 9 years of PSI in a statistics course, he was still using the method. However, he laments that, despite presentations, articles, and videotapes, he is not aware of a single other colleague at his institution who had adopted the method.

There are thus many competing and complementary educational innovations. In order for the Virtual Classroom to be a "success," it must not only "work," but its use must diffuse among educational institutions. In the long run, diffusion of the innovation may be much more difficult and problematic than the technological progress on which it is based.

COMPUTER-MEDIATED COMMUNICATION SYSTEMS

CMCSs use a computer to facilitate communication among people who are dispersed in space or time. Although available since the early 1970s (Turoff, 1972), CMCSs were not widespread until the 1980s, when personal computers became widespread in offices, schools, and homes.

The most common form of CMCS is "electronic mail" or message systems, which deliver discrete text communications from a sender to one or more recipients via computer networks. Message systems are one-to-one or one-to-many replacements for the written internal memo, the letter, or the telephone call. Conferencing systems are structured to support cooperative group work and group discussions.

There is extensive literature on CMC, encompassing hundreds of books and articles. (For reviews, see Rice 1980, 1984, 1987; Kerr & Hiltz, 1982; Hiltz, 1986a; Steinfield, 1986; Culnan & Markus, 1987. For a general discussion of CMCS, see Hiltz & Turoff, 1978; Johansen, Vallee, & Spangler, 1979; Uhlig, Farber, & Bair, 1979; Rice, 1984. Hiltz & Turoff, 1985, discuss alternative structures for CMCS.)

Structure can be provided by software tools or by explicit statement of guidelines for interaction. Among the objectives of such structuring devices are message routing, message summarization, and social organization (Huber, 1982; Hiltz & Turoff, 1985). Conferencing software usually provides structuring devices such as key words and sequential or trunk-and-branch numbering of discussion items, and often includes special roles or powers for a group leader. If there are quantitative data, ranging from simple yes-no votes to large tables or files of information bearing on a decision, the computer can serve as a support tool by organizing, analyzing, formatting, and feeding back the data to the group. Finally, special structures can be designed for programs to be executed, such as a Fortran program to be compiled and executed, or a test to be administered.

Early research on the social effects of CMC was aimed at generalizations about the impacts of the new medium. For example, Johansen et al. (1979, pp. 180–181) summarize a number of studies with the statement that "computer conferencing promotes equality and flexibility of roles in the communication situation" by enhancing candor of opinions and by helping to bring about greater equality of participation. On the basis of early pilot studies comparing face-to-face and computerized conferences, Hiltz & Turoff (1978, p. 124) conclude that more opinions tend to be requested and offered in computerized conferences, but that there is also less explicit reaction to the opinions and suggestions of others. However, the democracy bordering on anarchy that characterizes unstructured or "free discussion" CMC makes it difficult for groups to come to agreement on complex issues or problems (Sproull & Kiesler, 1986).

A second generation of research on CMC seeks a better understanding of the conditions under which the general tendencies of the medium are stronger, weaker, or totally absent. For example, current work at the New Jersey Institute of Technology focuses on the development and evaluation of a variety of new capabilities for CMC. The goal is to discover the interactions among task types, communications software, and individual or group attributes that will allow the selection of optimal system designs and implementation strategies to match variations in user group characteristics and types of tasks or applications.

Much of the research on teleconferencing has focused on the question of the appropriateness of alternative communication modes for different functions. Media differ in "social presence": the feeling that a medium is personal, warm, and sociable rather than impersonal, cold and unsociable (Short, Williams, & Christie, 1976; Rice, 1984). The paucity of nonverbal cues in CMCS may limit information that serves to improve perception of communication partners, to regulate social interaction, and to provide a social context for communication. On the other hand, participants may explicitly increase overt social-emotional expressions such as greetings (e.g., Hi, Group!!) (Duranti, 1986) and paralinguistic cues (Carey, 1980), in order to compensate for the missing communication channels. Written versions of paralinguistic cues would include all-caps for emphasis and the liberal use of punctuation marks or phrases such as "boo-hoo," "HA HA!" or "my face is red" to convey feelings.

A controlled laboratory experiment on small group problem solving used Interaction Process Analysis (Bales, 1950) to compare the process and outcomes of computerized conferences vs. face-to-face discussions (Hiltz, Johnson, Aronovitch, & Turoff, 1980; Hiltz, Johnson, & Turoff, 1986). There were proportionately more of the task-oriented types of communication associated with decision quality, and proportionately less of the social-emotional types associated with ability to reach agreement, in the computer conferences. Some analysts have asserted that CMCS are unsuitable for social-emotional communication (e.g., Heimstra, 1982), whereas others have described high levels of social-emotional content which may get out of hand (e.g., Hiltz & Turoff, 1978; Rice & Love, 1987; Sproull & Keisler, 1986). Either extreme would hamper effective communication. A content analysis of two years transcripts from a computer conference used in professional education (Weedman, 1991) revealed variety and flexibility in patterns of interaction, supporting both task and nontask functions. "The computer conference environment was found to be very supple, supporting a wide range of topics and interactions between individuals who differed in status and in the degree to which they knew one another outside the conference" (Weedman, 1991, p. 303). In rating various motivations for using the conference, both task and nontask reasons were named as "major" or "very important" by a majority of students. These included "feeling in touch," "intellectual stimulation," to be able to freely discuss professional concerns, and "social exchange."

In designing the Virtual Classroom project, we desired to identify software structures and teacher behavior or approaches that would support the full range of communication necessary for effective education. This includes structures to organize and regulate student activities as well as structures or processes to encourage the social-emotional interaction necessary in order for students to establish cooperative relationships with their instructor and peers.

SUMMARY

The Virtual Classroom shares with Computer Assisted Instruction (CAI) the goal of using the computer to provide a more active learning environment, one that demands the involvement of the learner, and that is "self-pacing" in terms of the speed at which material is received and responses made. However, it differs from CAI in that the primary means used to increase motivation and mastery of both "facts" and skills is collaborative learning: cooperative work among a peer group of students, guided by the instructor.

Our goal was to create software and instructional styles and activities that would enable students and teachers dispersed in space or time to form an active, supportive, and effective learning community. The Virtual Classroom can be thought of as a means of "learning without limits." It was designed to overcome many of the limitations of traditional classrooms. There are no limitations on the time, place, or pace of learning; or on the ability to form a collaborative learning community that includes a diversity of people: different ages, different life experiences to share, from any part of the world.

CHAPTER 3
SOFTWARE TOOLS FOR A VIRTUAL CLASSROOM

> Education is the structuring of a situation in ways that help
> students change, through learning, in intentional (and some-
> times unintentional) ways. (Johnson & Johnson, 1975, p. 2)

The starting point for the design of software to support a Virtual Classroom was the variety of communication structures and physical facilities
to support those communication forms that are used in the traditional
classroom. Software structures were created that to some extent emulate
these physical structures, but the resulting communication is, of course,
different in many ways, constrained in some ways, and expanded in others.
The software development process and the resultant features which
create an online teaching and learning environment are described in this
chapter. They enable the instructor to structure a variety of learning
activities for participants in an online class.

USER-GUIDED DESIGN

Several evaluative methodologies were used throughout this project to
obtain feedback from prospective and actual users. In designing a new
application, it is not possible for prospective users to know ahead of time
what they will want. Rather, the users must gain some experience with
prototypes. Then they are in a position to critique those prototypes, and
make suggestions for improvements.

Gould et al. (1987) describe three "behavioral principles of system design" that were applied to the evolution of Virtual Classroom software features:

1. Early focus on users and tasks. Designers must understand who the users will be, and the nature of the work to be supported by the computer system. This was accomplished, in part, by hands-on experience by the project director/designer in using the evolving software for its intended purpose. In addition, other faculty members participated in the process of setting specifications and goals for the features to be developed.
2. Empirical measurement. Early in the development process for each new feature, intended users' reactions to the prototypes and documentation were gathered through protocol analyses and observations of attempted use in an actual course.
3. Iterative design. When problems were found in user testing, as they always are, they must be fixed. Some of these problems were identified by "bug reports," and user problems and complaints, which were sent to a "HELP" mailbox on a continuous basis, and preserved as a file for later analysis. Other problems were identified through feedback on postcourse questionnaires administered to students, and faculty course reports, at the end of each semester. "This means that design must be iterative: There must be a cycle of design, test and measure, and redesign, repeated as often as necessary" (Gould et al., 1987, p. 758).

Thus, the software features and the user interface for the Virtual Classroom™ are constantly evolving, based on an iterative design process that is guided by feedback from users. First a set of prototype features were constructed and used for three semesters on the original EIES conferencing system. Most of the field trials reported here took place using this prototype in 1986 and 1987. Then the functionality represented by the final form of these features was included as an integral part of a new full-screen, distributed conferencing system called EIES2. The new system has been used by courses from 1988 through 1993, and is constantly undergoing improvements based on feedback from users. It is a concept that is meant by the Virtual Classroom, rather than the specific software that embodies this concept at any point in time. Over a period of years, software development and formative evaluation occurred in the following cycle, which takes about six months to complete for each new feature or version of the Virtual Classroom:

SPECIFICATION: The project director, the development staff, and other interested faculty members develop and finalize ideas for the functionality and interface for a new feature. Generally, this specification is divided into necessary initial functionality, and additional functionality or options to be developed later, as resources allow. The lead systems analyst reviews all specifications and revises or adds to them based on overall system design and what is needed to integrate the feature into the total system.

CODING: One systems analyst takes primary responsibility for actually coding and testing the new feature. Sometimes this coding work is shared by a graduate student or another systems analyst.

QUALITY ASSURANCE (QA) testing: after development and testing on a "single user" development version, the new feature is installed in the "Quality Assurance" version of EIES 2 operated at NJIT. Here it is tested by the Project Director, with the participation of other staff members. Frequently this results in requests for revision of some aspect of the functionality or interface, or the discovery of "bugs," which results in recoding, then retesting on the QA version. The QA version is available only to the research staff.

FIELD TESTING AND EVALUATION: the code for the new feature, once it has passed QA testing by a few people, is integrated into the operational utility at NJIT. If resources permit, it undergoes "protocol analysis" with two or more representatives of a "typical user." For example, when Gradebook was first installed, a Protocol Analysis was carried out with two instructors who use Virtual Classroom. A Protocol analysis presents a specified task to a "typical prospective user." The user is then asked to "think out loud" while trying to use the software to accomplish the task. Confusions and difficulties are noted, which results in suggested revisions to the functionality, interface, or user documentation. (See Ericsson & Simon, 1984, and Carroll et al., 1985, for information and examples of the Protocol Analysis method for studying problems in human-computer interaction.) In any case, the new feature is used by at least one class as part of its online activities. The instructor and student using the feature report any difficulties or confusions, via messages to "HELP." A questionnaire (online as a form, or by paper) may also be distributed to the users, in order to systematically collect their opinions and suggestions about the feature. A postcourse questionnaire includes items on each of the currently available software features to support the Virtual Classroom, and is the source of further suggestions for enhancements. Bugs that surface with the 20–30 members of a class, which were not discernible with a small number of testers on the QA version, are fixed as they occur. Other suggestions are assessed as to their importance and the amount of effort it would take to make the suggested changes or enhancements, and the changes are made as the testing progresses, or put on the "do as resources allow" list of desirable enhancements.

RELEASE: Any major changes to the feature that result from user feedback are incorporated into the software between semesters, repeating the QA testing cycle. The new feature is then incorporated into releases of the software to other sites. The printed user documentation, consisting of a Starting Guide and Advanced Features Guide (as appropriate), are updated to include the new feature or enhancement.

Exactly how the Virtual Classroom "looks" and "feels" in terms of both functionality and interface thus changes from semester to semester. In the section that follows, features described and illustrated by examples thus represent "snapshots" of the system at a particular point in time. The initial prototype was constructed within the original EIES, a line-oriented system developed in 1976, when users had only 300 baud printing terminals as means of access. The VC enhancements had to use similar menu and command structures, in order to remain consistent with the larger software environment. Many of the EIES1 interface characteristics do not follow the current standard for good human–computer interaction (HCI) design (see Shneiderman, 1987). Obviously they should not be slavishly copied by system designers who want to create a similar system within a different conferencing environment. We were able to make many improvements in the HCI factors when we constructed the second version of the VC within the full-screen EIES2 environment.

OVERVIEW OF THE VIRTUAL CLASSROOM SOFTWARE FEATURES

One way to understand the software which comprises the Virtual Classroom is with an architectural analogy. Think of all the different kinds of learning tools and spaces and ritualized forms of interaction that take place within a traditional classroom, and within an entire college campus or high school. All of these things exist within a Virtual Classroom, too, except that all of the activities and interactions are mediated by computer software, rather than by face-to-face interaction. Exhibit 3–1 summarizes many of the types of software structures in terms of their counterparts in the traditional (physical) classroom.

Some of these features (messages, conferences, notebooks, and directory) are common to many CMCSs. We will first describe and illustrate how they are used in the Virtual Classroom. Then we will look at three kinds of software enhancements developed specifically to support online

EXHIBIT 3-1
Some Communication Structures in the
Virtual and Traditional Classrooms

VIRTUAL CLASSROOM SOFTWARE FEATURE	FUNCTION	TRADITIONAL CLASSROOM EQUIVALENT
Conferences	Class discussion & lectures	Classroom
Messages	"Private" student-student & student-teacher discussions	Office hours "Hallway" conversations
Notebooks	Individual & working groups composition & storage of documents	Paper & Ring-binders word processor & diskette
Document read activity	Scan & read "published" material	Books & journals
"Personal TEIES"	Create, modify, & share diagrams	Blackboard
Exam	Timed student-teacher feedback with no other communication permitted during test taking	Exam
Gradebook	Teacher may record & change grades and averages; student may access only his or her grades	Gradebook (paper)
Pen-names and anonymity	Encourage self-disclosure and experimentation	
Response activity	Force independent thinking & active participation	

courses: Activities, instructional management tools, and graphics. Finally, this chapter closes with a look at a total "online campus" or Virtual University, which includes a number of facilities that cut across and integrate the specific courses that are offered at any one time.

For individual questions, the VC student may communicate with the instructor or other students by private message. Usually, these messages are sent and received at different times, but there are also facilities for "real time" conversation, if people are using the system at the same time.

In my own experience, communication during these "electronic office hours" is generally more extensive and more personal than exchanges with students during conventional office hours, in courses that do not use the Virtual Classroom.

It is not only teacher–student communication that may be more voluminous and more "friendly" than it would be without the Virtual Classroom, but also student-student private communication, and contacts with new "friends" made online. One software feature that supports private communication is the Directory, which contains brief self-descriptions of the individuals and groups who have accounts on the system. Another is the ability to see who else is online at any time and available for a chat. Exhibit 3–2 is a partial log of an actual session recorded while I was teaching an online section of Computers and Society during Spring 1988. It illustrates the use of messages and the Directory.

In the class conference, the instructor presents supplementary *electures* (electronic lectures) and leads a discussion. Here, the students must put what they have learned into their own words, answering questions about the material raised by the instructor, responding to the contributions of other students, and entering new information for response by others. The class conferences are the heart of the Virtual Classroom, since they are a presentation and discussion space shared by the entire class. An instructor may use more than one conference. For example, in a management course, there was one "main conference" for the entire class. Then, each of two competing simulated corporations had its own conference for its "company business." In Computers and Society, with about 50 students in a joint section one semester, we chose to use one conference for most activities, but a second conference for two student-led activities (reviews of research articles made by each student, and the independent research report contributed by each student). Setting up separate conferences organizes activities by conducting them in different places. In addition, students can be given different privileges in the different conferences. For example, the moderator of a conference has a great deal of potential power. In the conferences for the simulated organizations in the management courses, it was the student-presidents, not the instructor, who were the moderators.

A necessary (but not sufficient) characteristic of a successful class conference is that the students are motivated to participate actively, to think about the material, and to respond to one another. Exhibit 3–3 shows some excerpts from a 1988 Computers and Society conference which illustrate extensive and thoughtful participation. The mechanism used to elicit this participation was the "debate." Students seemed to generally enjoy getting into the spirit of the debate format, referring to each other in the formalized manner of the debate as "Mr." or "Ms." so-and-so.

EXHIBIT 3-2
Sample Session: Sign-On, Messages, and Directory Search

WELCOME!

"Welcome" means you have made it online.

NAME OR NUMBER?120

Each person has a name, nickname and number as unique identifiers. I gave it my number, since that is the shortest to type.

CODE? DEMO

The access code protects the security of your account.
The user can change it at any time.
It is blocked out on the screen and printouts after typing, so others cannot see it.

NJIT Electronic Information Exchange System (102087)
Roxanne Hiltz on at 3/2/88 11:13 AM EDT via Newark Direct Access
Last Active: 3/1/88 10:49pm

System name and the date of the present software version.
Verifies who I am and the time and date of access.
An additional security measure to detect "break-in."
If I was not using the system last night, then it is time to change my access code!

LIST THOSE NOW ONLINE (Y/N)?y

This is the first question from the system. Choices to be made are sent by the system in all-capital letters, and ends with a question mark. I must answer this question with a Y (yes) or N (no).
The question asks if I want to see who else is online at this time.
I could engage in real-time "chat" with any of these people.
I answer "yes."

1: 11:10 AM Gurinder Singh Johar (Sal,1773)
4: 9:44 AM Ellen Schreihofer (EL,109)
5: 10:47 AM SAMIR ULLAL (2292)
6: 10:02 AM Debbie Hopkins (Debbie,2107)

In this list, there is one user whom I don't know and who sounds intriguing ("SOLIDARIOS"); also I think Debbie Hopkins is a Virtual Classroom student, but she is not one of mine and I am not sure.

EXHIBIT 3-2 (continued)

12: 8:41 AM Eileen Kelly (I,1240)
40: 10:38 AM ULEC (helping hand,340)
41: 11:13 AM Roxanne Hiltz (Roxanne,120)
43: 10:26 AM Barbara Eisenstein (205)
44: 11:08 AM Chris Spadola (juve,1972)
45: 10:59 AM William F.X. Reynolds (BILL R,1565)
51: 10:59 AM (Ms.) Gail S. Thomas (Gail Thomas,1983)
52: 11:11 AM S O L I D A R I O S (Solidarios,363)

Waiting:
12 Confirmations
7 Private messages

ACCEPT ABOVE COMMUNICATIONS (Y/N/#/R)?y

Pending:
M 14829 Received by Sam Later (Dude,1769)
3/ 1/88 10:23 PM
M 15558 Received by Murray Turoff (Murray,103)
3/ 1/88 10:39 PM
M 14549 Received by George W. Olsen (GWO,2291)
3/ 2/88 7:51 AM
[more confirmations here . . .]

The system tells me if there are any confirmations of private messages received by people to whom I have sent them since I was last online, and how many new private messages are waiting for me. It asks if I want them all (Y or Yes), None, a certain number of them, or if I want to use a special reply and message handling mode whereby the system will pause and ask me if I want to reply to each individual message before going on to the next one. I ask to see 14 of these communications, which is all the confirmations and two new messages.

Confirmations are very concise, and you have to know how to "decode" them. They show a message number, the recipient, and the date and time read. If I have forgotten what the message is about, I can ask to get the whole message. These confirmations happen to show two messages received by students and one by my co-teacher in an online course (Murray Turroff, who also happens to be my husband).

M 14517 (StudentX) (####) 3/02/88
10:30 AM L:39
KEYS:/EXPLANATION/
POSITION/
I have been wanting to send this message to you for some time but never got down to it till now. When I registered for this course I did expect a lot of course-work even though I did not know what to expect. When the course started I was totally lost . . . I had no experience(work) It was very difficult for me to write an example of resistance to information systems . . . I finally managed to get a practical example, which is what I presented. I could not recover from the time I lost in trying to get an example of resistance but some how managed to finish my review.

Honestly, and I say this without trying to be modest, I thought I had done a terrible job and was feeling down in the dumps because I expected that you would ask me to do it again. This feeling was further heightened when I saw everybody else's work, Anyway, I was pleasantly surprised to see that I got 90 on the review. Because I was upset I didn't study for the test as I should have, with the end result was that I got confused (mixing up the authors and their articles in my head) and got a grade I expected. Any additional work that you might have so that I may improve my under- standing of information systems. I do not mind if the work is not related to the course because, as I mentioned earlier, I am extremely interested in this subject. Therefore, please call me if you have any kind of work for me. I know this is lengthy but I hope I haven't bored you too much. I don't

I have deleted the student's name from this mesage. He/she is explaining a very poor mid-term exam score. This is the first message I had received from this particular student. It is formal in tone but also more self-revealing than remarks students tend to make in regular office hour visits.

EXHIBIT 3–2 (continued)

haven't bored you too much. I don't know why I exactly wrote this but maybe it is to tell you that I am doing my best and don't plan to give up come what may. By the way, the course is extremely interesting.

Yours sincerely,

M 15682 Eileen Kelly (I,1240) 3/ 2/88 9:26 AM L:5 KEYS:/JO OUT SICK TODAY/ TO: Bob A., Murray, EL, Roxanne, JJ
Jo just called, she sounds terrible. She will not be coming in today.
Access to:
  Messages (1)
  Conferences (2)
  Notebooks (3)
  Special Systems (4)
  Directory (5)
  Explanations (6)
  Reviews (7)
  Composition (8)
  Monitoring (9)
INITIAL CHOICE?5
There are 1877 members, 59 groups.

Do you wish to:
  Get items (1)
  Display titles (2)
Search/Find by:
  Name parts (3)
  From-To dates (4)
  Word/Phrase (5)
  Zipcode (6)
  Update your entry (7)
DIRECTORY CHOICE?1
MEMBER/GROUP
(NAMES/#'S)?363

Last modified: 9/18/84 3:55 PM
This is an administrative message, from one employee and about another. People have to tell you if they are not available. You can't see if they're "not there."
This is the "main menu" or "Initial Choice." It asks you which part of the system you want to go to. Once you know the menus you can "turn them off" and use commands. I type a "5" to indicate choice 5, the directory. I would like to check on who some of the people are who are online now.

Each part of the system has its own menu to choose actions that can be undertaken there. In the directory I first see that there are a total of 1877 individual "members" or users of the system as of today; and that they belong to 59 different groups. (Each class is a group, for instance. you can send a message to all the members of a group to which you belong; Put them all in a conference or define special commands or software structures for a group.) Then I choose to "get" directory items. I have to know the ID (name, nickname or number) or the person whose description I want to see. I ask for "363" (SOLIDARIOS).

S O L I D A R I O S (Solidarios,363)
Nickname: Solidarios

Telephone: (809) 566-5641 -2 /
567-6313
Last active : 3/ 2/88 11:22 AM
Established : 6/10/83 3:18 PM
Last modified: 9/18/84 3:55 PM

Address: P.O.BOX 620 GUSTAVO
MEJIA
RICART 68 Piso 2 SANTO
DOMINGO
DOMINICAN REPUBLIC Telex
ITT 3460597
RCA 3264295
* * *

Description: SOLIDARIOS, Council of American Development Foundations is a consortia formed by 17 development organizations in 14 Latinamerican and Caribbean countries. Members promote low income groups development projects. Development is understood as an ample ideological concept that implies reorientation of political & social power & income redistribution.

Group membership:
Group: CARINET/PFP (53)
Title: CARINET/PFP

MEMBER/GROUP
(NAMES/#'S)?2107

Debbie Hopkins (Debbie,2107)
Nickname: Debbie
Telephone:
Last active : 3/ 2/88 10:02 AM
Established : 1/18/88 12:48 PM
Last modified: 3/ 1/88 2:23 PM
Address: 52 8th street Ridgefield Pk., N.J. or box 454, rd#1 Pine Bush, N.Y.,12566 07660

Directory descriptions are entered by the members themselves; also displayed are the group or groups to which the member belongs. I note that "SOLIDARIOS" is actually a South American Organization, and that it belongs to "Clarinet PFP" (If I looked up this group description I would find that this stands from Caribbean Network/Partners for progress, and that there are over 200 people in this international development oriented group), and Debbie is indeed a student in the Virtual Classroom taking the course OS 471.

EXHIBIT 3-2 (continued)

Description:
I am a 5th year arch student(out in may!!) Ican usually be found in studio 408 colton, on mon, wed, thur. & fri. I enjoy fishing, sailing,hiking (actually walking in the woods but there aren't any real woods down here). I also like talking and am beginning to like conversation on eies.

The Computers and Society excerpt also illustrates another characteristic of the online class . . . the ability to have "guest" experts drop by. The topic of the debate was whether there should be a new federal commission to regulate computer applications. The closest existing regulatory body is the FCC, which regulates the use of communications technology. A former FCC commissioner, Nicholas Johnson, agreed to briefly look in on the debate and offer the students some insights on the problems as well as the advantages of a federal regulatory bureaucracy. He was teaching another course online at the time, for the Western Behavioral Sciences Institute.

Attached to the conference may also be various computer-mediated "activities" to be performed by students. For instance, there may be a quiz to take, or a computer program to write, compile, and run. Such activities are actually programs, rather than text, which are triggered to run when the student chooses to "do" the activity. This concept of activities, above and beyond the exchange of text, is one of the key software innovations of the Virtual Classroom project. Activities will be explained and illustrated further below.

For individual or joint writing assignments, an online notebook may be used to create and edit material, with the results subsequently shared with the instructor and/or other students in the class. For example, teams of approximately four students in one of my courses (Information System Evaluation) were required to develop and carry out a research procedure called *protocol analysis*. They used a notebook to draft and critique the subject instructions, questionnaires, task, etc. that they all would use. Each student generally took responsibility for the first draft of each part of the project. Then the other students would present either suggestions for changing the draft, or more usually, would directly edit the existing draft and enter it for the others to compare to the original, which was also left in the Notebook.

Most instructors choose to make themselves observers or even participants in notebooks being used by students for joint projects. This way,

EXHIBIT 3–3
Excerpts from a Class Conference: The Debate
Computers and Society, Spring 1988

Notes: The last names of contributing students have been shortened to show just the initial, in order to achieve a balance between protecting the privacy of the students and their "ownership" of the intellectual contributions. Some comments have been shortened, but otherwise they appear as they were entered.

The first two lines are the "headers" which are added at the time the comment is created, to aid identification and later search and retrieval. They show the conference number, comment number in that conference, full name of the author, nickname, system ID number, date and time of entry, length in lines, and, if the author supplied them, key words and an associated comment number.

:C1717 CC236 Murray Turoff (Murray,103) 3/ 9/88 9:52 AM L:42
KEYS:/ASSIGNMENT/DEBATE ON ROLE OF GOVERNMENT/

A. At this point in the course you have had some fairly extensive exposure to issues in the area of Computers and Society and you should be feeling better about how these issues are dealt with. Hopefully you can begin to distinguish at this point what is significant insight from advertisements.

"C1717cc236" is the *address* or *identifier* for the comment. "C1717" means the comment is conference number 1717.
"CC236" means it is the 236th comment (this number is assigned sequentially).

B. We are now going to launch a major formal debate on the role of Government in determining the future of Computer and Information technology. The proposition is stated below. However, before that the rules of this debate.

Detailed instructions are given for what the students are to do. They should be as complete as possible, since students will not be able to get immediate response to questions about things that are unclear. Note that there are grading guidelines designed to encourage the students to carefully read and respond to one another's entries.

1) You must take a clearly pro or con position in a comment in the conference. Not in a branch.
2) The comment should be concise, and different from the ones before it in terms of the argument or point you are making.

EXHIBIT 3–3 (continued)

3) Comments can be no longer than 50 lines.

4) Once you have made your own position comment on this issue, then you must enter a comment that is a specific rebuttal to another student's comment. Therefore the total assignment requires at least two comments by you. This rebuttal should attempt to wipe out the other student's position as effectively as possible.

5) After these two comments have been entered, you are free to engage further in the debate. You may wish to respond to whomever rebutted your initial position.

6) The grade will be based upon the initial two comments you entered; however, I will take account of other additions especially if they improve upon what you said initially and do not duplicate things that others have said.

Now for the issue:

BE IT RESOLVED THAT THE FEDERAL GOVERNMENT SHOULD ESTABLISH A FEDERAL INFORMATION COMMISSION (hereafter known as FIC) FOR THE EXPLICIT PURPOSE OF REGULATING ALL ASPECTS OF COMPUTER AND INFORMATION SYSTEMS IN THE BEST INTERESTS OF THE GENERAL WELFARE.

Today there are many concerns that indicate that perhaps the government should adopt a regulatory posture towards Computer and Information Systems.

This debate is in effect for the whole of March; however, you must have your initial position argument in by one week from today.

:C1717 CC242 Donald E. K (DEK,2083) 3/15/88 10:04 PM L:45
KEYS:/DEBATE/INITIAL COMMENT/
A:236
*** I am opposed to the idea of the creation of the FIC. ***

As proposed, the Federal Information Commission (FIC) would regulate all aspects of information systems. I believe this is too drastic a measure. Certainly there are some issues involving computers and information systems that should be government regulated. Among these, the most notable is the privacy issue in regards to personal information. However, there are still many other areas in which government regulation is the incorrect solution.

An article in Information WEEK reports that the federal government is considering licensing computer programmers to insure safer software as a result of two deaths caused by a software malfunction in a cancer treatment system [1]. An approach such as this is completely missing the point. There are many other people involved in this situation. Some deal with computers and informations systems and others that do not. With regards to computers, the system designers, the software support systems (compilers,operating systems, etc.) manufacturers, and computer hardware manufacturers are not considered in this approach. Why should it be that only the programmer is held responsible? Also, what about the doctors, the manufacturer of the cancer treatment machine and the technicians who operate the apparatus who are involved in this situation? Couldn't they have also been a factor? I believe that this scenario is very likely with an FIC.

The computer system is the wrong level at which the government should become involved. In the case cited above, it is clearly a medical situation and it should be the medical community and possibly, the Food and Drug Administration that should intervene.

If we regulate programmers, would we not stifle advancement of the state of the art? Suddenly all those who write any computer code would have to be concerned with liability. There would be considerably less experimentation with new methods because of the risk of being blamed for an unforseen coding flaw. The same fears would be held by the researchers and developers of new computer hardware, system designers, etc. Advancement in the entire field of computers and information science would be greatly impeded and the FIC would not be working in the 'best interests of the general welfare.'

1. Information WEEK, 'Government,' January 11, 1988, p.16.

:C1717 CC243 Sam L (Dude,1769) 3/16/88 8:15 PM L:37
KEYS:/DEBATE/

I support the idea of creating the Federal Information Commission(FIC) for various reasons. First of all, information interchange is becoming a threat to peoples privacy.

Almost everything about an individual is stored today in a computer system. That individual has no idea who has access to that information or who may alter it. The abuse of uncontrolled information exchange could result in many annoying, confusing, and even potentially dangerous situations for people involved. Getting tons of garbage mail just because their name was in the computer is quite annoying and I think all would agree. But this is nothing compared to what could happen if this gets out of hand. People would be able to find out anything about others for good or bad purposes. A child could find out about his parents past and his impression of his parents could change dramatically (remember "Back to the Future"). A teacher would be able to find out his students' backgrounds which could result in prejudiced grading.What's worse, a murderer could find out exactly where his potential victim lives and works, when he leaves home, and what route he takes to work, just by dialing in from his computer.

EXHIBIT 3-3 (continued)

FIC would be as good with information exchange as the FCC is with regulating radio and TV communications. Imagine radio or television without FCC? It would definitely be a chaos. Information exchange will turn into chaos too if the FIC is not established. The lack of communication standards, absense of privacy protection, and other similar aspects could turn computers into enemies just as well as friends. I think privacy is the main issue to consider when deciding whether or not to establish FIC. But there are other aspects of uncontrolled information exchange which could lead to disasters.

Altering of bank accounts, access to military information, foul up of credit buying, and even triggering of a nuclear war could result from uncontrolled information exchange. The FIC should be established as a safety measure and an organizing factor of information interchange. It should regulate who has the access to what kind of information and for what purposes. Without the FIC today's world of communications will probably soon turn into a world of crime and foul play.

:C1717 CC252 charles L (chucky,1900) 3/17/88 10:20 AM L:29
KEYS:/DEBATE/

I am opposed to the creation of the FIC. I believe in the laissez-faire policy that permitted the early growth in this country. The computer industry is developing at a very fast rate. I believe that government intervention would substantially slow the rate of progress which our computer hardware and software industries have been moving with. American companies would lose competitive ability in world markets if they had to wait for government approvals and reviews. I also believe that there would not be as many developments because many companies simply would be more reluctant to invest in applications which might not get approval. Aside from time loss and less development, I don't believe that the government will have employees who have adequate knowledge of computer applications or their social implications, to regulate such a critical industry. I am sure many pro-regulation advocates would still believe that regulation would still prevent corruption or developments which are not in everyone's best interests. However, there is also alot of corruption and social injustice going on in regulated industries. President Reagan has proven through the deregulation of the airline and trucking industries that government regulation was not in the best interests of everyone. Airline rates have dropped and service has improved through competition, which is an important part of maintaining quality and preventing corruption in U.S. industry. Again pro-regulation advocates will say that industry will act in it's own self interests and not for the good of the public. I believe that companies must do what they can in order to be competetive. For example, automating a production facility might cause widespread unemployment, but if an American company cannot do it because of regulation it's Japanese competitors will destroy them because they will be automated. In a sense the companies best interests are everyones best interests in the American system.

:C1717 CC262 Chris S (juve,1972) 3/21/88 3:52 PM L:15
KEYS:/DEBATE/REBUTTAL TO D. KLEMP (CC242)/
A: 242

I agree with Mr. K . it would probably stifle the growth of computers and software for fear of repercussions from "FIC". It would be the same fear for a doctor of a malpractice suit.

Guidelines would have to be flexible, make this field breath with life, not put it into an early grave. There will always be people totally against or for computers. What is really needed are people who care, understand, and grasp the real potential of what computers can and will do for us in the future. Have both sides represented when making laws, have them see the many sides of computers, and not the black and white of problems, but also the grays, and the beautiful colors that will bring a new generation of computers and software.

:C1717 CC276 FRANCES R (FRAN,1925) 3/29/88 11:04 PM L:25
KEYS:/DEBATE/REBUTTAL/
A: 252

This is a rebuttal to Charles L 's debate(CC252).

In your debate, you said that government intervention would substantially slow down the rate of progress which computer hardware and software industries have been moving with. It is true that government intervention may slow down the process, but I don't think by that much. Don't you think the computer industry is moving at too fast a pace, anyway? I do. We need to slow down and take the time to inspect and test all new hardware and software.There would be less mistakes and I think people would benefit from it more. That is what the FIC would be there for, to make sure that people get the most out of their hardware or software. You also stated that there would be less developments because companies would not invest in applications that might not get approval. What is the use in investing in something that doesn't get approval from the government. If it doesn't get approval, then obviously the application or product does not meet the required standards. You also mentioned that President Reagan had deregulated the airline and trucking business. True, airline rates have dropped and service has improved, somewhat, but also look at all the accidents and near misses that occurred in the past couple of years. Who knows, if the airline industry was still under regulation, all the accidents and near misses could have been prevented, maybe not all, but a good percentage of them. What I'm trying to say is that I strongly believe we need an FIC.

EXHIBIT 3-3 (continued)

:C1717 CC285 charles L (chucky,1900) 3/31/88 10:53 AM L:25
KEYS:/DEBATE/RESPONSE TO R 'S REBUTTAL/

****RESPONSE TO FRANCES R 'S REBUTTAL****

Yes, I do believe that the government intervention would slow down the process, not simply because of the pace of computer progress but because of the sheer number of applications in the United States. This agency would have to be humungous, and would be as widespread and beurocratic as the Division of Motor Vehicles. It would also consume vast amounts of tax-dollars, and the time of private companies. You claim that we need to slow down the process in order to inspect and test new hard and soft wares. Let the companies themselves inspect and test, they are better judges as to the quality of the work, and will be more critical than an uninvolved government administrator. Furthermore, a government agency would not "make sure that people get the most out of their hardware or software," they cannot make value judgements on a program or hardware, only check if standards are met, a program could be garbage and pass standards of security. Your final argument that airline safety may have been better if the industry were still regulated is an argument against regulation. The deregulation I was referring to was price regulation, and as you admitted prices have dropped and service has improved. Airline safety (your main beef), is still regulated by the FAA and other agencies, the inadequacies of these agencies in providing safety was clearly explained by you in your comment. However I also believe that the air traffic controllers strike had alot to do with this. The government has therefore proven ineffective at both price and safety regulation.

:C1717 CC311 Nicholas Johnson (Nicholas,703) 4/15/88 12:30 AM L:88
KEYS:/DEFROCKED FCC COMMISSIONER ENTERS DEBATE/

Hi, I'm Nick. Roxanne introduced me a comment or two ago. In a message from Murray, he urged me to enter your "debate." So that's why you are suddenly confronted with this scrolling comment from some stranger.

Hopefully you will forgive me, as I am neither professor nor student in this conference, for being unprepared. Ideally, I would want to read all your comments from the beginning, pick up themes, identify you by name and comment, weave them together, and add some thoughts of my own. Since I am teaching my own courses here at the University of Iowa Law School, travelling, and otherwise engaged that's not possible – at least not this evening.

Good comments. I assume you will all get As < grin >.

As some of you pointed out, there are really two separate questions here. One is: what are the range of public policy issues raised by the presence of

48

computers in our society (or, otherwise phrased, by our passage from an industrial to an information society)?

The other is: of those issues, which can be appropriately dealt with by a regulatory commission?

It is absurd (from my limited perspective), or at least intellectually and analytically quite limiting, to put the all-inclusive proposition that we should "get the government off our backs" and have no regulation of anything whatsoever. (That is, in practical effect, merely a self-serving argument for increased domination of our lives by large corporations.) It may be quite reasonable, however, to argue that the regulatory commission form is inappropriate, inefficient, or whatever, to deal with some given, very specific policy question (say, using the FBI instead of the FIC to investigate hackers breaking in to government computers).

We need standards. Without them the trains would not only not run on time, they would not run on tracks. Government can set standards (the FCC has "type acceptance" for TVs and regulates the amount of radiation your computer can splash on you). But trade associations can also do it. Large buyers (like the Defense Department or General Services Administration) can do it.

Many of you have pointed out threats to privacy. We have general, and electronic, privacy acts on the books. This may be an area where the combination of legislative standards from Congress, and their interpretation and enforcement by the Justice Department and courts, is superior to a regulatory commission.

And, of course, information age industries are subject to the range of regulation that confronts any business: IRS regulations, labor relations (NLRB), export regulation (especially for computers to communist countries), safety and health of workers (OSHA), workman's comp, zoning restrictions, sales taxes, etc.; it's endless.

The normal rationale for regulatory agencies, as at least one of you pointed out, involves the failure of the marketplace. The first regulatory commission, the ICC, was created to regulate the railroads. Railroads are natural monopolies; seldom do competing railroads run tracks side by side. That was the rationale for regulating the airlines (the old CAB), the telephone company and broadcasters (FCC), natural gas pipelines (the old FPC), etc.

To what extent is the computer industry such an oligopoly (handful of dominant firms restraining competition) or monopoly? How about the conduits (our equivalent of the natural gas pipelines) called Tymnet and Telenet? Are the details of overseeing their pro/anti-social activities so numerous, changing, and dependant on expertise that a full-time agency makes more sense than using Congressional committees and courts?

As a concession to the shortness of life (mine as well as yours), I'm going to cut this off in mid-thought and go to bed. Hope there's enough here to at least give you a glimpse into my approach to these problems.

I only wish we had more time together. Good luck to you. Goodnight. - Nick.

they can directly observe the quantity and quality of contributions being made be each member of the team. More importantly, the students know that their group work is being observed. This motivates each student to do his or her share, and not assume that they can loaf along as a "lurker" (somebody who reads but does not write) and let the other members do all the work while sharing the credit. The Virtual Classroom also offers several other unique possibilities:

Pen names or anonymous entries may be used in contributing responses to questions or assignments, or to role-play during a simulation or debate. Pen names may enable the student to share ideas and experiences without embarrassment or revealing confidences. For instance, in a sociology course, students used pen names in applying concepts of different types of socialization to their own childhood, and in applying concepts about factors related to interpersonal attraction to one of their own relationships.

Students may learn by *taking the role of teacher*, being responsible for summarizing the important points of a topic or "outside reading" for the benefit of the rest of the class.

Students may be forced to think and respond for themselves rather than passively listening to the instructor or other students. For instance, in one variety of the *response branch* activity designed for this project, students must independently answer a question before they can see the answers of the other students.

Putting questions and answers into *a written form* may aid comprehension for some students. It may also improve their writing skills.

Commands can be used to *"tailor" the interface* and to customize the environment for each course. For example, Connected Education has created an entire "campus" by using commands to define various conferences and notebooks and special-activity programs with easy-to-remember names (see Exhibit 3–4).

The specific types of learning activities online vary a great deal depending on the subject matter and the skills and preferences of the teacher. Included in Appendix 3 is a narrative description of some of the classes that used the "Virtual Classroom" during the 1986–1987 year. These were prepared by the instructors in response to a list of issues and topics to be covered, and explicitly include "lessons learned" about effective and ineffective procedures and assignments.

The software features illustrated and described in detail so far are the "standard" features of EIES, and similar features exist on many other computer conferencing systems. In experiencing the use of these features (messages, conferences, notebooks, special group commands), to supple-

EXHIBIT 3–4
Activities Screens

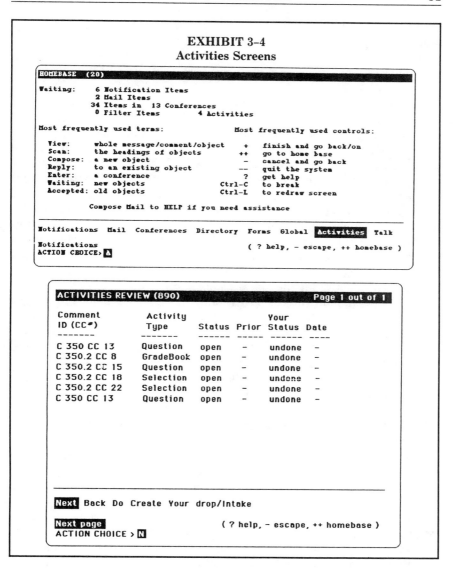

ment traditional courses or to deliver noncredit continuing education courses, it was evident that there were many limitations to be overcome, particularly for standard college-level courses that required numerous assignments and examinations as part of the course work. Conceptually, we divided these software needs into a set of structures called Activity branches which could be attached to a class conference in order to support special types of assignments or delivery of material that involved the whole class; a set of teaching support tools to help the instructor manage assignments and grading and quizzes for individual students; and microcomputer based software for the integration of graphical information with text information. These are described in the next three sections.

Activity Branches for Class Conferences

Activities may be attached to comments in a conference. In our implementation of software to organize student participation, the root conference comments form a linearly numbered *trunk*; and the *branches* attach to one of the root conference comments. All of the responses related to that activity are gathered together there, instead of being scattered throughout a conference as many separate comments. Rather than automatically receiving everything that has been entered by any participant, as with comments, participants choose to undertake Activities only when they are ready to do so, and explicitly give a command. A record is kept of DONE activities, and a review choice for branches helps users to keep track of which activities they have completed.

While students may access only their own records of done and undone activities, the instructor can review the branch activities status of any of the students. Most graded assignments in courses are presented as Activities, because of this extra help to students and instructors in finding and viewing both done and undone branch activities. Activities were developed specifically to support online classes or a Virtual Classroom, but they are also useful for other applications.

For our initial year of experimentation, there were three types of activities: Lectures or Documents to read, Selections to choose, and Questions requiring a response.

Exhibit 3–4 shows the 1992 version of the main menu choices for the Activities on EIES 2. At homebase (the first screen), any new undone activities are noted. Typing "A" for Activities then lists them. Then choosing "D" for "do" will take you into a specific waiting activity. At any choice, entering a question mark in reply to a system prompt results in display of online help information. It was necessary to make the system one that students could "learn by doing." Even though a printed manual for activities was distributed, students practically never had it with them during their sessions on the system.

The most frequently used activity type for online classes has been Question/Response. One or more questions for response by other conference members is contained in the main conference comment setting up a response branch. All of the responses are attached to this comment. Each person *must answer before seeing the responses of others*. This is very important for making sure that each student can independently think through and enter his or her own ideas, without being influenced by responses made by others. Alternatively, the author of a question activity can choose not to let participants to see responses of others until they are "opened" for viewing.

Between the conference comment describing the activity and the attachments containing that activity is a software "gate" that executes a program unique to that type of activity. For instance, in the Question/ Response, the software checks, did this person respond yet? If not, ask for their response. If yes, are there any new responses from others that they have not seen yet?

A DOCUMENT READ activity branch is a very simple hypertext structure that allows essay or lecture-type materials to be divided into sections. Each section has a title, and can be read by selecting that section from the table of contents for the document reading activity. When you do a reading activity, you can choose to read just some sections that particularly interest you, or the whole thing.

SELECTION activities allow the members of a conference to choose selections from a list (such as a list of available topics for student assignments) and indicates who has chosen which item so far. Without such a mechanism, allocating selections to students would require either dictatorship by the instructor, or a barrage of message traffic. The selection branch procedure also has the advantage of motivating students to make their selections early, since whoever makes a selection first gets it. Finally, as soon as a valid selection is made, it is confirmed for the student, who may immediately begin work on the topic.

Some activities may be set up to allow the use of a PEN NAME, so that students may feel more free to communicate about personal feelings. If the conference moderator decides not to allow pen name responses to branches, then everything will be entered with the regular account signature.

Finally, Branch Activities may be *sequenced*. This means that the instructor in a class conference or others who are authorized to create branching activities may specify that two or more branches must be done in a specified order. This allows the instructor to control the order in which various activities or course modules are completed by a student.

Conceptually, there is no end to the kinds of Branch Activities that can be added to a Virtual Classroom. The Branch Activity software consists of a set of programs that lead the author through the process of setting up the activity, a set of programs that lead the participants through actually doing each type of activity, and a common interface for accessing, tracking, and managing the whole set. For instance, for decision support tasks, voting and polling activities are available.

We found that adding this new branch activities subsystem does create an additional level of complexity and learning time for the student (and faculty member!) However, in large classes with a number of assignments, trying to do everything in a linear conference structure quickly results in a disorganized and unmanageable situation for both students and teachers.

Instructional Management Tools

This next set of special tools relates to individual assignments, rather than to shared activities in conferences; thus it also differs in that the use of these tools was channeled through messages and notebooks, rather than through the shared class conference. In the current implementation on EIES2, it should be noted, the instructional management tools are also integrated as activities (e.g., a *gradebook activity*.)

As both a systems analyst familiar with EIES1 and Interact, and an instructor in the Virtual Classroom project, B.J. Gleason was in an ideal position to develop a series of instructional management routines (see Gleason, 1987, for a manual and full description). These included:

- Makequiz, Quiz, and Grader — *Makequiz* allows an instructor to create an online quiz, which may consist of a variety of forms of questions (e.g., multiple choice or other objective questions, essay questions, or short answer responses such as the answer to a computation problem). *Quiz* allows the student to take an online quiz, and *Grader* guides the automatic grading and issuing of messages to students reporting their grades on the quiz. There is also a spreadsheet-like program, *Gradebook*, which organizes and computes weighted averages for all grades for each student, and which students can consult to see their grades and average at any time.
- *Assignment* and *Handin* automatically organize and track all student responses to a single assignment in a designated page in the instructor's notebook. For large classes with many assignments, this can be very important, since otherwise the instructor would have to find, sort, and transfer each of the individual assignments arriving as messages.
- Pascal, Fortran, and Debug provide for compiling Pascal or Fortran programs in a "batch" or "background" mode on EIES. This set of tools for courses involving programming allows the instructor to see the program as well as the compiled result, in order to improve ability to help students and to comment on the quality and correctness of their code.

Personal TEIES: Integrating Graphics and Text

The objective of Personal TEIES® was to allow an instructor or student to compose and display, on a microcomputer, text that is integrated with simple graphics, including pictures and mathematical symbols. The program also acted as a PC front end, which enabled users to dial and connect, upload, and download items between the central system and the PC.

The graphics are composed using a subset of the Graphical Kernel System and are then encoded in NAPLPS, the North American Presentation Level Protocol Syntax, for transmission and storage in EIES, EIES2, or any other CMCS that accepts ASCII code. The initial version was implemented for the IBM PC and compatibles.

The graphical items created and displayed in Personal TEIES are meant to emulate a blackboard in the traditional classroom, with class members not only able to look at one another's drawings, but also able to "erase" and "redraw" an item. Because it is encoded in NAPLPS, rather than communicated as a bit-map, it can be transmitted over a telephone line; and, if versions for different micros are completed, a graphical item drawn on an IBM-PC compatible could be displayed by a user of another brand of micro computer. The way the Personal TEIES® screen looks on the student's or professor's microcomputer is shown in Exhibit 3–5. Some interesting things to note are the following:

- Icon sets may be created, which are stored in *libraries*. For instance, these may be a set of symbols for mathematics or for chemistry or electrical engineering, which do not appear on the standard keyboard. When the user calls up an icon library, then these symbols may be selected by pointing to them with a mouse or by using the < alt > key on the keyboard which is mapped to the icon set. For example, if a mathematics icon set is in use, < alt >-A would produce the Greek letter alpha, and < alt >-B the Greek letter beta. Usually, the instructor would create or select appropriate icon sets for use in his or her course, and these would be distributed with the diskettes for Personal TEIES used by students in that course.
- Modification of graphics occurs at a conceptual level, rather than at the bit-mapped level. This is akin to what happens on a blackboard. So, for instance, anyone who receives a diagram may modify it, by, for instance, inserting, erasing, or moving figures or symbols in the diagram. The modified diagram may then be posted in the class conference, so that the members of the class can see, compare, and discuss the alternative versions.
- Unlike the physical blackboard, which runs out of space, there is no practical limit to the number of diagrams that can simultaneously be present in a class conference. Therefore, a group of students and faculty can create new graphical images without having to erase access to the older ones.

- The computer can enhance artistic presentation. All the student needs is a mental image of the diagram he or she wishes to create; the software helps him or her to draw it. Artistic ability and a steady hand are not required, and the user can redraw and modify things until he or she is happy. Of course, the subtle variations that make "art" are difficult-to-impossible to create; the software makes everybody's work appear to be of about equal quality. In a classroom environment, however, this may be an advantage, since even students who feel that they "cannot draw" can produce diagrams that look just about as good as anybody else's.

Unfortunately, Personal TEIES was much more difficult to implement in the IBM-PC environment than we had anticipated. A completely operational version was not ready until the end of March 1987. This version was used for a few exercises in Math 305; the other courses had to get along without the graphical capabilities we had hoped to provide.

Future systems to support a Virtual Classroom should deal with the need for shareable graphics for remote users. This will become much

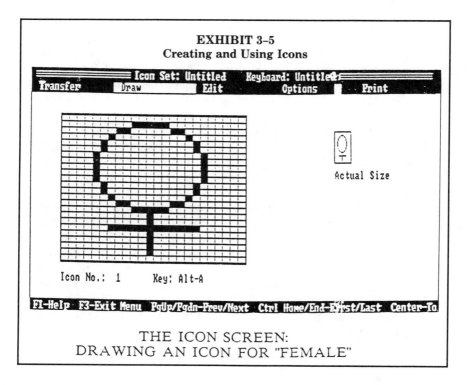

EXHIBIT 3–5
Creating and Using Icons

THE ICON SCREEN:
DRAWING AN ICON FOR "FEMALE"

easier as the microcomputers available to students require more memory and higher resolution screens, and as fiber optics overcome the current barrier of 1200 baud transmission over telephone lines.

THE VIRTUAL UNIVERSITY

Of course, a college campus is made up of much more than individual classrooms. There are libraries, counseling centers, and extracurricular activities such as student hangouts, special campus-wide public lectures, the bookstore, and the campus newspaper.

Paul Levinson (1988) has used the software features available on EIES to create an entire "electronic campus," which offers an online program of courses and related activities leading to a master's degree in Communications. In particular, he created a number of *defined commands* for his students and faculty members using the Connect-ED® campus to be able to jump straight to a desired activity, with one command. These commands are invoked and recognized by a special symbol (*a* + *sign*), which means that the system interprets the word typed as a command.

Exhibit 3–6 shows the facilities of the "virtual" Connect-Ed campus during the Summer 1988 term, as an example. Particularly interesting was the course in "Issues in International Telecommunications." Co-taught by instructors located in Washington, DC; Cape Cod, Massachusetts; England; and Norway, its students came from Asia and Latin America as well as North and South America. This is an example of a natural "match" between subject matter and mode of course delivery in which, in McLuhan's terms, the medium is (at least part of) the message. Crucial in the operation of an international campus in which students and faculty never see each other is the availability of human support and assistance online, developed and coordinated for Connect Ed by Tina Vozick.

Besides a number of formal courses, Connect-Ed offers access to two different online "hangouts," a library, a book order service, information one might usually obtain from a student counselor, and noncredit workshops or tutoring for writing. Frequently, campus-wide special lecture events are offered, in which visiting celebrities or scholars lecture on and discuss topics of general interest for a few days. In Spring 1988, the first Connect Ed student successfully completed an entire master's degree online. The Connect-Ed program is offered through the New School, which issues the course credits and degrees for the enrolled students. The Connect-Ed application demonstrates that the variety of learning students can be provided through a Virtual Classroom system can indeed offer new opportunities to obtain an education.

EXHIBIT 3-6
Connect Ed Campus

To go to the places listed on the right, type the commands listed on the left at any EIES prompt.

CLASSES (Summer 1988)
New School for Social Research

+CYBER   Cybernetics & Poetry (C2564) (Gerri Sinclair & Lionel Kearns)
+ISSUES   Issues in International Telecommunications (C2245) (P. Levinson - J. Glenn - T. Wright - M. Paulsen)
+OLJ   On-Line Journalism (C2763) (Brock Meeks) (S. Lerch)
+PROFWRIT Computer Networks & Professional Writing (C2539)

Polytechnic University

+DOCU   Intro to Software Documentation (C2518)

Connect Ed Not-for-Credit Workshops

+SHOP   On-Line Writer's Workshop (C1978) (S. Lerch)
Type +prev for list of courses from previous terms.

HANG-OUTS

+cafe   Connect Ed Cafe: socialize with students and faculty, read comments by and interact with special Connect Ed guests, meet next term's faculty and discuss their courses
+tech   Technical Forum: discuss problems you may encounter with personal computer equipment and software, telephone lines, and EIES RESEARCH AND INFORMATION
+library   read online papers by Connect Ed faculty and associate writers, extensive collection of original papers of computer conferencing
+synapse   Periodic Newsletter discusses new Connect Ed commands, upcoming courses, news of students, special events (type +archive for back issues)
+bookorder order required and recommended course texts, books by Connect Ed authors, specials, audio and video tapes, and antique scholarly books via Connect Ed's online book service
+copypol   Connect Ed policies on copyright and reproduction of text
+credit   Options and requirements for Connect Ed students
+esl   Connect Ed's online tutoring in written English as a second language
+jobs   employment opportunities in computer conferencing and related fields

58

SUMMARY

Messages, conferences, notebooks, and the directory are standard types of CMC structures, which have been used to support different forms of interaction in the Virtual Classroom. In addition we created some special types of software structures to support a learning environment. These include *Activity Branches*, which are actually programs attached to pieces of text; *instructional management programs* to support exams and grading; and a PC *front end* (Personal TEIES®) to enable students and instructors to include graphics in their communication.

The Branch Activities tools were designed to specifically support a collaborative learning environment in which students become actively involved in "teaching each other," under the guidance of the instructor(s), rather than being passive recipients of material entered by the instructor. For example, When a Question/Response activity is used, each and every participant must independently think through and enter an answer before being able to see the answers of others. This helps to create an equalitarian learning environment. The *read activity* supports the convenient delivery of substantial pieces of text to the class. It allows individual students or groups of students to deliver their written presentations or "papers" on selected topics to the others, without causing undue overload. When a contribution is in a read activity, it is a signal that it will be somewhat lengthy. The recipients may simply press function key 4 on Personal TEIES™ for capture of the material to disk or printer.

These special Virtual Classroom® software tools are not just for the. *teacher* to present *electures* (electronic lectures) and ask questions. Students also use them to carry out their assignments to present information about a selected topic related to a course and lead a discussion about that topic. An example of the use of the activity branches by students in a Computers and Society course comprises the final exhibit (3-7). This shows very active and thoughtful involvement by the students.

EXHIBIT 3-7
Excerpts From Student-Led Presentation And Discussion
Computers and Society Course, NJIT

Notes: This assignment was carried out using the "activity branch" software. In a response branch, each student must answer the question before being able to read the answer of others. Each response is attached to the main comment containing the question for response; e.g., 63.1 is the first response to the question in comment 63, 63.2 the second, and so forth.

EXHIBIT 3-7 (continued)

C105 CC61 Tal Barnea (TB, 2246) 4/14/86 11:04 AM L:2
(ORIG.) 4/14/86 10:19 AM L:2
KEYS:/BRANCH/READ/POETRY AND COMPUTERS/

Contents:

----

1 Computers and poetry
2 Pro and Con
3 Applications
4 Summary

ITEMS TO READ (#,#-#)?4
    Item: 4 (Summary)

Viewing all that has been said, I think that there is almost no doubt about the fact that the computer, although capable of creating lines that look like poetry, is incapable of creating real poetry that comes from senses and emotions. The impact of computers on poetry should be found in other aspects such as analysis, education, and freeing the poet to do the creating.
As a final note, I put down part of two poems, one written by a man (who???) and the the other by a computer. Can you distinguish between them? (See response branch.)

1. The gray sea and the long black land
    And the yellow half-moon large and low
    And the startled little waves that leap
    In fiery ringlets from their sleep
    As I gain the cove with pushing prow
    And quench its speed in the slushy sand.

2. The sunrise is coming, breathing but secret,
    Singing or weeping its joy or its terror;
    The planet's impulse is this night's gift:
    Tender, wicked, knowing, now forgotten, now treasured,
    Sometimes buried, sometimes remembered, always grasping
    As we are compelling earth and thighs and fields of violets.

C105 CC63 Tal Barnea (TB, 2246) 4/14/86 10:51 AM L:13
KEYS:/RESPONSE/POETRY AND COMPUTERS/

Read comment 61 in conference 105 before answering these questions.

1. Can you distinguish between the two poems cited?
Which is which?

2. Does poetry created by a computer have any meaning (literally speaking)?
Does it make any sense?
Can computers create real poetry?

3. If you found it difficult to distinguish between the man made poem and the computer made poem, what use is there for poets and the field of poetry?

Response CC63.1 chantalak Lacharoj (chantalak, 2375) 4/14/86 9:25 PM L:29
KEYS:/ANSWERS TO TAL BARNEA'S COMPUTER GENERATED POETRY/

1: I admit that it's difficult to distinguish which poem was by human which was by computer. I'm not at all fimiliar with poetry but I could guess that the first one "The gray sea..." was written by computer. Not that I can write better that but by examining the sentence structure, we can see that all it's doing is picking nouns and adjectives and joins each pair with "and". The second poem is far more beautiful and I guess computers can never come up with lines like that.
2: Computer generated poetry does have meaning and thus can be called real poetry. I even think it's a good poem. It makes sense because I can understand it.
3: I feel that computers are more useful in this field as an aid to a poet rather than being "poets" themselves. As of now, they are better at analysis than generating poems, but surely days will come when one can not distinguish "which is which."

Response CC63.4 Joseph Tagliaferro (TAG, 2268) 4/16/86 6:14 PM L:18
KEYS:/RESPONSE TO POEMS AND COMPUTER/

1) It is very hard to distinguish between the two. But I feel I can give a pretty good estimate which is the computers. The first seems to me to be the computer. It's phrases like: slushy sand, gray sea and black land. These phrases sound like something that was put in, to fill a spot in the poem, with no real thought about what the adjective means. Those phrases are just unclear.
2) No, as I stated above, the computer has no meaning. It just finds a word that will fit and puts it in the appropriate spot. It cannot have the ability to have meaning, because it doesn't have any intuition.
3) Not being a poetry major and really unserstanding what goes into developing a poem, I can only give you my gut feeling. I can not see how an artificial intelligence can have feeling and experience to arrange a piece of poetry so as to make someone sit back and either laugh or cry!!

EXHIBIT 3-7 (continued)

Response CC63.6 Sanjay Patel (STICK22,2273) 4/23/86 6:26 PM L:10
KEYS:/RESPONSE FROM STICK22 TO TAL-BABY FOR POETRY/

Yes, I agree that the introduction of computer in various fields has altered the performance of those in the area and also changed the quality of feedback and information associated with the specific field. Nevertheless, the use of computes in poetry has causes poets (modern day) to be a bit more lazy. This is, with the use of tape recorders and word processors, the same gifted poets of the universe have perverted their thoughts by allowing the machines to do the work. In this sense, the mind is not acting in a creative manner, instead the power of the word processor is taking control over the power and gifted talent of the poet. I do not see a reversal in the trend; that is. I don't see the quality of poems increasing again since people will always,if not to a greater degree, continue to use the computer.

Response CC63.7 Hiseog Tagkuaferri (TAG, 2268) 2/24/86 12:07 AM L:6
KEYS:/RESPONSE TO STICK22'S RESPONSE/

I don't agree with Sanjay about word processor's talking away from creativity of the poet.The poet proper still has to write out all his thoughts. The word processor is therre just as a tool to help him. It is not controlling his ideas, but just making it easier to copy and move it around and change it, if it has to be.

Response CC63.9 SANJAY PATEL (STICK22,2273) 4/26/86 PM L:9
KEYS:/HATRED TOWARD THE USE OF WORD PROCESSORS IN POETRY/

YES, THE WORD PROCESSOR IS A TOOL TO HELP THE WRITER. BUT MY CONCERN IN THE USE OF THIS MACHINE FOR COMPUTER POETRY IS THAT THE USE OF THE PROCESSOR PREVENTS THE POET FROM EXECUTING THE BASIC FORMS HE PRACTICES IN WRITING POETRY; THAT IS, THE PHYSICAL WRITING AND SCRATCHING OUT OF THE WORDS ON PAPER IS MISSED. ALSO, AS CORRECTIONS ARE MADE, THE PREVIOUS WRITING IS NOT SEEN IF THE PROCESSOR IS USED; HOWEVER, WITH THE USE OF THE OLD PEN, PENCIL, AND PAD THE USER CAN SEE HIS MISTAKES AND LEARN FROM THEM EASIER THAN FROM THE DRAFTS DONE ONTHE PROCESSOR. SURELY, HE CAN SAVE THE VARIOUS DRAFTS IN DIFFERENT FILES, BUT THE CORRECTIONS AND HOURS OF SWEAT, MUSTARD STAINS AND SCRATCHES ARE NOT APPARENT ON THE PROCESSOR AS THEY ARE ON THE APD AND PEN.

Response CC63.11 Paul Elder (Cheech, 2370) 4/28/86 4:56 PM L:30

I write poetry so I guess it's sort of a challenge to try figure out who (or what) wrote which poem. They were both very nice works but my vote for the human authored poem goes to poem #2. Please let me know whether I am correct. When I read poem #1 I said, "Hmm, this could have been written by a human." It did make sense. However, when I read the second one I noticed that there was a smoother flow to it, and the image produced by it was more "alive" and descriptive of what it was talking about. If my guess is wrong, well..., then the computer fooled me! I really doubt it though. I believe that a computer is capable of making phrases rhyme and matching the rhythm from line to line, but I cannot agree that a machine, no matter how sophisticated, can put feelings and emotions into its output.

:C105 CC103 Tal Barnea (TB,2246) 5/2/86 8:28 AM L:13
KEYS:/COMPUTERS AND POETRY/FOLLOWUP/SUMMARY/
A:61

I am adding a few lines to sum up the presentation on computers and poetry. For all those who read it, the first poem (The gray sea ...) which many people though has phrases with little meaning put together by a computer, was actually written by a human poet named Robert Browning, and is called Meeting At Night. The second poem, which I too found to be more meaningful, was created by a computer. Paul, you weren't the only one fooled, nobody, and I mean nobody, got it right. Maybe David is right in his opinion that it does not really matter what the author meant or felt when writing the poem. What should matter is what we feel when we read it, and if it has a meaning to use or it "moves" us then why should we care who or what wrote it.

CHAPTER 4

THEORETICAL FRAMEWORK AND HYPOTHESES

> The release of productivity is the product of cooperatively organized intelligence.
>
> (Dewey & Tufts, 1939, p. 446)

What is a successful implementation of a computer-mediated system to support educational delivery, and what variables determine this success? The Virtual Classroom project built upon previous work on acceptance of computer-mediated communication systems and on teaching effectiveness, both in conceptualizing the variables that can be expected to affect the process and outcome of online courses, and in operationalizing the measures of outcomes.

DEPENDENT VARIABLES: MEASURING THE SUCCESS OF THE VIRTUAL CLASSROOM

"Acceptance" or "success" of computer systems is sometimes assumed to be both unidimensional and determined mainly by functionality and human factors design considerations (Rushinek & Rushinek, 1986; Goodwin, 1987). For instance, if employees use an interactive computer system, then it may be defined by management as "successful." "Technicists" (see Mowshowitz, 1981) or "systems rationalists" (see Kling, 1980) may assume that, if a system is implemented and being used, then the users must like it and it must be having the intended beneficial impacts. However, many social analyses of computing assume that it is much more problematic whether or not systems have beneficial effects on users as individuals and on productivity enhancement for organizations (see, for instance, Keen, 1981; Hiltz, 1983; Markus, 1983; Kling & Iaconno, 1984; Attewell & Rule, 1984; Strassman, 1985; Baroudi, Olson, & Ives, 1986).

Three components of acceptance of Computer-Mediated Communication Systems (CMCS) were found to be only moderately interrelated in a previous study of users of four systems: use, subjective satisfaction, and benefits (Hiltz, Kerr, & Johnson, 1985; Hiltz, Johnson & Turoff, 1986; Hiltz, 1989). The same three basic dimensions of success were used in this study. However, amount of use of the system is conceived of as an intervening variable rather than a truly dependent variable. The other two dimensions are subjective satisfaction with the Virtual Classroom and with various aspects of the software system; and benefits, or educational outcomes. The possible benefits are greater convenience of access to education, and improved quality of learning.

THE INDEPENDENT VARIABLES

Among the theoretical and empirical approaches to studying the acceptance and diffusion of computer technology and its impacts on society, four major approaches were identified: Technological Determinism (characteristics of the system); the Social-Psychological approach (characteristics of the users); the Human Relations school—characteristics of the groups (courses) and organizations (colleges) within which systems are implemented); and the Interactionist or Systems Contingency perspective. This classification of four alternative theoretical approaches represents a selection and blending of perspectives presented in the work of Kling (1980) and Mowshowitz (1981) on theoretical perspectives on computing, and from Zmud (1979) and others, who have looked at the effects of individual differences on the adoption of MIS and other technologies.

From the theoretical approach which may be labeled TECHNOLOGICAL DETERMINISM, characteristics of the hardware-software *system* determine user behavior and the degree of success of a computer application. Rob Kling, in his review of theoretical approaches (1980), identifies the "systems rationalists" as those who tend to believe that efficiently and effectively designed computer systems will produce efficient and effective user behavior. Mowshowitz's typology of theoretical approaches to the study of computing issues has a parallel category, the "technicist," who "defines the success or failure of particular computer applications in terms of systems design and implementation" (Mowshowitz, 1981, p. 148). For example, Turner (1984) showed that the form of the interface of the applications system used by social security claims representatives affected both attitudes toward the system and job satisfaction and performance. Applying this approach to prediction of success of the Virtual Classroom, the technological and rational economic factors which would be expected to be important in explaining user behavior include access and reactions to particular aspects of the hardware and software (both on the personal computer or terminal though which the student and teacher access the system, and on the central mainframe), and the cost in time and money of using the new system compared to other alternatives for educational delivery.

To the extent that these assumptions are correct, we would expect to find that reactions to the particular hardware used would account for a great deal of the variance in success. For instance, we would hypothesize that students with a microcomputer at home and a high speed baud modem would be most likely to fully benefit from this technology. In addition, we would expect to find high correlations between subjective satisfaction with the system, and amount of use and benefits. We would also expect to find few differences among courses; the same technology should have the same impacts on all classes and students. The relative power of technological determinants can be assessed by examining the results to see if they support these predictions.

Individual Differences as Predictors

The PSYCHOLOGICAL or "individual differences" approach to predicting human behavior when confronted with a new technology would emphasize characteristics of the *individual*: attitudes and attributes, including "personality type," expectations, beliefs, skills, and capabilities (Zmud, 1979). Attitudes consist of an affective dimension involving emotions ("Computers are fun") and a cognitive dimension based on beliefs ("Using this system will improve my education"). As applied to this study, we predicted that preuse expectations about the Virtual Classroom would be strongly correlated with subsequent use of and reactions to the system. Among the individual attributes which might affect success are ability (measured by SAT scores and previous grade point average), age, gender, ethnic group or nationality, previous use of computers, and typing skills.

The personality-level attributes that might affect success include motivation or self-discipline, which may be related to perceived *Sphere of Control*; we predicted a moderate relationship between measures of Sphere of Control and acceptance of the Virtual Classroom.

Sphere of control – Work on the conceptualization and measurement of "locus of control" built for many years on the work of Rotter (1966), who devised a single scale to measure Internal vs. External Locus of Control. Paulhus (1983; see also Paulhus & Christie, 1981) devised a new set of 30 items based on a theory of three separate "Spheres of Control" (SOC) that could vary independently. Personal Efficacy as a subscale measures control over the nonsocial environment, as in personal achievement being a result of one's effort rather than "luck." *Interpersonal control* measures control over people in dyads and groups. Sociopolitical Control refers to control over social and political events and institutions. A confirmatory factor analysis, correlations with measures on other scales, and experimental research that predicted behavior on the basis of SOC subscale scores supported the reliability, validity, and utility of the three subscales.

For this study, only the personal efficacy and interpersonal control scales were included in the baseline questionnaire, in the section labeled "images of yourself" (see Appendix 1).

Group or Course Differences

The HUMAN RELATIONS approach "focuses primarily on organizational members as individuals working within a group setting" (Rice, 1984). The small groups of which an individual is part are seen as the most powerful determinants of behavior. From this perspective, existing ties among group members, and the style of teaching (electronic or otherwise) and the interactions among the members of a class would be the most crucial determinants of the acceptance and impacts of this new computer-communications technology. We would expect large differences in outcomes among the courses in which the students are enrolled.

The Interaction or Systems Contingency Model

The INTERACTIONIST (Markus, 1983) or SYSTEMS CONTINGENCY (Hiltz, 1986a) approach to the social impacts of computing was adopted for this study. In this model, no single one of the above three classes of variables was expected to fully account for differences in success of the Virtual Classroom; all were expected to contribute. However, these sets of variables are not simply additive; they interact to form a complex system of determinants. For example, both student ability and attitudes, and the way the Virtual Classroom is implemented in a specific course, are presumed to interact with educational technology: Favorable outcomes are contingent on certain levels of student ability and motivation, and on the skill and level of effort of the teacher. This theoretical perspective can be equated with what Kling (1980) calls the *package* or interactionist approach to the social impacts of computing. This would be termed a *pragmatic* approach by Mowshowitz, since it assumes that "the use made of computers is determined in part by the social or organizational settings in which they are introduced" (Mowshowitz, 1981, p. 150).

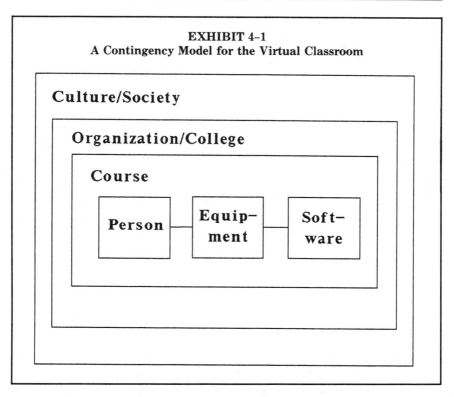

EXHIBIT 4-1
A Contingency Model for the Virtual Classroom

Culture/Society

Organization/College

Course

| Person | Equip-ment | Soft-ware |

A contingency model is diagrammed in Exhibit 4-1. Any use of the VC is nested within a particular social context. At the lowest levels, characteristics of the user and of the hardware–software system shape the dynamics of human–computer interaction during a session in which a teacher or student uses the Virtual Classroom. Equipment access is one crucial element. Do the instructor and student have a PC at home, or must they travel to reach one? Does this equipment include a printer, the ability to upload and download, and a screen with good resolution for reading? If not participants will be handicapped in their use of the system.

However, this use is within the context of a particular "group," in this case, a particular course. Courses vary on a number of dimensions, including the nature of the subject matter (from technical subjects such as Statistics or Computer Science through "liberal arts" courses such as Sociology or a writing seminar), the way the teacher uses the system in designing materials and assignments for the students, and the size of the class. Courses are in turn delivered within a particular institutional context, which includes the computing facilities made available to students, the educational goals and requirements of the college or university, and the amount of institutional support for participation in the project. The latter includes released time for faculty to prepare courses to be delivered via computer, and such factors as teaching load and the reward structure. (For instance, will time invested in utilizing this innovation count as a positive or a negative factor in decisions about promotion and tenure?)

This study does not move beyond the variables at the organizational or institutional level. Though one course was offered primarily in Canada, we did not measure cultural and societal differences as they might affect the success of the innovation. However, cultural differences should be taken into account in the sense that they may be important in introducing this technology in other societies, where the structure of higher education and educational philosophies may differ from those in the United States. For instance, one could speculate on whether or not the technology could be used in Japan, where the different system of writing would pose special technical difficulties, and where there is more emphasis on group interactional and educational achievements than in American society.

EDUCATIONAL OUTCOMES TO BE MEASURED

Educational outcomes of a delivery medium can be looked at for both students and for faculty members. The quantitative data that was collected focuses upon outcomes for students. Qualitative or anecdotal data were relied upon to document effects on the instructors, since with only a small number of faculty members participating, statistical analysis would not be fruitful.

The quality of education provided by a course should be measured by how much a student learns, retains, and later uses as a result of taking the course. Learning is a complex and multidimensional phenomenon (see, for instance, Anderson, 1983; Bloom, 1956). There are at least four basic types of learning:

- Rote learning, whereby a student memorizes facts or acquires specific skills; the student is able to "play back" the inputs presented in the course materials.
- Integrative/critical knowledge-building, wherein the student is able to pull together or synthesize diverse facts, ideas, or procedures by analyzing and organizing them into larger conceptual frameworks.
- Attitudinal change, whereby a student acquires, for instance, an "appreciation" of literature or art, standards for ethical behavior in their occupation, less prejudiced feelings about other racial or

cultural groups, or increased interest in pursuing further knowledge in a particular field.

• Application, whereby the student is able to use the knowledge, skills, or attitudes gained through the course in new situations. For example, if a student takes a course in management, is he or she able to apply the material from the course to management situations and become a more effective manager?

Courses vary a great deal in terms of which types of learning are emphasized and tested. We were not able to control for differences in learning objectives in this project, but have included courses, questions, and other measurement procedures which tap a variety of learning objectives.

The hypotheses about expected impacts of the VC which will be presented in this chapter guided research during the year of initial extensive study, using a "quasi-experimental" design comparing a wide variety of VC courses to traditionally delivered courses. Subsequently we extended the research to gather data on larger numbers of students in a few specific courses; the hypotheses for these follow-up studies will be presented in a later chapter.

General Premises

The following statements are not formal hypotheses, because they do not predict relationships between two or more variables. However, they are assertions for which we sought support or refutation throughout the research:

PREMISE 1: The Virtual Classroom is a viable alternative for delivery of college-level education. By *viable* is meant a means of delivery that will result in acceptable levels of satisfaction and performance for both instructors and students.

PREMISE 2: Computer-mediated communication as a mode of course delivery will require changes in teaching and learning strategies.

Mastery

Shavelson et al. (1986, p. vi) stated that

Telecourse evaluations must ultimately focus on outcomes and address the exchangeability of these outcomes with those attained by students in traditional courses. By "exchangeability" we mean the extent to which the knowledge, skills, and attitudes acquired by students from a telecourse are interchangeable with the knowledge, skills, and attitudes that are: (a) valued by faculty and administrators, and (b) acquired by students enrolled in the same course offered as part of the traditional curriculum.

The most basic outcome for a course is mastery of the fundamental facts, concepts, and skills the course is designed to teach. Such mastery is usually measured by examinations and assignments, which are graded. Students can also be asked to report their impressions of the extent to which a course improved their mastery of the subject or changed their attitudes. Postcourse questionnaire items drawn from widely used measures of teaching effectiveness were included for this purpose. We will use instructor-assigned grades, instructor's reports, and student self-reports to measure achievement of learning goals in a course. If there is no difference in test scores for material presented online vs. material presented in traditional face-to-face courses, we may consider this a criterion for minimal "success" of the Virtual Classroom.

Given that previous studies of courses delivered by television or other noncomputer media tend to indicate "no difference" in mastery as measured by grades (e.g., Schramm, 1977), we did not expect significant differences in grade distributions between VC and TC sections of a course. Though there may be some variation from course to course, depending upon the nature of the subject matter and the characteristics of the students, we expected that overall:

HYPOTHESIS 1: Scores measuring *mastery* of material taught in the Virtual Classroom will be equal to or better than those for the Traditional Classroom.

Why bother with an innovation like the VC if we expect no significant differences in scores? Mastery as measured by tests tends to treat mainly the lowest level of knowledge, rote learning. We expected that the VC would prove superior for higher levels of learning. Since many people feel that learning via computer could not possibly be as good as learning in a traditional classroom, it is important to establish that, at least, it does no harm.

For the first year of experimentation, we did not have a large number of students in matched sections of courses. Without a large "N," it is difficult to achieve statistically significant results, unless the outcomes for the VC and the TC are very different. The first time teachers and students use a new technology, there are likely to be unanticipated problems or difficulties, which will be overcome by time and experience.

Thus, we did not have confidence that the VC would always be significantly better.

Other Outcomes

There are many goals related to educational process and outcomes that are desirable to achieve, other than high scores on examinations. These less tangible but higher level changes may actually be of more long-term value than the ability to score well on a test covering a specific set of subject matter at a particular point in time. The capitalized words or phrases in the list below will be used in the remainder of this document to refer to the indicated outcome. The variables are given a brief conceptual definition below; their operational definitions are specified in the chapter on research methods.

HYPOTHESIS 2: VC students will report higher subjective satisfaction with the VC than with the TC on a number of dimensions:

2.1 *Convenient access* to educational experiences.

2.2 Improved *access* to their *professor*.

2.3 Increased *participation* in a course. This may be due to convenience or ease of participating, and may be reflected in the regularity and quality of their assignments, reading, and contributions to class discussion. Though this may be considered a "process" rather than an "outcome" variable, student participation in the activities of a course is usually considered a desirable objective in and of itself.

2.4 Improved ability to apply the material of the course in new contexts and *express* their own independent *ideas* relating to the material.

2.5 Increased level of *interest* and involvement, which may carry beyond the end of the course.

2.6 Improved ability to *synthesize* or "see connection among diverse ideas and information" (Davis, Dukes, & Gamson, 1981). Kraworth et al. (1964) define *synthesis* as "The putting together of elements and parts so as to form a whole, arranging and combining them in such a way as to constitute a pattern or structure not clearly there before."

2.7 *Computer comfort*—Improved attitudes toward the use of computers and greater knowledge of the use of computers. This was measured by repeating questions on attitudes toward computers before and after the course, and by directly asking the students if they have improved their computer competence.

2.8 Improved communication and cooperation with other students in doing classwork (Group *collaboration*).

2.9 Improved Overall *quality*, whereby the student assesses the experience as being "better" than the TC in some way, involving learning more on the whole or getting more out of the course.

One or two questions were included to measure several other possible desirable outcomes of a course; these were not embraced as an explicit objective of any of the experimental courses in this study and were therefore measured in only a minimal way. These include better "critical thinking" skills (Ennis, 1962), greater self-understanding, and greater understanding of ethical issues in a field.

Impacts on Writing

Since all communication in the VC is in writing, and students will see one another's writing, practice in written communication may improve skills. Good writing in fact combines a number of skills, including organization, sentence structure, grammar, and the almost indefinable elements of "voice" and of "style" that make it interesting or engaging. Thus, improvements in writing skill are very difficult to measure.

Computers in the form of text processors and spelling checkers have been used from elementary school on up to try to both speed up and improve the writing process. As Daiute (1985) points out, if electronic mail or computer conferencing is added to word-processing capabilities, one can expect some additional possible improvements, because, after all, writing is supposed to be a "social" process, a process of communication. Using the computer not only to assist in the manipulation of text but also to communicate it to others may help to provide motivation, a source of collaboration or constructive criticism, and a defined "audience." "Setting writing in a wider communication context can help students express themselves more naturally, even when they are writing formal essays" (Daiute, 1985, p. 5). Moreover, "The computer conference can be a tool for consolidating and transmitting ideas in writing at a time when the writer feels most communicative, most excited, or most confused" (p. 25).

As Daiute (1985, p. xiv) pointed out:

> With the computer as the instrument, writing is more like talking. Writers interact with the computer instrument, while the pen and the typewriter are static tools. The computer enhances the communication functions of writing not only because it interacts with the writers, but also because it offers a channel for writers to communicate with one another and because it can carry out a variety of production activities. Writing on the computer means using the machine as a pencil, eraser, typewriter, printer, scissors, paste, copier, filing cabinet, memo pad, and post office. Thus, the computer is a communication channel as well as a writing tool. The computer is a language machine.

Freed from the need to constantly recopy when revisions are made, the student using a word processing program can supposedly revise more easily and thus produce a better final version. However, using the computer in the writing process can have disadvantages as well as advantages. (For some case studies and reviews, see Bridwell, Sirc, & Brooke, 1986; Collins, 1982; Daiute & Taylor, 1981; Hansen & Haas, 1988; Kiefer & Smith, 1984; Malone, 1981.) Nontypists may be able to write much faster by hand than by using a keyboard. In addition, in order to write using a computer, the student has to access and "power up" the equipment and software, and learn to use the commands of the text editing system as well as of the larger computer system in which it is embedded; this imposes an added burden. The few studies of comparative writing quality have shown that writing on the computer is sometimes rated lower than writing done by the same people with traditional tools. It may be more "sloppy," because it is more like talking. Spoken sentences often are loosely constructed, and there tend to be more grammatical errors in speech and more use of phrases such as "sort of" and "kind of." Computer drafts also tend to have more spelling errors (which may be "typos") and syntax errors caused by omitted and repeated words. Finally, "this research is not conclusive, because none of the studies have been done after the writers have become as comfortable with the computer as they are with pen or typewriter" (Daiute, 1985, p. 113).

The major objective of the Writing Seminar at Upsala College is to improve writing. The students in one of these classes had the Virtual Classroom available for part of their work. All of their writing assignments were done in small groups online, and the students were asked to critique one another according to guidelines provided by the instructor. The impact on their ability to write clearly and well was assessed using data generated by standard before-and-after testing procedures at Upsala. Every freshman is given a "holistically graded" written essay exam upon entrance, and again a semester later, after the writing course has finished. (This means that the essay is graded as a whole, rather than given separate grades for grammar, organization, argumentation, persuasiveness, etc.). We took advantage of this existing data to attempt to compare changes in writing scores for the experimental online section with changes for students in the other sections.

HYPOTHESIS 3: Use of the Virtual Classroom will lead to improvement in writing.

Of course, there are other factors which may affect the validity of any such conclusion. Students will not be randomly assigned to the various sections, and the teachers and specific topics used for writing assignments will vary. There is a methodological question as to whether this single "holistic" assessment of writing quality may be able to capture specific types of improvements that may occur. Moreover, there is a serious question as to whether any single semester-long course can significantly improve writing. However, statistical tendencies toward a difference associated with system use would be as promising for more controlled experimentation with writing courses in the future.

In addition to this attempt to quantitatively measure overall improvements in writing, we asked students in all courses whether or not use of the system improved their ability to communicate their ideas. In addition, we asked faculty members to observe and report any changes they noticed in the writing of their students as an online course progressed.

Collaborative Learning as an Intervening Variable

Group collaboration experience has been mentioned as a possible desirable outcome of a course. It is listed as a desirable objective in itself, because in "later life" people will often have to work together on team projects, rather than carrying out separate competitive efforts. *Group* or *collaborative learning* was defined in Chapter 2 as learning that occurs through interaction with a peer group. It is conceptualized as a key means or process in the Virtual Classroom environment, that may aid in achieving other objectives such as mastery of the material. For instance, when all students are entering their assignments online, it is much easier to encourage them to look at and learn from one another's work than in the TC, where massive amounts of photocopying would be necessary to attain the same objective. However, some students may not take advantage of these opportunities to learn from their peers.

Group learning was measured for all participating students with a set of four items included at the bottom of the "general information" page of the postcourse questionnaire. In addition, for those students using the system, a number of items on the section labeled "comparison to traditional classrooms" were used as indicators.

HYPOTHESIS 4: Those students who experience *group* or *collaborative* learning in the Virtual Classroom are most likely to judge the outcomes of online courses to be superior to the outcomes of traditional courses.

Correlates of Outcomes

In accordance with the theoretical framework adopted, there are many factors in addition to collaborative learning experiences that are expected to be associated with outcomes.

HYPOTHESIS 5: Differences among students in academic ability (e.g., as measured by SAT scores or grade point average) will be strongly associated with outcomes in the Virtual Classroom. High-ability students will report more positive outcomes than low ability students.

Although this may not be desirable outcome, it is true in the TC and may be magnified by the VC. Good reading and writing skills are a precondition for collaborative learning in this environment. An online course replaces all oral explanation with a writing-based discussion. Learning depends on asking questions and receiving responses from the instructor and the other students. Students who lack basic communication skills are likely to be unable or unwilling to formulate questions about any difficulties they are having. Since many of the courses included have a mathematical foundation (the two statistics courses and the computer science course), basic ability to comprehend mathematical material in a written form may also be correlated. In terms of equity the main issue of importance is not whether better-prepared students will learn more via the VC than less prepared or less able students, but whether those with weaker academic skills will be able to perform at an acceptable level at all. Because of self-pacing we expected that they would.

Another individual-level set of characteristics that is likely to be related to outcomes is attitudes and expectations. Students must be motivated in order to discipline themselves to sign on regularly and participate actively. The relevant expectations include attitudes toward computers, toward the system that will be used, and toward the course.

HYPOTHESIS 6: Students with more positive precourse attitudes towards computers in general and towards the specific system to be used will be more likely to participate actively online and to perceive greater benefits from the VC mode.

As discussed in the section on theoretical perspectives, the personality attributes related to self-discipline and achievement motivation that are expected to be correlated with student behavior in the VC may be tapped by measures of *sphere of control.*

HYPOTHESIS 7: Students with a greater *sphere of control* on both the personal and the interpersonal levels will be more likely to regularly and actively participate online and to perceive greater benefits from the VC mode.

Students do not take courses online within a homogeneous context. They take a particular course, which develops a social structure, heavily influenced by the style and skill of their instructor in conducting the course. According to our contingency perspective, we would expect process and outcomes to differ among these groups or courses.

HYPOTHESIS 8: There will be significant differences in process and outcome among courses, when mode of delivery is controlled. (Another way of stating this hypothesis is that there will be an interaction effect between mode and course.)

In other words, some courses will be more successful in the VC than others. By describing these differences, we hope to understand how to best use this technology in the future.

Implementation Issues

Adoption of this innovation is not likely to be strongly influenced by findings on comparative outcomes of traditional and virtual classes. It is more likely to be decided on "political" and practical economic grounds. As Shavelson et al. (1986) note,

> The telecourse is a controversial, emotionally charged issue in higher education. To some it represents a threat – indeed, the greater the sophistication of the course, the greater the competition and threat to traditional educational institutions, their curricula, and instructors.

Case study methods were used to document implementation issues. In particular, opposition to the experiment was recorded as well as dealt with. The practical problems of implementing the courses, and the costs in terms of time and hassles to faculty and staff, were described. This recording of largely qualitative aspects of the implementation can be used to suggest the sorts of problems and possible solutions that may be relevant for future implementations.

There are two aspects of implementation that can be explored with our quasi-experimental design and examined using quantitative rather than purely qualitative data. These are the effect of course repetition and the effect of the nature of the educational environment, as it varies among colleges. Some of the online courses were repeated a second time. Because the VC is a new approach to teaching, we expected that instructors would learn from their first attempts and improve their skills for teaching online with practice.

HYPOTHESIS 9: Outcomes for the second offering of a VC course by an instructor will be significantly better than those for the first attempt at teaching online.

In addition, the Virtual Classroom was implemented within several very different educational environments. One major difference is between the campus-based populations of NJIT and Upsala, where the quasi-experimental design was conducted, and the distance education students who took courses through Connected Education, the Ontario Institute, or WBSI. The number of cases for these data is probably too small to do more than see if, on the whole, the distance-education implementations are more or less successful than the campus-based courses. It will probably also not be possible to disentangle which differences between Upsala and NJIT may be most important in explaining any differences in outcomes. However, it can be expected that these outcomes will be influenced by differences in access to equipment, skill level and computer experience of the students, and the general "educational environment" within which the experiment took place.

HYPOTHESIS 10: There will be significant differences between the Upsala and NJIT implementations of the Virtual Classroom, in terms of both process and outcomes of the online courses.

HYPOTHESIS 11: There will be significant differences between the campus-based VC courses and those offered through totally distance learning programs

Two Modes or Three?

In the hypotheses above, mode of delivery is dichotomized: courses using VC vs. courses conducted totally in a Traditional Classroom environment. The initial design for this field study anticipated only two modes of delivery. In fact, as actually implemented, we had three modes of delivery: totally VC, totally TC, and mixed. Is the mixed mode simply a variant of the VC, some sort of average of the other two modes? We have no prior studies to serve as a basis for answering this question, but we suspect that it is not.

Hypothesis 11: Results for the "mixed" mode will not represent a simple "average" of results for totally VC and totally TC modes, but will represent a distinctive set of strengths and weaknesses.

This is an admittedly vague statement. What it means is that, in each of the preceding hypotheses, we will be aware that there may be significant differences between VC courses offered totally online and those offered in a mixed mode.

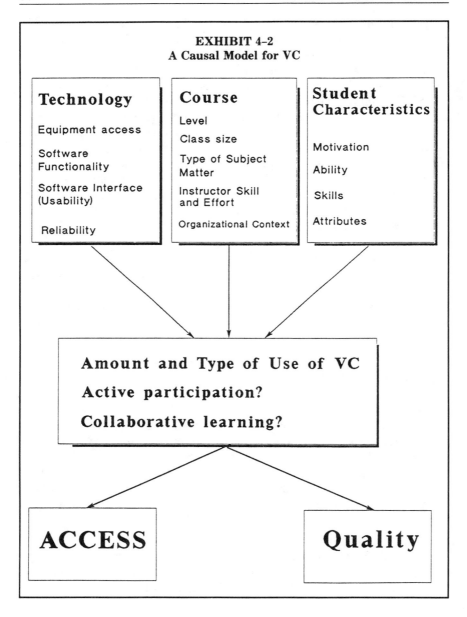

EXHIBIT 4–2
A Causal Model for VC

Technology

Equipment access

Software
Functionality

Software Interface
(Usability)

Reliability

Course

Level

Class size

Type of Subject
Matter

Instructor Skill
and Effort

Organizational Context

**Student
Characteristics**

Motivation

Ability

Skills

Attributes

Amount and Type of Use of VC

Active participation?

Collaborative learning?

ACCESS

Quality

SUMMARY

The independent, intervening, and dependent variables used to assess the effectiveness of the Virtual Classroom are displayed in the causal model in Exhibit 4–2. Overall, it was expected that providing the Virtual Classroom as a learning environment would result in learning experiences that were, on the average, better than those available in the traditional classroom. This is because of the increased convenience of interaction with the materials and activities of the course at any time, and the increased possibility for collaborative or peer learning activities. However, favorable outcomes are predicted to be contingent on a number of conditions. These include the adequate academic skills of the learner, adequate functionality and usability of the software, effective use of the medium by the instructor, and the support or lack of support for this mode of course delivery provided by the host institution.

PART II

TEACHING IN A VIRTUAL CLASSROOM: THE PERPETUAL PROFESSOR

If ever I am a teacher it will be to learn more than to teach
—Madame Deluzy (1747–1830)

CHAPTER 5

BASIC PRINCIPLES AND GETTING STARTED

> Whatever you would have your children become, strive to
> exhibit in your own lives and conversation
>
> — Lydia Sigourney (1791–1865)

We have seen that a Virtual Classroom is a teaching and learning environment located within a computer-mediated communication system. As a teaching environment, it provides a set of tools, strengths, and limitations that are available to an instructor for delivering course materials and structuring learning experiences. Its characteristics are merely potentials, just as the empty classroom with its chalkboards and desks awaits the efforts and creativity of the instructor and the students to make it "come alive."

This section looks at the Virtual Classroom from the teacher's point of view. Its purpose is to present the lessons learned by the faculty members who have participated in the project, particularly in terms of guidelines or generalizations that may be of use to future instructors who are considering using computer-mediated communication as a mode of educational delivery. It is directed primarily toward the prospective educator.

However, understanding the pedagogical guidelines and instructional designs and processes that apply to a Virtual Classroom is also of fundamental importance for those whose interests in online learning lie elsewhere. Prospective *students* in online courses can gain insight into what their experiences are likely to be by seeing how the teaching process differs between the Virtual Classroom (VC) and the traditional classroom (TC). *Scholars and administrators* who want to know about the outcomes of online courses also need to understand the teaching processes that weld the opportunities provided by the medium and a set of instructional goals into a particular online "course."

Just as there is no single recipe for successful teaching in the traditional classroom, there are diverse techniques which can be successful in the computer-mediated environment. Whatever strategy is initially chosen will have to be modified on the basis of observations about the level of ability and motivation of the students; this is true in any medium. However, there are some fundamental differences in teaching between the VC and the TC, stemming from the differences between the communication channels.

There are three basic principles to keep in mind for successful teaching in the Virtual Classroom, dealing with media richness, timely responsiveness, and interaction:

1. *Media richness*: In the traditional classroom, a pleasing voice, occasional jokes, dramatic gestures, and interspersed questions can help to enliven a long lecture. In CMC, there is only the screen and/or the printed pages. Even if the work station supports color graphics and sound, long segments of lecture-type materials are boring. To maintain interest, the instructor should use written language in a skillful way (including the use of humor and metaphor), orchestrate active participatation by the students, and stimulate collaborative assignments that involve both social and task-oriented activities.

2. *Timely responsiveness*: Unlike the face-to-face medium, students will not receive an immediate response to their questions and comments. This can be very frustrating, especially if they are "stuck" in the middle of a mathematics problem or other assignment. However, whereas they may have only a limited opportunity to ask questions during a few set hours a week for a traditional class, they can participate and receive feedback on a daily basis in the Virtual Classroom. But this depends on the instructor, who needs to sign on every day except for occasional announced exceptions to this policy, and respond to all waiting material. Most faculty report that this takes them about 30 minutes to an hour a day, depending on the number of students and the level of their activity. This is what is meant by the "perpetual professor"; teaching is continuous, like parenthood, rather than being confined to a few specific hours during the week.

3. *Interaction*: Probably the greatest determinant of the extent to which students feel that the online mode of delivery is better or worse than traditional modes is the amount and quality of interac-

tion between the instructor and the students, and/or among the students. This is not easy, as can be deduced from reading the course reports included as Appendix III to this volume. But, as B.J. Gleason notes, if you can cajole or coerce the students into this collaborative approach to learning, they will share ideas with each other in a way that is seldom or never seen in a traditional classroom. Herein lies both the key and the challenge for being an effective teacher in the Virtual Classroom environment.

This section of the book provides a brief overview of some techniques that can be used to improve the probability of providing a valuable learning experience for students in online courses. It is based on qualitative data: observing and teaching online classes, looking at the comments and suggestions made by students, and case reports by instructors. Exhibits will give exemplary excerpts and illustrations of these techniques from actual courses. A deeper understanding of the techniques and problems of instructors in specific courses can be gained by looking at the selection of narrative case histories of instructors' experiences in using the Virtual Classroom included in Appendix III. These exhibits and case histories will give the reader a feeling for the diversity of teaching techniques and experiences which underlie this summary. You may wish to look through the course reports before reading the rest of this section.

The appendices and reports on this project refer to some features of the particular software used, such as the Activity Branches described in Chapter 4. In utilizing other CMC systems which do not incorporate these features, it may be possible to devise analogous procedures. For example, additional conferences might be set up for specific types of exchanges or assignments related to a course, rather than organizing and segregating them as an "activity."

In many ways, teaching a course online is merely a variation of moderating any computer conference. As in any computerized conference, the outcomes are dependent upon both the skills and hard work of the moderator, and the skills and level of motivation of the members of the conference.

CMC can be used to deliver an entire course online, or as an adjunct to other media. A later chapter will describe some of the ways in which it can be used to support face-to-face classrooms or distance education delivered via media such as television or print materials.

CHOOSING AN APPROPRIATE COURSE

We have noted that interaction among the members of a class is an essential characteristic of successful application of the Virtual Classroom approach to education. There are several preconditions for success related to this aspect of the medium.

In order for interaction to occur, students must be motivated to learn and able to communicate by typing and reading. In some educational settings, this may not be a problem. In others, it may be a severe obstacle. It is pretty hopeless to try to use CMC to develop higher level cognitive skills if the students are having trouble with reading and writing. Likewise, if a course is a "required" one, which many students resent taking, and about which they profess feelings ranging from lack of interest to fear and hostility, the Virtual Classroom is not recommended. It requires more effort from students than the traditional classroom, where all they have to do is show up and take notes.

CMC is not as effective as books or lectures for the one-way delivery of information, for most students. If the objective of a course is to follow a lock-step syllabus that requires students to memorize or master a great deal of information or specific skills, and it does not aim at having them discuss the material in any depth or to apply it in a creative way, the medium may be inappropriate. Finally, courses that require visual material (such as art history), manipulation of physical objects (such as an experimental chemistry course, where simulated experiments will not suffice), or audio interaction (such as a language course) will have to be supplemented by other media rather than being offered totally online.

GETTING STARTED

If students are to participate effectively in the Virtual Classroom, they must have adequate access to the system, feel comfortable with the medium and with each other, and know what is expected of them. The instructor must be competent using the system and have a course design worked out ahead of time which is appropriate to the medium and the capabilities of the specific system.

Assuring Access

Instructors should have access to a microcomputer, modem, word processing software, and printer from their homes as well as from their offices. In preparing for, and offering, an online course, especially for the first time, they will be spending several hundred hours online. In order for daily exchanges with students to be an enjoyable experience rather than an onerous burden, it is essential that faculty members be able to have the convenience and comfort of working nights and weekends from home.

If many hours are going to be spent online, instructors (and ideally students, too) should consider installing a second telephone line for the computer. Family members do not appreciate being cut off from the outside world for hours at a time! In addition, it is very likely that an instructor will want to be able to talk on the telephone to a student while signed online, to watch what a student is doing. Fortunately, second or "teen" lines are generally priced very reasonably. If you are not within a local phone call of the system or network node you are dialing, also look into extended calling arrangements with your local telephone company. These generally allow up to about 20 hours a month of connection to a specific set of telephone numbers for a flat fee, such as $5.00.

Ideally, each student would also have access to online course material through a micro and modem at home, as well as equipment at school or work. In the ideal set-up, the micros and communication software would all be the same, so that a single set of instructions for connecting to and using the CMC system would suffice. You cannot expect each individual student to master several kinds of hardware and communications software.

If you are going to rely on access through microcomputers at the university, make sure that there are adequate numbers of machines with modems and telephone lines available, that there are evening as well as daytime hours when students can use the equipment, and that any assistants who are available to help students use the equipment know how to establish a connection to the CMC.

What is an adequate number of work stations? The problem is that student use does not distribute itself evenly through the week; many members of a class will wait until a few hours before an assignment or activity is "due" to sign online. A safe guideline would be to have at least half as many terminals or micros available as there are students in the largest online class. With any fewer, there is likely to be occasional frustrating queuing. There must also be adequate capability to send material to a printer; students should be able to easily obtain a print of anything which they may want to reread in the future, after having seen it once on the screen. Check out all components of equipment access carefully before deciding to use CMC. For instance, it could take months to have new phone lines installed, if you discover that there is a microlab but no capacity for the machines to dial out to a remote host.

To help remote students with their own microcomputers, develop a set of printed materials which show how to use the most widespread combinations of hardware and software they have. Don't forget to provide instructions for reaching the system through packet-switched networks (including interuniversity links such as Telnet) or local area networks, as well as direct dial. Recommend a single communications software package, or perhaps two, for them to acquire if they are buying one, and give instructions for how to correctly set the communications parameters for these packages. For instance, we have found that SMARTCOM is a superior package, but it is relatively expensive; we also recommend the "shareware" program Procomm for those who do not want to spend much money on software. Adequate and affordable communications software is a problem, so we included communications management in the Personal TEIES microcomputer software, which we developed. Diskettes of Personal TEIES can be sent to each student with the correct defaults and calling numbers already set. This could also be done with diskettes of other communications software distributed to students.

Have a telephone number students may call if they have trouble getting connected. Do not consider a person actually "registered" for a course until he or she has signed on and sent a communication. Call students who have failed to appear online for more than a few days past the scheduled starting date, and find out what the problem is. Likewise, if a student "disappears" from an online class for a week or more, call to find out what the problem is. Try to help the student solve the problem, and work out a "contract" or schedule whereby the student can catch up with the course.

Decide how you are going to introduce the students to the system and ease them online. You may send printed instruction or tutorials, provide a videotape, or have a face-to-face meeting in a computer laboratory. If the students are computer novices, they may need an introduction to PCs and DOS first, as a separate laboratory.

An initial face-to-face meeting where students meet you and the others and learn the basics of using the system is a good idea if geographical dispersion makes this practical. If you decide to try "hands on" training in system use rather than just a demonstration, there should be no more than two students per terminal, and one assistant to help every four to six learners. Ideally, such a training session would be 3 or more hours long; certainly, 50 minutes is too short to accomplish anything except confusion. If your class is small, another idea is to schedule a first "synchronous" session, where the entire class is online at the same time for about an hour and a half, so that you are available for immediate response to questions. If you do this, have a second phone line available so that students who have difficulty connecting can call for advice and successfully join the session. If there are more than about 15 students, consider breaking up the class into smaller subgroups for the first face-to-face session or the synchronous online session.

COURSE DESIGN AND PREPARATION

First, you as instructor must feel comfortable with the software and your hardware. Before trying to teach a course online, it is a good idea to participate in other conferences, practice using the editor, and observe some other online classes. Note, for instance, Robert Meinke's course report in Appendix III. Casual use of a system is not sufficient preparation for delivering an entire course online. If you have not thoroughly mastered the software and equipment you will be using, you may find, as he did, that the first month or so is "absorbed in coping with the mechanics of computing," and is exhausting and frustrating.

Plan out the entire course ahead of time, and prepare and store your "fixed" material such as lectures and assignments. Decide how you are going to organize the course, in terms of the use of structures such as multiple conferences for different activities, branch activities, notebooks, etc. Make sure that you or a technical assistant has correctly added all students to the groups, conferences, and other work spaces they will need to have access to when they sign on. Be sure to plan lots of activities where the students will be working together collaboratively and actively contributing to the online material, rather than just reading what you provide and doing assignments on an individual basis. Then you should be able to concentrate on the dynamics of the course and on being responsive to the students, rather than staying up half the night preparing materials for the next day.

How long will it take to prepare a complete course for presentation online the first time? One guideline is that it will take about as long as it takes you to prepare a new course for presentation in a traditional classroom the first time; perhaps 100 to 300 hours. Even though you have offered a course "face-to-face," reorganizing and rethinking and preparing it for the new medium is almost like starting over again with a topic area for a course. In many institutions, instructors receive reduced teaching loads or other special considerations such as summer pay for "new course preparations." Such considerations or allowances should be extended to faculty teaching courses via CMC.

In planning how a course can best be delivered online, you will find that you are forced to clearly identify its basic objectives, and to think a great deal about the types of instructional strategies and assignments that can be used to attain these learning objectives for the students. Designing a course for the Virtual Classroom can "introduce novelty and excitement" for the instructor as well as the students. The result, as Robert Meinke points out in his course report, is that you are likely to end up altering the way you teach courses in the traditional classroom in the future.

The second time you offer a course online, the amount of time and effort required on your part will be much less. The total time required will probably be comparable to that required for preparation, delivery, grading, and counseling students in courses in the traditional classroom environment. However, the time will be distributed differently, spread throughout the week rather than being concentrated on one or two days.

Even though you start the course with a complete plan, be prepared to modify it depending on the ability of the students to maintain the pace and level of effort you had anticipated in your plan. This is really no different than teaching a face-to-face course, when you should have the whole course planned ahead, but be ready to modify the plans based on feedback from the students.

Decide which set of special instructional support tools you will use, e.g., response activities, selection activities, the Electronic Gradebook, or forms on EIES 2. Though each kind of special software tool may be useful, too many of them will become confusing to students, so you may need to go back and decide that some of the special commands or subsystems that might be helpful are really not necessary. Whenever students are requested to use a new command or software routine for the first time, explain it step-by-step. Make their first use of a new facility fairly easy substantively, and make sure that each student has mastered it.

Many instructors give a first assignment which consists of sending a private message, reading waiting conference material, entering a comment or response in the conference, and handing in a fairly simple assignment. (For an example, see Exhibit 5-1.)

Consider setting aside a special place for technical problems, such as a branch in the class conference or a separate conference. Encourage students to help their peers with their questions in this side discussion, rather than taking on the burden of answering all of the questions about system use yourself. This will help to build group cohesiveness and improve the self confidence of the "helpers," as well as taking a considerable burden off you.

INITIAL COMMENTS AND ACTIVITIES

Have an individually addressed message waiting for each class member when they sign on. This might welcome them, ask them to send a message back to you describing any impressions or difficulties so far, and direct them on how to go to the class conference after sending their return message. The purpose of this message and requested response is to help you keep track of which students have "made it" and which may be having difficulties. If the system you are using does not automatically store a record of when messages are received, keep your own list of the progress of your beginners in finding their electronic way to the class.

Spend some time planning and writing the welcoming and orienting comments that will await the students when they first enter their Virtual Classroom. Try to make your use of language both interesting and

EXHIBIT 5-1
Some Initial Segments of Introduction to Computer Science

Note: Students' names changed to preserve confidentiality
:C213 CC1 VC - BJ Gleason (BJ/VC,213) 1/21/87 3:24 PM L:55 KEYS:/WEL-
COME/ CIS 213 ONLINE! /

Welcome to CIS 213 - Section 15109 - Spring 87 ONLINE!

The Ground rules are simple: This is a class, just like, more or less, one that
you would attend normally. The only real difference is that there is no dress
code. But many of the normal rules still apply. No cursing, swearing and no
telling off color jokes. You must remember, even though it seems that you
are the only person online, many other people use this system.

Another important rule: This is an experimental section. In other words, not
everything may work properly. If you run into any problems, TELL ME!
The only way we will be able to correct the problems is if we are told when
they happen.

Finally: There is no such thing as a stupid question. If you do not understand
something, ask. You can leave the question in this conference, or send me
(BJ/VC,213) a private message.

Well, that's about it. Feel free to roam about the system, and don't worry,
you can't "break" anything. Feel free to join other conferences, and there are
quite a few, but be sure to follow the rules established by the moderator.

So, relax, sit back, and we will all have a good time.

But most off all - in the words of the Hitchhiker's Guide to the Galaxy:

DON"T PANIC!!!

:C213 CC3 VC - BJ Gleason (BJ/VC,213) 1/21/87 3:27 PM L:20 KEYS-
:/GRADES FOR THE COURSE/ A BRIEF OUTLINE /

In this course we will have:
Midterm - 33% of the grade
FINAL - 33% of the grade

The other 34% will be Labs, assignments, and a research paper.

Every week, you will have to answer a quiz. This week it is a sample quiz, but
starting next week, they will count. The quizzes before the midterm will be
applied to the grade you receive on the midterm, and the quizzes from the midterm to the final will be applied to the final exam grade. So don't miss them!

EXHIBIT 5–1 (continued)

There will be one quiz a week, about 5 to 15 minutes long. The quizzes will be open book open notes. You can only take the quiz once.

:C213 CC5 VC - BJ Gleason (BJ/VC,213) 1/21/87 3:33 PM L:20 KEYS:/
FIRST ASSIGNMENT/
As discussed in class:

1. change your name

2. enter a nickname

3. send me (BJ/VC,213) a private message

4. enter a comment in this conference, and give me a little background about yourself

5. when your notebook is established, you are to enter it and compose the FORTRAN assignment I gave you in class. You can then run it using the + FORTRAN command.

6. take the sample quiz, using the command + QUIZ, and when it asks where is the quiz, type N213NP10

:C213 CC8 Harry Doe (har2,2440) 1/21/87 8:03 PM L:1 KEYS:/TEST/

Hey Class- G O O D   L U C K

:C213 CC24 Ralph Doe (ral,2279) 1/21/87 8:17 PM L:3 KEYS:/NO.1/

MY NAME IS RALPH.I AM CURRENTLY TAKING CIS-213 +
AS MY TECHNICAL ELECTIVE. +
MY MAJOR IS MECHANICAL ENGINEERING AND I WILL GRAD-
UATE IN MAY 1987 +

:C213 CC28 VC - BJ Gleason (BJ/VC,213) 1/22/87 7:00 PM L:2 KEYS:/TEST/
A: 8

a thoughtful wish harry . . . thank you, and from me, good luck to all . . .
:C213 CC44 VC - BJ Gleason (BJ/VC,213) 1/22/87 7:28 PM L:6 KEYS:/NO.1/
A: 24

Hey Ralph!

Glad you picked this course . . . You do not, however, have to type a + at the end of every line. It is only needed as the first character on a new line if you want to finish the message!

Keep up the good work!

friendly; you are modeling the informal and friendly atmosphere you wish
to encourage. Summarize what you are going to do in the course, and tell
them what to do first.

Students must form a "group," a "we," if an online course is to proceed
well. One way to facilitate this is to ask students to enter medium-length
introductions in which they mention, not just resume-type facts like their
major or their job, but also personal things like their hobbies and their
marital status. This might be entered either as a regular conference
comment or as a question/response activity during the first week, as part
of their first assignments.

Exhibits 5–1 and 5–2 show excerpts from the first few days of entries
and interaction in two very different conferences, one for undergraduates
using the system for the first time and unfamiliar with one another as well,
and the other for Western Behavioral Sciences Institute participants who
are "veterans" of many prior month-long seminars on EIES together. In
the former case, for the neophytes, much more instruction has to be given
on the mechanics of carrying out the assignments, and the initial entries of
the students are quite short and generally at an intellectually disappointing level. However, both instructors responded quickly and positively to the first responses from the participants, with the positive
reinforcement displayed to motivate others in the conference to join in too.

During the first week especially, give lots of positive feedback to
students, so that they know their efforts have been read. Throughout the
course, try to make the emotional tone of your communications positive
and supportive. Let the students know that, while they are expected to
use an editor on papers or assignments, a more casual style is acceptable
for discussion comments or questions, and that a few typos are okay as
long as the meaning is clear. Consider establishing a separate conference
for informal chatting online. For instance, Connected Education on EIES
includes a *cafe*, where students and faculty as well as other members of the
system talk about current events, restaurants, or travel, or any other topic
of interest.

Remember, especially at the beginning, to use welcoming phrases
("Great to see you onboard and participating in the class, Ellen!"). Use first
names to establish a climate of informality. Keep directive statements
sparse and light-handed. Use some self-deprecating humor if that feels
comfortable to you, and model peer behavior by exposing some of your
personal characteristics, feelings, or experiences (Harasim & Johnson,
1986).

MAKING EXPECTATIONS CLEAR

A syllabus or course outline showing the schedule of topics, readings, and
assignments should be entered as one of the initial entries in the course,

EXHIBIT 5-2
The Welcome and Introduction

At the beginning of any class conference, the moderator-instructor should welcome the students, describe the content and basic procedures for the course, and tell the students what to do first. The excerpts below show Jay Forrester doing this for a WBSI course, with a language style that is intriguing and engaging. Note the style of responding to several comments in one response; in an active conference, this may not only be necessary but also helpful in synthesizing some diverse opinions and entries.

:C1737 CC1 Jay W. Forrester (Jay F.,2916) 2/27/87 12:34 PM L:22 KEYS:/
ORGANIZATIONAL DESIGN/MARCH TRIP/

Welcome to Conference 1737, "Concepts of Organizational Design." It is now time for all amphibious types to come out of John Craven's oceans to contemplate what may happen in the future on land. For those who cannot survive out of water, try to put up a periscope for observation and at least be a lurker from the deep. The tour guide for March is planning a trip through possible future kinds of organizations, some dimensions of leadership that were not covered in the February CEO conference, the idea of designing organizations rather than letting them happen, how to increase organizational effectiveness, questions about productivity of the national economy, making organizations a more personally satisfying place in which to work, and a look at why the economy is behaving the way it is and where it may be going.

That is a lot of territory to cover. There may be washed out roads, mudholes, and detours along the way. Indeed, that is too crowded an itinerary for one month, so there will be shortcuts, and some of the advertised attractions may be missed. We will see where the conversations lead.

Some of the ideas to be presented have been well tested, others will be highly speculative. Most of them have not yet penetrated far into the corporate culture. We can debate concepts, validity, and practicality.

We will not divide the month into blocks for the various subjects but try to carry on several themes in parallel. Only after we get started can we judge whether or not that will work.

:C1737 CC3 Jay W. Forrester (Jay F.,2916) 2/27/87 12:42 PM L:13 KEYS:/
PUZZLES IN MANAGEMENT/

As a way to start, let me suggest that each of you put in a brief statement of about 15 lines on some troubling or perplexing aspect of management that you feel arises out of social and/or economic interactions. Here we mean management in the broadest sense of the term – management of : one's own self and relations to job and others; school systems; corporations . . .

:C1737 CC11 (Doug C.,384) 3/ 1/87 11:10 PM L:16 KEYS:/STRUCTURE EXAMPLE/

I once ran a quality of work-life project at the World Bank. We created a more participatory management for a Regional Vice President. All went well for about three months. Then some odd events and the VP got scared and we stopped but studied the situation.

What we found was that this "development agency" was really organized as a factory to produce loans, and participation (discussions of development and more planning) got in the way, because they could only slow down the assembly line.

So I learned a crucial lesson about organizational structure; if you want something good, like participation (because it develops people and would be good for the Bank in the long run) you have to make sure the underlying structure of the organization requires it, and if not, to change that first.

:C1737 CC14 Jay W. Forrester (Jay F.,2916) 3/ 2/87 10:14 PM L:24 KEYS-:/WORLD BANK/ORGANIZATIONAL DESIGN/

Reference CC11, CC12, and CC4). The World Bank is so far from the kind of organization suggested in "New Corporate Design" that "participation" probably means very different things in the two settings. What would "Individual Profit Centers" on page 6 and "Objective Determination of Compensation" on page 8 mean in the context of running the World Bank? Certainly it would mean a different and more responsible organization. Perhaps it would mean that an individual would be personally responsible for the success of a loan and for its being paid back. He would receive financial compensation accordingly . . .

:C1737 CC16 (Doug C.,384) 3/ 2/87 11:52 PM L:21 KEYS:/MORE RE-QUIREMENT TO ACCOUNTABILITY /

Jay, I didn't expect you to take the path you did on the World Bank. What you say makes analytical sense, but how does it fit the reality?

The bank actually pays staff salaries on the interest earned. And all loans have been paid back. The accountability in this regard is quite good. And the staff works like a taxicab company and bank staff go to the countries and try to come up with formidable bankable loans

The problem is that because of the tie in with the IMF, etc., the countries are extremely likely to want to pay the loans back, even when the financed projects fail.

EXHIBIT 5-2 (continued)

So, as a tight business it does very well, self financing itself and all. But in terms of developmental significance and providing interesting work for its staff it falls way short of its potential

So the lesson I see is that good organizational design must heed to standards of broader human significance than just bottom line.

Otherwise we could have an economy that is doing very well while the people are doing very poorly.

---

mailed to students, or handed out at the face-to-face meeting. While a sequential set of topics or modules is the most common form of organization, the instructor may decide alternatively to structure the course as a limited set of *multilogues* (activities and discussions that are to proceed simultaneously); if this is the case, also make that clear, as does Jay Forrester in his initial conference comments shown in Exhibit 5-2.

For courses organized in terms of modules or topics, you should establish a regular rhythm of activities and deadlines, so that students know how to plan their time. For instance, you might regularly enter material on a new unit over the weekend, and give them until midnight the following Monday to finish all assignments for a unit. If you are on a system like EIES, which is busiest on Mondays, consider entering new materials on another day such as a Thursday, with the deadline for completion the next Wednesday night. If there are two or more courses being offered for which students are using the same microcomputers, make sure that they do not have the same usual deadline day during the week. Generally speaking, it is a good idea in a semester-length course to have modules that are a week or two in length, so that students can establish a regular pattern of participation and activity for each week during the course.

Exhibit 5-3 shows a typical entry by an instructor in the Virtual Classroom project who received very high ratings from the participants. Notice that there are some informal comments (e.g., "Hope your spring recess was wonderful") mixed in with the clear list of expectations for the next segment of the course.

Generally, faculty and students should not enter material in all-capital letters. This makes it harder to read. However, all-caps can make things stand out. Note that the instructor who created the material in Exhibit 5-3 used all-capital letters for the assignment. Thus, for instance, if students keep a transcript or a downloaded file of course material, the assignments can be located very quickly if they are identified by the all-capital letters format. Another use of all-caps is to make a word or a phrase stand out in

EXHIBIT 5–3
The Course Leader Makes Expectations Clear

:C2585 CC185 Rose Dios (ROSEANN,2547) 3/23/87 4:46 PM L:44
KEYS:/WEEKS 9 AND 10/DISCUSSION OF LECTURE/
ASSIGNMENTS/

HELLO! Thank you for the kind words—I HOPE YOUR SPRING RE-
CESS WAS WONDERFUL! . . . Thank you for correcting my example on
the probability of rain during the world series . . . this year the victory was
ours!

YOUR ASSIGNMENT FOR THE NEXT 11 DAYS IS AS FOLLOWS:

1. READ COMMENTS 185–202 IN CONFERENCE 2585.

2. READ PAGES 129–146 AND 163–171 IN YOUR TEXTBOOK.

3. USE + BRANCH TO ANSWER THE QUESTIONS IN COMMENTS
   200, 201, 202.

THESE 3 QUESTIONS ARE YOUR HOMEWORK FOR THIS
MATERIAL.

4. TAKE THE SECOND TEST BY USING +QUIZ. THE LOCA-
   TIONS OF THE QUESTIONS ARE

   N2585NP303
   N2585NP304
THE FIRST QUESTION IS ON PERMUTATIONS AND
COMBINATIONS.
THE SECOND QUESTION IS ON EXCLUSIVE AND INDEPENDENT
EVENTS.

YOU CAN TAKE THE TEST ALL AT ONCE . . . OR DO EITHER OF
THE QUESTIONS IN ANY ORDER AND ON ANY DAY YOU WISH SO
LONG AS YOU DO BOTH OF THEM BEFORE THURSDAY 04/02/87
MIDNIGHT!

5. THE HOMEWORK (3 QUESTIONS) AND THE QUIZ (2 QUES-
   TIONS) MUST BE COMPLETED BY THURSDAY 04/02/87 MID-
   NIGHT!! THIS ALLOWS YOU ABOUT A WEEK AND A HALF TO
   GET EVERYTHING DONE!

HAVE A GREAT WEEK!

order to emphasize it or convey excitement or emotion. In systems that support highlighting, different sized fonts, or reverse video, these more sophisticated uses of typography can be used for the same purposes.

SUMMARY: GETTING STARTED

A checklist for the instructor provides a summary of the main points in this chapter.

1. ASSURING ACCESS

    A. For Instructor
    Home PC access
    Separate phone line installed
    First participate in someone else's course
    Thoroughly master mechanics of system before you use it to teach.

    B. For students
    Check number of PCs, modems, phone lines, printers, communications software, hours available
    Train assistants to give help with different types of equipment

2. COURSE DESIGN AND PREPARATION
    Prepare and store fixed material
    Choose strategies and structures

3. INITIAL ACTIVITIES
    Welcome and orient
    Call "no shows"
    Short simple assignments
    Immediate positive feedback
    Make expectations clear
    Establish Predictable cycles
    Use friendly language and humor to build cohesion

CHAPTER 6

MODERATING CONFERENCES AND STIMULATING ACTIVE PARTICIPATION

> "If you only spoke when you were spoken to, and the other person always waited for you to begin, you see nobody would ever say anything," said Alice.
>
> — Lewis Carroll

A class conference is an exchange of ideas and information. As with any group discussion, the moderator or leader needs to engage in several kinds of behavior that will facilitate the group's participation and productive collaboration.

BASIC PRINCIPLES

The most basic premise from which all online teaching should begin is that the goal is to build a learning community and to facilitate the exchange of ideas, information, and feelings among the members of the community. Every *electure* (electronic lecture) should be designed to include questions for discussion or response, rather than simply representing one way transmission of "knowledge." The students, as well as the instructor, should be encouraged to raise new topics and ask questions of the class, and to respond to one another's contributions.

One set of experts about online faculty behavior that is conducive to an exciting and productive learning experience is students who have taken several courses online and who are, thus, in a position to generalize about desirable types of instructor behavior.

Students in the Western Behavioral Sciences Institute's School of Strategic and Management Studies were practicing executives, many of whom had advanced degrees. Those who had taken at least six of the month-long seminars were asked to complete a questionnaire aimed at pinning down just what makes a "good" online course. It included this open-ended question:

"Suppose a new WBSI faculty member were to ask you for advice on teaching online. What is the one most important thing that a faculty member should do to facilitate a good learning experience?"

Exhibit 6–1 displays the students' replies. Note that they emphasize, over and over again, *responsiveness*. Several comments also touch upon the need to be competent online, and also to organize the interaction. These themes are expanded in the sections that follow.

THE INSTRUCTOR AS DISCUSSION LEADER

The key activity in the Virtual Classroom is the exchange of ideas and information among students, with the faculty member as an organizer and facilitator of the activities and discussions. The minimum amount of time devoted to a topic area should be a week. Otherwise, there is not sufficient time for participants to read the initial materials presented by the instructor, compose their responses, and engage in a discussion based on the variety of student contributions. This may mean that you must choose to focus more "in depth" on a smaller number of topics or modules than you would cover in a face-to-face course that meets two or three times a week. As Robert Meinke points out in his course report, in the traditional classroom one can skim quickly and sequentially over a number of topics in a single hour-long session. Trying to treat a number of topics simultaneously in a Virtual Classroom is likely to be confusing. Harasim (1987, p. 123) describes the following kinds of instructor moderator activities, which should be applied to any class discussion:

- *Introducing* the discussion topic by relating it to readings or other course materials and clearly posting the issue or question to which the students are to respond.
- *Probing*, as in an unstructured interview situation, to get students to expand and build upon comments made by themselves or others.
- *Providing Information*: As the subject matter expert, the teacher should talk about studies or sources or facts that can help shed light on the issues raised in the discussion and provide short electures that supplement the printed materials assigned to the class to read.
- *Integrating* or weaving the discussions by synthesizing points

---

EXHIBIT 6–1
(Verbatim) Advice to Faculty From Experienced WBSI Students

Promote interaction.

Ask questions and genuinely respond to answers.

Be responsive, Keep comments short, be flexible - not stick rigidly to a predetermined outline.

Frequent, direct responses. Directed questions relevant to topic or readings. Interact with student ideas. Put students together online.

Stimulate responses by providing unique or oblique alternatives.
Respond to or acknowledge in some way on line the comments made by each participant.

Learn to type (use the system), write a lot. Respond to each query or comment in timely fashion.

Be responsive in a substantive way to what is said by others.

Encourage specific responses or comments.

Know the stuff, give positive responses/recognition to member comments.

Reinforcing feed back; have supplemental reading material available via + READ [an activity branch or attachment, which hides long pieces of text until participants are ready to deal with them].

Make concise presentation of points, be responsive to comments and alternative viewpoints, and encourage those students who are lurking to comment.

Recap (summarize sort of where we are, once a week) and respond.

Try to guide discussion towards some consensus if you can, but don't panic if you can't.

---

which students raised, building upon and developing themes which emerge, and linking them to the literature and the topic.
- *Asking questions* and raising issues, based on contradictions or inconsistencies or gaps created by the student's contributions.
- *Focusing* the discussions on crucial points, prior to wrapping up a topic and moving on.

- *Coaching* students on communications skills. If you notice that some of them are constantly making entries that are difficult to read because they are full of control characters, poorly formatted, or badly edited, point it out, and suggest that they always review and edit draft entries before adding them. Do this in a private message, so as not to embarrass the student. Try to put this in a positive frame of reference by noting that good ideas might get more response from others if they were easier to understand.

The course leader has to stay flexible and tuned into the dynamics of the group, above all. If a discussion is going well, do not cut it off arbitrarily, just to fit a predetermined syllabus. (See, for instance, the admirable example of moderator nonintervention by WBSI instructor Harlan Cleveland, in Exhibit 6–2.) If there is no fixed set of materials that must be covered in a certain period of time, let the lively and successful discussion roll on, without distraction. In a course that has a fixed syllabus, let it continue while simultaneously introducing the next topic or activity. In the latter case, where several things are happening simultaneously and become interwoven in time sequence, it is especially important to provide some organizational cues and tools for the participants.

Often, students are so interested in the topic being discussed that they do not want to stop when the course is "over" according to the calendar. Plan for this contingency and try to allow a few extra weeks for the course to wind down after it is officially ended, if possible.

Organizing Material and Keeping Track

As material builds up, there is a problem in finding and reviewing old entries and keeping track of all that is going on, unless the instructor establishes some procedures at the beginning to help with this. Consider making an index in the first comment that is updated weekly. The index might include a list and location for all "lectures," assignments, and activities.

Other organizing procedures depend upon the software features available in the central conferencing system, and the hardware and software available at the individual work station. Most systems support "key words" for items, and a method of searching and finding related items via these keys. If the system does accept key words for entries, establish a key for every topic raised, use it consistently, and encourage students to do the same.

It is necessary, when anyone responds to an entry, to make explicit exactly what you are replying to. Some systems provide software features to support the automatic self-organization of the conference proceedings in

---

EXHIBIT 6-2
Letting Well Enough Alone

Though the instructor should have general plans to integrate a number of comments, and bring a discussion that is flagging to a close and move on to other topics, these must remain contingencies. If other students take on part of the integrative role, and if a discussion is vigorous and productive, then the instructor's intervention will only be frustrating. As WBSI instructor Harlan Cleveland puts it in the following comment, "If it ain't broke, don't fix it!" Note that this particular course had gathered 144 comments in only two weeks. Obviously, the students were engaged in the topics and did not need new stimuli or re-direction.

:C1746 CC145 Harlan Cleveland (Harlan,481) 2/19/87 2:02 AM L:24 KEYS:/ MIDCOURSE CORRECTION?/ A: 109

Peter: In your cc109 you ask, in effect, whether we need any mid-course correction in this teleconference. I had prepared some provocations in case what you call the polylogue (is that word better than multilogue?) was languishing by mid-month. It isn't languishing. If I added new themes just now, the circuit would surely scream "OVERLOAD." My other option was to try to prepare an integrative summary of the comments so far—but then Lynne O'Shea rescued me with her wonderfully integrative cc129, with its 30 speculations about the CEO of the future based on this teleconference. I tend to judge an enterprise such as this conference the way I judge faculty colleagues: if they're not stimulating me when I talk with them, they're probably not stimulating their students either. And vice versa: if I react (with ah-HA, or appreciative laughter) to what they tell me, it's fair to assume that they're stirring up their students too. So far, I'm enjoying you and Brad and John and the WBSI participants very much. So . . . the oldest principle of management applies: If it ain't broke, don't fix it. . . . . .Harlan.

---

this manner. For example, EIES 2 has a "reply" function. Whenever a user chooses to "reply," this is attached to the parent item in the conference organizational tree structure. (The second reply to conference comment 33.6, for instance, would be numbered 33.6.2 and would be placed in this position in the proceedings.) The key words and subject headings of the parent item are retained for the reply, as a default.

Some systems also support the explicit creation of an "association" or "link" between any new item and any preceding item or items. This is coupled with the ability to retrieve the entire set of associated items.

If features such as key words, replies, and associations are available, use them and teach students how to use them. A conference is not a disjointed collection of items to be read once and then forgotten. It should be reviewed and reorganized by each participant frequently so that ideas build upon one another and themes and topics become inter related. One way to get students to do this is to give them an assignment after a few weeks in the course, to find and summarize everything said to date about a particular topic or issue.

PC-based tools should be used as much as possible to aid each participant in organization. Download the conference, store it in on the PC, and reorganize it into different files by topic. If there is a hypertext capability on the PC, so much the better for documenting the rich web of relationships between items that grows in a good class conference.

If the central system does not have features such as key words, associations, or a hierarchical conference structure, model how to substitute for this manually, by always stating the relationship explicitly. For example, "In comment 64, John says . . . " If the user has no hard disk on the PC for downloading and organizing materials, then she or he should get a print of materials and use a highlighter and marginal notes to describe the associations among entries.

The branching activities software constructed on EIES appears to be very valuable in keeping a course organized. Even though these software features were very "buggy" and slow as initially implemented, those instructors who used activities were sold on the advantages of the approach, and those who did not were sorry. For example, Robert Meinke concludes, "Branching should be introduced as early in the course as possible. It is the only way to maintain a sense of order and encourage creative interaction."

The instructor and other participants should generally make conference entries relatively short (25 lines is good because it fits on one screen; 50 at the most), and on one topic. Use a separate comment for each separate subject. This also facilitates review and reorganization of the proceedings by students; encourage them to do the same thing. If an item is going to be longer than about 50 lines, enter it in a different format that can be retrieved on demand, such as a "read branch" or a " + read" document on EIES.

Some students will fall behind, due to sickness or other problems. Review conference status and available data such as last sign on to stay aware of "absentees." If you use a mechanism such as Branch Activities for all assignments and subdiscussions, their late entries can enable them to catch up without disrupting the flow of the current conference topic.

Consider establishing separate conferences for distinct activities. For example, the Management Laboratory on EIES had one "general discussion" conference for all class members, and separate conferences and notebooks where each simulated company carried out its work. In Computers and Society, separate conferences are usually set up for general discussion, article reviews, a debate, and student presentations. It is useful for any member of a system to be able to set up a conference any time the need arises. In particular, students should be able to establish a conference that initially includes just those working together on a presentation or writing assignment, and then later add the rest of the class to view and discuss the finished product.

STIMULATING ACTIVE PARTICIPATION

Techniques related to success in the Virtual Classroom have to do with stimulating a form of participation which is very difficult within the traditional classroom: the active engagement and participation of all students in a collaborative learning community. Though CMC can be considered to be a "narrow-band" medium of communication, the fact that materials are written and searchable, and that communication is asynchronous, also opens up new possibilities for enabling all students to actively participate, at their own pace, in dealing with the concepts, skills, and ideas in a course. As Harasim (1987, pp. 118–119) puts it, "The electronic medium opens new educational options for both learners and teachers, not only in expanding educational access, but also in redesigning teaching strategies and learning activities." The most basic redesign is to think of asking questions and stimulating student activities to find and share "answers," rather than "giving all the answers." Though students may derive some benefit from simply reading materials online, conferencing as a mode of course delivery can only provide its full potential benefits if students actively contribute to a group learning experience.

Active participation is an objective that may be difficult or impossible to elicit from all students. To some extent, active student participation is a matter of students being made comfortable with the medium, but it is also related to cognitive maturity (McCreary & Van Duren, 1987; Perry, 1970). The spectrum of type of student participation ranges from "absentees," who seldom or never sign on even to receive waiting material, through "lurkers" or "read-only" participants, to those who make a few comments, to those who make regular scattered contributions, through those who are regularly actively involved in contributing to the course, often on a daily basis. The level or quality of student contributions ranges from the illiterate and incorrect to the truly insightful and skillful presentation of ideas.

Generally speaking, students at an upper level undergraduate or graduate level have attained a level of cognitive maturity and writing skill which predisposes them to active and highly readable engagement with ideas and new skills. The cognitively immature student tends to want the faculty member to "give the right answer." There may be an intermediate stage where students discover that different books and authorities give different "answers," and feel that "there are many different and equally good answers, including mine." The cognitively mature student has learned to critically analyze and apply alternative theories or techniques, and to develop criteria for judging which are the relatively better and relatively poor "answers." A skillful faculty member can lead the cognitively immature student toward a more critical and active involvement with course materials as part of the learning that takes place. If none of the students start out with a level of cognitive maturity and writing skill that facilitates active involvement, this will be a difficult process to get off the ground, but not impossible. Compare, for instance, the levels of cognitive and stylistic skill evidenced in the initial entries by students in CIS 213 (Exhibit 6–1) with those by the mature and CMC-experienced students in Jay Forrester's Western Behavioral Sciences course (Exhibit 6–2). There is simply "no comparison."

The instructor might feel discouraged by initially sparse and not very brilliant comments by students. However, by the end of a semester, students who started out with first comments just like those in CIS 213 were making mature and well-written contributions such as those that can be seen in Exhibits 3–7 and 6–3. Note, however, that the latter two exhibits are from courses in which the students were at least sophomores. Below a certain level of ability, motivation, and competence with microcomputers, the Virtual Classroom approach is not recommended as an educational delivery mechanism.

Robert Meinke and Lincoln Brown give detailed accounts of problems with freshman-level courses at Upsala (Appendix III). As Professor Meinke commented,

> Online courses emphasize those very skills in which many of our students are most lacking, reading and writing. Reading and comprehending a textbook is very difficult for many, and the online course intensifies this difficulty by requiring even more reading. Further, it eliminates the very means by which many students actually do their learning, through the spoken word. For this reason alone I believe that online courses are most adaptable to advanced courses where students are experienced and more likely to come with better developed study skills.

Anthropologist Kendy Rudy summed up her observations of the interaction of the medium with student characteristics as follows: Students are like themselves, only more so, when online. The chatty ones write long responses, the worriers modify their messages, the dutiful ones do what is required reliably but without brilliance, and the irresponsible are conspicuous by their absence.

Suggested Techniques

The following techniques may aid students in becoming actively involved in making contributions to an online course.

1. *Requiring Regular Participation*: For the cognitively immature or the poorly motivated student, it may be necessary to present activities which force the student to sign online and participate regularly. One such mechanism is the weekly quiz, which must be taken during the indicated week, and is then "closed." This typically makes the student sign on at least twice a week—once to get the new material and assignments, and once to take the quiz based on the reading assignment. Without at least twice a week participation, an active dialogue is not possible; the quiz is an admittedly authoritarian type of mechanism for forcing participation, but one that may be helpful for cognitively immature students and those who lack self-discipline. If the quiz is objective, it can be automatically graded and the answer returned immediately, during the same session, thus giving the student some immediate feedback on how well the facts or concepts have been mastered. B.J. Gleason's report on Computer Science, and Robert Meinke's report, both conclude that weekly quizzes worked very well as a mechanism for motivating regular participation.

2. *Making Material Relevant*: Ask questions or make assignments that enable students to connect the course materials to current events or to experiences in their own lives, and to respond on that basis. For example, in a statistics course, the idea of probability estimates was introduced with a problem having to do with a current baseball World Series. In a sociology course, the concept of role conflict was explored by asking each student to describe an incident of role conflict and its resolution that had occurred in their own life, using a pen name to protect privacy.

3. *Response Activities*: The response "branch activities" on EIES were developed to force active participation. When a question is asked in a response branch, each student may be forced to independently enter a response to the question, before being allowed to view the responses of other students or to see the summation and integration of the different responses by the instructor.

4. *Conflicting Opinions*: Two instructors from different disciplinary or theoretical backgrounds may present conflicting points of view or arguments for different techniques in the conference, with the students asked to respond in terms of which they think is more applicable, and why. Another mechanism is to set up a debate, in which the students form teams and/or are challenged to critique one another's opinions.

5. *Responding and Weaving*: Instructors should explicitly respond to contributions by students. They need not respond to each one individually.

Even better is to respond to several at once by weaving them together, summarizing, and posing a further question based on previous responses. Students should be referred to by name.

6. *Request Responses*: In the conference or in private messages, instructors may urge specific students to respond to specific comments or issues, based on knowledge of their relevant experiences.

7. *The Simulated Agent Provocateur*: An instructor can use a pen name to question or challenge an entry which he or she made, thus setting an example that the students may follow and/or setting up a debate. If the instructor makes such a pen named entry, he or she should follow it up shortly afterwards with an entry explicitly thanking the pen-named entity for the comment. Great fun!

8. *The Visiting Expert*: Guest "lecturers" may be invited in for a period of time to present material or case studies. Students may be asked to each present one question to the guest, and be graded on the quality of the question.

9. *Role Playing*: Almost everybody likes to "act" or play roles. Little children play the roles of teacher, doctor, mother, or soldier. By taking on the words and actions of others, they learn something about what it is like to occupy that occupational role, or are able to explore fantasies and ideas. Role playing can range from a single week's assignment to a semester-long simulation.

COLLABORATIVE LEARNING

The above examples apply to active student involvement in discussions which are led by the instructor. However, students can play an even more active role by working in collaborative groups and/or taking some of the responsibility for presenting material and leading discussion. Some possible formats and types of collaborative learning assignments were listed in Chapter 3 and above; more detailed examples are described below.

1. *Students as Teachers*: In its simplest form, each student may be asked to make the equivalent of a seminar presentation. For example, in a Computers and Society course, each student selected a specific area from a list, such as computers and music or computers and poetry, located relevant literature, and made a short summary for the rest of the class. Student presentations can be taken one step further by making the student responsible for stimulating and leading a discussion on the topic. The way this was handled in the Computers and Society course was to assign half the grade based on the presentation-type material, and half to the discussion leadership. Each student was required to pose one or more

interesting questions for response, based on the presentation and its relationship to other material in the course. The grade for discussion leadership was based on how many responses by other students were made. This motivated the student to ask an interesting question, to respond to responses from students in order to get them to comment further, and to respond to one another's questions and presentations by setting up a kind of reciprocity. Since the students were contributing to one another's grade by responding to one another, if student A responded to student B, then B felt some obligation to respond to A's question. An example of the innovative and stimulating exchange that was generated by the presentation and question on computers and poetry was shown in Exhibit 3-7.

2. *The Role Play or Drama*: Students may be assigned roles to play which will dramatize and give life to opposing points of view or enable them to apply general concepts or techniques. For instance, you might assign the statuses of management, labor, and arbitrator for a case in a labor relations course. In a Connected Education course, the high point was a "trial" for murder of an android, with the issue being whether an artificially created being is "alive" and can be "murdered." The students played the roles of attorneys, judge, and jury.

Exhibit 6–3 shows students playing the roles of employees in a simulated organization. More about this "Virtual Management Laboratory" will be described in a subsequent chapter. By playing the role of "Vice President for Marketing, West" or "Vice President for Personnel," students of management get an opportunity to practice their managerial skills. In addition, just like dressing up for Halloween is fun, it is enjoyable to take on an alternate identity, and interact with others who are also playing roles. Even though it is "fun" and stimulates active participation by students, role plays can also explore serious topics and develop students' skills. Over the course of the semester, the students simulated a fiscal year in the operation of the organization, including creating their organization, developing product and marketing plans, and creating MIS and long range plans. By simulating the operations of an organization, they were able to apply the concepts described in their textbook; they took their roles as "corporate officers" very seriously.

3. *The Formal Debate:* Students may be divided into teams to present opposing viewpoints, perhaps with some members of the class acting as respondents and "judges." Kendy Rudy's course report describes one successful use of a debate format. Rather than being formally divided into teams, the issues may also simply be presented, with two opposite "resolutions," and the students may self-select which side to argue. When there are multiple sections of a course online, the sections may debate each other, with a prize given for the "winning" side. For example, during

EXHIBIT 6–3
ROLE-PLAYING

Excerpts From Student Discussion of MIS Requirements
for "The Imperial Corporation" Simulation

C2024 CC140 Paul Y. (Yogi,2212) 3/28/87 12:54 PM L:19 KEYS:/MIS/
REQUIREMENTS/MARKETING WEST/

MIS Department, This is a brief description of the features that I believe are
essential to the functioning of my Department (Marketing West). First of all,
I will need a database manager to keep track of appointments, companies to
be visited, companies already visited. It will have to maintain records on all
Marketing campaigns.

Secondly, the system will have to be able to keep me up to date on all of our
figures—Unit cost, Selling price, Maintenance costs, latest sales figures,
quantity on hand, etc. We have to know what we are working with before we
go to try and show it off. Lastly, the system will have to keep up to date with
the latest sales figures so that I can formulate a strategy as to my next
prospective buyers. If I know who has been buying lately, I can attack more
of them. I can not think of anything else off-hand, but I'm sure I'm missing
some major needs. Thank You Paul Y. (V.P Marketing West)

:C2024 CC148 Grace C. (Gio,2046) 3/30/87 11:12 AM L:29 KEYS:/MIS/PER-
SONNEL DEPT./

TO: Imperial Computer Company President, VP's and managers
FROM: Grace C. , Personnel Manager
RE: MIS system in the Personnel Department
The MIS system in Personnel only needs to comprise the following: 1) A huge
DATABASE (in the form of a mini-computer, not sure?) in order to contain
all the employee files. 2) Four computers (two in the Personnel Dept. and two
in the Records Dept.) that can access this employee DATABASE. 3) Four
computers (two in Personnel and two in Records) mainly used for word-
processing functions. 4) Finally, the two word-processing computers in
Personnel will be equipped with modems in order to communicate with
various employment agencies so as to keep an up-to-date account of potential
employee prospects. A modem can be very useful in my department since we
can also keep the employment agencies informed of openings as they occur -
this should prove to be a much more efficient and speedy system than the old
process of advertising job openings in newspapers and waiting for responses. Of course, job openings will still be advertised in papers for the
general public. However, I am all for electronic communication with employment agencies and even agencies such as Affirmative Action and EEO.

:C2024 CC152 PAUL B. (Ozzy,2027) 3/30/87 12:44 PM L:22 KEYS:/MIS REQUIREMENTS/

FELLOW EMPLOYEES, AS I WAS LOOKING THROUGH THE MESSAGES I CAN SEE THAT WE ARE MAKING GOOD PROGRESS. I THINK RON DID A GOOD JOB ON OUR BREAK-EVEN POINT AND OUR COMPANY DID A GOOD JOB IN GETTING STARTED THAT WE CAN MAKE A PROFIT AFTER 4 MONTHS.
I WOULD LIKE TO EXPLAIN THE MIS REQUIREMENTS FOR MY DEPARTMENT (MARKETING-EAST COAST). PAUL YURGA HAS ALREADY PUT HIS IN. SINCE HE IS IN CHARGE OF MARKETING IN THE WEST COAST WE HAVE BASICALLY THE SAME NEEDS BUT I WILL TRY TO RESTATE THEM IN DIFFERENT WORDS. FIRST,I THINK IT WOULD BE A GOOD IDEA IF PAUL'S SYSTEM AND MY SYSTEM WERE HOOKED TOGETHER SO THAT I COULD GET AN OVERALL PICTURE OF WHERE OUR PRODUCT IS NEEDED. IF WE AREN'T SELLING SO GOOD IN THE EAST I COULD SHIP SOME COMPUTERS TO THE WEST. BASICALLY,I WOULD NEED A COMPUTER TO SEE HOW MY SUBORDINATES ARE SELLING THEIR PRODUCT IN THEIR SPECIFIED AREA TO BE ABLE TO DISTRIBUTE EFFECTIVELY. THIS COULD ALSO TELL ME IF WE NEED TO IMPROVE OR CHANGE OUR ADVERTISING SCHEMES. ALSO, A COMPUTER COULD GIVE ME LISTINGS OF NEW BUSINESSES AND SCHOOLS THAT COULD BE POTENTIAL CUSTOMERS. THIS WOULD BE AN IMPORTANT PART OF EXPANSION OF OUR COMPANY.

Spring 1991, two sections of Computers and Society debated the issue of whether or not computer professionals should be licensed, as doctors and lawyers are. This was part of a curriculum component on professionalism and ethics. The "losers" (as judged by the quantity and quality of arguments) had to provide refreshments for the "winners" during their final exam.

4. *Writing Groups*: Students may be asked to present drafts of written assignments to one another (perhaps using pen names), critique one another's drafts, and then revise the draft on the basis of suggestions and reactions from the other students. This was the basic approach in the Freshman Writing Seminar at Upsala College that used the VC for part of the coursework. Mary Swigonski's report on this experiment points out that there were at least three problems in her initial implementation of this approach to teaching writing. The first was that students were not given sufficient time to master the mechanics of the system and its editor before being asked to use it for a complete written assignment. The second

was that the group size used (six or seven students) turned out to be too large. Dr. Swigonski suggests writing groups of three or four students in future implementations, so that the students are not overwhelmed by the volume of material to which they are supposed to respond. Finally, there was the *politeness syndrome:* students did not get beyond saying polite, nice things about one another's writing.

Solving the training and group size problems seems straightforward; how to overcome the "politeness syndrome" will require more experimentation with alternative approaches to structuring assignments, modeling "constructive criticism," and motivation strategies. For example, as long as the students in the writing seminar said something about one another's drafts, they received full credit for that portion of the assignment. Perhaps a significant portion of the grade should be awarded for the quality of their critiques and suggestions for improvements for one another's drafts.

5. *Group or Team Projects*: Many courses use the VC to facilitate groups of students working jointly on assignments, for which all or part of the grade is given to the group as a whole, rather than grading solely on the basis of individually handed-in work. For example, Introduction to Computer Science online included a substantial programming task assigned to small groups of six students, as the final course assignment. The assigned program had a fairly obvious division into six subroutines, but the subroutines would have to be coordinated by an overall structure and set of standards and documentation, in order for the program as a whole to run successfully. Working together on a project provided the students with a practical illustration of principles they had read about, such as the need to make programs readable by others by including comments and using indentation, and the need to generate test data to make sure that each part of a program not only completes its task, but also passes on the correct outputs to a subsequent part of the overall program

In NJIT's CIS 675 (Evaluation of Information Systems, offered in mixed-mode from 1987 through 1991), there are several assignments where students are given the option of forming groups of two to four to work jointly and hand in a single result, rather than undertaking the assignments as individuals. The students who work jointly on assignments use the system to plan and coordinate their work, to draft and revise their report, and to allow the instructor to look at "work in progress" when they feel they need advice or feedback.

6. *Team Building* : One way to form collaborative groups for joint projects is to start with an individual assignment which enables each student to demonstrate mastery of the system by successfully presenting material or responses to the class as a whole. Then have the students form pairs for the next assignment, and work out their own division of labor and joint presentation. For the third assignment, students may elect to keep

the same partner or switch to a new partner, if the collaboration has not worked well. By the fourth assignment, each pair may be instructed to join with another pair to form a small group of four (or two pairs, to form groups of six, depending on the nature of the assignment.) These small groups may then be used for a number of activities during the rest of the course, such as reviewing one another's draft papers, working on assignments or reviewing for an exam, or forming a team for a debate or role playing exercise. Davie (1987) reported a very positive experience with these learning partners and "team building" strategies. "It seems that the necessity of discussing the topic in-depth with one's learning partner helped to identify important issues to a greater extent than writing alone" (p. 17). The students themselves indicated that it was important for each partnership or group to set explicit expectations for tasks and to set specific due dates for particular parts of the assignment to be completed. The students also found that it was helpful for the two partners to spend some time working online at the same time, passing drafts back and forth.

In order for learning teams or learning groups to work well, the teams need a joint notebook or other working space for their projects and discussions. The instructor should be able to observe all entries in these spaces, but should not intervene unless the students seem to be completely on the wrong track, or are "stuck" and explicitly ask for help. A useful scheme for motivating participation by all members seems to be to base a portion of the grade (e.g., 50%) on the quality of the group or team product, and another part of the grade on the instructor's observations of the amount of effort expended by each team member. The students should be aware of how their joint work will be graded, in any case.

SUMMARY:
CHECKLISTS FOR ONLINE INSTRUCTIONAL TECHNIQUES

1. THE INSTRUCTOR AS DISCUSSION LEADER
   a. INTRODUCE EACH NEW TOPIC AND CLEARLY DESCRIBE ISSUES AND ACTIVITIES FOR STUDENT RESPONSE.
   b. TIMELY, FREQUENT RESPONSES TO STUDENT COMMENTS AND ASSIGNMENTS.
   c. BE FLEXIBLE: LET LIVELY DISCUSSIONS CONTINUE.
   d. ASK QUESTIONS, RAISE ISSUES.

    e. RECAP AND WEAVE RESPONSES.
    f. ORGANIZING – USE:
      KEY WORDS OR TITLES FOR ENTRIES
      BRANCH ACTIVITIES
      SEPARATE CONFERENCES
      SHORT, SINGLE-TOPIC COMMENTS
      INDEX

2. STIMULATING ACTIVE PARTICIPATION
    a. REQUIRE REGULAR PARTICIPATION
    b. WEEKLY QUIZZES OR ASSIGNMENTS
    c. USE SOFTWARE THAT FORCES RESPONSES
    d. RELATE MATRIALS TO CURRENT EVENTS OR STU-
      DENTS' EXPERIENCES
    e. PRESENT CONFLITING VIEWS
    f. RESPOND AND "WEAVE"
    g. USE :
      TEAM AND GROUP ASSIGNMENTS
      STUDENTS AS TEACHERS
      ROLE PLAY AND SIMULATION
      DEBATES
      GROUP PROJECTS

CHAPTER 7

COLLABORATIVE TEACHING IN A VIRTUAL CLASSROOM*

Man is a social animal, formed to please and enjoy in society.
— Montesquieu

There is a sort of economy in Providence that one should excel where another is defective, in order to make them more useful to each other, and mix them in society.
—Joseph Addison (1672–1719)

The traditional classroom can be a lonely place for the teacher. After the stimulation of graduate school, surrounded by others who are interested in the same area of scholarship, teachers often find themselves the only ones on their campus who teach and do research in a specific area that corresponds to a course offering. After several years, they may feel "burned out" of inspiration and excitement about teaching; they need a colleague to help them rethink and innovate to keep "teaching" an enjoyable and rewarding learning experience for them, too. The Virtual Classroom can provide an environment for faculty to collaborate in teaching in a variety of ways.

We designed the Virtual Classroom specifically to support collaborative learning activities. It is not surprising that instructors used the same facilities to collaborate with one another in exchanging ideas and services to deliver courses. This was a spontaneous development. This chapter

---

*Portions of this chapter are adapted from Hiltz, Shapiro, & Ringsted (1990, pp. 37–55). Reprinted by permission.

describes some of the forms of *collaborative teaching* we have observed, including:

1. *Informal collaboration.* Instructors at different institutions work together to develop and exchange ideas and materials for courses that have some content in common, "sit in" on one another's classes electronically, and/or act as "guest lecturers" in one another's online courses.
2. *Formal co-teaching.* Two or more instructors, from the same or different institutions, share teaching responsibilities for an online course, or join their online sections in some joint activities.
3. *Collaborative Degree Programs.* Faculty and staff from two or more institutions pool faculty resources via CMC to offer majors or degree programs which are richer than any one of the institutions could offer alone.

INFORMAL COLLABORATION

Just as there are teachers' lounges and teachers' meetings in traditional institutions, there is a conference called "Teachers' Lounge" on all of our Virtual Classroom systems. There, instructors have informal, sociable discussions and also provide an online support group for difficulties encountered: a place to exchange problems, observations, and solutions.

For example, one teacher complained about some of the students procrastinating and not regularly signing on several times a week. Such sporadic participation meant that the students tended to get "behind" the active participants. Another instructor reported that he had found a solution for that problem. He observed that, with the pressures of work and family, some students only make time to do things when they are "due." His solution was to make things "due" twice a week, through using activities that were open for only three to four days. Students knew that they had to sign on at least once in the first half of each week and once in the second half, or it would be too late to do those activities. Other instructors tried this and found that it does result in more regular participation.

Similarly, a writing instructor reported that she had problems getting students to offer constructive criticism of one another's drafts. Other instructors suggested that she base part of the grade for each writing assignment on the number and quality of constructive suggestions that each student offered to others. This did result in the students devoting more effort to responding to one another's drafts, rather than being mainly concerned with their own drafts.

Perhaps in some better academic world, students do not have to be motivated by due dates and grades. In the institutions in which we have experimented with undergraduates, that is not the case. What happens in the Teachers' Lounge is that instructors share ideas about how to use the tools available in the Virtual Classroom to motivate active participation among the students. The basic choices are the same . . . "carrots or sticks," but the form that these motivators can take is different. You cannot use the "stick" of calling on a student by name to answer a question, as Professor Kingsley did in the television series "The Paper Chase." Through this technique, Kingsley motivated the students to regularly study the materials of his law course, in order to avoid the embarrassment of not knowing an answer when called upon. Though the technique of using activities which are available for only a few days is different in form, it accomplishes the same objective.

Another form of informal collaboration is the "guest lecture," or other forms of guest membership by one faculty member in another faculty member's class conference. The best way to learn the techniques of teaching online is to observe an experienced teacher, and almost all "new" or "prospective" Virtual Classroom teachers begin as an invited observer in the electronic classrooms of their colleagues. Usually the guest faculty member is a fairly passive observer for awhile, but eventually begins to participate in the discussion, too. Often, there are formal guest lectures by faculty members in one another's courses. For example, as illustrated in Chapter 3, while former US Federal Communications Commissioner Nicholas Johnson was online as a teacher of his own course for the Western Behavioral Sciences Institute, he made a guest appearance in an online NJIT Computers and Society class. The NJIT class was debating whether or not a "Federal Information Commission," similar to the FCC, should be established to regulate computer and information technology applications in order to protect the privacy and well being of the public.

Another interesting example was a "cameo role" played by one instructor in another instructor's role simulation. Upsala Professor Glenn Halvorson had his Business French class undertaking a simulation of the establishment of a business in France by two U.S. partners. Other roles included representatives of French government agencies and French businesses. All communication took place in the form of "letters" in French, among the participants, who signed their letters with their "pen names" (the roles they were playing). NJIT faculty member Enrico Hsu, who was teaching an online management laboratory at the same time, made sporadic and dramatic "appearances" in the role-playing exercise in the French course. He had learned that some unexpected drama added interest to online simulations, and lent that insight to pique the interest of students in his (electronic) colleague's course. These two examples show how the Virtual Classroom can make it easier for a multidisciplinary perspective to be added to courses by facilitating the participation of visiting faculty members, who may spend only a few hours total in their "guest appearance."

Informal online collaboration among faculty members can also be used as a method for planning implementation of the technology. For example, in 1992, faculty members at Eastern Oregon State College are working online with colleagues at other universities that belong to Oregon Ed-Net to plan and develop curriculum modules for a series of courses that will use EIES 2 during the 1992–1993 academic year. Facilitated by seasoned online instructors Peter and Trudy Jonson-Lenz, the online collaboration was preceded by a two-day, "hands on," face-to-face workshop.

Faculty also collaborate online to develop and test curriculum ideas. For example, in one project on EIES, high school science teachers used the system to pool their ideas about how to implement the AAAS science curriculum in high schools. They gave one another ideas and feedback about experiments, demonstrations, assignments, and teaching examples.

CO-TEACHING

One way to bring more interest to a course is to have more than one instructor, each representing a different discipline or point of view. Usually, this is difficult, because the instructors who wish to teach together must be co-located at the same college, and coordinate their schedules so that they have the same times free. In addition, both need to sit through all classes, so that they are up to date on what is covered and do not duplicate or omit material. This in essence requires "double work," while the pay or teaching credits are split. No wonder co-taught courses are relatively rare in the traditional classroom. In the Virtual Classroom, these disadvantages do not occur.

Co-teaching can take the form of two or more instructors teaching a single "section," in which case the instructors are often from different disciplines, or different locations. It can also take the form of linked online sections of the same course, in which some activities are shared in common conferences, and some are conducted in separate section conferences. For example, in Spring 1991, Roxanne Hiltz offered a partially online section of a graduate course, CIS 675, Evaluation of Information systems, in which the face-to-face meetings took place at NJIT. Murray Turoff was teaching a section which met face-to-face at a branch campus. Both sections had a joint online conference, where they presented and discussed reviews of research articles, received some lecture-type material, and discussed their ongoing, common assignments. Each section also had its own conference, for discussion of topics not common to the two sections, and its electronic gradebook. Finally, groups of students set up conferences to work on joint assignments.

Another experiment was not so successful. During 1988–1989, Murray Turoff combined his "day" and "evening" sections of Computers and Society with a section for which Roxanne Hiltz was responsible, to offer a joint online "triple section" of the course with a total enrollment of 96 students. We were attempting to explore the limits of the present technology in terms of class size. As will be described in the next chapter, we did experience some problems with "electronic anomie" in this online triple section.

Learning on the Job in Denmark

At the Danish Institute of Technology, Aarhus Technical College, and other members of an educational and research consortium in Aarhus, Denmark, the emphasis in learning and teaching at a distance has been on the ways in which new interactive information technologies comply with new vocational learning requirements. The introduction of new technologies and techniques has increased the need for employee versatility and co-operation. This has minimized the possibilities of once-and-for-all acquiring sufficient and life long job qualifications. Jobs involve learning, and learning encompassing technical, social and organizational aspects have become a sine qua non to organizational development. Both for quantitative and qualitative reasons it is no longer possible to meet continuous vocational training needs in traditional educational settings.

Addressing this problem, the consortium has for a number of years in Denmark been involved in a series of experiments focusing on how computer conferencing can redefine traditional distance education concepts and methodologies. The medium is used to produce courses which emphasize collaboration between "academic" and "applied" experts, and peer exchanges of problems and solutions. The learning objectives are defined in close cooperation with the learners. The learners become more responsible for their own learning processes, and the teachers function as "facilitators" helping the learners to structure the learning process rather than acting as traditional deliverers of knowledge.

For example, the theme of the one course supported by the COM conferencing system was food, environment, and new health strategies, seen in relation to new production methods, changing socioeconomic conditions, and changes in the outer environment. The course was developed and implemented as a cross institutional venture among three departments at two universities. The purpose of the course was to update the knowledge of professionals teaching home economics and nutrition, and professionals working in the primary health sector, using an interdisciplinary, problem-oriented approach.

The contents of the course corresponded to a traditional two-week (full time) course. Organized as open learning, it ran over three months, with an initial and a final face-to-face weekend seminar where all the participants and organizers of the course were gathered. The course divided students into groups of four or five, and emphasized group work, debate, and exchange of knowledge and experiences within the groups and between the groups. The logic was that the network could update the knowledge of participants through exchange and discussion of professional experiences with geographically dispersed colleagues working in related fields (peer-group learning). The teachers of the course functioned as consultants rather than as traditional tutors. The course had an "open curriculum" structure, with projects and subthemes being defined by the participants in the initial phase, and developed through the guidance and support of the teachers.

Though each group had one main counselor (teacher), each student could still access the other teachers. All teachers could "see" the work taking place online in all of the groups. The consultant from Aarhus Technical College's Center for Distance Education helped with technical and system problems and functioned as a counselor, both for the teachers and for the participants, in establishing communication structures and flows.

The course was structured in such a way as to create maximum synergy between a knowledge acquisition approach and a learner defined, experience based approach. Throughout the course the participants were to a great extent responsible for their own learning processes in so far as they were the ones to formulate problems, define themes, and agree on suitable methodologies and ways of presenting their results. Each working group undertook a project. At a final weekend face-to-face seminar the projects were presented and evaluated.

Evaluation. Evaluation questionnaires were sent out before, midway through, and after the course. These data showed that the course gave the participants a lot of useful knowledge, new methodologies, insight and approaches in relation to new local health strategies and initiatives. Furthermore, the users felt that they also gained insight into the use of new technology and its possible application to their own work. Many also pointed out that the online nature of the course had been especially useful in the planning phase. It was easier to access each other, comment on each other's work and, make use of the different qualifications within the group in building up and structuring the course.

ELECTRONIC CONSORTIA FOR COLLABORATIVE DEGREE PROGRAMS

The Danish course just described is an example of collaboration accross institutions to produce a joint course. An entire degree program may also be established on a consortial basis. Using the Virtual Classroom and videotapes and broadcasts, it is easy to share faculty and other resources. For example, NJIT does not have the resources to offer an entire degree program via distance education. However, it is currently negotiating with Mind Extension University to provide a complete set of major courses in computer science, following the new ACM curriclum guidelines and drawing on its over 30 faculty members in computer science. These courses would be offered via a mix of Virtual Classroom and videotapes. Mind Extension University is making similar arrangements with other universities to provide courses in areas where they have rich faculty resources; it acts as the "broker" to put together a complete list of courses to comprise an undergraduate degree program. This is an example of a Virtual University (one that has degree programs without having a traditional campus or large faculty of its own), which we will return to in the last chapter.

On a less ambitious and less "tradition-breaking" level, technology such as the Virtual Classroom can be used by cooperating departments in two or more universities to expand the offerings available to their majors, and/or to pool teaching resources. This has sometimes been done in the past by faculty members physically travelling to a "partner" campus to offer some courses; it is a lot easier on the faculty to be able to teach students from the "sister" institution online than to travel to them.

SUMMARY

This chapter has reviewed a number of educational efforts using the Virtual Classroom as a mechanism for collaboration among faculty members and institutions in the development and delivery of courses. Some of the examples presented are completed and evaluated, some are underway, and some are still in the planning phase. Examples range from a course co-taught by two instructors on the same campus to multi-institutional courses and degree programs.

In an era of constant budget crises in higher education, the Virtual Classroom type of system will become an important mechanism for making more effective use of faculty resources, through its ability to allow faculty to cooperate in developing and offering courses and degree programs. Though the incentives for the institutions are primarily economic, those for the faculty are primarily in terms of an increase in the quality of their teaching life, and opportunities for professional renewal. It is both stimulating and enjoyable for faculty to interact with other faculty members from other disciplines and institutions in an online learning community.

CHAPTER 8

ELECTRONIC ANOMIE AND OTHER IMPLEMENTATION PROBLEMS

"Reeling and writing, of course to begin with," the Mock Turtle replied, "and the different branches of arithmetic–ambition, distraction, vilification and derision."

—Lewis Carroll

Not everything in the Virtual Classroom turns out exactly as the planners and instructors envision. Sometimes things get very confused, like the Mock Turtle's version of mathematics.

This chapter describes some of the problems which arose in implementing the Virtual Classroom for online delivery of undergraduate courses for credit. Particularly during the first semester, when the quasi-experimental design of matched online and face-to-face classes was carried out, many problems deleteriously affected the online courses. In subsequent semesters, most of the problems were lessened, if not solved, and the results began to improve. Some of the implementation problems encountered in later experiments, particularly with a large multisection mixed-media course on computers and society, will also be described.

One implication of our experiences is that other institutions should "start small." That is, start with only one or two courses online and build from there. With a first semester set of offerings that included eight different completely or partially online courses and five "control" classes, spread over two campuses, we found ourselves in the situation of being unable to deal adequately with all of the minor crises and glitches that occurred.

RECRUITING AND ENROLLING STUDENTS

The ideal student for the Virtual Classroom would be mature in terms of motivations about learning (seeking to learn as much as possible rather than to do as little work as possible), informed about the characteristics of this mode of delivery, and the owner of a PC and modem at home (in order to maximize their access). The ideal faculty member at an institution offering such courses would be informed about the advantages and disadvantages of VC delivery in order to advise prospective students, and supportive of a new means to deliver education to students who might benefit from it. The ideal university bureaucracy would be flexible and have good internal communications, so that steps could be taken to assure ease of implementing an enrollment decision by a student once that occurred. In fact, students, faculty, and administrators are likely to be resistant, if not resentful or hostile, towards such an educational innovation, which they may perceive as a threat or an imposition.

None of these ideal conditions prevailed during the first semester of formal experimentation with the Virtual Classroom. In fact, it sometimes seemed as if the whole process was being run by the Mock Turtle, or perhaps Murphy's Law. These problems are described here for two reasons. One is that doing so may help others to be aware of some of the pitfalls that can occur in implementing a new course delivery technology. The second reason is that these problems undoubtedly affected the quantitative results, to be reported in the next section of the book, particularly by decreasing the number of subjects in the study below what had been planned.

In Spring 1986, a one-page description of the Virtual Classroom experiment was developed. The plan was to include it as a page in registration materials at Upsala and NJIT, and to footnote VC courses with references to this information. The information included a provision that the student must speak to the faculty member in charge of the course to review the consent form, and sign and turn in such a consent form in order to register for the course. This information page was included with Upsala registration materials, which is provided to about 2,000 students each semester.

At NJIT, because of the expense, it was ruled that this page of information could not be included in the registration information that was sent to thousands of enrolled and prospective students. Instead, each VC course carried the following notation: "experimental course delivered via computer; see instructor for information." The registrar's office stated that procedures would be developed to make sure that students did not register for the course without a signed consent form. The NJIT campus newspaper did carry the full project information that was prepared and sent to them, as a "front page" article.

By August, pre-enrollment figures were dismal at both schools. There was one student enrolled for Introduction to Sociology at Upsala, and three for Introduction to Computer Science at NJIT. By erecting barriers to enrollment, even potentially interested students were discouraged. These barriers were inadvertently quite effective at NJIT. We discovered this when students who had intended to enroll in a VC section told the instructors that they had been informed that the VC section was closed, so they had enrolled in another section instead. Investigation of this mystery revealed that the registrar had decided to handle the consent form in the following manner. Capacity for the course had been set at zero; therefore, when a student tried to register, she or he would be told that the section was closed and that they would have to see the instructor for permission to register. However, the assistants actually present at registration did not know the special circumstances under which the computer was showing the sections as "closed." They simply told prospective students that the section was closed. As soon as this situation was discovered, the capacity was reset at 30, with the result that students began registering without understanding what it was that they were registering for. They simply would not take the trouble to seek out the instructor, as suggested in the registration material. Since instructors have only a few office hours a week, and students usually allocate just an hour or two to register for a semester, this is quite understandable.

When the dismal enrollment situation was discovered in August, posters and flyers were prepared and distributed on both campuses. The poster listed all VC sections and had a pocket for the flyers. There was a separate. flyer for each course, with other VC courses available listed on the flyer also. The color was bright yellow. The posters were put near registration areas, in classroom buildings, and in bookstores and dormitories.

In addition, at the final Upsala registration period, the project director visited each faculty member advising students, explained the project, distributed brochures, and made a plea for them to "advise in" students who might benefit from this approach.

The result of the last-minute flurry of recruiting activity was that adequate numbers of students registered for the courses to be offered, though less than would have been desirable for purposes of obtaining statistically significant results. However, in many cases, these students were either totally ignorant of the experimental nature of the mode of delivery (having simply registered for an open section, without bothering to find out or perhaps even to notice the statement about "delivered via computer"), or unsuited for it.

For instance, a number of the students registered in the online section of Introduction to Sociology were ice hockey players. The project director advised two of these players when they attempted to register. The ice hockey players reported that their team met in the chapel basement, which was also the location for Upsala's registration. They had seen the poster and flyers there. Their coach took it as a way out of a scheduling dilemma. It seems that the team could only "get the ice" for practice from 1 pm until 4 pm, 5 days a week. It was impossible for most students to find a full schedule of classes within these limitations, since they also could not take classes at night, when games were scheduled. The coach noticed from the posters and flyers that the VC section did not meet at any specified time, and therefore would not conflict with other courses, and advised any player who needed another course to sign up for it. These students had come to college largely to play hockey rather than for academic reasons; they basically had no interest in sociology but simply "needed a course;" and they attended other classes in the mornings and then went straight to hockey practice. After attending the initial training session, most of them signed on little or not at all. They certainly were not "ideal" students for the Virtual Classroom.

Soliciting in the Chapel. Advertising and recruiting students for specific courses is simply not done in academia. Thus, our posters and flyers and personal communications were considered "unfair competition" by many faculty members. On both campuses, outrage was expressed at the means used to recruit students for the VC sections.

At Upsala, the Project Director was accused in a meeting of the faculty Educational Policies Council (EPC) of "soliciting students – in the chapel, no less." Questions were raised about the project's being illegal (in the sense of not following college regulations for course approvals) and unwise. Many members of the EPC felt that anything delivered via computer could not be as effective as a traditional course, and that educational quality was being endangered. Though, in the past, EPC approval had been required only to introduce a new course, many members felt that this means of teaching was so radically different from their concept of "teaching" that approval should have been sought in order for the experiment to be offered. These same members indicated that they probably would not have given such approval. Though the Dean's approval for the project had been secured, their reaction was that the Dean should not have approved the project and should have brought it to them for approval. In retrospect it was a tactical error on the project director's part not to seek out members of the EPC before the meeting to discuss the project with them.

During the same week in September, the project director received an irate call from a representative of the Organizational and Social Sciences department at NJIT. This department offers Introduction to Sociology at NJIT. They had been asked if they would offer one section online, but had declined. Upsala and NJIT have cross-registration agreements, whereby a student at either school can register for a course at the other. On all of the course brochures, other VC sections were listed. Therefore, for instance, Upsala students were informed that they could register for Introduction to Computer Science online, and NJIT students were informed that Introduction to Sociology, offered by Upsala, was available to them.

The OSS representative was angry and outraged, and implied that we could be stealing their students. This was unfair competition. Moreover, they had not approved the course offered by Upsala for credit at NJIT.

I explained that any NJIT student who tried to enroll for the Upsala course would have been required to check with his or her advisor and obtain approval for this course before enrolling. In fact, no NJIT student had requested enrollment. This latter fact mollified the OSS faculty member. However, he indicated that he felt that the approval of the OSS department should have been sought ahead of time, before listing this course as available to NJIT students; and that it was very, very unlikely that such approval would have been given.

Despite the publicity that so roused the ire of faculty members on both campuses, many students showed up at the first VC session for many of the courses with no idea what they had signed up for. This theme comes out in several of the interviews with students included in Appendix II, particularly for students who felt negatively about the means of delivery. They simply did not see the material included in the registration information or the posters and flyers and newspaper articles available. Though they were offered the opportunity to transfer to another section, they generally stated that the alternative section was scheduled at an inconvenient time. They started their training in a negative and resentful frame of mind . . . and in many cases, their attitudes slid downhill from there. Since they were surprised and/or angry during the training session, they did not even hear some of the relevant information. For instance, all training sessions included a discussion of where and how to obtain a modem and a special telephone line, if students had a PC at home but no modem. Students who were "inadvertent enrollees" tended not to hear, or to remember having heard, this information.

HARDWARE AND SOFTWARE PROBLEMS

Computer-Mediated Communication depends on many different pieces of equipment; if any one of them fails, the student is "shut out" of the "classroom." There is the central conferencing system itself, which may have hardware or software failures; its communications hardware and software for accepting incoming traffic from various sources; the telephone lines and/or packet network system through which the user reaches the system; and the microcomputer, modem, communications software, and printer at the user's end. Our implementation was severely inadequate in terms of providing sufficient equipment at the user's end, and we also had some serious limitations with EIES.

Ideally, every student taking a course partially or completely online would have a micro and a modem at home and/or at work, and could dial in anytime. At the very least, there should be adequate access to high-quality and compatible equipment on a campus offering such courses. Such was not the case, particularly at Upsala.

Practically no Upsala students had microcomputers. On campus, there was a motley and inadequate collection of equipment. We had anticipated a major donation to the project from IBM, but they pleaded a change in financial resources vs. needs for their own new facility for corporate technical training at Thornwood, New York, and reneged. In the Upsala microcomputer laboratory, there was one ideal piece of equipment – An IBM PC-XT with a hard disk, 1200 baud modem with SMARTCOM software, and 1200 baud printer that was reliable. We also had three Radio Shacks that had no hard disks and completely different communications software; plus a shared printer for all three that only operated at 300 baud. There were three Apples with modems; they had still different communications software. Moreover, the Apple configuration did not support continuous printing while online; the user had to print one screen at a time. In addition there were a few 300 baud 'dumb' printing terminals spread around the campus; access procedures using this equipment were different from those required for use of the microcomputers, which further confused the students.

To make matters worse, the operating budget of the Upsala microlab was such that it could only stay open about 50 hours a week, instead of a desirable minimum of 12 hours a day, 6 days a week. The result was that many students found it very difficult to match their need to use equipment to 'attend' their classes with the limited opportunities available. As will be seen from data presented later in this report, the Upsala students did not spend a great deal of time online at least partially because access was so inadequate. (These access difficulties are described in more detail in Bob Meinke's report on the Introductory Sociology course at Upsala, in Appendix III.)

At NJIT, freshmen and sophomores had been issued their own PCs. However, they were not issued modems or printers, and many were not willing to buy them for this course. In the Virtual Classroom laboratory at NJIT, there were only seven micros, and only one of these with an attached printer. Students without micros at home needed to use an awkward and time-consuming "remote print" facility to get printouts. In the regular microcomputer laboratories, the administration refused to provide connections to EIES. Their argument was that the labs were already overcrowded, and that they did not have the facilities to add connections to the local area network for these machines. Thus, many of the NJIT students ended up on dumb CRTs placed in a big hallway, sending remote prints to a fast printer several floors below. This is hardly convenient or optimal access.

Problems reported by students who did have micros and modems at home included difficulties with tying up their phone lines for hours at a time, and with lack of adequate documentation for communications software. One of the best communications software packages, SMARTCOM, is expensive. Instead, students made use of a variety of "shareware" or inexpensive programs with less functionality. We could not even tell them how to use much of this software to connect to EIES, since we had never seen it ourselves.

A related problem was with student assistants, who were supposed to be available to keep the labs open and to help online students. Many of them proved unreliable for various reasons. Their priorities were elsewhere. For instance, if they had an exam or an assignment due in a course, they just didn't show up for their hours, and students found locked doors on the micro lab. One assistant at NJIT, who had been scheduled for 15 hours a week of the time the lab was to be open, went to Taiwan for one month in the Fall and another in the Spring, because his parents died. Our project staff was so small that we had no "backup" personnel to cover consistently when such events occurred.

EIES itself was running on a minicomputer that is not very large or powerful by today's standards. It slowed noticeably when more than about 30 users were online simultaneously, which tended to occur during the initial training sessions and at midday on weekdays. It could accept only limited numbers of users coming in through each possible channel: local area network at NJIT, 300-baud local, 1200-baud local, and TELENET. The local area network access lines and/or the 1200-baud dialup lines were sometimes saturated during this experiment, forcing the students to try another access method or wait on a queue for a free line. In addition there was one serious crash during the fall semester, which came at the very worst time: during the last week of classes, when everything was "due." The EIES disks had filled up, and it took about two days to straighten out the mess and delete some noncrucial files. This was very frustrating and disruptive for the students, needless to say. (Note: We had been requesting additional storage capacity for over a year; the purchase order was not approved until its necessity was demonstrated by the system coming to a complete halt. Such mechanisms for determining the true need for additional hardware resources are probably not unusual in universities, where there is competition for limited hardware budgets.)

Five years later, the equipment problems are less severe, but they still exist. Though all full-time NJIT students are issued microcomputers, part-time students do not receive them. They still have to use the crowded microcomputer laboratories. Problems with "lost" remote prints for these students still persist. In sum, equipment access and problems seem to be a problem which needs constant attention for courses delivered via computer.

UNFINISHED SOFTWARE

For a variety of reasons that will not be described in detail here, the actual signing of the contract for this project did not occur until November 1986; meanwhile, the project supposedly started in January 1986. The start of software development was postponed while the question of whether the whole project was a "go" or "no go" was at issue. As a result, the special software which we had intended to have completed fell about six months behind schedule. Only an incomplete and very "buggy" version of the branch activities was available at the beginning of the fall. The Personal TEIES graphics package was not completed until almost the end of the Spring.

Perhaps the decision should have been "no go." However, it was not possible to postpone the experiment, since academic offerings are scheduled an entire year in advance. The choice was to proceed with unfinished special software tools, or to cancel the entire project.

Five years later, after several years of use of the new system, EIES 2, to deliver Virtual Classroom courses, we have reached the conclusion that software glitches are also endemic to this mode of communication. The software is constantly evolving, based on feedback from users, as explained in Chapter 3. Whenever a new function or subsystem is added, the first few weeks are likely to turn up "bugs" and problems. Hardware failures and software problems still occasionally occur, such as problems with overflowing memory during an end-of-semester flurry of activity, or system outages due to power failures or inadequate air conditioning when an unexpected 80-degree day occurs during the normal heating season. We now warn students that short system outages or problems can occur at any time, and that they should think of these like "snow days" for traditional classes. They are told to think about the fact that it is a lot less disappointing and inconvenient to dial in and find that the system is temporarily unavailable, than to make a long trip to a class only to find that it has been canceled because the instructor is ill. Ideally, there would never be any interruptions in access to the Virtual Classroom, but hardware and software are not currently 100% reliable.

RESISTANCE TO COLLABORATIVE LEARNING

Most students are used to instructional designs that are based on either completely individual activity, or competition. The widespread practice of grading on a curve emphasizes competition and penalizes students for helping one another. When faced with an instructional design which calls for them to work with others in a cooperative or collaborative manner, particularly if they are expected to play a teacher like role such as giving criticism of draft papers, many students are resistant. They may also feel that any grading scheme that makes their performance and grade dependent on collaborative work with others is "unfair." Finally, many students apparently place little value on the opinions of their peers.

This attitude of little regard for or interest in communication from other students was apparent among some students at the very first training session. When asked to practice using the system by entering comments for one another, they were impatient about reading material contributed by their peers, asked how to break the output, and wanted to know how to go straight to the assignments and lectures contributed by the instructor. If this attitude toward communicating with and working with their peers persisted, they were unlikely to feel positively about the Virtual Classroom approach.

Materials in Interviews 2 and 4 in Appendix II are relevant to this generalization. Note that the student in Interview 2 complains about VC being "self-study." When asked about his reactions to the contributions of the other students, he said, "I usually just blew off the other class members' comments and went straight to the professor's lecture. I wouldn't say that the other students' comments were a waste of my time; I just didn't read them."

On the other hand, students who worked hard on collaborative assignments and then were "let down" by other group members also had very negative feelings, at the time. As a student in Organizational Communication who had finished her part of a group activity on time put it, "I don't think it's fair that those of us who worked so hard to get our information on the computer have to suffer for those who don't bother to get their assignments in on time!" A subsequent message assuring her that she would receive an "A" for her excellent and lengthy contribution did not make her feel a whole lot better about it. She messaged back about still feeling disappointed when she came to the lab looking forward to reading contributions by others, only to find that the "others" had not appeared. The students who were late completing their parts of an online collaborative activity were the same ones who were chronically late doing traditional individual handwritten or typewritten assignments. In the latter case, however, their tardiness did not interfere with the learning of other students, whereas in a collaborative online assignment, it did.

Another problem is getting students to offer constructive criticism to one another; this is an unfamiliar role. In the partially online writing course at Upsala, for instance, Mary Swigonski required each student in a writing group to respond to specific questions on one another's draft essays. On a particular writing exercise, they might have been asked to suggest a better opening, suggest a better organization, and to suggest a better closing. Each student was to use these comments to produce an improved final draft. Dr. Swigonski reports that, in responding to these questions on each peer's essay, she could not get the students beyond "being nice" to one another. They felt comfortable saying what was good about the draft essay, but did not feel comfortable offering criticism. She encouraged the students to use pen names, but reports that they still did not feel comfortable making critical comments.

In future studies, the reasons for students' reluctance to offer constructive criticism to one another should be investigated with unstructured interviews focused on this issue. Perhaps, for instance, students feel that their peers would be upset by critical remarks, even if offered in the context of suggestions for improvements. They may be reluctant to risk causing hurt or anger, which would negatively affect their relationships with one another. Perhaps they feel unqualified to make such suggestions, especially in a "public" forum. Or, alternatively, they may feel that, by helping one another out, they might be negatively affecting their own grade, if the class is graded on a curve. Finally, the observed problem may be related to student grade-oriented motivations. In the Upsala writing course, students were required to say something about each peer's draft essay in the small writing groups. However, they were not graded for the quality of their suggestions. In many courses, instructors have observed that the students at these two colleges allocate their effort roughly in proportion to its importance for their grades. Since anything above "zero effort" counted the same, they may simply have taken the rational time-allocation choice of making the minimal effort needed to maximize their grades. If the reasons for the failure of students to offer constructive criticism on drafts are understood, it may be possible to change the social dynamics in future online classes.

ELECTRONIC PRANKS

For some students, CMC represents a fascinating opportunity for mischief, minor and major. It is inevitable that students will be tempted to abuse the medium.

As Keenan (1987) points out, on the public and private BBS systems, some people are posting information that goes beyond the obscene and annoying and becomes truly dangerous and/or criminal. For instance, a BBS allegedly operated by a Ku Klux Klan chapter gives the names, addresses, and license plate numbers of KKK "enemies," including rabbis and suspected FBI agents. A BBS in Calgary contained plans for causing the city's Light Rail Transit train to crash; other entries have included things from directions for making an atom bomb or drugs to credit card numbers and instructions for "phone freaking."

Nothing quite this dire happened during the Virtual Classroom experiment. Students were warned orally and in one of the first messages they received that irresponsible behavior would result in loss of their accounts, just as disruptive behavior in a traditional classroom would result in their being asked to leave the class. They were specifically instructed not to send messages, anonymous or otherwise, to anyone who was not in their class and whom they did not know. Of course, some ignored this and sent personal and sometimes obscene messages to strangers they saw online. We have no idea how often this happened without complaint from the "victim," but in over half a dozen cases there were complaints, and steps were taken to warn the offending student and/or to remove the account, depending on the severity of the breach of standards for acceptable student conduct.

Some students figured out how to steal an ID and use it to misbehave without much threat of exposure and punishment; they obtained other people's accounts from users who were careless about not protecting their passwords. In one case, several fraternity "brothers" of a sick student "helped him out" by signing online for him while he was in the hospital, and took the opportunity to send obscene messages to whatever females happened to be online at the time, under their fraternity brother's name, of course.

Another student went this one better. He or she observed an instructor's password during a demo; the instructor evidently did not change his code after the demo. In the middle of the night, the perpetrator got online using the ID of the instructor, sent a series of extremely objectionable propositions to just about everybody online, and also posted several comments in public conferences under the instructor's name, making scandalous remarks about the purported behavior of the president of the university. All of the latter were erased by the next morning; EIES users are for the most part a self-policing community. One of the recipients immediately sent a message of complaint about "Professor X's" message to the system monitor and user consultants; the system monitor then used his emergency privileges to delete all the conference comments and freeze the account. However, this should serve as an important cautionary tale for instructors and others. *Do* be careful to protect your access code! Use a temporary code for all demonstrations, and then change your access code immediately afterwards.

In sum, it is inevitable that the freedom and new opportunities for communication offered by CMC will be abused by some immature and/or irresponsible students. Policies must be developed which provide guidelines, and describe the consequences of unacceptable behavior online. These must be communicated clearly to the students, and enforced. Students and faculty must also be warned to protect their passwords, and coached on how to change them if they think that someone else may have seen their password. Special places such as a "student center" or a "jokes" conference should be set up where a certain amount of horseplay is acceptable, and students told to confine their "fooling around" with the system to these recreational conferences. Finally, if incidents do occur, they should be made the subject of a metadiscussion on responsible behavior. Often, the students are more incensed by the misbehavior of their classmates than is the instructor. A discussion of an incident such as an obscene comment entered anonymously is a good opportunity for building the cohesion and norms of the electronic community.

ELECTRONIC ANOMIE

There are currently limits to the size of an online class. These limits are social, not technical. Beyond a certain size, the amount of material generated in a class leads to information overload, and the number of people involved gets too high to foster a sense of community. The result may be *electronic anomie,* or normlessness.

Our initial experiment with combined multiple sections online experienced these problems. During 1988–1989, Murray Turoff combined his "day" and "evening" sections of Computers and Society with a section for which Roxanne Hiltz was responsible, to offer a joint online "triple section" of the course with a total enrollment of 96 students. We were attempting to explore the limits of the present technology in terms of class size. There was a main class conference for all three sections combined, secondary conferences for special activities such as a debate and student reviews of articles, and also separate conferences for "Turoff's students" and "Hiltz's students." However, even this attempt to segment the activities did not create enough organization to allow the course to run smoothly. Most of the students constantly complained of "information overload" (such as 100 or more new comments waiting if they had not signed on for several days). Since each student was given assignments which required entering a minimum of one comment a week, and since the instructors were entering perhaps 40 comments a week between them, most of them responding to student contributions, it is not hard to understand how the amount of material generated might have seemed overwhelming.

There were so many students that the participants had trouble getting a "personal feeling" for each other. About the middle of the semester, we had a "student revolt" on our hands, with about a dozen complaining comments suddenly entered, demanding that one of the upcoming assignments be canceled to allow everybody a chance to catch up. This was puzzling until we discovered that one of the students had chosen a very unusual topic for his project. The research project was based on the hypothesis that large online communities would be easy places in which to foment "rebellion against authority." The project took the form of an experiment. He sent personal messages to all classmates, urging them to follow his lead in the class conference and to complain and demand a reduction in work. Enough of his classmates complied so that his experiment could be considered a "success." The real subjects of the experiment, the instructors, gave a week's extension on an assignment in the face of what seemed to be overwhelming student opinion. This decision was based partially on their feelings that they were also having trouble keeping up with, and responding to, the barrage of comments, which was stimulating but exhausting.

However, phase two of the student's diabolical (from the point of view of the instructors) experiment "failed." The second phase was to try to prove the hypothesis that the technology could be used to foment ethnic or subcultural conflict. The student entered nasty ethnic attacks in the class conference, which made disparaging remarks about just about every ethnic group represented in the class except for his own. The other students did *not* follow this lead, but rather expressed feelings of strong disagreement and censure. So there are some limits to anomie, even in a large Virtual Classroom.

Our tentative conclusions on the basis of this experiment are that additional software and organizational strategies might make it possible to teach large online sections successfully, but that it will be difficult. Too many hours sitting in front of the CRT can strain anybody's eyes. We plan to try a very large joint section again, but with mixed media, delivering most of the "lecture" type material via videotape rather than via online texts.

During 1989–1991, two sections of Computers and Society were offered each semester, with both joint and separate class conferences and activities. For most purposes, the classes are kept separate for online electures, assignments, and discussions. For several special activities, they are joined in a special common conference set up for this purpose. For example, the "debate" assignment has evolved to a format in which the topic for the semester is debated between the two sections, with each section assigned a position, "pro" or "con," on the issue. Final projects are typically presented and discussed in a joint conference, so that the students can benefit from the widest possible number of presentations by their peers. These double sections, with a maximum of 50 students total and a limited number of joint activities, have worked quite well.

Andrew Feenberg, who frequently taught courses in the WBSI program, also reports problems with "information overload" when the number of students gets to high. At a presentation at which the author attended at Simon Fraser University (Feenberg, 1991), an audience member noted that WBSI class size reached about 100 participants at one point, and asked how this was handled. Feenberg replied:

> We tried many things. Most of them failed. This is one thing we tried. We said, "This is too many people", I think we had about 75 people; it's too many people; 25 is about an optimum size. So we will divide the group into three subgroups of 25 and they will not be able to read each other's comments. And then we'll have the teacher's comments in a separate conference that they'll see. So they can read the teacher's conference, in which only the teacher speaks, but they'll respond in their own conference . . . This was the problem. The teacher would see an interesting comment in his three conferences and he wouldn't really separate them clearly in his mind, and he would comment on different things that people said in their conferences, in HIS conference, and so, the, 'so-and-so' over here knows that 'so-and-so' over there, said something interesting, but he can't read it, and he'd say, "I would like to be able to read 'so-and-so's' comment, but I can't." In each session there'd be a hint, a remark, that maybe this sub-division was a stupid idea and finally we took the hints and we collapsed it back into a single group.

> No good plan was ever figured out, to deal with this problem. What we did instead of having a good plan to deal with the problem was to multiply offerings, so that in any given month, there would be more things to do and people would tend then, to migrate towards what interested them the most, so the size of the individual conferences would be reduced somewhat and opportunities to participate would be spread. Obviously, if you are dealing with a much larger population, that wouldn't be good enough. You couldn't have, say, a thousand people, picking and choosing among sixty different topics, the things they wanted to do that day. I don't have a solution to this problem. It's an interesting question. Maybe it isn't a problem because universities don't recruit students the way we did. We built an institution from scratch. Universities recruit from a large base, they recruit enough people to have a class which is a temporary entity which dissolves, but we just kept adding people on.

The conclusion reached is that individual class conferences, where most discussion and work takes place, should be kept to 30 people or less. There may also be special purpose "plenary sessions" or joint lectures where two or more classes participate. Though you can jam more and more people into a lecture hall without seriously hindering everyone's ability to participate by listening, you cannot put large numbers of students into a single Virtual Classroom, where active, generative, and collaborative learning techniques are emphasized. The flood of contributions becomes too large for participants to deal with, and both communication and norms of polite social interaction tend to break down.

SUMMARY

The implementation of Virtual Classroom was far from optimal. Problems included:

- Recruiting sufficient numbers of students for the experimental online sections.
- Opposition from faculty members who believed that the medium would fail to adequately deliver college-level courses, and/or that it would be unfair competition which would decrease enrollments in their courses.
- Failure to adequately inform all students enrolled in the experimental sections of the nature of the educational experience in which they would be involved, despite explanations in registration material, campus newspaper articles, flyers and posters.
- Inadequate amounts and quality of equipment for student access.
- Limited capacity of the central host (EIES), which was sometimes saturated.
- Unfinished software tools to support the Virtual Classroom, including the graphics package that had been considered so important for some of the courses.
- Resistance by some students to collaborative learning.
- Deliberate misbehavior by some students.
- Emergence of "electronic anomie" when attempting to deal with approximately 100 students in a single conference.

These problems interacted. For instance, we had initially anticipated only four courses involved in the experiment. Partially because of the low enrollments in the experimental sections, many other courses were added to the study. Each additional course had its own unique problems and demands, which added to the overload on the limited staff for the project. We were working under a contract that specified tight deadlines for completion of phases and "deliverables." It would have been far better to spread out the implementation over a longer period of time. However, the rigidity of the academic calendar and scheduling conventions (whereby courses and teaching assignments are scheduled as much as a year in advance) and of the project contract requirements made this impossible.

One lesson learned is not to underestimate the public relations effort that will be needed in implementing a new course delivery technology. Do not assume that, because you have the support of the President and/or Dean, faculty and staff members not directly involved in the project will be understanding or cooperative. Instead, expect what Peter Keen (1981) calls "counter-implementation." Deflect and co-opt possible resistance by sending a description of the project to everyone whose cooperation may be needed, and then meet personally with each of them to answer questions and to plan or negotiate their participation. You may need to personally orient all of the staff of the registrar's office and the computer labs, for instance, to help to assure that all will go smoothly. Include facts that will deflect criticisms before they arise. For instance, use data from this study, cross-referenced to the account in the Chronicle of Higher Education (De Loughrey, 1988) to show that the quality of the education received by students will not suffer.

To forestall disruptive behavior by students, make it clear that while the Virtual Classroom is less formal than the traditional classroom, it also has standards for acceptable, considerate behavior. Make it clear that students who misbehave will lose their accounts on the system and their membership in the class, just as they would be ejected from a traditional classroom for disruptive behavior. When students do behave in an inconsiderate or unethical manner, make it a topic of discussion so that the group itself develops norms and sanctions their peers. This helps to build an electronic community. Finally, do not put more than about 30 students into an online section/main class conference. Just as traditional classes are closed when the classrooms run out of seats, so must online classes be limited in size, in order to provide a manageable communication environment.

The implementation problems are most severe the first year that a campus tries the Virtual Classroom approach. Unfortunately, that was also the year in which we conducted our first quasi-experiment and collected data on "matched" sections of online and traditionally offered courses. This should be kept in mind when examining the results of the comparisons. Had more time been allowed to phase in the use of this new medium before collecting comparative data, the statistics for the Virtual Classroom would probably appear more favorable.

However, after five years of additional experimentation, there are still occasional problems with hardware or software or institutional support. These problems are no worse than those encountered by the teacher using a traditional classroom, where sometimes the school is totally shut down by weather or vacation periods, and sometimes the instructional equipment ordered and needed (such as an overhead projector, VCR, or even chalk and erasers) is missing, and makes it difficult to teach.

Despite the fact that teachers tend to have to work "around the clock, 7 days a week" in the Virtual Classroom, and despite the endemic technical problems involved whenever one has to rely on a complex computer and telecommunications network, most teachers who have tried teaching this way would prefer never to give it up. They feel that they have more regular and better communication with their colleagues, as well as their students, than with traditional media.

PART *III*

LEARNING IN A VIRTUAL CLASSROOM: RESEARCH METHODS AND FINDINGS

A man may well bring a horse to the water, but he cannot make him drink without he will.

—John Heywood, Proverbs, 1546

CHAPTER 9

RESEARCH METHODS

"Measure twice, cut once."

−(Folk saying)

The purpose of evaluation is to provide knowledge to guide subsequent implementations of an innovation. In order to explore the evaluation questions raised in the first chapter, and to test the specific hypotheses developed and presented in Chapter 3, it was necessary to observe a variety of courses, students, and implementation environments.

Institutions vary a great deal in the computing facilities which they provide for students, and in the characteristics of their students. Three types of learning environments were included in this study. NJIT is a comprehensive technological university enrolling about 8,000 students, which provides a microcomputer to each of its full time undergraduates. Upsala College is a small, liberal-arts oriented college with about 1,000 students, which at the time of this project possessed only a single micro-computer laboratory with seven machines. Two distance learning programs (described below) enroll part-time adult students, who supply their own equipment.

The primary research design rested upon matched but "nonequivalent" sections of the same course taught online and in the traditional classroom. Though the same teacher, text and other printed materials, and midterm and final exams were used, the classes were nonequivalent because the students were able to self-select delivery mode. The matched courses included:

- Introductory Sociology at Upsala College (Soc 150);
- Freshman-level Computer-Assisted Statistics at Upsala (CC140y);
- Introduction to Computer Science (CIS213) at NJIT; and
- An upper-level introductory course in statistics for engineers at NJIT (Math 305, Statistics for Technology).

Introduction to Sociology (SOC 150) is taken by most students in their freshman year. Introduction to Computer Science (CIS 213) is a second-level course at NJIT, with a course in FORTRAN as the prerequisite. A statistics course was offered in two versions: the freshman-level course at Upsala that was a required "core" course for all students and had no mathematical prerequisites except acceptable scores on a Math Basic Skills test; and an NJIT upper level first course in statistics for engineers, with a calculus prerequisite.

However, these introductory courses are not representative of the range of possible applications of the Virtual Classroom, or for exploring variations in process and outcome in such an environment. For these purposes, the sample was expanded to include many other courses which used the VC mode of delivery. For example, whereas all the instructors had extensive experience delivering courses in the traditional mode, this was a "first time" experience teaching an entire course in a Virtual Classroom. On the basis of this experience, they might change their minds about effective procedures in this new mode. It was possible to schedule online sections of the computer science and the two statistics courses to repeat in the spring semester; but not possible, given teaching load limits, to also schedule a second "control" course in Spring 1987. Therefore, the sample was expanded to include a repeat of three courses online.

Secondly, there are many potential applications of the VC in a "mixed-modes" format. Some part of the course is conducted face-to-face, and a part occurs online. A total of five courses using this mixed mode of delivery were included during the initial, funded year of experimentation: an introductory management course, a writing course, organizational communication, anthropology, and business French.

In both Fall and Spring, there was an experimental and a control section of the management course. The control section completed all course activities in the traditional manner. The major course assignment involved the organization and simulated operation of a start up company over a "fiscal year." The control sections did this by meeting periodically during one of the scheduled class times, and by communicating by telephone or written memo or out-of-class meetings in between. The experimental sections carried out their management laboratory assignment completely online. There was a class conference for general discussion and separate conferences and notebooks where the simulated organizations conducted their business. In looking at some of the data on this course, we found that the amount of usage was actually heavier than in several of the courses that were totally online. For many analyses, therefore, this course was included along with totally online courses.

The third expansion of the sample and study design was based on the fact that there are many ongoing sets of courses which are currently being offered by other institutions online, but for which there is no traditional equivalent. These include graduate level courses in media studies, offered through Connected Education™ on EIES, with registration and credit at the New School. Begun in October 1985, a series of two-month-long master's level courses is offered throughout the year. At least one student has already completed an entire master's degree online. Each student was included in the study only once, even though they might have taken six or more courses during the year. The response rate for the mailed questionnaires to this group was much lower than the response rate for questionnaires administered or collected during the face-to-face meetings on the first and last days of the NJIT and Upsala courses that were delivered online. Thus, the total number of subjects for Connect-Ed (29) does not reflect the total size of their student body.

A postgraduate course offered for teachers by the Ontario Institute for Studies in Education (OISE) on their PARTI system serves as an example of continuing professional education online. Another example is a two-year program offered online for executives by the School of Strategic Management of the Western Behavioral Sciences Institute. Materials and results these programs will occasionally be displayed and included in the analyses.

After the initial funded project, particularly as the new version of the Virtual Classroom system was developed on EIES2, some instructors continued to experiment with offering courses partially online and partially in the traditional classroom, despite the lack of any financial support for their efforts. This included sections of the management course, where a "Virtual Management Laboratory" was developed and elaborated from 1986 through 1990. The nature of this subsequent experimentation with the Virtual Management Laboratory and the results obtained will be described in Chapter 13.

In addition, several sections of NJIT's CIS350, Computers and Society, used the system from 1985 through the present; some data and examples for this course will be included in selected analyses. Finally, a graduate level course in computer science, CIS 675, continued to use successive versions of the system from 1988 through the present, and will also serve as the source of some qualitative data. Other courses have continued to use the system, but did not complete any formal evaluation questionnaires or procedures. For example, an introductory psychology course was offered by NJIT during Spring 1991, using broadcast course tapes on public television for lectures, and the Virtual Classroom on EIES 2 for contact among the dispersed students and instructor. Occasional anecdotal data or examples will be included from such ongoing efforts.

The purpose of including these additional courses in the study was to increase the overall sample size, and thus the chances of obtaining statistically significant results. The expanded sample of courses also increases the generalizability of the findings to a wider range of online offerings, and facilitates exploration of variations among online courses.

There is an unfortunate confounding in the design; both of the totally online courses at the Freshman level were offered at Upsala, and the two totally online courses at NJIT were at a higher level. With only four totally online courses supported by the project, however, it is inevitable that not all relevant variables could be adequately controlled.

Table 9-1 lists the courses included in the initial quasi-experimental study and notes both the number of students in each, and the number for which we have complete data.

How did this diverse set of courses offered in different modes and at different schools translate into research designs for statistical analysis? This question is answered in the next section.

THE QUASI-EXPERIMENTAL DESIGN

The standard experimental design of random assignment to matched sections of traditional and experimental courses is neither practical, ethical, nor particularly relevant for evaluation of the Virtual Classroom. Students cannot be randomly assigned to sections of a course meeting at different times, given the constraints of their other obligations, and the same instructor obviously cannot teach two sections of the same course at the same time. It is not ethical, because in an experiment, there is some risk that the outcomes will not be favorable, and students should voluntarily agree to assume the risk of using an experimental form of delivery for an entire course. Finally, it is not methodologically sound in terms of estimating future impacts. Students who choose telecourses, especially telecourses delivered via computer, are likely to differ from students choosing traditional courses in nonrandom ways. They are more likely to have out-of-class obligations which make it difficult for them to attend regularly scheduled classes, for instance, and to have more positive attitudes toward computers. Random assignment is also not methodologically sound when one of the objectives is to explore variations among online classes. There are many online courses for which there simply are no "face-to-face" equivalents, because they are designed specifically for distance education; and many traditional classes requiring laboratory equipment, such as biology or chemistry, for which there is no online equivalent possible at the present time.

TABLE 9-1
NUMBER OF STUDENTS, BY COURSE

Course	Period	Mode	Enrolled	Completed Postcourse
AT NJIT				
CIS 213	Fall	Online	17	9
CIS 213	Fall	Offline	20	12
CIS 213	Spring	Online	21	10
Math 305	Fall	Online	13	9
Math 305	Fall	Offline	22	19
Math 305	Spring	Online	27	23
Management (OSS471)	Fall	Mixed	28	23
Management (OSS471)	Fall	Offline	21	13
Management (OSS471)	Spring	Mixed	32	23
Management (OSS471)	Spring	Offline	26	20
AT UPSALA				
Intro Soc	Fall	Online	17	11
Intro Soc	Fall	Offline	19	18
Statistics	Fall	Online	14	12
Statistics	Fall	Offline	20	17
Statistics	Spring	Online	12	9
Organizational Communication	Fall	Mixed	12	6
Anthropology	Fall	Mixed	12	8
Writing Seminar	Fall	Mixed	18	12
Business French	Spring	Mixed	8	6
OTHER				
Connected Education	All Year	Online	43	11
Ontario Institute	Spring	Online	12	7

Shavelson et al. (1986) state that three designs can be identified as relevant to evaluating student outcomes from telecourses. These are:

1. *Uncontrolled assignment to form nonequivalent groups,* in which students self-select into tele- or traditional courses. Before and after knowledge and skills are measured. This is the primary evaluation design chosen for this study.
2. *Patched-up design* is "appropriate when institutions regularly cycle students through the same course, such that students from one cycle can serve as a control group for students from another cycle." Unfortunately, this is not the case at NJIT or Upsala, and the design can be used only to a very limited extent.

3. *Case study methods* provide narrative (descriptive and qualitative) accounts. Elements of the case study method were included.

The above set of alternative methods, however, ignores the important question of variation in success within telecourses. In examining the question of "assessing interactive modes of instruction," Davis, Dukes, and Gamson (1981) reach the following conclusion:

> Low priority should be given to conventional evaluation studies that compare a control group using a conventional classroom with an experimental group using some interactive technique . . . We doubt that fruitful, context-free generalizations can be found demonstrating that one technique is uniformly better than another, even for specific learning objectives.

> Our alternative approach accepts the fact that these techniques show no evidence of general inferiority to conventional techniques. . . . The focus should be on the conditions under which given interactive techniques are most and least appropriate. We need to know the contextual variables that maximize the effectiveness of a given method. (pp. 321–322)

Given that the Virtual Classroom is a new educational technology, it is necessary to prove that it is just as good as a traditional classroom for *mastery* of facts and information. For this purpose, we followed the traditional evaluation approach of experimental and quasi-experimental design. For each of five target undergraduate courses, we matched a section of a course in traditional classroom mode with a mode employing the Virtual Classroom. Examination scores and other outcomes can then be compared for the two sections. In other words, at the core of the evaluation design is a 2 x 5 factorial design, with each of five courses offered in two different modes of delivery (see the top of Table 9-2).

However, this basic design was supplemented with data from other courses which used the Virtual Classroom in a variety of ways, in order to gain a better understanding of the contingencies which influence variations in outcome:

1. The online courses which are repeated fall and spring can be analyzed as a quasi-experimental factorial design with a 4 (course) by 2 (first vs. second offering) design (middle display of Table 9-2).
2. We can look at differences among modes in terms of totally online courses vs. traditional classroom courses, vs. mixed mode courses; in other words, a one-factor, three levels of treatment design. During the time that the quasi-experimental design was implemented, a number of other courses also used the Virtual Classroom in a mixed mode of delivery, as described above. There were

TABLE 9-2
QUASI-EXPERIMENTAL DESIGNS FOR ASSESSING
DIFFERENCES IN OUTCOMES BY MODE

Design 1
COURSE BY MODE

COURSE	ONLINE	Face-to-face (FTF)
CIS 213	13	18
MATH 305	12	22
MANAGEMENT	28	24
INTRO SOC	16	19
STATISTICS	11	15
TOTAL	80	98

Design 2
REPETITION OF ONLINE COURSES

COURSE	FALL	SPRING
CIS 213	13	19
MATH 305	12	24
MANAGEMENT	28	30
STATISTICS	11	11
TOTAL	64	84

Design 3
SCHOOL BY MODE

	ONLINE	MIXED	FTF	TOTAL
UPSALA	41	38	26	105
NJIT	71	58	63	192
CONNECT-ED	29			29
Ontario Inst.	7			7
TOTAL	148	96	89	331

Number of Students for Whom Data are Available Shown in Cells

no "matched" sections without the software for these courses, but the students can be asked to compare their experiences in the Virtual Classroom with experiences in prior, traditionally delivered courses. This gives us the largest number of subjects; the number for whom at least some data are available is shown at the bottom of the diagram for "design 3."

3. We can examine contextual factors related to the conditions under which VC was most and least effective. These include differences among courses and organizational settings, and differences related to student characteristics, attitudes, and behavior. One of

the major contextual variables considered was the institution
within which a course is conducted. The third display in Table 9–2
shows the basic 3 (modes) by 4 (colleges) design for this analysis.

The quasi-experimental design described above used matched face-
to-face and online sections of these courses, all offered during Fall 1986. The
design is quasi-experimental rather than a fully controlled experiment for
two major reasons: students self-selected mode of delivery, and the nature
of assignments differed between matched sections. Efforts were made to
encourage students to register in the experimental sections, but only with
full information about the nature of this "unproven" method of delivery.

Initially, it had been intended to use exactly the same assignments in the
matched online and Virtual Classroom sections of courses. However, the
faculty members pointed out that this would be totally inappropriate, and
would fail to take advantage of the unique opportunity offered by the VC
for collaborative activities. So, the faculty members were freed to devise
whatever assignments they thought most appropriate for this medium,
provided the textbooks and the midterm and final exams were the same.

Each instructor incorporated collaborative activities in the online section which were different from the individual assignments given in the
traditional section. This varied widely depending on the nature of the
course. For example, in the upper level statistics course, students could
see one another's homework assignments after they had done their own, in
order to compare approaches. In some assignments, each student chose
one problem to work on instead of doing them all; the rest of the class could
see their solution. In Introductory Sociology, many assignments made use
of pen names and required students to enter analyses of how general
concepts, such as role conflict, applied to their own lives. The use of pen
names prevented embarrassment in using examples from their own experiences to share with the class. In Computer Science, the VC section had
a final assignment requiring a group to complete a complex program by
breaking it into subroutines, and then making sure that all the subroutines
worked together to produce the correct overall result. Such an assignment
was possible only for a group able to work together constantly, and to have
an integrated facility online for showing programs to one another, compiling, and executing them. The traditional section had only individual
programming assignments.

EVALUATION INSTRUMENTS AND PROCEDURES

Data collection and analysis was conducted under "protection of human
subjects" guidelines, whereby all participating students are informed of

the goals and procedures followed in the project and confidentiality of the data is protected. A variety of methods were used for data collection, including questionnaires for students, automatic monitoring of online activity, participant observation in the online conferences, use of available data such as grade distributions or test scores for participating students, descriptive case reports by the instructor for each course, and a small number of personal interviews.

Questionnaires

Pre-and postcourse questionnaires completed by students are the most important data source (see Appendix I). The precourse questionnaire measures student characteristics and expectations. The postcourse questionnaire focuses on detailed evaluations of the effectiveness of the online course or course segments, and on student perceptions of the ways in which the Virtual Classroom is better or worse than the traditional classroom.

The precourse questionnaire was administered and collected at the beginning of the first "training" session in which the Virtual Classroom use comprised or supplemented the instructional delivery mode. For Connected Education students and OISE students, the precourse questionnaire was included with the mailed system documentation, with immediate return requested.

Postcourse questionnaires were mailed to online students one week prior to the final examination. They were asked to bring the completed questionnaires to the final exam. The instructor collected each questionnaire as the final exam was handed to each student. If the questionnaire was not completed, the instructor handed a new one to the student and asked him or her to complete it after finishing the exam. Students were told that they could stay extra time if necessary to complete the questionnaire. If a student refused to complete a questionnaire, this was his or her right under the protection of human subjects regulations, and did not affect the course grade in any way.

For courses in "mixed" mode, the postcourse questionnaire was distributed and collected in class, towards the end of the semester. A mailing with two follow-up requests was used for Connected Education students and for students who were absent during an in-class administration.

Measuring Course Effectiveness. The items used to measure students' subjective assessments of courses were included in the postcourse questionnaire. They were developed on the basis of a review of the literature on teaching effectiveness, particularly Centra's (1982) summary. Copies of the available student rating instruments described in that book were obtained, and permission to use items from these standard questionnaires was given. Effectiveness was conceptualized as being related to four dimensions: course content, characteristics of the teaching, course outcomes, and comparisons of process in the virtual and online formats. These dimensions are presented as separate sections in the postcourse questionnaire.

Almost all of these items from standard teaching effectiveness questionnaires suffer from the potential methodological problem of response bias. Likert-type items are worded positively, and the semantic differential type items are arranged so that the most positive response constantly occurs on the same side of the page. Though rewording for approximately half of the items was considered, it was decided to leave them in their original forms so that the results might be more directly comparable to those for other studies using the same items.

Course evaluations by students are admittedly a controversial means of measuring course outcomes. They have been observed to vary with many things in addition to teacher competence and student learning, such as an interaction between faculty status and class size (Hamilton, 1980). Student evaluations are strongly related to grades received in the course. There is argument about which is the cause and which is the effect. If grades are "objective" measurements of amount of learning, then we would expect that students with higher grades in a course would also subjectively report more positive outcomes. However, it may be that a student who has a good grade in a course rates that course and instructor positively as a kind of "halo effect" of being pleased with the course because of receiving a good grade. Such distortions of teaching evaluations are probably more prevalent when the student raters know that their responses are being used as input for evaluating faculty in personnel decisions. In this case, the participants knew that their ratings were used only for this research project, and the ratings were made before final grades were received. Despite the limitations of subjective ratings, the students were probably in a better position than anyone else to report on the extent to which they had or had not experienced various positive or negative outcomes from a course.

Survey of Dropouts. All students who dropped an online course or who requested transfer to the traditional sections were surveyed with a special questionnaire designed for this purpose. The questionnaire probed the reasons for the action by the student and whether they constituted a "rejection" of the technology or other factors (see Appendix I). Among these reasons might be dissatisfaction with the software or with response time; inadequate access to equipment; or reasons not related to the mode of delivery, such as personal problems, dislike for the subject matter in the course, or the work load required.

Dropouts who did not respond to the mailed questionnaire (with two mailed follow-ups) were contacted several times in order to try to interview them by telephone. They turned out to be very hard to reach; we were able to obtain only one such interview.

Automatic Monitoring of Use. CMCS automatically capture and store a complete transcript of the entire conference. Printouts of all courses were retained for subsequent analysis. This provided a wealth of qualitative data for use in describing and understanding the different forms of interaction that occur in the VC, the techniques used by instructors, and the reactions of students.

In addition, we used software built into the EIES systems for measuring the amount and type of online activity by participants. A routine on EIES 1 called Conference Analysis permits the tabulation and display of the number and percentage of lines and items contributed by each member of a conference, either for a specified part of the conference or for the entire conference. This automated analysis was run for each class conference.

Monthly data available for each member of the system included the following:

- Total number of logins to the system.
- Total hours online.
- Total number of conference comments contributed. This is not a complete measure of student activity related to the class, since it excludes contributions made in "branch activities"(which were numerous for some courses), or in notebooks or private messages.
- Total number of private messages sent.

By recording these data monthly, we can aggregate to obtain the total for the whole course, but we can also examine the extent to which these measures of activity change during the course.

Other Types of Data

In addition to standard questionnaires, the monitored data on participation, and grades on tests and the final grade for the course, several other types of data were gathered.

Institutional Data. During the 1986–1987 academic year, measures of general verbal and mathematical ability (the SATs) and level of academic performance (the grade point average) were obtained from college records for each student, if the student agreed and signed a formal release. These enabled us to measure students ability.

Feedback from Faculty. An online conference for faculty, messages exchanged with the project director, and 2-day-long face-to-face faculty workshops were used to exchange information about experiences conducting classes in the virtual classroom. Each faculty member also produced a description of their experiences in teaching online. This feedback from faculty, along with direct observation of the online classes, was used to generate the mostly qualitative data that served as the basis for generalizations about effective online teaching techniques.

Interviews with Students. Personal or telephone interviews were conducted with 10 students. Most of these students were selected from a list of 15 students who had given the most positive and 15 who gave the most negative ratings of VC on the postcourse questionnaire, or who had dropped out and had not responded to the "dropout" questionnaire. A few "moderately negative" or "moderately positive" students were included in the personal interview sample in order to try to fill in the spectrum of reactions. The purpose of the interviews was to probe the reasons underlying the students' evaluations, and to explore the full context of experiences and circumstances which resulted in their opinions of the Virtual Classroom. The interview guide and some sample interviews are included in Appendix II.

MEASURING THE VARIABLES

A summary of the independent, intervening, and dependent variables used in this study, and of their operational definitions, is included in Exhibits 9-1 to 9-3. The independent variables have been classified according to the theoretical framework which guided the study, as related to characteristics of the technology, the individual students, and of the courses (class groups) and institutional contexts (colleges) through which the courses were offered. Note that the frequency distributions are shown for many of the items; they give an overall picture of the results, which will be discussed in subsequent chapters.

Many of the variables in this study are fairly simple and straightforward, such as age or gender, and were measured with single questions on the questionnaires. Others measure complex concepts, and were con-

EXHIBIT 9–1
Independent Variables and Indicators

CHARACTERISTICS OF INDIVIDUALS
(Measured at Baseline)

VARIABLE	INDICATOR
Attitudes	
Attitudes toward computers	Index
Expectations about system	Index
Personal Sphere of Control	Index
Interpersonal Sphere of Control	Index
Skills and Characteristics	
Academic standing	(Freshman to Post-doctoral)
Age	
Ethnic Group	__Black/Afro-American __Hispanic (Mexican, Puerto Rican, etc.) __White __Asian or Asian-American __Other
English (First Language)	Is English your native or first language? ☐ Yes ☐ No
Typing	How would you describe your typing skills? (1) ___None (2) ___Hunt and peck (3) ___Casual (rough draft with errors) (4) ___Good (can do 25 w.p.m. error free) (5) ___Excellent (can do 40 w.p.m. error free)
Mathematical Aptitude	Math SAT
Verbal Aptitude	Verbal SAT
Academic Performance	Grade Point Average
Terminal Access Home Terminal	Question Do you have a micro or terminal at home (or in your dorm, wherever you live during classes)? (41% – yes)
Access Problem	Is access to a terminal or micro for the online class a problem for you?

	7%	15%	19%	20%	39%	
:	1 :	2 :	3 :	4 :	5	:
	Serious Problem		Not a Problem			

$N = 176$ $\overline{X} = 3.7$ $SD = 1.3$

ceived from the beginning as composed of a number of dimensions, represented by a series of questions.

For all courses in all modes, a set of postcourse questionnaire items measured student perceptions of general characteristics of the course content, the quality of the instruction, and course outcomes. An additional extensive set of items measured student perceptions of the nature and

EXHIBIT 9–2
Intervening Variables

CONTEXTUAL VARIABLES

Mode of Delivery | Traditional Face-to-Face
 | Virtual Classroom
 | Mixed

Course

School | NJIT, Upsala, Other

Instructor's Experience | First or Second Offering

INTERVENING VARIABLES

<u>System Use</u> Monitor data

    Number Times Online "

    Total Hours Online "

    Total Messages Sent "

    Number and Percent of Comments "

<u>Collaborative Learning</u> <u>Index</u>

Assignments Useful

I found reading reviews or assignments of other students to be useful to me.

12%	24%	26%	21%	6%	7%	4%
: 1 :	2 :	3 :	4 :	5 :	6 :	7 :

Strongly Agree   Strongly Disagree

N=177 $\overline{X}$=3.2   SD=1.6

Inhibited

I felt more "inhibited" in taking part in the discussion.

12%	24%	26%	21%	6%	7%	4%
: 1 :	2 :	3 :	4 :	5 :	6 :	7 :

Strongly Agree   Strongly Disagree

N=179 $\overline{X}$=4.5   SD=1.7

Less Work

I didn't have to work as hard for online classes.

3%	9%	9%	16%	20%	24%	19%
: 1 :	2 :	3 :	4 :	5 :	6 :	7 :

Strongly Agree   Strongly Disagree

N=181 $\overline{X}$=4.9   SD=1.7

Communicated More

I communicated more with other students in the class as a result of the computerized conference.

13%	21%	13%	19%	10%	12%	11%
: 1 :	2 :	3 :	4 :	5 :	6 :	7 :

Strongly Agree   Strongly Disagree

N=179 $\overline{X}$=3.7   SD=1.9

Increased Efficiency

Did use of the System increase the efficiency of your education (the quantity of work that you can complete in a given time)?

11%	18%	15%	23%	10%	15%	6%
: 1 :	2 :	3 :	4 :	5 :	6 :	7 :

Definitely yes   Unsure   Definitely Not

N=175 $\overline{X}$=3.7   SD=1.7

EXHIBIT 9-3

DEPENDENT VARIABLES

Mastery

midterm exam grade
final exam grade
course grade
writing scores

Improved Access
Access to professor

Having the computerized conferencing system available
provided better access to the professor(s).

18%	21%	19%	14%	10%	9%	8%
: 1	: 2	: 3	: 4	: 5	: 6	: 7

Strongly   Strongly
Agree   Disagree
$N = 179$ $\overline{X} = 3.3$ SD = 1.9

Convenient

Taking online courses is more convenient.

25%	24%	16%	12%	8%	8%	7%
: 1 :	2 :	3 :	4 :	5 :	6 :	7 :

Strongly   Strongly
Agree   Disagree
$N = 175$ $\overline{X} = 3.7$ SD = 1.8

Subjective (student)
Assessments of Quality
   VC Overall
   Course Rating
   Instructor Rating
   Increased Interest
   Synthesis

Index (see exhibit 9-4)
Index
Index
Index
Index

Increased Motivation

The fact that my assignments would be ready by the other
students increased my motivation to do a thorough job.

16%	25%	14%	20%	6%	11%	8%
: 1	: 2	: 3	: 4	: 5	: 6	: 7

Strongly   Strongly
Agree   Disagree
N=179 $\overline{X}$=3.4   SD=1.8

Stop Participating

When I became very busy with other things, I was more likely to
stop participating in the online class than I would have been to
"cut" a weekly face-to-face lecture.

15%	20%	14%	15%	8%	15%	14°
: 1 :	2 :	3 :	4	: 5 :	6 :	7

Strongly   Strongly
Agree   Disagree
N=177 $\overline{X}$=3.8   SD=2.0

More Boring

The online or virtual classroom mode is more boring than
traditional classes.

8%	6%	8%	16%	17%	24%	21°
: 1	: 2	: 3	: 4	: 5	: 6	: 7

Strongly   Strongly
Agree   Disagree
N=177 $\overline{X}$=3.8   SD=2.0

More Involved

I felt more "involved" in taking an active part in the course

16%	22%	18%	18%	13%	6%	6%
: 1	: 2	: 3	: 4	: 5	: 6	: 7

Strongly   Strongly
Agree   Disagree
N=177 $\overline{X}$=3.3   SD=1.7

Comments Useful

I found the comments made by other students to be useful
to me.

11%	28%	20%	20%	10%	7%	4%
: 1	: 2	: 3	: 4	: 5	: 6	: 7

Strongly   Strongly
Agree   Disagree
N=177 $\overline{X}$=3.3   SD=1.7

quality of the online courses as compared to traditional courses. Some sets of dependent variables (items dealing with course content and quality of the teaching) were treated only in terms of a combined index in this study, since they were not conceived of as being substantially influenced by mode of delivery. The two sets of variables measuring course outcomes and VC ratings were treated both individually, and in combined indexes.

Constructing Indexes

Many of the conceptual constructs used in this study are measured by multiple items. It is more valid to use several items, each measuring a slightly different aspect of the variable, and then combine them, rather than relying on one question. In building *indexes* or measurement *scales*, items were included in the questionnaires that appeared to have "face validity." That is, conceptually, they appear to measure some attitude or behavior that is included in the concept. After the data were collected, these intended scales were subjected to an item analysis to see if they were indeed correlated. A reliability analysis was conducted, which computes Cronbach's Alpha as an overall measure of the reliability of the composite measure. In this procedure, each designated component is left out of the total index and the Alpha level computed for an index without the item included. In arriving at the final indexes, we omitted items that did not correlate well with the index as a whole, and/or items which substantially lowered the Alpha value if they were included.

Four of the items asking the students to directly compare the VC with the TC form a composite "VC OVERALL" index. This variable will appear very frequently in the discussion of results of the study, so its components are shown in Exhibit 9–4.

Similar tables showing the items comprising other indexes used in the study are included in Appendix I-D. Composite independent variables include the Personal Efficacy and Interpersonal Control scales devised by Paulhus and Christie (1981) for measuring a person's perceived *sphere of control*. The questions appear in the section of the preuse questionnaire called "Images of Yourself."

The set of items on "current feelings about using computers" form an index of Computer Attitudes (see Appendix I). The same items were repeated on the postcourse questionnaire, with that index labeled as "Computer Attitudes-2." Similarly, the items on "expectations about the EIES system" combine into an *EIES EXPECTATIONS* index. Other scales were formed by combining items from the *course rating* and *instructor rating* portions of the postcourse questionnaire.

Multiple items measuring the course outcomes of increased interest in

---

EXHIBIT 9–4
THE "VC OVERALL" INDEX

Not choose another
I would NOT choose to take another on-line course.

11%	9%	6%	10%	10%	19%	35%
: 1 :	2	: 3	: 4 :	5	: 6	: 7 :

Strongly agree   Strongly disagree

$n = 182$ mean = 5·0   S.D. = 2·1

Better learning (R)
I found the course to be a better learning experience than normal face-to-face courses.

17%	15%	14%	25%	10%	9%	10%
: 1 :	2	: 3	: 4 :	5	: 6	: 7 :

Strongly agree   Strongly disagree

$n = 183$ mean = 3·6   S.D. = 1·9

Learned more (R)
I learned a great deal more because of the use of EIES.

10%	20%	15%	27%	9%	11%	8%
: 1 :	2	: 3	: 4 :	5	: 6	: 7 :

Strongly agree   Strongly disagree

$n = 182$ mean = 3·7   S.D. = 1·8

Increase quality
Did use of the system increase the quality of your education?

12%	22%	22%	22%	8%	6%	7%
: 1	: 2	: 3	: 4	: 5	: 6	: 7 :

Definitely
yes   Unsure   Definitely not

(R) indicates item was reversed for scoring. index range = 4 (worst) to 28 (best);
Mean = 18·3, S.D. = 6·1, $n = 203$, Chronbach's alpha = 0·85.

---

the subject matter and in ability to synthesize material were combined
into INTEREST and SYNTHESIS indexes. There is also a COLLABORATION INDEX
of whether group or collaborative learning took place, such as making
friends and working cooperatively.

RELAXING EXPERIMENTAL CONTROLS

The initial quasi-experimental design called for the "matched" sections of
four courses to be "the same" in every way except that one section would
be completely online (meeting face to face only for training, the midterm,
and the final) and the other section would be completely face to face. They

were to have the same content and the same assignments. The assumption that this could be done without crippling the potentials of the medium or raising ethical issues turned out to be incorrect. In fact, in all of target courses, adjustments had to be made.

Even before the semester started, the instructors pointed out that to require the same assignments in the matched sections would severely limit their ability to make use of the unique characteristics of the medium. The VC supports collaborative assignments and in-depth discussions, whereas the TC does not. So, though the offline reading assignments and the exams remained the same, the assignments given students were quite different for the two modes. This was true even for the Upsala statistics course, for instance, where the online section began with students filling out a questionnaire in the class conference and then using the data provided by the other class members to carry out a statistical analysis. The offline section did this assignment using a presupplied data set.

The instructor for the NJIT statistics course found that many of the students wanted to work together in parallel, taking the opportunity to ask questions of her or the other students face to face, while working online. She scheduled a once-a-week, 2-hour session when she was available in the NJIT micro lab. About a third to a half of the class seemed to show up each week (unfortunately, we did not keep records of which ones). Generally, there would be periods of one or two students working silently at each of the terminals in the lab; periods where subgroups would be in animated discussion around a terminal, pointing at the screen; and short periods when several or all of them were conferring with the instructor about a question raised by the online material. We had not anticipated this "group lab" adaptation of the medium, but the instructor felt that it worked well for her and her students.

In computer science, the instructor found that the students could read through and understand the written version of his lecture material in a much shorter time than was required to cover the same material by talking and listening and taking notes. Therefore, he supplemented the online section by adding some additional activities and material which was not included in his traditional section.

In Sociology, the online assignments were totally different than those for the matched face-to-face section. These online assignments involved role playing and discussions. However, the midterm exam was based mainly on the textbook. There were many more failures on the midterm in the online section. The instructor felt that perhaps this was not fair to the students, since they had been tested on material that was not similar to the assignments they had been doing. Therefore, two optional face-to-face exam review sessions were held, and those who attended were given the opportunity to retake the midterm. This incident underscores the impossibility of complete "matching." The two media are suited to very different types of learning and assignments, and it does not make sense to try to test the students using the same examination. Nevertheless, we stuck rigidly with the use of the same midterm and final in all courses for this study.

This relaxation of rigid "matching" of activities in online and traditional courses does confound the medium of delivery with the pedagogical approach of collaborative learning, for the initial study. In a subsequent study described in Chapter 13, we are able to disentangle the two. One of the instructors, Enrico Hsu, became so enamored of collaborative learning through role playing and simulation that he continued to incorporate this technique into all subsequent offering of his management course, whether offered in the VC or the TC, and with and without various other computer-based technologies.

Additional Methodological Hindsight

The personal interviews with students proved very valuable. They were extremely time consuming, in terms of reaching the students, conducting and recording the interviews, and then transcribing them. However, they provided a great deal of insight into the personal experiences that underlay the statistical results. It would have been useful to obtain even more of these personal interviews.

SUMMARY

A variety of data collection methods and research designs were used in this project, to serve different evaluation objectives. A small number of courses were offered in a quasi-experimental design, with the same teacher, text, and exams. This enables us to assess the "exchangeability" of traditional and virtual classrooms, in terms of outcomes such as the performance of students on exams. However, a much larger number of courses was included in order to explore a range of "unique uses" of the technology in different types of courses. The data from these courses will provide a rich basis for understanding the contingencies which influence acceptance and impacts of the technology.

CHAPTER 10

WHAT HAPPENED IN THE VIRTUAL CLASSROOMS?

> The whole object of education is, or should be, to develop the mind. The mind should be a thing that works. It should be able to pass judgment on events as they arise, make decisions.
>
> —Sherwood Anderson

In this chapter, we will review the level of activity which occurred in the Virtual Classrooms during the quasi-experimental study and the students' ratings of, and comments about, their experiences. We will examine how the VC mode of delivery seems to have affected educational process and outcomes, both on "average" and as it varied among courses.

REASONS FOR TAKING A VIRTUAL CLASSROOM COURSE

Table 10-1 displays the results of questions about the importance of reasons for enrolling in a course. For all students in all modes, among the most important motivations given for enrolling in a course are that the course is required for graduation (56% reported this reason as "very important"), or required for a major (47%). Job-related interests or general interest in the topic also characterize a substantial number of enrollees (32%). In deciding whether to sign up for a traditional vs. a virtual classroom section, two additional motivations may come into play: curiosity about (or attraction to) the medium, and convenience.

It should be noted that the reasons given for taking a course are not necessarily reasons for enrolling in a VC section. As reviewed in a prior chapter, many of the students who enrolled because the course was required ended up in a VC section inadvertently, without understanding the mode of delivery.

There were significant differences among courses in the extent to which mode-related motivations characterized the students' reasons for taking a particular course and a particular section of a course. For the two "distance education" courses included in the study, greater convenience and curiosity about or attraction to the medium was a very strong factor (see Table 10–1; distributions for partially online courses with no matching section were omitted, since these students had no choice of section or mode). These factors also played an important role for the totally online courses at NJIT. At Upsala, they were important for many or most of the students who enrolled in Sociology online, but not for the students in the statistics course.

Given the problems with fall publicity recounted earlier, the proportions reporting "more convenient" as a "very important" reason for choosing a section for the two online courses offered at NJIT in the spring, and for the online distance education courses, are most informative. These are 71%, 67%, 64%, and 58%.

INTERACTION IN THE VIRTUAL CLASSROOM

One way to begin to understand what happened in the Virtual Classroom is to look at sample transcripts of parts of courses. Several excerpts have been included as exhibits in previous chapters. In this chapter, Exhibit 10–1 includes a fuller excerpt from a typical week-long "module" in the Introductory Sociology course. Typically, the instructor presents an electure on some key concepts or skills to be mastered by students, and then presents the students with the assignment or questions and activities they are to do online to help them achieve that mastery. The Introductory Sociology excerpt illustrates many of the problems as well as many of the potentials of using the VC mode of course delivery.

There is a great deal of variation in perceptions of characteristics of the Virtual Classroom, both among courses and among students in the same course. However, some "central tendencies" include the following:

- Greater candor among those who participate; and
- A tendency towards procrastination.

Both of these tendencies are illustrated in Exhibit 10–1. The instructor reports that the students seemed to feel more at ease about revealing

TABLE 10–1
Reasons for Taking Courses
% Choosing "Very Important"

	Job	General Interest	Required Major	Required Grad	Instructor Reputation	No Choice	Curious	More Convenient
CIS213-Sp	54	54	31	25	8	0	54	71
CIS213-F	56	29	59	53	19	0		
CIS213-FTF	43	62	19	19	14	0	33	52
Math305-S	17	42	67	67	46	20	50	67
Math305-FT	14	4	73	77	24	10		
Math305-FTF	33	50	62	70	29	8	56	42
OSS-Fall	32	14	57	64	4	0	19	12
OSS-FTF	50	42	83	74	4	10		
OSS-Spr	40	23	67	73	14	10	27	14
SOC-Fall	19	31	38	47	20	7	63	44
SOC-FTF	21	21	26	42	11	0		
STATS	27	27	36	46	27	0	27	36
STATS-F	13	27	27	53	40	0		
STATS-FTF	0	8	27	58	33	9	33	9
CONNECT								
ED	71	71	8	8	31	0	64	64
OISE	42	25	8	25	0	0	75	58

personal experiences in relating examples to apply and illustrate sociological concepts. Certainly, many of the responses in the exhibit relate to very personal aspects of the students' lives. About half the students chose to use their pen names. The half who signed their assignments with their names do not seem any less candid than the half who used the privacy protection provided by a pen name.

Some of the entries are so poorly written that it is difficult to understand them. This should not be attributed to typing errors; many of the basic skills essays hand written by freshmen show the same types of pervasive grammatical errors. As we will see later in this chapter, these students had fairly low levels of skill for college-level work, as measured by SAT scores and grade point averages for other courses.

EXHIBIT 10–1
EXCERPTS FROM INTRODUCTION TO SOCIOLOGY

Note: Only minimal editing of student comments has been done, in order to preserve the tendency towards mistakes in grammar and spelling that pervade many of the entries. A name in quotes means that the student chose to enter a response with a pen name. Other names have been removed. The instructor's comments have been greatly shortened, in order to give just the essence of the material to which the students were responding.

:C2039 CC148 Robert Meinke (Bob M,1571) 10/ 9/86 10:08 AM L:145
KEYS:/ROLE STRAIN/ASSIGNMENT #9/ (YOU MAY WANT TO MAKE A PRINTOUT OF THIS LONG MINI-LECTURE AND ASSIGNMENT)
 Your text briefly discusses the topic of ROLE STRAIN. I would like to amplify that discussion because role strain is one of the most prevalent sources of discomfort in people's lives, probably also in yours.
 ROLE STRAIN: The difficulty experienced by an individual in meeting the expectations of his or her roles.
 Role strain has two major causes:
 ROLE CONFLICT: Conflict due to incompatible demands of one's roles.
 ROLE AMBIGUITY: Discomfort because what is expected of one in certain roles is not known or not clearly understood.
 (over 100 lines of "mini lecture" deleted here)

ROLE STRAIN: ASSIGNMENT #9
 ENTER AS A CONFERENCE COMMENT. DUE: TUESDAY MID-NIGHT, 10/14.
 USE YOUR PEN NAME. USE KEY: ROLE STRAIN/ASSIGNMENT #9
 1) Describe in detail an experience of real role strain that you have experienced sometime in your life.
 2) In sociological terms, what was its cause? Was it due to:
 a) role conflict
  -a role incompatible with your personality
  -conflict between the role demands of two different status's
  -conflict between two roles in one role set
  -conflict between the demands within one single role
  -conflict with a role partner over the meaning of that role
 b) role ambiguity
  -because the role was a new undefined role
  -because the expectancies of the role were rapidly changing
  -because you were entering a new life status which you didn't feel prepared for
 3) How did you try to resolve the strain?
 a) compartmentalization
 b) hierarchy of obligations

c) banded together with others to change the social definition of the role
d) re negotiated the role definition
e) left the status
f) chose an emotional outlet to escape

:C2039 CC173 "MONIQUE" 10/13/86 11:31 AM L:18
Keys:/role strain/assignment #9/
An example of role strain that I am experiencing now is between school and work. I work for a major corporation while going to school full-time. However, my employer would like me to put in more hours than I do now. The strain that I feel is that I know I need a four-year degree to advance in the company, yet they expect me to work more while in college. Without the degree, I will never get anywhere in the company.
2) The cause of the role strain is role conflict- conflict within the demands of one single role.
3) I tried to establish an hierarchy of obligations to resolve the conflict. I will not go to college less than full-time, so all of my spare time is devoted to working. This way I can gain work experience, and, hopefully, be hired at a high level after I get my four-year degree. :C2039 cc177 "money" 10/14/86 11:47 am 1:12 keys:/role strain/ assignment 9/
One experience of role strain was as an employee of Upsala college. The problem was role ambiguity, I came into a job whose duties were not clearly defined. It was also at the time of a change in supervisor. I was hired by an acting director, but when I reported to work, I found a new director. The job description was non-existent and the new director never took the time to develop one. I tried to resolve the conflict by establishing a hierarchy of obligations, and also by renegotiating with my supervisor what the role should be. I finally left the position for a more stable one.

:C2039 cc179 (name, nickname, id) 10/14/86 1:48 pm 1:24 keys:/role strain/ assignment #9/
One of the most difficult role strain that I have experienced is what is expected of a young women. This happen to me a couple of years a go. I real ly enjoy rackets ball and my mother and boyfriend knew this. They did not seem to mind me playing, but once they found out that I had join a club which had racket ball tournaments the idea of me playing was wrong, and I was considered out of place. My mother said that it look bad for a lady playing ball with men, or competing with men in a sport. My boyfriend gave me little talks about how unlady like it is playing against men then he told me that perspiration does not help women but hinder them. A this was a conflict of role, the type of role conflict is role ambiguity, he and my mother did not want to accept that role expectancies are rapidly changing. 2 2)In sociological cause was b) role ambiguity because the expect encies of the were rapidly) I tried to resolve the strain by re negotiating the role definition of what is expected of a young lady.

169

EXHIBIT 10-1 (continued)

:C2039 cc181 (name,nickname, id) 10/14/86 8:04 pm l:16
keys:/role strain/

A daughter to a mother is an example of role strain. Daughter which is me as a teenager growing into an adult. I have an different opinion on things that my mother cannot relate too. I guess there is an rebellion stage within the teenage years. My mother states her opinion and expects me to agree as a good daughter should do. This causes a great conflict.

Her role of a daughter is one who listens and obeys to whatever she may say. 2.) The cause was due to role conflict. A role incompatible with my personality conflict between the demands within one single role and conflict with a role part over the meaning of that role. 3.) I tried to resolve this strain through re negotiation. I would listen to her opinions and take them into consideration but also have her to listen to my opinions as well. With both maybe we could come to some reasonable result.

:C2039 cc183 (name,nickname,id) 10/14/86 8:26 pm l:8
keys:/role strain/ass.#9/

1. I experienced role strain when my mom remarried and my stepfather -father was introduced into my home. I had to assume a new role as a step-daughter which included asking him for permission to go out or to use the car. Asking for money when I or my mom didn't have any, etc. 2. In sociological terms my role strain was caused by role ambiguity. 3. I resolved this role strain by renegotiating my role as a step-daughter with my step-father. He is my mother's husband and I will give him respect from time to time but then I will look upon him as a father in certain situations.

:C2039 cc184 (name, nickname,id) 10/14/86 8:28 pm l:19
keys:/role strain/assignment#9/

I experienced role strain when I entered Bucknell University as a freshman. I had no previous problems in assuming the role as a student in high school (roles included being sociable and studious, which lead to academic achievement), but I experience difficulty at bucknell because I could not assimilate the college life. As a result, I was unable to be sociable, studious, and achieve academic success. My grades, of course suffered drastically, and I began to feel socially confined. Support was not given to me by other students and bucknell faculty. As a student I was entitled to this support.

Role ambiguity caused my role strain, for I wan not properly prepared for life as a college student. I had no former experiences to rely on preparation for this newly acquired or achieved status.

I resolved my role strain by leaving this status. I dropped out of college after the first semester of my sophomore year vowing never to return to school, especially bucknell university. Obviously, I did not keep this vow. I now feel that the two years I had taken off from my formal education has enabled me to make a more mature approach to being a college student.

The excerpts also show the tendency of students to put off assignments and other forms of online participation. The first assignment was due by midnight on a Tuesday night. Several of the entries were made after dinner on that evening. Since the students did not have computers at home or in their dormitories, this meant that they had to make a special trip to a computer terminal in the evening.

The close times of several of the items suggest that the students were in fact in the laboratory together. It was a common practice for two or three students in an online course to develop a "buddy system" and sit next to each other and talk over things that were coming across the screen, and help one another with the mechanics of using the system or the contents of the material. Though this was supposedly not allowed during quizzes, it undoubtedly occurred then, too.

VARIATIONS AMONG COURSES

Course is not a unidimensional variable. It includes differences in type and level of subject matter, differences in type of use of the system (totally online vs. partially online courses), cognitive level of the students (mostly freshmen vs. upper classmen or graduate students), and differences in teaching style and procedures. It is also confounded with differences in access to the system, since some courses were offered through Upsala, where equipment access was relatively poor. It is not possible to separate out which aspect of *course* may account for significant differences in outcomes among courses. But this much is clear: on almost every measure of process and outcome, there are substantial and statistically significant differences among courses.

Variations in Student Ability, by Course

In addition to differences among courses in the initial motivations of students, there were also differences in ability levels. We collected data on overall grade point average and on SAT scores for those students included in the quasi-experimental research design. These data are shown in Table 10-2. Note that the Introductory Sociology students in the online section were fairly weak students. Their average GPA was only 2.0 (the minimum average required for graduation), and both their verbal and math SAT scores were fairly low. In addition, there was a difference among the Upsala statistics sections. Those students in the fall VC section were relatively good students with better grade point averages. The Spring VC section students in the Upsala Statistics course, by contrast, were not particularly strong, and in fact had a Math SAT average just under 400.

TABLE 10–2
DIFFERENCES IN STUDENT ABILITY, AMONG COURSES

OVERALL GRADE POINT AVERAGES OF STUDENTS, BY COURSE
QUASIEXPERIMENTAL DESIGN

COURSE	FALL ONLINE	FACE-TO-FACE	SPRING ONLINE
CIS 213	2.9	3.1	2.7
MATH 305	2.6	2.8	2.5
MANAGEMENT	3.1	2.5	2.8
INTRO SOC	2.0	2.5	–
STATISTICS (CC140)	2.7	2.2	2.3

MEAN SAT VERBAL SCORES, BY COURSE

COURSE	FALL ONLINE	FTF	SPRING ONLINE
CIS 213	333	400	444
MATH 305	375	455	364
MANAGEMENT	454	430	435
INTRO SOC	365	361	
STATISTICS	427 A	332 A	371

SECTIONS WITH THE SAME LETTER SIGNIFICANTLY DIFFERENT, $P < .05$, DUNCAN MULTIPLE RANGE TEST

MEAN SAT MATH SCORES, BY COURSE
QUASIEXPERIMENTAL DESIGN

COURSE	FALL ONLINE	FTF	SPRING ONLINE
CIS 213	640	580	571
MATH 305	590	480	458
MANAGEMENT	580	542	573
INTRO SOC	409	374	–
STATISTICS	492 A	346 A	399

SECTIONS WITH THE SAME LETTER SIGNIFICANTLY DIFFERENT

ACCESS PROBLEMS AND ACTIVITY LEVELS

The less than ideal access conditions described in Chapter 8 were reflected in postcourse ratings of access problems. On a 1-to-5 scale, where 1 is "serious problem," and 5 is "not a problem," those who responded with a 1 or 2 rating can be considered to have experienced difficulties. Overall, 22% said that access to a terminal or micro was a problem, 19% had problems with busy ports to EIES, and 33% complained of slow system response. As would be expected, these problems were much more prevalent at Upsala.

Differences in access problems, as well as in the mode of employment of the system, are reflected in Table 10–3, which shows computer-monitored statistics usage activity of students in the different courses. The results of the analysis of variance are shown in the bottom lines of the table, which indicates the probability that there were really "no differences" among the courses. Activity levels varied tremendously among courses, with the highest activity levels occurring for the fall computer science course, and some very low levels of use for several of the Upsala courses where the system was used as an adjunct to face-to-face instruction. Consistently, both frequency of participation and total time spent online are much lower for the Upsala courses.

Two points should be kept in mind in examining these data. One is that the Connected Education students were specifically coached on how to upload and download from their micros, in order to decrease connect time, and that many of the NJIT students also used this technique. Secondly, the Upsala statistics course was only a "half-course" lasting 7 weeks, including the orientation meeting and the final exam. Even adjusting the data for the statistics course for the length of time, the average participation was very low, especially for the Spring online course. On the other hand, it is apparent that in some of the courses, such as the two online sections of computer science, the Spring Math 305 course at NJIT, and the Spring Management Lab at NJIT, the average student was checking in almost daily, and sent many private messages in addition to participating in the class conference.

Table 10–4 shows that the amount of participation in class conferences differed among the courses from a low of less than 50 comments in the main class conference for the mixed mode courses at Upsala to almost 1000 comments in the Spring management lab conference. The pattern of balance between instructor contributions and student contributions also differs markedly. The most technical of the courses – Computer Science and the two Math/Statistics courses – tended to be teacher dominated in terms of the proportion of contributions, whereas the courses in "softer" subjects tended to have the majority of comments contributed by students. Overall, in 12 of the 15 sections, the number of comments by students exceeded those by the instructor. Though we have no comparable counts of student and instructor comments in the TC, we know that they tend to be teacher dominated. Thus, the participation data support the premise that the VC will encourage active participation of students.

STUDENT PERCEPTIONS OF THE VIRTUAL CLASSROOM

The following pages summarize students' reactions to their VC experience across all courses that were offered totally or partially online. It must be

TABLE 10-3
DIFFERENCES IN MEAN (PER STUDENT) ACTIVITY LEVELS,
BY COURSE

COURSE	TOTAL HOURS	TOTAL TIMES ONLINE	TOTAL MESSAGES SENT
CIS FALL	74.8	143.0	43.0
CIS SPRING	30.2	97.2	21.1
MATH 305 FALL	25.2	58.3	20.9
MATH 305 SPRING	44.9	80.3	14.7
MANAGEMENT FALL	17.7	39.4	9.1
MANAGEMENT SPRING	43.2	90.1	22.7
SOCIOLOGY FALL	18.2	37.0	23.2
STATISTICS FALL	7.9	25.2	8.2
STATISTICS SPRING	5.5	16.3	4.5
CONNECTED ED	13.0	41.7	8.1
ORG. COMMUNICATION	14.0	30.7	9.0
WRITING SEMINAR	8.3	14.4	2.5
ANTHROPOLOGY	4.3	7.1	1.2
FRENCH	8.0	20.7	4.2
F	2.3	3.9	2.5
P	.01	.001	.01

kept in mind, however, that "average" responses and reactions are obtained by combining results for courses which varied a great deal.

Included in Appendix I are the complete distributions for responses to the postuse questionnaire on the items that asked all students who used the Virtual Classroom to compare their experiences to previous experiences in courses delivered entirely "face-to-face." These questions were 1 to 7 Lickert-type scales, with responses ranging from "strongly agree" to "strongly disagree." In the discussion below, the responses from 1 to 3 were summed as indicating agreement, and those from 5 through 7 as indicating disagreement. Rather than constantly repeating the full text of the questions, each one has been given a short label, which appears in Exhibit 9-2, along with the more detailed distributions. In addition, the analysis will draw on excerpts from interviews with selected students, which are included in Appendix II.

Convenience. The majority (65%) felt that taking online courses was more convenient. Even those students who generally prefer traditional courses tended to comment on the advantages of being able to work on the course at times of their own choosing. For instance, a student from the fall statistics course at Upsala commented,

TABLE 10–4
PARTICIPATION PATTERNS IN CLASS CONFERENCES

COURSE	N	STUDENT COMMENTS	INSTRUCTOR COMMENTS	% COMMENTS INSTRUCTOR	% LINES INSTRUCTOR
CIS FALL	17	148	242	62%	71%
CIS SPRING	21	93	173	65%	73%
MATH 305 FALL	13	55	119	68%	65%
MATH 305 SPRING	27	366	111	23%	49%
MANAGEMENT FALL	28	367	56	13%	11%
MANAGEMENT SPRING	32	826	173	17%	17%
SOCIOLOGY	17	265	115	30%	64%
STATISTICS FALL	14	70	55	44%	81%
STATISTICS SPRING	12	45	33	42%	81%
CONNECT-ED-1	13	330	62	14%	12%
CONNECT-ED-2	13	310	102	25%	28%
ANTHROPOLOGY	12	40	19	32%	18%
WRITING SEMINAR	18	33	6	15%	21%
ORG COMMUNICATION	12	58	35	38%	32%
FRENCH	8	50	11	18%	23%

N – Total number of students enrolled
STUDENT COMMENTS – Total number of comments entered by students
INSTRUCTOR COMMENTS – Number of comments entered by the instructor
% COMMENTS INSTRUCTOR – Percentage of comments entered by instructor
% LINES INSTRUCTOR – Percentage of lines entered by instructor

I liked that I was independent and that I could go whenever I wanted to. And I like how the conferences were written down and I could get my notes. It also helps if you miss a day or two, because the computer always has your assignments there for you.

Those with computers and modems at home were, of course, most likely to appreciate the convenience. For example, a management lab student said,

It's also good because there is easy access whenever you want. I have a modem at home. I can go on at 3 o'clock in the morning. That's usually when I do most of my work.

Themes related to the greater convenience and comfort of attending class online also appear in the comments offered by students about what they "liked best" about the Virtual Classroom. "Being able to do the assignments at my own pace and not being obligated to sit in a very confined classroom," "the freedom," "being able to put the information into the computer whenever it is convenient," "flexible class hours," and "not having to go to class" are some of the attributes mentioned.

On a related item, the majority of students (58%) felt that they had better access to their professor in the Virtual Classroom. This interaction was also more "friendly" and egalitarian than would be typical of the traditional classroom. For example, a Math 305 student said:

She'll put a message in and say, "Have a great week . . . " Especially, if you have a message or a problem, she'll write back and say, "Hi there, how have you been? You have a problem with this . . . " It's really almost like talking on the phone. I try to send messages back the same way, real casual. It's not a strict teacher-student kind of thing. Because of her, you feel a lot closer, because it's so easy just to pop a question. She'll answer the next day, or whenever you come online. (Excerpt from "Interview 1" in Appendix II)

The result of the questions on convenience and access to professors support the hypotheses that compared the traditional classroom:

H.2.1. The Virtual Classroom offers more convenient access to educational experiences.

H.2.2. VC students will perceive improved access to their professors.

Participation/Motivation. The majority (63%) disagree that they "didn't have to work as hard for online classes." The fact that most felt that they worked much harder also comes out in the interviews with students and the course reports from instructors. However, it should be noted that the instructors did not unanimously agree with the student perceptions that they were working harder for online courses.

It is definitely true that the most enthusiastic students spent a great deal of time in their online courses. For example, a very positive student who participated in the Management lab reports:

I sign on every day. I usually spend about an hour; it depends how much other work I have. Sometimes as little as half an hour; sometimes two or three hours. Sometimes I sign on several times a day. I spend a lot of time online. I love it . . . I don't mind putting in the hours, the time just flies by.

Irregular Participation. Almost half (49%) admitted that when they became "busy" with other things, they were more likely to stop participating in an online course than to "cut" a traditional class. This is the flip side of self-pacing. Many students just did not have the self-discipline to stick to a regular, frequent schedule of signing online and working. For instance, see the second student interview in Appendix II. This student remarked, "I don't feel that I have the self discipline for it. I don't have enough time in my day as it is. To sit down and make myself do something like that. . . ."

The students who did not participate regularly recognized that they were not able to get much out of the course by letting everything go until the last minute. For instance, a student who got a "D" in Computer science got into the habit of staying late at work only one night a week to use the computer from there. He explains his apparent inability to make time for regular and leisurely participation in the course as follows:

> My downfall was in trying to minimize reading of the comments during the time I had to devote to it. I didn't read them on the screen, I printed them out and took them home. Then things would happen. I work long hours, I live alone and have to cook dinner.. I did look at a few of them . . . but I tried to do everything as fast as I could in order to maximize what I could finish during that one night. I tried to bring the paperwork home, but you bring home a book and often it does not happen . . . I read maybe 60% of it.

As a result, instructors began devising strategies to force frequent signon, such as weekly quizzes due on a different day than the assignment, or raising the proportion of the grades allocated to online participation. (See, for instance, the course narratives in the Appendix III by the instructors for Introductory sociology, Computer science, Statistics, and the Management lab.)

Increased Interest, Involvement, and Motivation. For those who did participate, the level of interest and involvement tended to be high: 55% agreed that the fact that their comments would be read by other students increased their motivation, 62% disagreed that the Virtual Classroom was "more boring" than traditional classes, and 56% agreed that they felt more involved in taking an active part in the course. The word *fun* was frequently used by those students who reported high levels of interest and involvement.

Thus, though there were some problems with irregular participation

(for which instructors devised strategies to counter the tendency to
procrastination), on the average, students reported that they worked
harder in VC classes that in TC classes, that they were motivated by the
fact that their comments would be read by other students, and that they
were more involved in the course. Thus, the results of the initial field trials
in terms of students perceptions support the following hypotheses:

H.2.3. VC students will report increased motivation and participation in
courses.
H.2.5. VC students will report increased interest and involvement.

Less Inhibition. The questionnaire item was worded negatively, in
terms of feeling "more inhibited": 44% disagreed, 29% perceived no difference between modes, and a quarter did feel inhibited. This was obviously
an aspect of online participation which varied a great deal among students,
and perhaps among courses, as a result of levels of writing skill, self-
confidence, and the atmosphere established by the instructor.

Sociology instructor Robert Meinke reports, in his course narrative,
that

> Online courses do encourage students to write better responses to their
> assignments. The fact that other students will read what they have written
> often stimulates more effort. I also found that students seem to feel more at
> ease about revealing personal experiences. The options that EIES provides
> of sending anonymous or pen name responses encourages the more shy
> person to express him or herself more openly.

A Math 305 student (Appendix II), said that he felt "more free" to say
things online:

> I may seem gregarious, but I'm pretty shy. It's easier from here. Because it
> seems like one-on-one.

Related to the general perception that the written word allows people to
be somewhat more "free" in expressing themselves, is the feeling expressed by several students that the medium makes grading more "fair." A
CIS student remarked:

> All he knows is what you type. He can't be prejudiced against you based on
> the way you look . . . It's more fair this way. You're being judged really on
> your work, not on your personality.

On the other hand, some students felt more inhibited, especially about asking questions that might expose them as "ignorant." While students might join in a discussion or a simulation, they were more reluctant to ask questions about the reading or a lecture. Some of this reluctance may be due to a false assumption that they might be penalized for a "stupid" question. The Upsala statistics student explained:

> Sometimes you don't feel comfortable asking the teacher questions through the computer. In class, you can raise your hand, or you can ask questions after class. It is not as comfortable to ask a question online, so you don't ask. . . . Maybe he will take off credits or something. Sometimes it is too late to put a question in – the assignment is already due. It's more personal when you see the teacher.

Especially in the more technical courses, such as statistics and Computer science, the instructors also experienced a difficulty in eliciting and responding to student questions and assignments online. For instance, Lincoln Brown explained the relative lack of instructor responses to student comments in his class conference as follows:

> Where students had problems, I sent them messages.

> While I plead guilty to not providing positive feedback, note that there's not much which can be said about many of their comments. For example, when simply asked to look at a graph and comment on which bar is higher, they all made some appropriate but innocuous comment.

> And look at the timing problem I mentioned in the report. I gave an assignment on March 27th; the first solution was entered on April 6th; most came in on April 15th (future taxpayers practicing with this deadline!) I had been collecting responses on paper as they came in, but didn't grade them or comment until after the due date (a mistake on my part.) In a few cases I believe I responded to each with a grade and a one-line comment via one of BJ's +quiz - related programs.

> I believe the whole idea of "comments" is fundamentally different in a math course and, say, a sociology course. Maybe Rose found it not to be so – I wish I had time to follow her conference while mine was going on – but probably most of the time there will be this difference.

Group Communication and Collaboration. Opinion is more mixed about whether the Virtual Classroom led to more communication with other students in the class: 47% agreed, but 19% perceived no difference between delivery modes on this criterion, and 32% disagreed. On related items, 55% agreed that the fact that their work would be read by other students increased their motivation, 59% found the comments made by other students to be useful, and 62% found reading the reviews or assignments of other students to be useful.

Those who were most enthusiastic about the medium tended to value the contributions and comments of other students highly, and to enjoy reading them. Among the phrases that are used in describing what students "like best" about the Virtual Classroom (in response to the open-ended question on the postcourse questionnaire), students mentioned "class participation," "being in touch with other students constantly," "working as a group and extended communications online," and "the openness—I liked to hear other students' ideas." A Math 305 student reported that the comments of other students were

> . . . entertaining. Some of those people have some witty comments. That makes the class more interesting. If you find that there are a lot of comments, then you get online just to see them.

By contrast, a negative student in the Upsala statistics course refused to read anything written by students, and referred to student contributions as "junk." A classmate in the same course reported, however,

> Most of the students who made comments were the ones who really understood the class and they were about the lectures. And they were pretty helpful, especially when the homework could be checked.

An Organizational Communication student commented as follows about the value of reading the comments of other students:

> I felt that they were really helpful. It gave me another perspective on what I was doing. If I did not see a point and they did, I was able to incorporate it into my thinking . . . It was really a good way of learning different ideas.

In sum, though there was a considerable minority who did not perceive these effects, on the average, student perceptions support the following hypothesis:

H.2.8. VC students will perceive improved ability to communicate with and cooperate with other students (group collaboration).

Overall Quality and Efficiency. Overall subjective assessment by students of the Virtual Classroom, as determined the question on whether it increased the quality and efficiency of education, also tended to be favorable. The complete results for these items were included in Table 9–2; 56% of the students agreed that the VC improved the quality of their education, while 21% disagreed. There were more mixed feelings about whether it increased efficiency. The modal response on this item was that the students are "unsure"; 44% agreed that the amount of work they could accomplish in a given time was greater online, and 31% disagreed. This is congruent with the report that they worked harder online than for traditional courses.

Results for the item on overall quality thus support:

H.2.9. The VC will be perceived by students as improving overall quality of education, as compared to the traditional classroom.

Interitem Correlations. We have reviewed responses to 11 questions asking students for comparisons between the traditional and Virtual Classroom environments. Only 1 of the 55 interitem correlation coefficients was particularly high: finding the comments of other students useful and reading the assignments of other students correlated at .70. The other dimensions were clearly distinct in the students' minds, in the sense that response patterns were different. For example, the next highest coefficient was .57, between increased convenience and whether the VC was more boring. Thirteen of the coefficients were under .10. This suggests that the students did tend to read each of the statements carefully and responded to each one individually, rather than adopting an automatic "response set."

EVIDENCE ON DROPOUTS

One of the most important behavioral indicators of dislike of the Virtual Classroom approach is the rate at which students drop courses offered via this mode, as compared to the dropout rate for similar courses offered offline. There definitely was a greater tendency towards dropout in VC sections. This seems to be related to the tendency of students with poor study habits and a lack of self-discipline to procrastinate, then realize that they are hopelessly far behind, and drop the course. (There may be a disproportionate tendency for students with many family and job obligations to elect a course via this medium in the first place, but this is only speculation.)

Unfortunately, students who were not very reliable about completing their online work regularly and who dropped out of courses offered via this mode were also very elusive when we tried to get data from them. All dropouts were sent two copies of the special questionnaire prepared for them, with the second letter pleading the importance of having their responses. Only nine returned it; none from Upsala. All dropouts who did not return a questionnaire were called for an interview. Only one could be contacted by phone; the others were never at home. Thus, the evidence we have is incomplete.

Table 10-5 shows the results for the nine dropouts who did respond to the questionnaire. Some of the reasons, such as "family problems" and "had a similar course already" are not related to mode of delivery. Of the nine, three would not choose to take another course via this mode. Two of the nine agreed that they "did not like the Virtual Classroom approach." On the whole, then, the reasons given by dropouts who responded tended not to be strongly critical of the medium, but instead reflected the types of reasons given for a decision to drop any course. Thus, they support the overall premise of the study that the Virtual Classroom is a viable mode of course delivery.

SUMMARY

Average subjective ratings of the Virtual Classroom by students are shown in Table 10-6, rank ordered from those items on which students were most enthusiastic or positive to those on which they were least positive. Among the attributes of the Virtual Classroom experience rated highly are increased access to the professor, increased interest and involvement, and being able to see other students' assignments. On the downside, students were more likely to procrastinate and stop actively participating online when they became "busy with other things." They also felt that they worked harder in the VC; though the students might not perceive this as an advantage, the faculty do.

There was a great deal of variation around these averages. In some courses, students were much more active and involved than in others. About 20%-25% of the students disagreed that the VC is superior to the TC on the dimensions measured.

The data presented in this chapter support several of the premises and hypotheses that framed the study. The subjective ratings by students tend to be favorable. None of the "dropouts" who responded to questionnaire named their dislike of the Virtual Classroom approach as their main reason for doing so. Specific hypotheses supported by data presented in this chapter include:

H.2.1. The VC will improve convenience of access to education (pre-course questionnaire frequency of choosing "convenience" as a "very important" reason for choosing the section; postquestionnaire).

H.2.2. VC students will report improved access to their professors (postquestionnaire, interviews).

TABLE 10-5
Reasons Given for Dropping Virtual Classroom Courses
(N = 9 Students responding)

Question: How important were each of the following factors in your decision to drop the course?

Reason	Very Important	Somewhat Important	Not Important
Health problems or personal problems	22%		78%
The course was too hard for me	11%		89%
The course was too much work		11%	89%
I did not like the instructor	22%	22%	56%
The subject matter was boring or irrelevant	22%	78%	
I had too many other courses and needed to drop one (or more)	22%	78%	
I was doing poorly	11%	11%	78%
I did not like the "Virtual Classroom" approach	22%	11%	67%
I had too many outside demands (other classes, full-time work)	33%	67%	

MOST IMPORTANT REASON
    (1) 38% CONFLICTING DEMANDS
    (2) 12% SIMILAR CLASS
    (3) 12% FAMILY PROBLEMS
    (4) 25% TOO HARD
    (5) 12% DISLIKE INSTRUCTOR

If I had the opportunity, I would register for another class which used the "Virtual Classroom" approach:

11%	22%	22%	0%	44%
:1	:2	:3	:4:	5:
Strongly Agree	Agree	Don't Know	Disagree	Strongly Disagree

H.2.3. The VC will result in increased motivation and participation (questionnaires, participation data).

H.2.4. The VC will result in improved ability of the students to apply the material of the course and express their own independent ideas relative to

TABLE 10-6
SUMMARY OF STUDENT PERCEPTIONS OF THE
VIRTUAL CLASSROOM

Characteristics of VC	Better		Neutral	Worse
	2.0----------3.0----------4.0------------5.0			
More From Traditional(R)	2.4			
Choose Another (R)	3.0			
More Convenient	3.1			
(Not) More Boring (R)	3.2			
Others' Assignments Useful	3.2			
More Involved		3.3		
Comments Useful		3.3		
Better Access to Professor		3.4		
Increased Quality		3.4		
Increased Motivation		3.4		
(Not) More Inhibited (R)		3.5		
Better Learning		3.6		
Learned More		3.7		
Increased Efficiency		3.7		
Communicated More With Students		3.7		
Stop Participating (R)			4.2	
Less Work				4.8

Key: Ratings could vary from 1.0 to 7.0. In computing means for this display, scoring of negative items was reversed (R)

the material (Direct observation, example exhibit from Introductory Sociology).

H.2.5. The VC will result in increased levels of interest and involvement (questionnaire).

H.2.8. The VC will result in improved communication and cooperation with other students (questionnaire).

H.2.9. The VC will improve overall quality of education (questionnaire).

On almost every criterion, there was a difference between Upsala and NJIT, with NJIT students viewing their experiences more favorably. In the next chapter, we will examine the results in a more statistical manner, examining outcomes in terms of access and quality, relating them to the hypotheses, and exploring differences among courses and schools in more detail.

CHAPTER *11*

EFFECTS OF MODE OF COURSE DELIVERY: ACCESS AND QUALITY

Learning by study must be won;
'Twas never entailed from sire to son.

–John Gay (1685–1732)

The previous chapter showed that the subjective reactions of students to the Virtual Classroom tended to be favorable. This chapter will begin with an examination of whether or not there were differences in mastery of course material between the traditional and virtual classrooms, as measured by grades on examinations and course averages. It will then present a number of results related to the relative effects of mode of delivery, and institutional context (school) on both subjective and "objective" outcomes. The data used are primarily from the five courses included in the quasi-experimental design with matched sections using different modes of course delivery.

DIFFERENCES IN OBJECTIVELY GRADED PERFORMANCE

For those courses with matched online and traditional sections, one "objective" measure of the influence of mode of delivery on course outcomes was the grades obtained. As can be seen in Table 11-1, grades differed significantly by course, but there was only one significant difference in grades by mode, when course was controlled.

Many things need to be considered in understanding what produced

TABLE 11-1
DIFFERENCES IN GRADES BY MODE AND COURSE

MEAN MIDTERM EXAM GRADE

COURSE	ONLINE	FTF	BOTH
CIS 213	90.7	80.1	85.4
INTRO SOCIOLOGY	75.2	75.9	75.5
STATISTICS	68.8	69.5	69.6
ALL	78.5	75.2	

Mode F = .91 p = .34
Course F = 6.43 p = .003
Mode by Course F = .98 p = .38
NO SIGNIFICANT DIFFERENCES WITHIN COURSES

MEAN GRADE ON FINAL EXAM

COURSE	ONLINE	FTF	BOTH
CIS 213	79.3	78.8	79.1
MATH 305	79.0	81.6	80.3
INTRO SOCIOLOGY	68.4	68.7	68.5
STATISTICS	53.6	56.4	55.0
ALL	70.1	71.4	

Mode F = .13 p = .72
Course F = 11.28 p = .001
Mode by Course F = .06 p = .98
NO SIGNIFICANT DIFFERENCES WITHIN COURSES

FINAL COURSE AVERAGE

COURSE	ONLINE	FTF	BOTH	p
CIS 213	3.11	1.93	2.52	.02
MATH 305	3.25	3.16	3.20	.85
SOCIOLOGY	1.62	1.47	1.54	.74
STATISTICS	2.23	2.35	2.29	.78
MANAGEMENT	2.68	2.85	2.76	.68
ALL	2.58	2.35		

Mode F = 1.23 p = .27
Course F = 7.58 p = .001
Mode by Course F = 1.3 p = .27

these results and whether or not they can be generalized. First of all, the number of subjects in each section was small, and thus differences would have to be large to be statistically significant. Secondly, despite the original plan to give exactly the same midterm, final, and assignments in matched sections, and to grade them the same way, the instructors found that they could not do this. For example, in the management course, the instructor reported that the assignments completed by students in the section with the online management lab were far superior. However, he felt that he should not penalize the students who did not have this facility, so he did not grade them on the same standard. In the required freshmen-level course in statistics at Upsala, all grades in all sections tended to be low. It became a matter of which failure rates were highest! Performance was equally poor, on the average, in both sections.

In the computer science course at NJIT, the instructor gave additional activities and assignments online, because he found that the students could complete the core material contained in the lectures much faster online. For this course, the difference on midterm exam scores was not significant (p = .12), but the online students did better. There was no difference in the final exam scores, but when the quality of assignments was factored in, the instructor judged the online students as having done significantly better work, on average. The online students averaged a solid "B" (3.11 on a 4-point scale where A = 4.00 B = 3.00, etc.), whereas the face-to-face students averaged a C- (1.93).

Thus, the overall conclusion is that online students learned the required material for a course as well as or better than students in face-to-face classes. In a course where computer usage is intrinsic, the performance may tend to be significantly better. At the freshman level, in survey courses in which many students have difficulties passing, even though there is no statistically significant difference in objective measures of performance, the instructors felt that totally online delivery was not beneficial. The better students did very well in these freshmen-level courses online, but the weaker students tended to drop out or do even more poorly, according the perceptions of the instructors in their course reports.

Effects on Writing Skills

One of the online courses was a freshman writing seminar at Upsala. A pretest of essay writing skill was administered to all freshmen before they took this course. During the Spring semester, after they completed the course, a similar essay examination was given to the students. Both were graded on a holistic basis, as follows. The faculty is first "normed" by having all graders evaluate some sample essays which are photocopied, and then discussing differences in the scores assigned. Two faculty members assign a score from 1 to 10 for the essay. These two scores are averaged if they are reasonably consistent. If the two scores are more than two points apart, a third faculty member scores the exam, and then the two most similar scores are used.

If the students in the section which did assignments online improved more than other students as a result, this ought to be reflected in a more positive change in their writing scores than would be characteristic of students in the totally offline sections. However, this was not the case. The measure showed no change in holistically scored essays for the entire set of courses. There were no significant differences between the experimental section and the traditional sections.

Instructors in the nonwriting courses were asked if they had noticed any changes in their students' writing over the course of the semester as they used the system. Most agree that there was definitely a tendency for students to write a lot more as the semester progressed. Paul Levinson, of Connected Education, offers the following observations:

> Connect Ed has had one dramatic case of a woman with dyslexia or similar problem. When she first signed up for our courses, she was concerned lest her disability prevent her from participating. Her first comments were intelligent, but short and not very flowing.
>
> Less than a year later she was uploading 300 line term papers that read beautifully.
>
> Other more common consequences of on-line writing seem to be a general increase in the flow and smoothness of the writing over a few month period of time.

Because of the insensitivity and unreliability of the holistic scoring methods used for the Upsala course, we are not ready to conclude that Virtual Classroom makes "no difference" in students' writing. A much more carefully controlled study would be necessary in order to determine what changes in student writing, if any, are more likely or less likely to emerge when writing assignments are shared with others online, as compared to other modes for teaching writing.

Case Study of an Online Writing Workshop

Subsequent to the initial experiment with a partially online writing course, Rosenthal (1991) undertook a study of a totally online writing tutorial offered through Connected Education, as part of her dissertation research. In this case study, the descriptive data and conclusions are qualitative in nature, since there were no "control" groups and no standardized before and after writing tests were administered. However, the results were judged to be a successful application of computer-mediated communication to achieve a collaborative process for the improvement of writing. All of the students were mature and highly motivated; all did submit drafts and engage in peer-critiquing of each other's drafts. Revisions to their drafts were based on the suggestions received. Excerpts from the abstract to the dissertation (Rosenthal, 1991) report:

The application of computer-mediated communications (CMC) technology to writing instruction is in the developmental stage and little is known about how students and instructors use the technology in the process of learning and teaching writing. A qualitative research design was undertaken to address this gap in knowledge. A qualitative design provided explorative, systematic, and descriptive procedures to examine the archival record or written transcript of all the discourse content and written drafts generated by six graduate students and an instructor in an 8 week writing workshop that was conducted entirely, asynchronously through the EIES computer-mediated conferencing system.

The findings indicated that there was a match among the participants, the task, and the technology. . . . Participants . . . had access to the technology in their homes; were competent using it; and had a positive attitude toward it as a means of educational delivery. The instructor, a professional writer and experienced in the electronic classroom . . . explicitly employed a number of strategies to implement a student-centered, collaborative composing approach. She exploited communications opportunities available through the CMC medium to support this approach. Students' activity in the workshop focused largely on feedback exchange on their drafts and related rhetorical and process problems. They exploited communications opportunities to negotiate meanings in their drafts which evolved through collaborative effort as collaborative products. Participants . . . adopted informal, congenial, and humorous discourse norms that contributed to a rich social environment and friendly, interpersonal exchanges.

The findings of this case study indicate that a supportive and effective interactive writing environment can be created within the CMC context. The details of the case study provide suggestions as to how the skills of the instructor, the maturity and motivation of the students, and the nature of the roles and processes established may lead to such a successful outcome in a collaborative online writing environment. The extent to which the processes and participant characteristics are necessary and sufficient to produce the observed outcomes need to be established through further replications of studies of groups writing together in a Virtual Classroom.

OUTCOME DIFFERENCES AMONG COURSES

We have seen (in Chapter 10) that student characteristics and activity levels varied among courses. In looking at the results, there were statistically significant differences among courses for almost every dependent variable, as determined by a oneway analysis of variance. A few of these differences will be presented and reviewed here.

Table 11–2 shows differences in courses on some of the indices of process and outcome. On the collaboration index, high scores correspond to higher levels of perception of collaborative or "group" learning. The highest levels of collaborative learning occurred in the management course; it was also high for Organizational Communication, Business French, the online writing seminar, and Math 305. The level of reported collaborative learning appears to differ much more among courses than among sections of the same course offered in different modes.

For the Instructor Rating and Course Rating indices, high scores correspond to the least favorable ratings. Once again, differences among courses appear to be much larger than differences among sections of the same course offered via different modes of delivery. The only course for which there is a significant difference among sections is the introductory sociology course, where the students rated the instructor and outcomes as better in the face-to-face mode. In the computer science course, by contrast, the instructor and course ratings are higher in the Virtual Classroom mode. There is also a tendency for some of the best ratings to occur for the repetition of an online course by an instructor.

Table 11–3 shows results by course for the items which deal with overall comparisons between modes of delivery, including the index "VC OVERALL" which combines four items. High values of this index are the most favorable. The best overall ratings are for the second offerings of the Computer Science and Math 305 courses, and the Ontario Institute course, which was offered by an instructor experienced in this mode of teaching. The ratings for the Upsala freshman-level totally online courses tend to be among the lowest. By contrast with the students in the three upper level NJIT courses, these students tended to feel that online courses are more boring, to disagree that they were more involved, and to agree that they would not choose another online course. However, these ratings are not characteristic of the upper level, partially online courses at Upsala.

It will be noted that differences among courses are associated with differences between the two colleges. Much of this has to do with the poorer access conditions present at Upsala. As with course as a variable, "school" was significantly related to differences for most outcome variables. Table 11–4 shows some of these results. The Upsala students perceived the system as less "friendly" and less "convenient." They were less likely to feel that they communicated more with other students or the professor, or that they learned more.

Thus, we have identified the source of most of the low ratings of the VC given by students on the postcourse questionnaire. They tended to come from Upsala, where the instructional context provided inadequate computer resources to assure convenient access. In particular, the lowest ratings were for the totally online freshman-level courses at Upsala.

TABLE 11-2
SUBJECTIVELY RATED OUTCOMES, BY COURSE
MEANS AND ANALYSIS OF VARIANCE

COURSE	INSTRUCTOR RATING INDEX	COURSE RATING INDEX	COLLABORATION INDEX
CIS FALL FTF	28.5	17.8	18.9
CIS FALL ONLINE	25.4	14.3	20.0
CIS SPRING ONLINE	20.5	14.8	18.9
MATH 305 FALL FTF	15.7	13.6	23.1
MATH 305 FALL ONLINE	14.8	12.5	22.1
MATH 305 SPRING ONLINE	19.2	14.5	21.7
MANAGEMENT SPRING FTF	21.4	15.0	25.3
MANAGEMENT FALL ONLINE	23.1	16.7	26.1
MANAGEMENT SPRING ONLINE	18.0	13.9	27.2
SOCIOLOGY FALL FTF	A 19.3	A 13.7	A 23.9
SOCIOLOGY FALL ONLINE	A 25.5	A 17.6	A 17.2
STATISTICS FALL FTF	26.9	19.0	22.9
STATISTICS FALL ONLINE	25.8	18.7	21.0
STATISTICS SPRING ONLINE	25.9	17.8	20.2
CONNECT-ED	25.0	17.0	19.1
ONTARIO INSTITUTE	19.0	13.6	22.6
ORG. COMMUNICATION	22.2	15.2	24.3
WRITING SEMINAR	18.4	13.7	23.4
ANTHROPOLOGY	18.6	14.1	20.9
BUSINESS FRENCH	20.8	13.3	24.6
F (differences among courses)	7.7	2.6	5.3
p	.001	.001	.001
degree of freedom = 20 and	246	248	241

A- The two sections are significantly different
   Duncan Multiple Range Test (p < .05)
KEY: Instructor Rating Index Range = 11 (best) to 55 (worst)
     Course Rating Index Range = 7 (best) to 35 (worst)
     Collaboration Index Range = 6 (least) to 34 (most)

Besides limited access to their totally online courses, other factors may have contributed to the negative subjective rating results for these courses. The students had the lowest SAT math scores, on the average, which is a very rough measure of academic skills. As freshmen, they may have lacked the level of self-discipline, writing skills, and general cognitive maturity necessary to fit in well with the Virtual Classroom as a delivery

TABLE 11-3
DIFFERENCES IN PERCEPTIONS OF THE VIRTUAL CLASSROOM, BY COURSE: MEANS AND ANOVA

COURSE	ONLINE MORE BORING	MORE INVOLVED	WOULD NOT CHOOSE	BETTER LEARNING	VC OVERALL
CIS FALL	4.8	2.8	5.1	3.4	19.4
CIS SPRING	5.7	3.1	5.7	2.7	20.5
MATH 305 FALL	4.6	3.6	4.3	3.6	17.0
MATH 305 SPRING	4.8	3.5	5.3	3.3	19.7
MANAGEMENT FALL	5.0	3.0	5.2	3.4	18.8
MANAGEMENT SPRING	6.2	2.0	6.1	2.0	23.0
SOCIOLOGY FALL	3.9	4.4	3.8	4.6	14.5
STATISTICS FALL	3.9	4.4	3.6	5.0	13.9
STATISTICS SPRING	3.9	5.0	3.6	5.0	14.3
CONNECT-ED	5.5	3.3	6.7	4.5	18.5
ONTARIO INSTITUTE	6.3	2.9	6.3	2.8	21.5
ORG. COM.	4.2	3.6	4.1	4.1	15.4
WRITING SEMINAR	4.1	3.0	4.1	4.1	16.6
ANTHROPOLOGY	3.9	4.0	3.3	4.9	13.6
FRENCH	3.5	3.2	4.5	4.2	16.5

F	3.0	2.7	3.7	3.7	3.4
p	.001	.001	.001	.001	.001
df = 14 and:	167	167	167	167	165

Key: 1 = Strongly agree, 7 = Strongly disagree
"VC" Overall index may range from 4(worst) to 28(best)

mode. Finally, their instructors were less enthusiastic about participating in the experiment than most, partially because they felt overloaded by other responsibilities and partially because they felt from the beginning that the VC might not be "right" for required freshman-level courses. This combination of factors, in any case, proved to result in many students who preferred the traditional classroom as a mode of course delivery.

PROCESS AND OUTCOME: RELATIONSHIPS AT THE COURSE LEVEL

A number of dimensions on which courses varied significantly have been displayed and discussed. One way to pull this information together is to

TABLE 11-4
SELECTED SIGNIFICANT DIFFERENCES IN VIRTUAL CLASSROOM
RATINGS, BY SCHOOL

QUESTION	UPSALA	NJIT	F	p
SLOW RESPONSE	3.4	3.7	7.32	.008
EASY TO LEARN	4.4	5.6	19.77	.001
EIES FRIENDLY	4.0	5.4	25.03	.001
EIES INCREASED QUALITY (R)	4.2	3.1	12.76	.001
CONVENIENT (R)	4.4	2.6	36.75	.001
COMMUNICATED MORE (R)	4.4	3.4	9.92	.002
ACCESS PROFESSOR (R)	4.0	3.0	9.91	.002
MORE BORING	4.1	5.3	14.66	.001
MORE INVOLVED (R)	4.1	3.0	16.87	.001
NOT CHOOSE ANOTHER	3.8	5.4	21.46	.001
BETTER LEARNING (R)	4.5	3.0	22.57	.001
LEARNED MORE (R)	4.4	3.2	16.34	.001

Note: Items are 1 to 7 scales. Those with an (R) indicate that score interpretation should be reversed, so that low scores are "better."

look at the extent to which rank ordering of courses on outcome measures is related to rank ordering on other variables. Some results of this analysis are shown in Table 11-5.

The first thing to notice is that all the Upsala courses are at the bottom on the "VC OVERALL" index. In other words, outcomes were better for every single NJIT course than for every single Upsala course.

A second noticeable tendency is that the "top three" courses in overall ratings were the second semester offerings of courses at NJIT; there is a con sistent improvement with experience by the instructor for these courses.

Looked at on the course level, with only 13 cases, student overall ratings of the Virtual Classroom are strongly related to amount of activity in their class conferences. The rank orders for average number of times each student signed online and for the total comments in the class conference are shown as examples. The courses with the best outcomes were those in which the students signed on frequently, and in which there was a lot of activity. (Which is cause, and which effect, is impossible to untangle with these data.)

On the other hand, we totally failed to be able to explain variations in course outcomes in terms of any codable aspect of instructor behavior. An example is shown in Table 11-5 for a simple measure, the total proportion of comments by students. (Table 10-4 showed the obverse, the proportion by the instructor.) We had thought that classes in which the professor

TABLE 11–5
RANK ORDERS OF COURSES: PROCESS VS. OUTCOME

	VC Overall Index	Mean Times Online	Total Conference Comments	% By Students
NJIT Management Spr (M)	1	3	1	3
NJIT CIS Spring	2	2	6	12
NJIT Math 305 Spring	3	4	2	5
NJIT CIS Fall	4	1	4	11
NJIT Management Fall (M)	5	6	3	1
NJIT Math 305 Fall	6	5	7	13
Upsala Writing (M)	7	12	13	2
Upsala French (M)	8	10	11	4
Upsala Org. Comm.(M)	9	8	9	8
Upsala Sociology	10	7	5	6
Upsala Statistics Spring	11	11	10	9
Upsala Statistics Fall	12	9	8	10
Upsala Anthropology (M)	13	13	12	7

Key: M denotes a mixed mode course
Spearman's Rho's:
VC overall with Times online: 0.82, p = 0.001
VC overall with Total comments: 0.70, p = 0.004
VC overall with % by students: 0.11, p = 0.36

stimulated the students to do most of the writing would have better results than those in which many of the entries were by the instructor. However, even on this basic measure of process, there is no significant relationship. Several of the more teacher-dominated sections of courses, in math and computer science, were among the highest ranking on overall student ratings of their VC learning experience.

EFFECTS OF MODE OF DELIVERY

The purpose of this section is to examine differences in the subjectively measured outcomes of courses, as they were affected by mode of delivery. We were concerned with three modes of delivery: completely online, mixed, and face to face. Since we have seen that outcomes appear to be strongly related to the course, to the school (including its computing environment), and perhaps to whether an online course was a first-time or a repeat experience for an instructor, it was necessary to use the quasi-experimental designs built into this study in order to examine the relationship between mode and outcome. Thus, though we will include some one-way analyses of variance which simply compare the overall means of outcome measures by mode of delivery, the primary method of analysis will be a two-way analysis of variance (using the SAS General Linear Models procedure), to identify interactions of mode with course, school, or semester (first vs. second offering).

Of the numerous variables used in this study, very few were significantly related to mode of delivery, when all courses delivered completely online, in mixed mode, or face to face were pooled into three groups. Table 11-6 gives the results of most interest. It includes the dependent variables based on subjective measures of primary interest (the indexes), plus individual items measured for all modes which produced statistically significant differences.

There were no significant differences among modes in the overall course rating index, interest index, or synthesis index. For the instructor rating index and the collaborative index, the mixed mode of delivery was associated with significantly better ratings. However, in looking at individual items, it was interesting that the mixed mode produced significantly worse ratings in two cases. Students in mixed-mode courses reported that the course requirements were less clear, and that they were less likely to have completed all the written assignments. Apparently, although the mixed mode of delivery is exciting and provides very good conditions for

TABLE 11-6
COURSE OUTCOMES BY MODE OF DELIVERY, MEANS AND ANOVA

VARIABLE	ONLINE	MIXED	F-T-F	F (2,280)*	p
COURSE RATING INDEX	16.0	15.0	15.3	1.38	.25
INSTRUCTOR RATING INDEX	22.1 A	19.8 A	21.2	3.02	.05
COLLABORATIVE INDEX	20.6 A	24.9 AB	23.0 B	20.7	.001
INTEREST INDEX	10.4	10.3	10.0	.7	.48
SYNTHESIS INDEX	10.8	11.3	11.2	1.7	.18
INCREASED COMPUTER COMPETENCE	2.1 A	2.1 A	3.1 AB	30.95	.001
NEW FRIENDSHIPS	2.6 AB	2.0 A	2.2 B	9.44	.001
COMPLETED WRITTEN ASSIGNMENTS	1.9 A	2.2 AB	1.9 B	4.11	.02
STIMULATED ADDITIONAL READING	2.7 AB	3.1 A	3.1 B	4.58	.01
DEVELOPED ABILITY TO COMMUNICATE	2.5 AB	2.1 A	2.3 B	11.24	.001
COURSE REQUIREMENTS CLEAR	2.1 A	2.4 AB	2.0 B	4.54	.01

ENTRIES IN THE SAME ROW WITH THE SAME LETTER ARE SIGNIFI-CANTLY DIFFERENT, DUNCAN MULTIPLE RANGE TEST
*approximate degrees of freedom for F ratios

collaborative learning among students, the combination of traditional and online activities can prove overwhelming and confusing for students.

As was expected, students who used the Virtual Classroom were significantly more likely to report increased computer competence. This supports:

H.2.7. The Virtual Classroom will result in greater knowledge of the use of computers.

Those who had completely online courses were most likely to have been stimulated to do additional outside reading related to the course, which support the hypotheses that the VC will increase motivation and interest. On the other hand, for all courses combined, the expectations concerning developing relationships with other students online were not borne out. Students in the totally online courses were less likely to report having developed new friendships in the class, and less likely to feel that they had developed their ability to communicate clearly about the subject.

OUTCOMES BY MODE AND COURSE

When a two-way analysis of variance was used for all dependent variables, employing the matched Fall courses in the quasi-experimental factorial design, the results of the previous one-way analyses were verified. Almost all differences in outcomes were associated with differences among courses, rather than with differences among modes. There was some interaction between course and mode, but given the small number of cases, interaction was generally not statistically significant. With such a small number of students in each of the course by mode conditions, differences had to be extremely large and consistent to reach statistical significance.

Table 11-7 presents the results for one of these analyses, the Course Rating Index, as an example of the results of this set of analyses. There is no overall difference in course ratings by mode of delivery, but there are significant differences among courses, and a significant interaction between mode and course. Ratings were better for the online sections of Computer Science and the upper level statistics course (Math 305), and worse for the online section of Introductory Sociology and the management course.

In sum, it was differences among courses that accounted for most of the differences in outcome measures. To the extent that there was some interaction between mode of delivery and course, the pattern was not consistent. Within courses, few of the differences in outcome by mode were large enough to be statistically significant, and the direction of the differences that occurred was mixed. There was a fairly consistent ten-

TABLE 11-7
Course Rating Index, by Mode and Course
Means and Anova

Course	MODE Online	MODE FTF	Both
CIS 213	14.3	17.1	15.7
MATH 305	12.5	13.6	13.1
STATISTICS	19.2	18.6	18.5
SOCIOLOGY	17.6 A	13.7 A	15.7
MANAGEMENT	16.7 A	14.6 A	15.6
All Courses	16.1	15.5	

* Conditions with letter A are significantly different at 0.05 level
Anova: F = 4.42   p = 0.001
Mode: F = 0.62   p = 0.431
Course: F = 6.22   p = 0.001
Mode x Course: F = 2.61   p = 0.038
Range = 7 (best) to 35 (worst)

dency for the ratings for Computer Science to be higher in the online sections and for the ratings for Sociology to be higher for the face-to-face section.

INTERACTIONS OF MODE AND SCHOOL

School, as we have previously noted, was related to differences in Virtual Classroom outcomes, not only because of differences in equipment access conditions, but also because it was confounded with differences in the level of the courses which were offered. At NJIT, the online courses were for undergraduate students in the sophomore to senior years; at Upsala, the totally online courses were freshman level, while the mixed-mode courses were for upper level undergraduate courses; and for Connected Education and OISE, the courses were at the postgraduate level, and all students had their own microcomputers. Thus, it is not surprising that there was an interaction between "school" and mode for most of the outcome variables. Included here are a few of the most important of the results of these analyses; most outcome variables showed results that varied simultaneously by school as well as by mode of delivery.

In the first table (11-8) in this series of selected significant interactions by mode and school, we see that the students' perceptions of problems with sufficient access to a terminal or microcomputer are in some ways different than might have been imagined. For the remote education students in Connected Education and OISE, as would be expected, access was not a problem. However, the surprising things were that student perceptions of access problems were higher at NJIT than we assumed they would be, and at Upsala, for unclear reasons, the access problems were considered more serious in the mixed-mode courses than in the totally online courses. This may be because those in the totally online courses were prepared to have to go to the microlab to use computers, while those in the mixed mode courses had not chosen that mode and resented the trip more.

The best overall scores on the "Increased Interest" index (Table 11-9) were for the remote education students, the NJIT totally online courses, and the Upsala mixed modes courses. For degree of collaborative learning, the index scores were highest for the mixed-modes condition, at both NJIT and Upsala. Instructor rating indexes tended to be highest for totally online courses at NJIT, and for the mixed-mode courses at Upsala (Table 11-10).

EFFECTS OF REPEATING COURSES A SECOND TIME

Four of the courses which were totally or partially online the first semester were repeated the second semester. The assumption was that, with experience, not only would the process of teaching online be easier for the instructor, but it would also result in better outcomes perceived by the students.

TABLE 11-8
Terminal Access Problem, by Mode and School
Means and Anova

School	Online	Mixed	MODE Both
NJIT	3.5	3.6	3.6
UPSALA	3.8 A	2.9 A	
CONNECT-ED	4.8		
Others	4.6		
All Schools	4.2		

* Conditions with letter A are significantly different at 0.05 level
Anova: $F = 4.08$ $p = 0.001$
Mode: $F = 0.74$ $p = 0.478$
School: $F = 4.27$ $p = 0.006$
Mode x School: $F = 8.30$ $p = 0.004$
KEY: 1 = Serious Problem 5 = Not a problem

TABLE 11-9
Interest Index by Mode and School
Means and Anova

School	Online	Mixed	MODE FTF	All
NJIT	11.0 A	9.9 A	10.2	10.4
UPSALA	8.9 A	10.6 A	9.6	9.7
CONNECT-ED	11.2			
Others	11.4			
All Schools	10.6			

* Conditions with letter A are significantly different at 0.05 level
Anova: F = 3.59   p = 0.001
Mode: F = 0.60   p = 0.550
School: F = 3.54   p = 0.015
Mode x School: F = 5.02   p = 0.002
KEY: Index range = 3 (low) to 15 (high)

TABLE 11-10
Instructor Rating Index by Mode and School
Means and Anova

School	Online	Mixed	MODE FTF	All
NJIT	19.4	20.4	21.0	20.3
UPSALA	25.9 A	19.0 AB	22.9 B	22.6
CONNECT-ED	27.0			
Others	19.9			
All Schools	23.0			

* Conditions with letter A & B are significantly different at 0.05 level
Anova: F = 4.20   p = 0.001
Mode: F = 3.80   p = 0.024
School: F = 4.17   p = 0.007
Mode x School: F = 4.70   p = 0.003
Key: Index range = 11 (best) to 55 (worst)

There was a tendency for courses to improve the second time they were offered online, but there are many exceptions to this generalization when specific courses and outcomes are examined. Taking the overall results first, outcomes for the overall student rating index for the Virtual Classroom are shown in Table 11-11. It was true that these overall ratings were better the second semester for all courses that were repeated. However, only the management lab showed a statistically significant improvement.

In terms of final grades assigned to students, which measured the instructor's perceptions of the students' performance, there were no significant differences. Perhaps this was to be expected, since instructors may tend to grade on a curve for any class.

SUMMARY

This chapter analyzed differences among modes of delivery by using data from a quasi-experimental design. Different students were given different courses in different modes, but asked the same questions (and within course, given the same examinations). The reasoning was that, if mode of delivery was a strong causal factor in influencing outcomes, this should show up as significant differences in the responses of the students receiving different "treatments."

Our samples of students within each mode and course condition were too small to provide much statistical power, but generally speaking, there were few variations in outcome associated with mode of delivery. There were constantly large and significant differences among the courses and among the schools. The findings support Hypothesis 8: There will be significant differences in process and outcomes among courses.

In terms of grades, the only statistically significant difference was for the computer science course, where grades were better in the online section. This was also the course for which students in the Virtual Classroom condition spent the most time online. This result supports

TABLE 11-11
VC Overall Rating Index by Semester and Course
Means and Anova

| | SEMESTER | | |
Course	1	2	Both
CIS 213	19.4	20.5	20.0
MATH 305	17.0	19.7	18.3
STATISTICS	13.9	14.3	14.1
MANAGEMENT	18.8 A	23.0 A	20.9
All Courses	17.3	19.4	

* Conditions with letter A are significantly different at 0.05 level

Anova: $F=4.10$ $p=0.001$
Course: $F=6.86$ $p=0.001$
Semester: $F=3.31$ $p=0.072$
Course x Semester: $F=0.70$ $p=0.556$
Key: Index may range from 4 (lowest) to 28

Hypothesis 1, that mastery of material in the VC will be equal or superior to that in the TC.

Self assessments of students of the degree to which they increased their computer competence were significantly better for both the totally VC and mixed modes of delivery than for the TC. This supports Hypothesis 2.7.

In many cases, results were significantly different for the totally VC and mixed delivery modes, with the mixed mode producing better ratings. An exception to this pattern is perceptions of whether course requirements were clear; for this variable, the mixed mode was significantly worse than either the totally online or totally face-to-face traditional modes. These results support:

H 11. Results for the "mixed" mode will not represent a simple average of results for totally VC and totally TC modes, but will represent a distinctive set of strengths and weaknesses.

An attempt to determine quantitatively whether the use of VC might help improve progress in a freshmen-level writing course was a failure. Holistically graded pre- and postcourse essays showed no changes for any sections. Thus we cannot determine whether the medium has no effect, or the results are due to an unreliable and insensitive scoring procedure. On the other hand, subsequent qualitative case studies of totally online writing workshops come to the conclusion that the medium can be very effective in developing writing skills, if the students are motivated and have their own PCs, and if the instructor is skilled in creating a supportive, student-centered, and collaborative online environment.

All of the outcomes for VC courses at "computer-poor" Upsala were below those obtained at computer-intensive NJIT. This may seem "obvious," but it also carries important lessons for implementation elsewhere: Students should have access to Personal computers in their homes if they are to participate regularly and benefit from an online course. The findings support:

H10. There will be significant differences between the Upsala and NJIT implementations of the Virtual Classroom, in terms of both process and outcomes of the online courses.

When looked at by mode and school, the poorest results occurred for the totally online, freshman-level courses at Upsala. The upper level, mixed modes courses at Upsala tended to be rated relatively well; for instance, these courses had relatively high ratings for items on developing ability to communicate clearly, to improve critical analysis ability, increased confidence in expressing ideas, and increased interest in the subject matter. Thus significantly different outcomes by school and mode may be partially an artifact of differences in the level of maturity of the students enrolled in totally online courses in the two schools. The mixed-modes courses at Upsala were all upper level; students in upper level courses tend to be more mature and more consistently "ready" for an intensive college-level learning experience than is the average student in the freshman-level courses that were totally online at Upsala.

There was a tendency for student ratings of courses to improve the second time they were offered online. There were many exceptions to this generalization, when specific courses and outcomes were examined. For instance, although the overall ratings of the Virtual Classroom experience were higher the second time for all four courses that were repeated, only the ratings for the Management course showed a statistically significant improvement for that index.

However, the results tend to support:

H 9. Outcomes for the second offering of a VC courses by an instructor will be significantly better than for the first attempt at teaching online.

CHAPTER *12*

PREDICTORS OF SUCCESS IN THE VIRTUAL CLASSROOM

Alone we can do so little;
Together we can do so much

— Helen Keller

We have seen in Chapter 11 that some of the differences in outcomes of either totally online or mixed-mode courses are associated with the context provided by the course, the school and the access conditions available there, and whether a course is a first-time or a repeat offering. In this chapter, we will see that there were also many significant differences associated with student attitudes, attributes, and behavior. In the analyses summarized here, students in traditional courses were eliminated, since they were not relevant to the analysis. Those in the partially and totally online sections were grouped together, in order to have the largest possible number of subjects for exploring the correlates of student success in the Virtual Classroom.

STUDENT CHARACTERISTICS AS PREDICTORS

Preuse expectations become self-fulfilling prophecies. This has proven to be true in other studies of CMC and is also true in the Virtual Classroom application of this medium (see Rice & Case, 1983; Hiltz & Johnson, 1990). Table 12–1 displays the correlations between preuse variables and course outcomes. As would be expected, those with more positive attitudes towards computers at the outset were more likely to report more favorable course outcomes, to spend more time online, and to log on more frequently. They were also more likely to report that EIES was "easy to learn," less likely to feel at the end that they would not choose to take another online course, and rated the Virtual Classroom mode of delivery more favorably in comparison to face-to-face classes.

These same correlations tended to repeat and to be stronger when preuse expectations about the EIES system in particular, rather than general attitudes toward computers, were used as the predictor. The implication is that participation in the Virtual Classroom mode of learning should ideally be a choice of the student, so that those with poor initial attitudes are not forced to take part. Several of the interviews in Appendix II with examples of the "most negative" of the students who participated support this interpretation of the correlations. For instance, one student mentioned a "lot of apprehension" at the beginning, followed by only once a week participation. As discussed in the chapter on implementation problems, in this and other cases of negative attitudes and inadvertent enrollment, there was a problem with effectively communicating with such students to "counsel them out." They seemed not to hear what they were told or to read or understand printed material directed at

TABLE 12–1
Pearson's Correlation Coefficients Between Student Characteristics and Selected Outcome Measures

	Computer Attitudes (N=219)	EIES Expec- (N=150)	Personal Sphere of Control (N=217)	Inter- personal (N=213)	Class Standing (N=221)
Course Outcome Index	−.12	−.19	−.16	−.08	−.10
(N = 227* p =	.04	.01	.01	.11	.07
Instructor Rating Index	−.02	−.06	−.10	−.13	−.04
N = 228 p =	.40	.25	.06	.03	.27
VC Overall Index	.34	.38	.07	.07	.16
N = 159 p =	.001	.001	.20	.20	.02
EIES Easy to Learn	.43	.40	.24	.22	.14
N = 156 p =	.001	.001	.002	.10	.05
Not Take Another	.31	.33	.10	.16	.25
N = 156 p =	.001	.001	.11	.02	.001
Total Hours On	.15	.25	.03	-.01	.09
N = 215 p =	.02	.001	.34	.43	.08
Total Times On	.21	.26	.11	.01	.14
N = 215 p =	.001	.001	.07	.44	.02

*Note: N's for cells in a row vary slightly by item

them. For instance, the apprehensive student complained about NJIT facilities not being open during the weekends; yet, both at training and in follow-up announcements, all students were informed of the special laboratory where Virtual Classroom students could receive assistance. This lab was open half-days on Saturdays, and unattended terminals were available all day on Saturdays.

Similarly, a negative Math 305 student complained that the fact that the course would be online was a total surprise to him, and that he didn't like that idea from the beginning. He claimed that it wasn't in the registration material (then admits, "Maybe it was, but I just missed it"). OFFERED VIA COMPUTER was prominently printed in all-capital letters next to the course name and section number for online courses in the registration material, and posters and flyers were placed around the registration area. Then there was the telling little detail in an interview with a dropout, who carefully spelled out the instructor's name – getting both the first and last names wrong.

It is probably not coincidental that all three of these students who started out with being "surprised" to learn about the online class at the first meeting, and with negative attitudes toward the experiment, work full time and normally were on campus only to attend class. They understandably felt overloaded and were likely to screen out anything that did not seem to "require" their attention. The Math 305 student stated, for instance,

> I don't have enough time in my day as it is . . . I usually go to work, then to school, then to work and then back to the house to study at 11 at night, and I didn't want to sit down and read some other stuff . . . To sit down and make myself do something like that . . . I don't have the self discipline for it.

Sphere of Control: Not a good predictor. Qualitative observations similar to those above led initially to the inclusion of the Sphere of Control indices as predictors. It was hypothesized that considerable self-discipline and ability to manage one's time and one's life would be necessary in order to participate regularly and successfully in a "sign-on anytime" Virtual Classroom experience, and the Sphere of Control measures were assumed to tap this dimension. However, the results for Sphere of Control indices were not as strong or consistent as was hypothesized (see Table 12–1). The Personal Efficacy Sphere of Control index was significantly related to the overall course outcomes index, and to the perception that EIES was easy to learn. Interpersonal Sphere of Control was significantly related to the Instructor Rating Index, and to disagreement with the statement that they would not choose to take another online course. However, neither Sphere of Control index was related to the overall rating of the Virtual

Classroom and even those correlations which were significant were not very strong.

Student maturity and ability are crucial. Class standing corresponded to the educational level of the student: freshman through graduate student. Thus, it reflected both age and previous academic experience, and could be an indirect measure of cognitive maturity. The higher the academic level of the student, the less likely they were to conclude that they would not take another online course, and the better their overall rating of their Virtual Classroom experience in comparison to previous face-to-face courses. Since many of the students were freshmen, we were missing many grade point averages, so Math and Verbal Scholastic Aptitude test scores were used to explore the relationship between academic ability and achievement (whatever combination of these were measured by the SATs), and process and outcomes in the Virtual Classroom environment. Selected results of these linear regressions are displayed in Table 12-2. Many of these correlations were moderately strong, and very interesting. On the whole, it was the Mathematics SAT score which predicted student success in the Virtual Classroom, much more than the Verbal SAT score. The first two correlations in Table 12-2 were included as a matter of general interest: high Sphere of Control indices were associated with high Verbal SATs but not significantly associated with Math SAT scores. Those with high Math SATs (but not those with high Verbal SATs) signed on significantly more frequently, and also spent more total time online and sent more private messages. They were less likely to feel inhibited online; more likely to feel that they were more involved in the VC course than in traditional courses. The high Math SAT students also earned significantly higher final course grades online, were more likely to rate course outcomes highly, and were much more likely to give the Virtual Classroom better ratings overall than the traditional classroom.

By contrast, many of the correlations for the Verbal SAT are either weak (e.g., the weak but insignificant correlation with course grade), *or actually reversed.* This is very intriguing and was not expected. The high Verbal SAT students were significantly less likely to feel that VC increased access to the professor or their active involvement in the course. One can speculate about the combination of high Math SAT/Low Verbal SAT as one for which students are especially likely to "bloom" in the VC environment, but until we combine several years' samples and have a larger number of cases to work with, this will have to remain speculation.

The next table (12-3) explores the SAT scores as predictors using an analysis of variance, so that possible curvilinear relationships can emerge. The Verbal SATs were broken into four groups, which might be called "extremely low" (under 320), Low (330–390); average (400–499), and High

TABLE 12-2
Correlations between SAT Scores and VC Process and Outcome (N = 103)

VARIABLE	SAT Math	SAT Verbal
Personal SOC	.18	.29**
Interpersonal SOC	.15	.29***
Total Times On	.39***	.04
(Not) Inhibited	.20*	.13
Access Professor	−.06	.20*
More Involved	−.15	.17*
Final Grade	.31***	.13
Course Outcome Index	−.24**	−.01
VC Overall Index	.36***	.04

*Significant at $p = <.05$
**Significant at $p = <.01$
***Significant at $p = <.001$

(500 and over). The Math SATs, which were not as skewed toward low scores, were divided into Low, Average, and High groups. (Note the kind of skewing introduced by inclusion in the study of students at a technical school such as NJIT; only 13% had Verbal scores over 500, but 39% had Math scores over 500.) We see that there was practically no relationship between Verbal SAT scores and subjective satisfaction. "VC Overall" ratings were slightly higher for the highest ability group, with scores of over 500 on the Verbal SAT, but not significantly so. Grades were significantly related, but even though they were markedly higher for students with verbal SAT scores over 400, even the lowest ability groups achieved, on the average, passing grades in VC courses. This is encouraging for the potential of the technology to serve low-ability students as well as high-ability students. These trends are much stronger for the Math SAT scores. Those with the highest Math scores, 500 and above, gave the Virtual Classroom significantly higher ratings and achieved significantly higher grades in online courses.

Both for Verbal and Math SAT scores, there is the suggestion of an interesting curvilinear relationship with outcomes. Satisfaction with outcomes is actually higher for the very lowest ability groups (those with Verbal scores under 320, or with Math scores under 390, representing about a third of the students) than for the students in the next highest score category. More data on the relationship between SAT and Virtual Classroom outcomes are necessary before any firm conclusions can be made However, one can speculate that although the lowest ability groups had the most difficulties online, their constant access to the professor and their ability to work at their own pace were an advantage, and allowed

TABLE 12-3
SAT Scores by Overall Outcomes

Verbal SAT	Mean VC Overall	Mean Course Grade	% of Students
220–320	18.3	2.1	31%
330–390	16.5	2.0	18%
400–499	18.5	2.9	33%
500+	19.4	2.8	13%
All	18.2	2.5	100%
F	.68	4.9	
df	3, 91	3, 138	
p	.57	.003	
MATH SAT			
220–390	16.4	2.0	37%
400–499	15.6	2.5	24%
500+	20.8	3.0	39%
All	18.3	2.5	100%
F	7.6	7.8	
df	2, 93	2, 140	
p	.001	.001	

them to pass their courses, on the average, when they may not have been able to pass a traditionally delivered course.

In terms of the association between other student characteristics measured and the outcomes, the results tended to be mixed and weak, and were not included in tables here. For gender, the males did slightly better on final course grades (point biserial $R = .13$, $p = .05$). Males were also slightly more favorable, on the average, towards overall assessment of the Virtual Classroom ($R = -.16$, $p = .02$). This seems to be related to the tendency for males to like computers better and to have higher Math SATs. The correlation between gender and postcourse computer attitudes was of a similar magnitude: $R = -.18$ (with females coded as "2"), $p = .01$. However, though statistically significant, the differences related to gender were so slight as to have no practical importance. In fact, if one wanted to take the "long view," giving females a computer-intensive experience in a VC course could be seen as one way to improve their computer-related skills and attitudes.

The only correlation of outcomes with nationality was a slight ($R = .17$ $p = .03$) tendency for non-Americans to feel that they were less able to improve their ability to pull together or synthesize the variety of materials presented in courses. In terms of native language, the only statistically significant difference was that those whose native language was not English were slightly less likely to report increased interest in the subject matter ($R = .18$, $p = .01$).

There was only one statistically significant correlation with typing ability at preuse. Those with better typing skills had slightly better attitudes toward computers as measured postcourse ($R = .17$, $p = .02$).

ACCESS, ACTIVITY LEVELS, AND OUTCOMES

The first three columns in Table 12–4 deal with aspects of "access" to the Virtual Classroom: having a micro at home, perceived problems with equipment access, and overall "convenience" of the VC mode. (Better access to the professor is also an aspect of overall educational access, obviously; this variable will be treated in the table that follows, which groups it with increased interaction with peers as well as the instructor.) There were fewer and weaker correlations between having one's own microcomputer at home, amount of use of the system and reactions to it, than might be supposed. Though the correlation with overall VC rating was statistically significant, it was only .18. A second measure of access was a question asked on the postcourse questionnaire about access to a terminal being a serious problem. Those who felt it was not a problem were more likely to feel that VC had increased the quality of their education, and to give more positive overall reactions to the Virtual Classroom mode.

However, access is more than merely problems getting a terminal or micro to use. It may include perceived problems with telephone lines; or perhaps, perceived problems in making time to participate. In terms of increased access to one's professor as a result of the Virtual Classroom, this depends on the professor's making time on a daily basis to respond to all students, not just on the technological possibility of daily contact. These two "subjective" aspects of access, increased overall convenience and better access to the professor, have much stronger relationships with Virtual Classroom outcomes than details about the availability of personal computers.

The overall "Convenience" question was significantly related to the final exam grade and final course grade. In addition, perception that the Virtual Classroom is more convenient than traditional classrooms is correlated with subjective ratings of extent of collaborative learning, increased interest in the subject, increased ability to synthesize material in the field, attitudes toward computers at the end of the course, rating of the instructor and the course, and in particular, overall rating of VC.

All of the measures of amount of use of the Virtual Classroom tended to

TABLE 12-4
Access and Activity Conditions, by Outcomes
Pearson Correlation Coefficients (N of cases = 163)

	ACCESS			ACTIVITY		
	HOME	ACCTERM	CONVEN	TTOT	ONTOT	PRTOT
FINAL GRADE	.06	.10	.33***	.16*	.22***	.17*
FINAL EXAM	.06	.01	−.30*	.25*	.34**	.28*
COLLABORATIVE INDEX	.02	.02	−.15*	.14*	.07	.01
INTEREST INDEX	.02	.14	−.33***	.12	.17**	.08
SYNTHESIS INDEX	−.12*	−.02	−.26***	.08	.07	.03
INCREASED QUALITY	.07	.31***	−.51***	.16*	.17**	.14*
COMPUTER ATTS2	.30***	.37***	−.53***	.26***	.31***	.31***
INSTRUCTOR RATING	−.05	−.12	.32***	−.08	−.11	−.13*
COURSE RATING	.06	−.14*	.38***	−.20**	−.20**	−.13*
VC OVERALL	.18**	.36***	−.63***	.22***	.25***	.22***

KEYS: HOME = Have a terminal at home, pre-use
ACCTERM = Post question on problems with terminal access
CONVEN = Agreement with statement that VC is more convenient
      (1 = Strongly Agree, 7 = Strongly Disagree)
*TTOT = Total time online during course
ONTOT = Number of sessions online during course
PRTOT = Number of private messages sent during course
INDEXES: See Research Design Chapter for components
  *Significant at $p = .05$
 **Significant at $p = < .01$
***Significant at $p = < .001$

be related to outcome measures; the number of sessions or total number of times a student signed online was most strongly related. For instance, the correlation between number of sessions and the final exam score was .34, which was moderately strong. Level of activity was also related to the final course grade, a perception that VC increased the quality of education, more positive postcourse attitudes toward computers, and the overall course rating index.

Table 12-5 shows the correlations between the items measuring perception of increased communication and collaboration with classmates and instructor, and the outcome measures. As in the pilot studies, there were strong and consistent relationships between perceptions of having communicated more with the professor and the other students online, and overall evaluations of the Virtual Classroom experience. Those who felt

TABLE 12-5
Process and Assessments of the Virtual Classroom

	COMMUN-ICATED	ACCESS PROF	INCREASE MOTIVE	INVOLVED	COMMENTS	ASSIGNS
FINAL GRADE	-.15*	-.17*	-.23	-.22***	-.11	-.11
FINAL EXAM	-.09*	-.28*	-.23***	-.23***	-.11	-.06
COLLABORATIVE INDEX	-.51***	-.35***	-.25***	-.40***	-.45***	-.30***
INTEREST INDEX	-.25***	-.41***	-.40***	-.38***	-.40***	-.39***
SYNTHESIS INDEX	-.32***	-.44***	-.43***	-.37***	-.34***	-.33***
INCREASED	-.31***	-.46***	-.36***	-.45***	-.35***	-.35***
COMPUTER ATTS2	-.24***	-.35***	-.39***	-.42***	-.31***	-.39***
INSTRUCTOR	.27***	.35***	.32***	.28***	.21***	.23***
COURSE RATING	.29***	.40***	.46***	.46***	.33***	.32
VC OVERALL	-.41***	-.60***	-.48***	-.64***	-.44***	-.48***

KEYS: COMMUNICATED = Communicated more with other students
ACCESS PROF = Provided better access to the professor
INCREASE MOTIVE = Fact that assignments would be read by other students increased motivation
INVOLVED = Felt more involved in taking an active part
COMMENTS = Found comments made by other students useful
ASSIGNS = Found reading assignments of other students useful

$* p = < .05$
$** p = < .01$
$*** p = < .001$

they had better access to their professor, and who read and valued the comments and assignments of other students, felt that the Virtual Classroom was a better mode of learning than traditional face-to-face classes. Those who did not actively take advantage of the communication opportunities for such a collaborative style of learning tended to prefer the face-to-face mode.

This is reinforced in the interviews with very positive and very negative students in Appendix II. There were two major determinants, thus, of outcomes of the Virtual Classroom experience. One was whether the students had the self-discipline to regularly sign online. The other was whether they used the system to interact with the ideas and suggestions of the other students as well as their instructor. These two aspects of online behavior were interrelated. For those who valued communication with other members of the class, motivation to sign online frequently was increased. Frequent, regular, and active participation helped them to do well in the online course, and contributed to their positive evaluations of the course, the instructor, the attainment of learning goals, and evaluations of this mode of educational delivery.

MULTIVARIATE ANALYSES

In various parts of this account of results, we have noted a series of bivariate relationships which took into account the interaction of two variables at a time. What happens when we put all our predictors together? Which ones make the biggest contribution to explaining the variance in the dependent variables, and which ones are not significant once the others are taken into account?

Because our sample size was fairly small, we did not conduct many multivariate analyses or try to push the variance accounted for too far. The problem is that, as you add variables with a small sample, you run out of degrees of freedom; for example, 9 variables will always explain the variance in 10 cases perfectly.

We used simultaneous regression, which takes all the variables in the equations into account at the same time. This does have the methodological weakness that, if two variables are strongly associated, then they will probably share variance accounted for between them, and neither one may end up statistically significant. However, without a prior theory that clearly predicted what variables would be the strongest causes, there was no basis for alternative regression procedures. In order to use *mode* and *course* as variables, a series of "dummy variables" were constructed with 0–1 values (e.g., in the dummy variable for the statistics course, it was coded as "1" and all other courses were coded "0," or "not statistics").

In the first equation (Table 12–6), all students in all modes at NJIT and

TABLE 12-6
PREDICTING COURSE RATING: MULTIPLE REGRESSION

Variable	b	Beta	T
Course = Statistics	10.93	0.81	4.78***
School	−6.93	−0.73	−3.72***
SAT Math Score	−0.02	−0.68	−4.68***
Mode = Mixed	5.00	0.50	3.23**
Course = CIS 213	2.90	0.24	1.89
SAT Verbal Score	0.01	0.18	1.82
Academic Standing	0.60	0.17	1.62
Mode = Online	1.50	0.16	1.54
Course = Math 305	−0.58	−.05	−0.40
(constant)	26.46		6.53***

−Multiple R = 0.52 Adjusted R Square = 0.21
DF (10,121) F = 4.53 *p = 0.001
*p = < .05 ***p = < .001
NOTE: Low Course Rating scores correspond to favorable ratings

Upsala were considered, and the dependent variable was the Course Rating Index. In interpreting the signs of the beta coefficients, which are the best overall comparative measure of the level of association with the dependent variable, one must be aware of how the variables were coded, which is shown in the questionnaire items in Appendix I. The course rating scale was first introduced in Chapter 5, on methodology. Because it consisted of a series of positive statements accompanied by Likert-type scales which were displayed and scored as "1 = Strongly Agree," the lower the total score, the more positive the total course rating.

The strongest predictors have nothing to do with mode of delivery. The required freshman-level statistics course at Upsala received the lowest course ratings. Another course taken by many freshmen to fulfill a requirement, Sociology, showed up as also significantly associated with relatively poor course ratings.

Only two schools were used in this analysis, with NJIT coded "1" and Upsala coded "2." The second strongest predictor of course ratings was school; despite the two specific courses with relatively low ratings, course ratings on the whole were better at Upsala. The third strongest predictor was a measure of general ability; students with high Math SAT scores rated their courses significantly better.

Mode of delivery does appear as making a significant contribution to predicting overall course ratings: the mixed mode courses have lower ratings than the other modes, when everything else was simultaneously taken into account. Since, on the majority of measures, mixed mode courses fared well, we will not make a great deal of its appearance in this particular equation.

The second and third equations are only for those students who had a partially or totally online course, since it uses variables available only for these students. The only two significant contributors to predicting final grade in these courses (Table 12-7) are SAT Verbal score and agreement that taking online courses is more convenient. However, it should be noted that, even with 12 predictors in the equation, we cannot accurately predict final course grades, with only 14% of the variance explained.

The most important equation for our purposes is the prediction of overall rating of the Virtual Classroom (Table 12-8). The total proportion of variance explained by the 18 predictor variables is a respectable 67%. The significant predictors are SAT Math scores, and perceptions that the Virtual Classroom is more convenient than the traditional classroom, that it increased access to the professor, and that the student was more involved in taking an active part in the course.

In a stepwise multiple regression approach to predicting overall VC ratings (not included here), the order of selection was feeling more involved in the course, feeling that the VC is more convenient, perception of better access to the professor, and the SAT Math score. These four variables accounted for 60% of the variance (adjusted R squared).

TABLE 12-7
Predicting Final Grade for VC Students: Multiple Regression

Variable	b	Beta	T
SAT VERBAL SCORE	0.00	0.29	2.21*
CONVENIENT	−0.18	−0.270	−2.07*
INCREASED MOTIVATION	−0.11	−0.162	−1.40
ACCESS PROBLEM	−0.15	−0.155	−1.40
TOTAL TIMES ONLINE	0.00	0.119	1.07
ACADEMIC STANDING	0.09	0.099	0.97
ASSIGNMENTS USEFUL	0.08	0.098	0.69
MORE INVOLVED	−0.06	−0.078	−0.60
EIES EXPECTATIONS	−0.01	−0.068	−0.63
ACCESS PROFESSOR	−0.04	−0.053	−0.43
SAT MATH SCORE	0.00	0.025	0.17
COMMENTS USEFUL	−0.00	−0.006	−0.04
(Constant)	2.61		2.48*

Multiple R = 0.49 Adjusted R sq = 0.14
DF (12,86) F = 2.29 p = 0.001
*p = <.05

TABLE 12-8
Predicting Overall VC Rating: Multiple Regression

Variable	b	Beta	T
SAT MATH SCORE	0.01	0.29	1.96*
CONVENIENT	−0.92	−0.28	−2.65**
ACCESS PROFESSOR	−0.78	−0.24	−2.65**
MORE INVOLVED	−0.79	−0.22	−2.22**
Course = MANAGEMENT	−2.18	−0.16	−0.41
Course = CIS 213	−2.66	−0.16	−0.49
ASSIGNMENTS USEFUL	−0.42	−0.11	−1.08
Course = MATH 305	−1.67	−0.10	−0.31
ACADEMIC STANDING	−0.46	−0.10	−1.06
COMMENTS USEFUL	−0.35	−0.09	−0.97
INCREASED MOTIVATION	−0.27	−0.08	−0.99
EIES EXPECTATION	0.05	0.08	0.98
TOTAL TIMES ONLINE	−0.01	−0.07	−0.94
Course = SOC 150	−1.45	−0.07	−0.75
Course = STATISTICS	−1.03	−0.06	−0.56
SCHOOL	−0.46	−0.04	−0.10
SAT VERBAL SCORE	0.00	0.02	0.21
ACCESS PROBLEM	0.03	0.01	0.06
(Constant)	24.35	–	2.44*

Multiple R = 0.82 Adjusted R sq = 0.67
DF (18,79) F = 8.82 p = 0.001
*p = < .05 **p = < .01 ***p = < .001

SUMMARY: PREDICTING STUDENT REACTIONS TO THE VIRTUAL CLASSROOM

Course is a much stronger predictor of differences in course outcomes than is mode of delivery. Bound up with course are differences in characteristics of the students enrolled, in the subject matter and thus content of the experiences, and especially, in teacher style or skill in various modes.

Our primary interest in this chapter was in pursuing the question of correlates of relatively "good" outcomes in Virtual Classroom courses. Some student characteristics, such as Math SAT scores, are strong predictors of relatively good outcomes. However, it should be noted that even students in the lowest ability groups, as measured by SAT scores, were able to pass the course, on the average, and that the very lowest ability groups actually had a slightly more positive attitude toward the Virtual Classroom than did students with only moderately low scores. We speculated that perhaps the least able students particularly appreciated the opportunities to work at their own pace and to communicate more with their instructor about their problems in the course.

Convenience of access is also very important, as is regular and active participation, and a perception of improved access to the professor. These latter two variables, while partially related to student characteristics such as self-discipline, could also be greatly affected by how the instructor conducts the online course.

In sum, though academic ability is related to outcomes such as grades in the Virtual Classroom, low academic skills do not prohibit the student from adequate learning via this medium. Convenience of access to other students, as well as the professor, are strongly correlated to both objective and subjective outcomes. Thus, there is evidence that access, collaborative learning, greater participation and involvement as a result, and improved learning do form a causal chain.

In terms of our hypotheses, we have the following findings:

H4: Those students who experience "group" or "collaborative" learning in the Virtual Classroom are most likely to judge the outcomes of online courses to be superior to the outcomes of traditional classes.

H5: Differences among students in academic ability will be strongly associated with outcomes in the VC.

Finding: Supported, but low ability students, as measured by their SAT scores, were able to perform at a "passing" level in the VC, if they had the motivation and self-discipline to participate regularly.

H6: Students with more positive precourse attitudes towards computers in general and towards the specific system to be used will be more likely to participate actively online and to perceive greater benefits from the VC mode.

Finding: supported by significant correlations.

H7: Students with a greater Sphere of Control on both the personal and interpersonal levels will be more likely to regularly and actively participate online and to perceive greater benefits from the VC mode.

Finding: Sphere of Control personality scales were not a good predictor of activity or outcomes. Class standing, which is a rough measure of the maturity and academic self-discipline of the students, was significantly related to the number of times the student was active in the VC, and their overall ratings of the Virtual Classroom.

CHAPTER 13

MANAGEMENT GAMING IN A VIRTUAL LABORATORY

Enrico Hsu and Starr Roxanne Hiltz*

Do not train boys to learning by force and harshness; but
direct them to it by what amuses their minds, so that you may
be better able to discover with accuracy the peculiar bent of
the genius of each.

—Plato

We have seen that, during the initial year of extensive experimentation
with a variety of courses, one of the most successful was a "mixed modes"
offering of an introductory course in management. Over a period of 3 more
years, systematic enhancement and further experimentation in this
course with the use of the Virtual Classroom as a "laboratory" for learning
managerial skills continued. A total of 14 sections of this course were
offered in five different conditions. This chapter describes the series of
iterative enhancements to the Virtual Management Laboratory, the
second quasi-experimental design and hypotheses, and the effects of these
enhancements on various measures of student effort and performance.

This additional experiment is important because it helps to answer the
question, "Does technology make a difference?" In the initial study, the
only "objective" measure of improved student performance which we were
able to gather was grades, and their validity is flawed in many ways,
particularly by the tendency of many instructors to "curve" grades within
each section. One of the methodological advantages of the extensive

---

*Portions of this chapter are adapted from Hsu (1991), written under the direction of Starr
Roxanne Hiltz.

further experimentation with the effects of various enhancements to a Virtual Management Laboratory was the use of a computer simulation-game that enables us to obtain comparable measures of student performance across sections using different combinations of technological and pedagogical tools.

Another methodological weakness of the initial trials was the small number of students in any one course. Though the overall results of using the Virtual Classroom in a variety of courses appear to be favorable, there are too few students in the replications of any one course to be able to separate out the effects of variations in the technology from the effects of differences in the skills of instructors and the subject matter of the courses. By repeating the same course with the same instructor in a series of offerings, we were able to see if each of the assumed enhancements really does make an improvement in outcomes.

EXPERIMENTAL TREATMENTS IN THE VIRTUAL MANAGEMENT LABORATORY

In order to teach management skills, it is necessary to give students practice in a realistic environment. The purpose of extensive experimentation with constructing an online environment for management simulations was to develop and perfect just such a supportive "laboratory" for students to play managerial roles and receive feedback on their performance.

Enrico Hsu taught 14 sections of OS-471 Management Practices at NJIT. The textbook and course content remained the same, and all used an organizational simulation, which was a semester-long role play wherein each student plays a functional role in a simulated company. This has been described in previous chapters. Further details are available in Appendix III. The students were treated in five different ways. The differences in treatment consist in the *use or nonuse of:*

1. Virtual Classroom software implemented on a Computer-Mediated Communication System (CMC/VC) to facilitate structured communication within and between organized groups;
2. A microcomputer-based management game – Business Simulator by Reality Technologies;
3. Additional productivity software, such as a database system and spreadsheet, on students' personal computers, interconnected with each other via a centralized CMC. The software was provided to facilitate any business-related information processing.

EXHIBIT 13-1
Matrix of Experimental Treatments, Measuring Instruments
and Subjects

Treatment	1:Conventional	2: VC	3:Game	4:VC+ Game	5:VC+ Game+Software
Organization Simulation	Y	Y	Y	Y	Y
CMC/VC	N	Y	N	Y	Y
Management Game	N	N	Y	Y	Y
Productivity Software	N	N	N	N	Y
Measuring Instruments					
Pre-course VC questionnaire	Y	Y	Y	Y	Y
Post-course VC questionnaire	Y	Y	Y	Y	Y
CMC activity	N	Y	N	Y	Y
Group/Game Questionnaire	N	N	Y	Y	Y
Game Performance	N	N	Y	Y	Y
Game Report	N	N	Y	Y	Y

Distribution of Students among Treatments						Total
No. of course sections participating	4	5	2	1	2	14
No. of simulation/game groups	4	5	8	6	6	29
No. of students/subjects	106	124	54	20	23	327

In Exhibit 13-1, the first five rows define the five treatments. Given that the productivity tools could only be used on a group basis in conjunction with CMC, these five combinations or treatments represent all those logically possible. The next six rows of Exhibit 13-1 summarize the instruments used in measuring different aspects of teaching effectiveness. The last four rows identify the distribution of sections, simulation groups, and students assigned to each of the five treatments. Thus, the matrix in Exhibit 13-1 serves to succinctly define the five treatments by technologies and measuring instruments used. For convenience, we may simply refer to a treatment by its number as defined in the matrix, in subsequent discussions.

In preceding chapters, the results for the first year, which contrasted treatments 1 and 2, were presented. (Two of 4–5 sections shown in each of these treatments were included in the results presented for the initial experiment.) In this chapter, we will first concentrate on the contrast between treatments 3 and 4 (Business Simulator with and without Virtual Classroom). Then we will describe the advanced productivity tools in more detail, and look at the overall results for all five conditions of teaching and learning.

It should be noted that, for years 2 through 4 of experimentation, the location of the Virtual Classroom moved from the prototype on EIES 1 to its permanent software "home" on EIES 2. The new version of the system allowed much simpler integration with PC-based tools, and also provided a basic conference structure more suited to educational applications. Whereas the conference structure on the original system was linear, that on EIES 2 is hierarchical. Suppose you are viewing comment 3, for instance, and you have a reply you wish to make. You simply choose "Reply" from the full-screen menu. If your reply is the second to comment on 3, it will be added as 3.2. Then you go back to viewing other waiting comments you have not yet seen. Thus, it is simple to respond to each comment as you read it, and the logical structure of the conversation is automatically preserved.

In addition, EIES 2 allowed the attachment of "binary files" to any item. This made possible the integration of PC-based tools with the central VC facilities and conferences, and formed the technological basis for the innovations reported here. The sections in condition 5 were also taught how to use two new features of the Virtual Classroom on EIES 2. *Forms* are standard formats for data collection and display which can be attached to any comment, and "filled out" by others. This provides a systematic way to collect and compare information. *Filters* help participants to quickly find items that may be of particular interest. You can set a filter to "catch" and call your attention to new items according to criteria such as who wrote it, or key word (e.g., "assignment" or "urgent"). The availability of these features and tools and the specific encouragement by the instructor to share the results of using this productivity software were expected to facilitate the group collaboration.

MEASURES OF DEPENDENT VARIABLES

The complete set of measurement instruments used in this study are shown in the second portion of the table. Not all instruments could or were used in all conditions, and not all hypotheses or results will be included in this brief overview.

The standard pre- and postcourse Virtual Classroom questionnaires, as included in the appendix, were completed by all students in this study of technological enhancements to delivery of the management course. In addition, a Group/game questionnaire, administered together with the general questionnaires, was used to explore the psychological effects of playing a management game on a group vs. group basis. However, because the initial experiment relied so heavily on questionnaire data, most of these results will not be reported in this chapter. Instead, we will focus on new treatments and new measures.

CMC activity, for those treatment conditions with Virtual Classroom, gives an indication of the students' interest and motivation, and implies related learning effectiveness. We chose the time online and the number of items written as an indicator of the participants' activity level.

Group Summary Report. The group summary report is a report to be written at the end of the semester according to a prescribed set of guidelines. Even though the reports do not allow us to compare students' skills before and after the simulation, they provide evidence of the students' synthesis and communication skills. Summary game reports were graded by three outside judges according to five criteria:

1. Business knowledge: The correct usage of business terms (such as market share, bond rating, etc.), and meaningful discussion of the business results (such as return on assets, income before tax, etc.), are used as indication of the business knowledge learned by the student while playing a management game.
2. Innovative ideas: An example would be a substantial expenditure of advertising money together with high R&D investment when the company reaches independent level.
3. Clarity in presentation: This criterion is self-evident. A good presentation in writing is obviously an effective tool in the real world.
4. Information-processing skills: A well-designed database could provide more meaningful summaries of business results. A generous use of a spreadsheet could improve decision simulation capabilities.
5. Use of graphics: Colored charts provided by most commercial software package also indicate students' familiarity with the information-processing tools.

Quantitative Game Performance Scoreboard. For the groups who used a packaged management game as part of their simulated management activities, a composite index is defined based on data created by the game software during its playing. This index will be explained below in detail after the nature of the simulation game is described. The students had access to the financial indices and were also taught the meaning and derivation of these component indices. Therefore, it is clearly an indication of the students' skill to be able to manage their companies so that the indices result in a maximum possible composite index.

THE BUSINESS SIMULATOR GAME

In introducing Business Simulator, some sections had access to the Virtual Classroom on EIES2 at NJIT, whereas the control sections did not. Within each section, the students were randomly divided into groups of three to four students. Each group has a name and an organizational structure, consisting of a CEO, a Financial Officer, an Operations Chief, and a Marketing Executive. A game-playing procedure manual was distributed at the beginning of the semester, detailing the responsibilities of the various officers and the format of an end-of-semester summary report. Three phases of the life cycle of a business were simulated: start-up, growth, and independence. The decisions to be made in each phase are shown in Exhibit 13–2.

The decisions made by each group (or company) were processed through Business Simulator, resulting in a set of operating results, including units sold, back orders, ending inventory, and market share, representing nine fiscal years. The performances of the different companies were evaluated based on the final outcome of the ninth year. Each student company was paired from another company from the same section. The pair competed against each other and against three companies played by the computer. All companies submitted their decisions on a predetermined day each week. The companies without CMC submitted their decisions on a piece of paper, while the companies using CMC announced their decisions in their group conference. The instructor ran the game and saved the results on a diskette available for the students to copy.

The students also had access to the results of all other companies for comparison and reference. The key results were recorded in a database so that the comparative results could be organized and published from time to time. This practice proved to be useful in maintaining interest and competitive spirit.

The companies with access to CMC were assigned a group conference to conduct the simulated business. Typical uses were the assignment of functional roles, discussion of the logistics and scheduling of game playing, formulation of general strategies of the business, and review of operational results. Each student company discussed the results in its private

---

EXHIBIT 13-2
Decision Phases in Business Simulator (R) Game

Phase I	Phase II	Phase III
Startup	Growth	Independence
Price	Price	Price
Advertising	Advertising	Advertising
Units purchased	Units purchased	Units produced
	Factory construction	Factory construction
	/expansion	/expansion
	Factory production	Factory production
	Long-term debt sold	Long-term debt sold
	Common stock issued	Common stock issued
		Sales force size
		Commisions paid
		% of sales on credit
		Research and
		development
		One-year loans
		Supplier payment period
		Common Dividend per
		share

---

conference to see whether the outcomes met expectations and to search for possible reasons for deviations.

All students with CMC also participated in two other conferences: the Student Center for social activities and the Managers' Corner for management related discussions.

Measuring Results with Business Simulator

The clearest indication that the Virtual Classroom improves student learning of managerial skills is if the companies run by students with the Virtual Classroom perform better than companies run by students without it. We defined:

Aggregate Performance Index = Profitability
+ ROA (Return on Assets)
+ ROE (Return on Equity)

as a composite index measure to rank the performance of a company.

HYPOTHESES

From the above description, it appears that the work load for both instructor and students would be overwhelming for a three credit non-major course. Whether or not such a work load would be accepted by students depends a great deal on the interest level of the participants. Therefore, the course teaching procedure had to be designed by incorporating many elements of interest wherever possible. The criteria of feasibility is twofold: (a) the level of mastery of management theory and concepts as compared to other sections of the same course taught in a conventional manner, and (b) students' acceptance. Hence, the first hypothesis, which is a special case of H1 for the earlier study:

H1b: Mastery of management theory and concepts in the experimental sections will be equal to or better than in the conventional sections.

By *experimental* sections we mean use of CMC/VC, a management game, and productivity software alone or combined. This hypothesis may be tested by comparing results of a common exam given to all sections of OS 471 during one of the semesters (Geithman & Slowinski, 1990).

An exploration of the usefulness of CMC as a communication medium shall be attempted in the following hypotheses:

H12: There will be increased *student interest/satisfaction* when a CMC is provided for organization simulation or role play.

This can be tested by examining the data measurements from treatments 2, 4, and 5 (with a CMC) against treatments 1 and 3 (without a CMC).

H13: There will be improved *game performance* when a CMC is provided for practicing managerial skills, particularly decision-making skills and information-processing skills.

This can be tested by comparing the game performance score between treatments 4 and 5 (with a CMC) against treatment 3 (without a CMC). Comparison can be made on objective performance measures resulting from skillful decision making and group collaboration.

Since CMC is a text-based system, it is natural to expect students to grow in writing ability. Therefore, we have the following hypothesis about treatments 2, 4, and 5 (with a CMC) vs. treatments 1 and 3 (without a CMC). It is a special case of the third hypothesis in the original study:

H3b: There will be an increase in *student written communication effectiveness* when a CMC is provided for practicing managerial skills, particularly decision-making skills and information-processing skills.

Support for this hypothesis may come from questionnaires, group game reports, or written comments made in the conferences.

Effects on Group Collaboration

One of the primary emphases of this research is to explore the degree of realization of "collaborative learning" when various computer-based technologies are used. Organization simulation is believed to be an important source of collaboration. However, additional technologies should have a significant impact on the level of collaboration. Thus we have a special case of H2.8:

H 2.8: There will be increased *collaboration in learning* in the experimental sections as compared to the conventional sections.

Here again, the "experimental sections" are those using CMC/VC, a management game and/or additional productivity tools, alone or combined.

Effects of Additional Productivity Software

Under the generic term *productivity software*, we include word processors, a spreadsheet and a database. Many brands and versions of productivity software on microcomputers are available. Students often use them for individual work. The data files resulting from the use of the productivity software are usually kept on an offline storage media. Even though EIES 2 is essentially a text-based system, a facility has been provided for binary file transfer among the CMC participants. In other words, any data files in any format can be sent and received among the Virtual Classroom members through the mail or conference structure.

In addition, the sections in this condition were taught how to use two new features of the Virtual Classroom on EIES 2, *Forms* and *Filters*. It was hypothesized that the addition of the use of these productivity-enhancing information-processing tools would further improve the results obtained by conducting the business simulation game within a Virtual Classroom environment. Specifically:

H14: There will be an improved *game performance* by providing additional information-processing tools.

H15: There will be an increased *student effort* as a result of providing additional productivity tools within the Virtual Classroom to aid the playing of the managerial game.

These hypotheses can be tested by comparing the game performance, the contents of the game report and the CMC activity logs for treatment 5 (with additional information-processing tools) against treatment 4 (without additional productivity tools).

Summary

For easy reference, we summarize the above hypotheses as a listing with abbreviated independent and dependent variables in Exhibit 13–3. The full study (Hsu, 1991) also includes hypotheses about the effects the management game, which have been omitted from this abbreviated account.

RESULTS

At the end of the Spring 1989 term, a common test for five sections of OS-471 was administered. One condition was the traditional classroom (three sections with a total of 73 students), another condition used was a telecourse with CMC/VC use in addition to video broadcasts (13 students), and a third condition was an experimental section of our treatment 3 (with a game but no CMC; 24 students). Test questions were of multiple-choice or true/false type. Geithman and Slowinski (1990) published comparative results of the test, which are reproduced here as Table 13.1.

Our experimental section was designated as "Virtual Lab" in the results shown in Table 13–1, even though CMC/VC was not used for this particular treatment 3 section, since it did have an organization simulation and a game. Table 13–3, below, shows that, for all four areas of knowledge covered by

---

EXHIBIT 13–3
Listing of Hypotheses

Hypothesis	Independent Variable	Dependent Variable
1B	Mode of delivery	Mastery of course information
3	Management game	Student interest/satisfaction
12	CMC	Student interest/satisfaction
13	CMC	Game performance
3B	CMC	Student written communication effectiveness
2.8	Mode of delivery	Collaboration in learning
14	Information processing tools	Game performance
15	Information processing tools	Student effort

TABLE 13-1
Summary of T-Tests of Student Results on Common Management Examination (Mean, Standard Deviation, and Levels of Significance), by Type of Instructional Mode and by Type of Question Asked.

Instructional Mode	Mean	Standard Deviation	T (Signif. Level)	Mean	Standard Deviation	T (Signif. Level)
	Questions on Leadership and Motivation			Question on Planning and Communication		
Traditional Class Students	10.00	2.92	1.63 (0.11)	8.60	2.30	2.11 (0.04)
X Virtual Lab	11.30	3.14		9.75	2.11	
Traditional Class Students	10.00	2.92	-2.45 (0.02)	8.60	2.30	-2.54 (0.02)
X Virtual Lab	12.30	3.04		10.54	2.47	
TeleCourse Students	12.30	3.04	-0.99 (0.33)	10.54	2.47	-0.97 (0.34)
X Virtual Lab Students	11.25	3.14		9.75	2.11	
	Questions on Coordination and Control			Questions on Organizational Structure		
Traditional Class Students	8.56	2.54	1.43 (0.16)	8.46	2.64	1.60 (0.12)
X Virtual Lab	9.46	2.48		9.5	2.53	
Traditional Class Students	8.56	2.54	-4.36 (0.0002)	8.46	2.64	-1.73 (0.10)
X Virtual Lab	11.31	1.84		10.23	3.44	
TeleCourse Students	11.31	1.84	-2.57 (0.02)	10.23	3.44	0.67 (0.51)
X Virtual Lab Students	9.46	2.48		9.50	2.64	

Source: Geithman and Slowinsky, 1990

the common exam, students in the two experimental modes outscored students in the conventional sections (though not all pairwise comparisons are statistically significant). Thus, H1b is supported by these data.

Management Game Performance

The results displayed in Table 13-2 are important because decision-making skill is measured objectively and quantitatively via the game performance. Their significance consists in the clear distinction among three different communication environments where the management game was played. Treatment 3 used the conventional environment of face-to-face meetings, telephone calls, and written communications such as memos. Treatment 4 used a CMC to provide continued, structured, and asynchronous communication facilities for discussion and decision making. Significant improvement in the performance was noted. Treatment 5 was similar to treatment 4 except that additional productivity software was provided to improve the business-related information processing, which was then shared thoroughly by the group members via CMC as an always present network. Here again significant improvement in the game performance was noted over treatment 4. All the component indices are taken directly from the financial scoreboard built into the Business Simulator game model.

The differences in management game performance among three treatments (3, 4, and 5) are all statistically significant at $p < .01$. The difference between treatments 3 and 4 support Hypothesis 13. The difference between treatments 4 and 5 support Hypothesis 14.

Table 13–3 lists the grades on the group game reports earned by different student companies under three different treatments. The grades

TABLE 13–2
Evaluation of Management Game Performance

Treatment 3: Game (No CMC)		Treatment 4: VC + Game		Treatment 5: VC + GAME + Software	
Company	Index	Company	Index	Company	Index
Bots 'R Us	33.215	FurureWare	59.875	TechTron	58.075
Robo–Tecknics	27.625	RoboTech	42.175	Innovations	95.425
Hysterical Corp.	27.85	Ma Chine	64.65	Cybornetic	92.875
Forte–Hildebrand	26.3	KJ&J	55.75	JESA Electronics	127.075
Robotron	43.875	Robots R Us	46.875	Tel Star	69.9
KST Technologies	41.6	Robbots	64.975	Techni–Maid	51.3
SWAT Engineering	39.225				
RJM Partnership	36.75				
Total	276.44	Total	334.3	Total	494.65
Average	34.555	Average	55.717	Average	82.44
F					14.04
P					0.000

TABLE 13-3
Comparison of Group Project Grades

Treatment 3: Game (No CMC)		Treatment 4: VC + Game		Treatment 5: VC + GAME + Software	
Company	Grade	Company	Grade	Company	Grade
Bots 'R Us	2.9	FurureWare	3.0	TechTron	3.0
Robo-Tecknics	2.1	RoboTech	3.0	Innovations	3.3
Hysterical Corp.	2.7	Ma Chine	2.7	Cybornetic	3.7
Forte-Hildebrand	2.0	KJ&J	2.3	JESA Electronics	2.7
Robotron	2.9	Robots R Us	3.3	Tel Star	3.7
KST Technologies	3.0	Robbots	2.7	Techni-Maid	2.3
SWAT Engineering	2.0				
RJM Partnership	2.0				
Total	19.6	Total	17.00	Total	18.70
Average	2.45	Average	2.83	Average	3.12
		F	3.63	P	0.049

for treatments 4 and 5 (with CMC) are higher than those for treatment 3 (no CMC) at $p < .05$. This is despite the fact that treatment 5 students had fewer years in college than the students in treatments 3 and 4 (a quirk, not a purposeful manipulation). Their higher achievement in the group project grades (written communication effectiveness) appears to be attributable to the provision of CMC. Thus, we have support for hypothesis 3b:

H3b: There will be an increase in *student written communication effectiveness* when a CMC is provided for practicing managerial skills, particularly decision-making skills and information-processing skills.

Virtual Classroom Support for the Business Simulation Game

Underlying the statistical differences in performance patterns are the ways in which the Virtual Classroom changed the process of communication within the companies, particularly in the sense of building a true collaborative effort among the "officers." A great deal of camaraderie as well as serious discussions developed in companies with access to the Virtual Classroom. As one of the questions on the final exam, the students were asked to list the names and nick names of the class members. The students who used the Virtual Classroom knew the names of their classmates 83% of the time, while the students without the VC scored only 67%. The students with the Virtual Classroom organized ski/skating trips and small parties, while nothing of the sort took place with the students without it. Both the Student Center Conference and the Managers' Corner Conference played important roles in developing this camaraderie.

One-third of the students who used the Virtual Classroom asked to remain on the conference for further socializing with the instructor and the students of the next semester, some of whom selected these particular sections as a result of recommendations from the veterans. More importantly, students with the Virtual Classroom clocked an average of 5 hours per week on one or another of the conferences outside of class time, while students without the VC met less than 1 hour per week outside of class. Perhaps the most interesting evidence obtained is a verbal report to the effect that some students participating in the experiment stuck together after the commencement ceremony. It is strongly contrasted with the usual phenomenon that the students usually stay with their family and relatives on such occasions.

Much of the discussion in the conferences served useful, real- life purposes as well, and provided examples of collaborative learning in dealing with managerial problems. A comparison of the American management style with the Japanese proved an inexhaustible source of discussion, while hot debate took place over the economic relationship between West and East Germany.

In the Manager's Corner conference, students discussed what to do about various manager/employee relationship problems. For example, what do you do if your boss does not seem to do any work some days, and this inhibits your own productivity? "WK" noted:

> My boss goofs off a lot since he became a partner in the design firm I work for. He also has a good sense of humor, so when he is goofing off I ask him 'How can I help You, Bob?' and he'll tell me he's not really doing anything and I'll tell him that it sounds good to me and I want to do my fair share. Something like this usually makes him self-conscious looking for something productive to do. I think most bosses got to be bosses by being responsible and capable (I said MOST O.K.?) and I think if you can find some good natured way to point out to them that their goofing off affects you, their sense of responsibility should take over without causing too much trouble.

In a situation where the boss is a female and the subordinates are males, role strains may be introduced because males are used to playing a dominant, and often sexually aggressive role, towards females. When the issue of sexual harassment was raised, "LC" made the following comments about this situation, representing one of the males' concerns:

> Boy, that's a tough one!!! If she gets the idea that I'm hitting on her, I would sit her down and try to explain to her in the most subtle way I know how that I really wasn't hitting on her and that I'm not the kind of person who uses relationships to get ahead in the business world. The problem with this is that some people are so sensitive that they might take offense to this as well!!! I know it sounds crazy, but did any of you guys ever have a woman get upset with you because you DIDN'T make a pass at them??? This has happened to me, and that is why I'm very careful how I act in these type of situations. If my female boss got mad at me, I would try to explain it to her without hurting her feelings. If she still got upset with me, then I really don't know what I would do. Somebody help!!!"

Discussion in the group business conferences was serious but of similarly high quality. OA's comment represents a typical entry:

> I agree with you about raising the price from $34 to $41. We don't have enough production to compete at a low price so we might as well make like Hewlett Packard. This will result in a lower market share but will maximize our profits until we are ready to expand. One suggestion: spend more on advertising. Instead of $500K maybe $525K. Our sales will be targeted to a higher income bracket which has not heard of us or has regarded our goods as lower quality because of the lower price range.

The groups with the Virtual Classroom also benefited from greater group coordination and continuity in the face of real-life disruptions. For example, OA, the CEO of FutureWave, disappeared for a time and abandoned his prerogative of finalizing business decisions. LC and GB used all three conferences to plead for OA's return by posting humorous comments: "Hey, OA, did you get stuck in traffic again. We missed you at the class today. We wanted to confer with you about the simulator but we will see you at another time. GB." "OA, First of all, I'm extremely gratified to hear that you are alive and well. I thought maybe you had been swallowed up by a garbage truck or something!!! Nice to hear from you!!! How come you weren't in class??? How come you don't talk to us anymore??? Do we smell??? Are we offensive??? C'mon, lets get together and talk about Year #4!!! GB and myself shared some thoughts this morning, but as our CEO we would like to get your thoughts on a plan of action. When you read this, answer me right away so we can get the ball rolling!!!" "OA the Toxic Avenger has 47 items waiting for him in Manager's Corner and 17 waiting for him in our Group Conference. I'm tellin' you, homeboy, The King is Dead!!! Long Live the King!!!" OA returned eventually to

FutureWave (not, however, as CEO). He participated actively in the game and shared the credit for the good performance of the organization. In fact, FutureWave was the top performer by all the objective measures.

JR, CEO of KJ&J, had a similar experience; however, he continued to maintain contact with his group through the Virtual Classroom. He was able to return to the game and resume his responsibilities as CEO. Both examples show that the Virtual Classroom provides critical support for students who have been temporarily distracted from their duties.

In contrast, the CEOs of Hysterical and RJM, both companies without the Virtual Classroom, also vanished from their posts. Neither returned for the duration of the semester.

Finally, the Virtual Classroom helped students prepare the end-of-semester summary report, as the groups that used the Virtual Classroom for the conduct of their business had the benefit of a complete record of the individual contributions of the group members. The preparation of the report was only a matter of editing the contents of the conference, while the groups without the benefit of the Virtual Classroom had to convene several meetings to assign the work and assemble the results.

STUDENT COLLABORATION

In addition to the qualitative evidence of extensive collaboration via the VC, the same collaboration index was used in this extended study as in the first stages, consisting of items from the postcourse questionnaire. The results for the individual items are displayed in Table 13–4. For all treatments using CMC, the mean responses indicated considerable "group" or "collaborative" learning, rather than students perceiving it as an individual learning experience. By combining the four items we produce a collaborative learning index ranging from 1 (low) to 6 (high). The difference in this collaboration index between treatments 3 (game only) vs. 4 and 5 is almost significant statistically. When comparing treatment 3 (game only) vs. 5 (game + VC + productivity tools), the difference is significant ($F = 4.43, p = .037$). This indicates the effect of a full-featured Virtual Classroom in providing opportunities for collaboration among students. Thus, we have some support for H 2.8:

H 2.8: There will be increased *collaboration in learning* in the experimental sections as compared to the conventional sections.

Student Interest/Satisfaction

The strongest evidence of increased student interest and satisfaction when the VC was used are spontaneous comments in conferences and

TABLE 13-4
Individual vs. Group Learning

Group Experience	Treatment	Individual experience 1	2	3	4	5	Group experience 6	Mean	SD
	3	12%	19%	6%	6%	44%	13%	3.9	1.7
	4	0%	0%	7%	14%	50%	29%	5.0	0.8
	5	0%	4%	4%	4%	46%	42%	5.2	1.0
Importance of Help	Treatment	Crucially Important 1	2	3	4	5	Useless or misleading	Mean	SD
	3	0%	38%	31%	13%	13%	5%	3.2	1.2
	4	29%	43%	21%	7%	0%	0%	2.1	0.9
	5	13%	54%	21%	4%	4%	4%	2.5	1.2
Cooperation	Treatment	Not co-operative 1	2	3	4	5	Extremely cooperative	Mean	SD
	3	0%	6%	6%	44%	44%	0%	4.3	0.8
	4	0%	0%	0%	14%	50%	36%	5.2	0.7
	5	0%	4%	8%	25%	42%	21%	4.7	1.0
Communication	Treatment	Never communicating 1	2	3	4	5	Constantly Communicating 6	Mean	SD
	3	5%	19%	13%	31%	19%	3%	3.8	1.0
	4	0%	0%	7%	7%	64%	22%	5.0	0.6
	5	0%	0%	4%	33%	54%	9%	4.7	0.9

Collaboration Index

Treatment	Collaboration Index	F	P
3: Game	4.06	2.82	0.062
4: VC + Game	4.94		
5: VC + Game + Software	4.74		

behavior. For example, the students from one simulated online "company" all got together after their commencement ceremony. That they would choose to spend their graduation day with the members of a former online class indicates that this course must have been very satisfying for them.

To obtain quantitative support for our hypothesis, we can look at comparative data from questionnaire items measuring different aspects of satisfaction. Two indexes which show differences are the Instructor Rating Index and the Computer Attitudes Index, as shown in Table 13-5.

The Instructor Rating Index ranged from 1 (best) to 5 (worst). All of the ratings were favorable, on the average, but there is a statistically significant difference, with those sections having both VC and the game most favorable towards the instructor.

The Computer Attitudes Index (from the postcourse questionnaire) ranged from 1 (low) to 7 (high). The mean responses are shown for all treatments except the conventional classroom, which did not incorporate computer use. There is a statistically significant increasing trend as VC and the game and productivity software were added to the course.

TABLE 13-5
Subjective Satisfaction Ratings

Treatment	Instructor Rating Index	Computer Attitudes Index
1: Conventional	1.945	–
2: VC	1.864	4.82
3: Game	1.564	4.97
4: VC + Game	1.313	5.08
5: VC + Game +Software	1.517	5.29
F	4.59	3.88
P	0.011	0.021

Thus, questionnaire data support H12: There will be increased student interest/satisfaction when a CMC is provided for organizational simulation or role play.

Student Effort

We theorize that students' willingness to spend more time in course-related activities is a positive indicator of their effort in learning. Three out of five treatments used CMC. A comparison of the CMC activity levels should provide a clear indication of students' effort.

Table 13-6 lists and compares the activity levels of the students under treatments 4 and 5. The activity levels are monitored in three ways: (a) the cumulative time in hours the student spent on the CMC system; (b) the number of items written, the items being either conference comments or private messages; and (c) the total number of lines of these comments or messages.

The students under treatment 5 spent 52% more time than those under treatment 4 and wrote 42% more items, containing 755 more lines. The difference is statistically significant at $p < .05$. Apparently, when the productivity software was provided, the students had a great deal more of business-related information processing to do and had a great deal more meaningful information to share with their colleagues. Consequently, they learned more by doing more. H15 is thus supported:

H15: There will be increased student effort when additional information-processing tools are provided in conjunction with a CMC.

As mentioned above, students in treatment 5 (CMC/VC + game + productivity software) had less years in college on the average (1.94–1.98

TABLE 13-6
Analysis of CMC Activities

Treatment 4: VC + Game			Treatment 5: VC + Game + Software		
Hours/Student	Items	Lines	Hours/Student	Items	Lines
Mean 23.8	88.6	842.6	36.09	125.52	1474.09
		F	14.82	3.93	4.67
		P	0.001	0.051	0.034

years vs. an overall average of 2.36 years). The higher level of CMC activity for the less mature students must mean a higher level of effort on their part.

Because of a large number of students involved in treatment 2 at different times, only average time online and average number of items entered are listed in Table 13–7. Also listed for comparison are the equivalent statistics collected from other nonmanagement courses using CMC/VC technology and Slowinski's OS 471 Management Practices course using cable television and CMC.

The course used in the case study, Management Practices, is the only required management course for the NJIT engineering students. Most engineering students expressed their disdain for social science and vowed to spend the minimum possible amount of time to pass the course. They were, at the start, unwilling to spend any time outside classes. The teaching method, using organization simulation, Virtual Classroom, and a management game, made the difference. It is also clear that the integration of PC-based software (the game and the additional software) enhance rather than detract from the use of the Virtual Classroom communication facilities.

TABLE 13–7
Summary and Comparison of CMC Activities

Treatment	2: VC	4: VC + Game	5: VC + Game + Software	Non-Management Courses Using CMC/VC	Distance Teaching Using Video and CMC
Average Hours Online per Student per Semester	17.70	23.80	36.09	16.00	12.20
Rank of the Above	3	2	1	4	5
Average Number of Items Written per Student per Semester	49.16	88.60	125.52	27.20	9.60
Rank of the Above	3	2	1	4	5

SUMMARY

The initial multicourse experimentation with the Virtual Classroom compared traditional classroom-based courses to VC based courses. The intensive experimentation with a single course which followed introduced two new innovations to the organizational simulation virtual "laboratory" to support a multimedia introductory course in management. The first was the incorporation of a PC-based game, the Business Simulator. This game produces measures of the overall performance of the simulated companies, which provides an objective basis for comparing the performance of student groups across different delivery modes which use the game. The second innovation was the integration of the use of PC-based productivity enhancement software, including a word processor, spreadsheet, and database. An additional methodological development was the use of group *game reports* which were graded on a standard basis across different treatments. Control conditions included four traditional classroom-based sections which used none of the innovations, and two classroom-based sections which used the Business Simulator game but had no access to the Virtual Classroom. Experimental conditions included five sections with access to the Virtual Classroom, but no game; one section with use of the Virtual Classroom in conjunction with the game; and two sections with use of the Virtual Classroom, the game, and the additional productivity tools.

The findings about the positive effects of ever increasing sophistication of the computer-based tools made available to the simulated student organizations as mechanisms for learning and practicing managerial skills included:

Collaboration: Providing the Virtual Classroom resulted in increased group cohesion and collaboration, as compared to the section which played the game without the Virtual Classroom support. The evidence for this is qualitative, including the content of the online discussions, the lesser likelihood that team members would permanently "disappear" in the middle of the semester and game, and expressed desire of many students to continue to participate in activities with their "company" members or with the game, even after the semester was over.

Game performance was significantly superior when both Virtual Classroom basic facilities and the advanced productivity tools were used to support the student companies playing the game.

Student activity and effort were greatest when the Virtual Classroom basic facilities, the advanced productivity tools, and the game were all provided.

The final group game reports were better for students who had access to the Virtual Classroom, and better still when the advanced productivity tools were added. The game report scores are a measure of the students' written communication skills.

This four-year field experiment, which extended the original experiment for the management course (using the same instructor, basic syllabus, and grading methods), demonstrates that "technology can make a difference" in motivating greater student effort and in the effectiveness of student learning. Those students who had access to the Virtual Classroom did better than those without. And those students who had access to additional software tools which were integrated into the "EIES 2," or second software version of the Virtual Classroom, did the best of all.

PART IV
VIRTUAL CLASSROOMS AND VIRTUAL UNIVERSITIES: PRESENT AND FUTURE

"As large as life,
And twice as natural"

– Lewis Carroll, *Through the Looking Glass*

CHAPTER 14
SUMMARY OF FINDINGS

> the release of productivity is the product
> of cooperatively organized intelligence.
>
> —(Dewey & Tufts, 1939, p. 446)

During an initial period of experimentation with the use of a Virtual Classroom, an extensive study compared the processes and outcomes, for a variety of courses, with those of traditional, classroom-based college courses. During the four subsequent years, there was intensive further development and study of its use in a smaller number of courses, particularly to support a Virtual Management Laboratory. These initial experiments are just the beginning of the possible applications. As the innovation spreads, there will be much more data, many more stories to tell.

As this final chapter was being drafted, for instance, Connected Education was just beginning its 1991 summer semester online. One of the courses which has been offered in the past, "Issues in International Telecommunications," was offered in yet another format, a kind of "virtual electronic academic three ring circus." Paul Levinson, founder and President of Connected Education, led a core conference on the topic. A Soviet scholar led another conference in the course, connecting directly from the Soviet Union. Harlan Cleveland, a former ambassador and syndicated columnist, led a third conference in the course. All three also participated in one another's conferences. Two of the student participants dialed in from former "satellite" countries "behind the iron curtain." Just as the Berlin Wall came tumbling down physically, the former manmade barriers to truly international courses and universities have collapsed.

Though the "same" course has been offered for several years, with the changing faculty teams and world situation, it is never really "the same" online. Each time a course is offered, the medium collects a unique set of instructors and students, who explore new issues from new points of view.

Several universities have installed versions of EIES 2 with Virtual Classroom enhancements on their own machines, and are planning to open their own "virtual university" programs. This includes an organization in Spain, where the interface has been translated into Spanish. Because of the distributed architecture of the system, courses in conferences hosted at various locations can be "shared" with other EIES 2 locations. Some very large and diverse student bodies can be expected to grow and to work together in a very multicultural educational environment through these systems.

Eventually, the very nature of the *university* as we know it will change. Before turning to speculations about the future, however, let us summarize the findings and conclusions that emerge from the completed studies that have been presented in this book.

THE QUASI-EXPERIMENTAL FIELD TRIALS: SUMMARY OF FINDINGS

The first extensive experimentation with the Virtual Classroom involved the comparison of a large number of courses that used this medium of communication. For some of the courses, there was a "matched" section of the same course offered by the same instructor in a traditional classroom and using the Virtual Classroom, as the sole means of delivery or in combination with a reduced number of face-to-face meetings. For other courses, there was no "match," and the comparison was subjectively made by the students and instructors to previous, traditional courses.

Despite a far-from-perfect implementation, the results of this field trial were generally positive, in terms of supporting the conclusion that the Virtual Classroom mode of delivery can increase access to and the effectiveness of college-level education.

This was followed by continued use in "mixed media" courses, including a second quasi-experimental field research design, focusing on different modes of delivery of a management course. The following review of hypotheses integrates findings from the various studies or phases of the project, and serves as a summary of what we know about the Virtual Classroom in its current form of implementation.

Originally, there was an hypothesis that the mixed mode results would not simply represent an "average" of the VC and TC modes, but might have some unique advantages and disadvantages. In the following summary, results related to this speculation are included in reviewing each of the other hypotheses.

H1: Mastery of course material in the Virtual Classroom will be equal or superior to that in the traditional classroom.

Finding: Supported. For the initial quasi-experimental design comparing five matched courses, VC final grades were significantly better for one course (Computer Science) and no different for the other courses. In a subsequent study of a management course, students in a mixed video/VC section scored significantly better on a common final examination than students in traditional sections.

H2: VC students will report higher subjective satisfaction with the VC than the TC on a number of dimensions.

Findings:

2.1. *Convenient access* to educational experiences (supported).

2.2. Improved *access* to their *professor* (supported).

2.3. Increased *participation* in a course (supported).

2.4. Improved ability to apply the material of the course in new contexts and *express* their own independent *ideas* relating to the material.

Finding: Questionnaire data showed that increased confidence in expressing ideas was most likely to occur in the mixed modes courses. Qualitative judgments by faculty are that this is generally characteristic of VC courses.

2.5. Increased level of *interest* and involvement in the subject matter, which may carry beyond the end of the course.

Finding: This was course dependent. Though the averages for measures of increased interest are higher for both the VC and Mixed modes, the overall scores are not significantly different. Interest Index scores were highest for the VC mode at NJIT and for the Mixed mode courses at Upsala.

2.6. Improved ability to *synthesize* or "see connection among diverse ideas and information."

Finding: No significant differences overall in scores for items which formed this index from the postcourse questionnaire; mode interacts with course. However, instructors report observing improved ability of students to synthesize diverse information and ideas and deal with complex issues.

2.7. *Computer comfort*–improved attitudes toward the use of computers and greater knowledge of the use of computers (supported).

2.8. Improved ability to communicate with and cooperate with other students in doing classwork (Group *collaboration* Skills).

Findings: Mixed and course dependent. Though 47% of all students in VC and Mixed modes courses felt that they had communicated more with other students than in traditional courses, 33% disagreed. The extent of collaborative learning was highest in the Mixed-mode courses.

2.9. Improved overall *quality*, whereby the student assesses the experience as being "better" than the TC in some way, involving learning more on the whole or getting more out of the course (supported).

Although the "average" results supported most of the above predictions, there was a great deal of variation, particularly among courses. Generally, whether or not the above outcomes occurred was dependent more on variations among courses than on variations among modes of delivery. The totally online upper level courses at NJIT, the courses offered to remote students, and the mixed mode courses were most likely to result in student perceptions of the virtual classroom being "better" in any of these senses.

H3: The VC will lead to in improvement in student writing.

Findings: The hypothesis that writing scores would improve more for Upsala students in a writing course with access to the VC than for students in similar courses who did not use the system, was not supported. This may be because the holistic measure used was not reliable or detailed enough. It showed no changes for students in writing courses in either the face-to-face or partially online modes.

In the subsequent quasi-experimental study of students in different modes of delivery of a management course, all groups that played a management game had a final assignment to produce a group report. The grades assigned by outside judges were significantly better for those who used the VC.

A case study of an online writing workshop at the graduate level (Rosenthal, 1991) concluded that the VC provided a supportive environment for collaborative writing.

Thus, the VC appears promising as an educational environment for encouraging more writing and better writing skills, particularly for group or collaborative writing projects. However, more research is needed in order to delineate its advantages and disadvantages in improving writing skills.

H4: Those students who experience "group learning" in the virtual classroom are most likely to judge the outcomes of online courses to be superior to the outcomes of traditional courses.

Finding: Supported by both correlational analysis of survey data and qualitative data from individual interviews. Those students who experienced high levels of communication with other students and with their professor (who participated in a "group learning" approach to their coursework) were most likely to judge the outcomes of VC courses to be superior to those of traditionally delivered courses.

H5: High ability students will report more positive outcomes than low ability students.
Finding: Supported for Math SAT scores. Results for Verbal SAT scores much more mixed and inconsistent. However, even students with the lowest SAT scores were able to achieve passing grades, if they participated regularly.

H6: Students with more positive precourse attitudes towards computers in general and towards the specific system to be used will be more likely to participate actively online and to perceive greater benefits from the VC mode (supported).

H7: Students with a greater *Sphere of Control* on both the personal and the interpersonal levels will be more likely to regularly and actively participate online and to perceive greater benefits from the VC mode.
Finding: Very weak support in terms of correlations with Sphere of Control indices from survey data. However, qualitative interview data indicate that inability to regularly devote time to online activities, to "make themselves" participate regularly when there is no externally imposed schedule of class meetings, was a common characteristic of students for whom VC outcomes were relatively poor.

H8: There will be significant differences in process and outcome among courses, when mode of delivery is controlled.
Finding: Strongly supported. Course is a much stronger source of variance in outcomes than is Mode.

H9: Outcomes for the second offering of a VC course by an instructor will be significantly better than those for the first attempt at teaching online.
Findings: Although there was some tendency for this to be true, results were not consistently better on all measures for all second repetitions. Other factors, such as lower levels of skill or motivation among the students, may come into play.

Some courses may not be suited to this mode, and a second repetition of the totally online mode of delivery would not improve matters. The Introductory Sociology instructor came to this conclusion, as did the instructor for the required freshman-level course in Statistics at Upsala. Both felt that many of the freshmen, at least in the "computer-poor"

Upsala environment, lacked the skills and the self-discipline to benefit from a totally online course. However, both instructors felt that the mixed-modes method of delivery could be superior, especially for upper level courses that examine a small number of topics in depth.

H10: There will be significant differences among organizations in the effectiveness of their implementation of the Virtual Classroom. (Tested by comparing NJIT-based courses to Upsala courses using the same technology and measuring instruments).
Finding: Supported. Results were better at NJIT for the totally online courses.

The most important reason for the better results at Upsala is probably differences in equipment access provided to students. However, there are other differences confounded with *school* which might have produced the significant differences in outcomes. The totally online Upsala courses were both at the freshman level, while the totally online NJIT courses were at the sophomore level or higher. Freshmen often lack the motivation and study skills necessary to do well in an online course with no specific hours when it "meets." In addition, as a "computer-intensive" university, NJIT's faculty was more comfortable with computers to begin with. This could have improved their effectiveness as teachers via computer-mediated communication.

In the future, almost all colleges will provide adequate computer access to their students, and almost all instructors will have become computer literate, especially as the computers themselves become more "literate" in terms of ease of use. Thus, future results are likely to be more similar to those for NJIT than those for Upsala. However, it is likely to remain true that students who lack the self-discipline to work regularly on a course even though it does not have regular hours of meeting times, will not be good candidates for distance education courses.

SOFTWARE ELABORATION AND INTENSIVE EXPERIMENTATION

Though the findings of the original field experiment were promising, they left many questions unanswered, including:

- So much of the variance was due to differences among courses. Would the favorable findings for VC hold up if the experiment were repeated in the form of multiple replications in various modes for a single course, with the same instructor and basic syllabus?

- The tendency for instructors to curve final course grades within a section may have created the general finding of "no difference" in grades among sections of a course using different communication modes. The students told us that they learned more and that the Virtual Classroom is a "better" mode of communication than the traditional classroom. Couldn't we find an objective measure of student skills and knowledge acquired during a course, which would show definite differences in mastery associated with different modes of course delivery?

- Are the "advanced features" of a fully developed Virtual Classroom truly beneficial, or could you obtain similar results using less special features, and thus use almost any conferencing system? Moreover, how much of the results are due to "collaborative learning?" Couldn't you obtain the same results without any technology at all, by having teams of students engage in collaborative learning assignments without a conferencing system to support them?

The course selected for this further experimentation was Management Practices, a one-semester introduction to management. A total of 14 sections of this course were taught by the same instructor, Enrico Hsu, over a period of four years. All sections had the same basic syllabus and teaching technique, an organizational simulation in which groups of students form a simulated startup company and plan and market a hypothetical product. They learn how to be managers by practicing all of the steps necessary to organize a company and compete in the marketplace. Some sections undertook the organizational simulation in a traditional classroom. Some had the Virtual Classroom to support the communication and decision making among the organizational members. Then a second innovation was introduced: the integration of a PC-based management game, Business Simulator, which produces objective results in the form of indices of the performance of the simulated organizations, such as profitability and return on investment. There were no notations in any registration material about the mode in which a particular section would be delivered, in order to prevent a self-selection effect.

As part of the software evolution of the Virtual Classroom, the second version of the system, on EIES 2, allowed the attachment of binary files to any item. This means that, if students have the same PC-based programs, they can pass around the files produced by these programs, even though they are only machine readable and would look like nonsense if you tried to print them out as straight text. This made it easy to integrate the use of the Business Simulator game into the online sections of the course. In addition, some more advanced features, such as *forms* and *filters*, were added to the EIES 2 version of the software. As a final experimental version of the management course, two sections were taught using all available productivity enhancing tools available through a combination of the central software and PC software used by all students. The latter included a common word processing program, spreadsheet, and database.

The results, which are presented in detail in Chapter 13, supported the following hypotheses:

H 12: There will be increased student interest/satisfaction when a CMC is provided to support simulation or role play.

H 13: There will be improved game performance, when a CMC is provided for practicing managerial skills. (Note: Game scores are a measure of students' decision making and information synthesis skills.)

H 14: There will be improved game performance when additional information processing tools are provided in conjunction with a CMC.

H 15: There will be increased student effort when additional information-processing tools are proved in conjunction with a CMC.

Thus, the breadth of the original experiment is methodologically balanced by the greater depth of the second experiment. Both studies, in different ways, support the viability of the Virtual Classroom as a mode of course delivery.

SUPPORT FOR CONTINGENCY THEORY

In many cases, results of the quantitative analyses are inconclusive in determining which is "better," the TC or modes employing the VC. The overall answer is, "it depends." Results are superior in the VC for well-motivated and well-prepared students who have adequate access to the necessary equipment and who take advantage of the opportunities provided for increased interaction with their professor and with other students, and for active participation in a course. Students lacking the necessary basic skills and self-discipline may do better in a traditionally delivered course. Whether or not the VC mode is "better" also depends crucially on the extent to which the instructor is able to build and sustain a cooperative, collaborative learning group; it takes new types of skills to teach in this new way.

We did see that there are significant differences among courses in grade distributions, and in all other outcome measures, including the "VC OVERALL" index. Underlying these differences among courses are differences in the number and types of online activities required or facilitated by the instructor, and in the frequency and style of online interaction between the instructor and the students. Probably the single most important behavioral practice which produces relatively good results in online courses is the timely and "personal" (in tone) response by instructors to questions and contributions of students online.

DISCUSSION OF FINDINGS

The Virtual Classroom is a viable mode for delivery of college-level courses. However, there is much to be learned about the software, teaching techniques, and contingencies which optimize outcomes for this use of interactive computer systems. For example, though most students and teachers found the special software developed to be useful, there are many improvements to be made in its functionality and usability. We have continued the process of iterative changes in the software, based on user feedback, while implementing the Virtual Classroom features as part of a new EIES 2.

Informally, we have experimented with the limits on class size and the relationship between class size and the need for special software. The medium is a "natural" for small (10–15 students) online seminars involving discussion and one or two long papers or presentations by students. For this liberal-arts small-group type of application, software such as the branch activities and the gradebook is not necessary: Everything can be handled manually by the instructor. However, as class size and number of assignments and the technical nature of the material being taught increase, the special software enhancements such as the branch activities and the integration of graphics become necessary in order for the instructor and students to be able to handle the communications load.

With the existing software, we have successfully handled joint sections with approximately 50 students, in the Virtual Classroom environment. However, when we offered a triple section with 96 students online, the communication overload became unmanageable, even with the software enhancements we have thus far designed and implemented.

Another area for further research is mixed media courses, which combine Virtual Classroom with modes other than face-to-face meetings, such as videotapes, audio elements, or PC-based software. It may be that an optimal mode of delivery for many distance-education courses is the use of videotapes or video disks for lecture-type material, with the VC and PC based tools such as games or spreadsheets, as appropriate, for discussion and assignments and the building of a supportive learning community.

CHAPTER 15
LEARNING WITHOUT LIMITS

INHABITED GARDEN
The world is so empty
If one thinks only of
mountains, rivers, and cities;
But to know someone
who thinks and feels with us,
and who, though distant
is close to us in spirit,
This makes the earth
for us
an inhabited Garden

—Goethe

The Virtual Classroom is an environment that facilitates collaborative learning—among students, between students and instructors, among teachers, and between a class and wider academic and nonacademic communities. It also supports independent learning and generative, active learning techniques that are self-paced by each participant. For distance education students, the increased ability to be in constant communication with other learners is obvious. But even for campus-based courses, the technology provides a means for a rich, collaborative learning environment which exceeds the traditional classroom in its ability to "connect" students and course materials on a round-the-clock basis.

MODES OF USE OF THE VIRTUAL CLASSROOM

There are several modes of employment of the Virtual Classroom. It can be used in a *mixed modes* manner on a local campus, to support a quarter to three quarters of the coursework for classes that also have some face-to-face meetings. This adjunct or mixed mode seems appropriate for a wide range of courses, including lower level courses. It can be used to deliver totally online courses, to remote or distance education students and/or students who are taking other courses at a campus in a traditional classroom. For totally online courses, it is recommended that the material be at a sophomore or higher level, or else that students be screened very carefully, to advise those with poor study skills against an introductory course offered online.

In addition, VC can be used in *multimedia* distance education courses, combined with video and/or audio graphical conferencing. For example, at the current time, it is being used in several courses at NJIT that are offered either via broadcast, videotape, or satellite. The broadcast courses use standard public television courses, such as "Discovering Psychology," produced by PBS, in conjunction with VC for interaction among the dispersed class members. The satellite-delivered courses are offered via the National Technological University. One section meets at NJIT, in the "candid classroom," where it is being broadcast to students enrolled in a remote section, either through NTU, or carried to small groups of students on remote campuses of NJIT, through special lines. Thus, the whole class watches the real-time lecture at once, though some are on-campus and some are remote. The Virtual Classroom is used for all assignments and additional discussions, among the remote and on-campus students.

VC can also be used, very fruitfully, for remote education at the graduate level, or for continuing professional education of employees within organizations. Though not the purview of this project, the application area of continuing professional education may be the biggest market for Virtual Classroom in the long run. Such courses typically enroll mature, motivated students; focus on a few related topics; and have students for whom convenience of access would be very important.

The 2-year program of the Western Behavioral Sciences Institute provided one model of the use of the VC for executive education. There were four 6-month terms, and at the beginning of each term there was a 1-week residential seminar in La Jolla. Each term was divided into month-long seminars on specific topics, while a number of conferences and activities (such as small informal discussions groups of about 10) were continuous. At the end of the 2-year program, about three-quarters of the participants elected to remain in the network as alumni Fellows. The WBSI president, Richard Farson (1987) notes the following major advantages of online education:

> A program of depth and intensity, without removing the executive from his job for extended periods of time . . .

The network permits the executive to form a genuine learning community on a relatively permanent basis, to sustain them throughout their careers.

Certainly, one aspect of the Connect-Ed and WBSI programs which should be emulated in future projects is that students take more than a single course online. Just as the instructors tended to improve their ability to work in this new environment with repetition, so it may be expected that students can improve their ability to use the technology effectively on the basis of experience.

Computer-intensive classrooms, with a PC for every student, can be used to support collaborative learning in a same place/same time format. Since the machines are connected on a high bandwidth LAN and are all of the same type, students can create, use, and exchange audio and video/graphics elements as well as text, without difficulty. Alavi (1991) reports good results using such a classroom for teaching MBA students using team strategies. The students have to be coaxed to leave when the class time is over. They would like to be able to continue their team projects on an anywhere/anytime basis. In the next few decades, we will see changes that will make this possible, such as fiber optic networks that span the globe, standardization of protocols for digitized audio and video components of communications, and decreases in price that will make multimedia work stations affordable for students. This will open the Virtual Classroom for support of courses that require multimedia formats to adequately support communication.

CURRENT AND FUTURE DEVELOPMENTS

With the increasing power of PCs and the extension of digital networks around the globe, along with further developments in areas of Computer Science, such as Artificial Intelligence and Expert Systems, we will see more and more "intelligent" applications of computers in teaching, combined with CMC. One example of the type of program which will become common in the decades ahead is a system called *Ceilidh* (which stands for Computer Environment for Interactive Learning in Diverse Habitats), developed at the University of Nottingham in the UK, for supporting the teaching of programming (Benford, Burke, & Foxley, 1992; Zin & Foxley, 1991).

The core of the system is an online facility for submitting coursework in the form of programming assignments, which are automatically graded on the basis of a number of sophisticated metrics that assess the quality of the submitted work. Among the functions provided are the ability to edit, compile, and run programs, using test data provided. The system also includes the ability to communicate with the instructor or tutors and to access course notes and model solutions (after the due date for the assignment), as well as a number of tracking facilities for use by the instructor and tutors. Of particular interest is the ability for the instructor to ask for an automatic analysis of the probability of existence of plagiarism; this routine checks for identical or very similar submissions by different students. Designed for use in very large sections of hundreds of students, the automatic and immediate grading can be quite a boon for the instructor, which more than balances out the considerable effort needed to create the model solution and metrics for assessment of each submitted solution. The system makes it likely that students in large sections will have the opportunity for more "hands-on" exercises and problems than would be likely if everything had to be hand graded, and in addtion, the system gives the student immediate feedback. As implemented at Nottingham, the student is permitted to resubmit work after a short period, based on the feedback received, and thus improve the quality of the solution to the problem presented.

In the automatic assessment metrics, those used for courses in C + + and UNIX™ include dynamic correctness (which tests the program against several files of test data to find any errors), dynamic efficiency, typographic analysis, complexity analysis and structural weakness. The assessment metrics and test data and assignments are supplied by the instructor, who also decides the weights to be assigned to each of the quality metrics in computing an overall grade. Though designed originally for programming courses, systems such as this can be used for any course in which many problems are given that have "correct" answers, or solutions whose quality can be determined according to known parameters. This would include courses in such areas as Mathematics, Physics, and Engineering.

Similar to the experiences with the Virtual Classroom, it is reported that there is actually MORE interaction between student and instructor online, than in traditional courses (personal interview with Eric Foxley). Much of this takes the form of messages sent during and after working on an assignment, including many messages which argue for the superiority of the solution generated by a student over the "model" solution; sometimes this is indeed the case, and the instructor substitutes or adds the new "model solution" for availability to others.

Another development of great import is the tying together of the world's computerized information resources, and their accessibility to students and instructors through such networks as Internet, which links most colleges and universities. This means that students can access the equivalent of the world's libraries of information in computerized form, in doing research for papers or projects. In order to make the wealth of information navigable, it is being organized in many cases into a "Hypertext" format. An example of such a system is the "World Wide Web," which is now incorporated as part of the facilities of the Virtual Classroom on EIES2. This provides access to the Internet gopher world wide information services, including the ability to search databases on many campuses connected to the Internet.

In addition, problems are being solved for representing non-English characters. For example, a new shareware program call Real Accents! brings foreign language support to networks (Goldfield, 1991). This will help to open the technology to participation by students who do not read and write in English.

LEARNING WITHOUT LIMITS

The field trials described in this book have been at the university level. However, CMC technology can and is being used at the K-12 level as well. Here it can have revolutionary impacts on the nature of education, if its potential to remove many current limits on educational delivery are realized.

We have been involved with the Union township school district in New Jersey in proposing a large-scale effort to change the school system through the use of computer technology, including the Virtual Classroom. This proposal is briefly described here because it indicates the way in which the technology may be used to "break the mold" of schools as we know them. Similar efforts are occuring in many school districts in the United States.

The long-term objective of the Union Township effort is the establishment of a "Virtual School System." The justification is not the fact that modern computer and communications technology make this possible with off-the-shelf technology, but that it provides the opportunity for "freedom for learning." The intent is to free the student, the teacher, and the community from any physical or mental constraints that would inhibit the potential of any member of the learning community within a total school system.

The physical reality of our proposed effort is the introduction of a modern computer-communications network for learning within the Township and the provision of portable computers to every student and teacher. This network or "Virtual School" will be available and operative 24 hours a day, 7 days a week. It will reach out to encompass the 6,000 public school students in the K-12 range and the students in the private schools within the township. It will also encompass all the other auxiliary organizations and services that support the learning process (e.g., public libraries, the

PTA and the family, learning clubs, etc.). It is intended to support the total community and to be open to any community members and organizations that wish to support the educational process.

The overriding goal is the provision of "freedom for the learner," whether that be the student, the teacher, or the family unit. This is based upon the reality that the current educational process in the U.S. suffers from severe constraints and limitations on the use and employment of effective educational processes.

The student is constrained by:

Lack of tailored individualized instruction that matches his or her needs as an individual.

Lack of suitable peer groups for collaborative learning because of the way current classes are formed.

The lack of suitable learning facilities outside of the times that the physical school plant is available.

The inability to learn at his or her own pace and match learning resources to needs and interests.

A resulting lack of enjoyment of and enthusiasm for the learning process

Teachers are constrained by:

The rigidities of the school year calendar, the "school day," and organization of learners by "grade" or chronological age rather than their ability levels in specific subjects.

A lack of adequate continuing peer groups within the specific learning areas fow which they are responsible.

An overburden of administrative and noninstructional oriented tasks.

A lack of learning opportunities to advance their skills consistent with realistic constraints on time and resources

The inability to get help when he it is needed.

The lack of time for real instructional activities.

The community is constrained by:

The lack of coincidental time for improved communications among participants in the learning community.

The inability of the family unit to undertake real involvement in the learning process.

The lack of coordination ability to be able to apply available resources in the most productive manner possible.

There is no lack of improved instructional methods and methodology. Given enthusiastic, well-trained educators, and an effective environment for learning, major improvements are possible; this has been demonstrated by isolated instances of excellence both in the United States and abroad. Methods such as *collaborative learning, generative learning, active learning,* and *parallel learning* are all significant enhancements if they are applied correctly. A learning network, based upon modern computer communications technology, provides the opportunity to incorporate all these approaches as the toolkit available to the teachers to be applied as appropriate to the learning situation. A learning network would employ electronic mail communication worldwide, computer conferencing with Virtual Classroom enhancements, and access to host computers with all possible resources such as CAI. Some examples of the ways these communication and computer facilities can be employed are:

Students may use conferencing to form peer learning groups to engage in collaborative learning at any time or place of their individual choosing.

Teachers may easily deal with facilitating multiple small groups of learners by being able to track student peer group discussions in separate conferences at a time convenient to them.

Teachers can facilitate and encourage generative type group student projects within these network-based learning groups.

Students may take advantage of network resources to explore areas of interest or gain individual help and tutoring.

Community and family members who wish to offer services for tutoring and facilitating learning clubs can do so at times convenient for them.

Teachers may engage in their own peer exchange conferences to exchange lore and experiences on techniques and methods.

Educators from anywhere in the country can participate electronically in providing seminars for other teachers in methods and techniques they have mastered.

Modern CAI packages can be available any time of the day or night for students.

Taken together, the components of a community Learning Network can implement a full program of Learning Without Limits, whereby each student can progress through each course according to his or her level of ability and motivation. Learning can occur around the clock and throughout the year. Opportunities to take advanced placement courses, college courses for credit, vocational training, or to "graduate early" will be introduced at the upper levels. . . . And of course, the same aspects of "learning without limits" that we have described as possible on the K-12 level, apply to the use of the Virtual Classroom and related computer-based technologies at any level, to support lifelong learning.

The integration of the physical school system with the virtual school system and the effective utilization of both components is going to require many significant changes to current practices. Learning is now a 24-hour activity. Teachers will be encouraged to be able to work from home as well as at school. Learning will be available year round for those students who desire it. The very nature of a teacher's job as rather rigorously defined today by administrative practices and union agreements is going to evolve along very different lines.

There is not a high probability that this project will be funded at the current time. It is probably "too revolutionary" and too costly. However, something like this surely will exist sometime in the 21st century. Clearly, to realize the potentials that the technology of Learning Network offers, the critical problems are going to be those of introducing change to the existing social and organizational system.

VIRTUAL UNIVERSITIES

The results of this comprehensive case study indicate that the Virtual Classroom is an exciting new option for enhancing education in the 21st century. The technology will continue to improve. The new systems make it possible to integrate audio and video components with text-based items, though it may be the middle of the next century before these conditions to support a multimedia, asynchronous Virtual Classroom are met throughout the developed world, let alone in less developed countries. However, the technology which exists today is completely adequate. Full-motion video can be delivered separately via broadcast or videotapes, and audio components can be delivered via audio conferencing or audio tapes.

The most important technological advance, in the author's opinion, will be a decrease in the price of existing personal computers with high resolution screens. Small screens with poor resolution do not provide a large enough "window" to easily write or read large documents. For instance, Hansen and Hass (1988) compared reading and writing performance of students using paper, an ordinary personal computer with a small screen and a dark background, and a work station with a large screen, high resolution, windowing, and black on white print. Reading from computer screens takes about 25% longer on the average than reading from paper—that is why students in the Virtual Classroom prefer to download and print large items. The overall quality of what students wrote was poorer on a personal computer than on paper, but better with a work station than with either a PC or paper as the mode of composition.

Thus, as work stations come down in price over the next 2 to 3 years, this will be an important advance in the ability of students to do their work online.

The most important changes over the next decade or two will not be in technological advances, but in institutional change. The university has been among the most conservative of institutions . . . hundreds of them have existed, practically unchanged, since the middle ages. Each has been like a feudal empire, sufficient unto itself, interacting with other universities mainly on football fields and basketball courts, the modern equivalent of medieval jousting tournaments. This will change. The thousands of small to middle-sized colleges and universities will need to form consortia to offer courses via distance media, or they will lose out in the competition for students.

We have seen that it is exceptionally easy to offer "joint courses" in the Virtual Classroom, taught by instructors from the same or different universities. It is also easy to put together a variety of course offerings, with the faculty drawn from wherever they may be located. What we are going to see in the future are more Virtual Universities like the National Technological University. It has no faculty or campus of its own. Instead, it puts together a rich offering of courses drawn from many different institutions. It maintains quality control and negotiates the agreements whereby the institutions accept one another's courses for credit.

There will be many more arrangements like this in the future, and they will mean greater choice and higher quality courses for students, no matter where they may be living and how far away they are from a good college campus. The meaning of the "university" will change, and the idea of a "campus" as we know it may disappear. It is now possible to run a university from a closet . . . a very large walk-in closet to hold all the equipment, to be sure.

QUALITATIVE OUTCOMES AND OVERALL CONCLUSIONS

The verdict on the Virtual Classroom comes down, in the end, to the qualitative reactions of students and instructors who were stimulated by this new type of learning environment.

The VC is not without its disadvantages, and it is not the preferred mode for all students (let alone all faculty). Students (and faculty) report that they have to spend more time on a course taught in this mode than they do on traditional courses. Students also find it more demanding in general, since they are asked to play an active part in the work of the class on a daily basis, rather than just passively taking notes once or twice a week. For students who want to do as little work as possible for a course, this mode of learning may be considered a burden rather than an opportunity. The VC is also not recommended for students who are deficient in basic reading, writing, and computational skills.

We have noted that increased interaction with the professor and with other students is the key to superior results in the Virtual Classroom. Thus, the selection and orientation of instructors who can orchestrate such collaborative learning environments becomes the key to success.

Faculty Perspectives

You are going to have to work harder in teaching a course online, at least the first time. Even after reading the advice and guidelines included here, to a certain extent, you can only learn to teach online by doing it. Being a "virtual professor" is a little bit like parenthood. You are "on duty" all the time, and there seems to be no end to the demands on your time and energy. For instance, as I write this, it is 11 o'clock at night, and I just got a frantic message from a student who is halfway through an assignment and needs help. On the other hand, it is also like parenthood in the sense that the rewards are similar. You can have a better opportunity to help minds and skills to grow, and to establish close "mentoring" relationships with many of your students.

One aspect of the Virtual Classroom experience that is not touched on in the individual course reports is that the technology can also support the growth of collegial relationships among faculty members who are working together in teaching through this medium, as described in the previous chapter. During this experiment, we had a conference where teachers brought their problems and observations and offered advice and solutions to one another. Though we met together face-to-face only twice during the academic year, a supportive community emerged, marked by cooperation and sharing of problems and solutions. We "sat in" on one another's online classes, exchanged many private messages, and helped one another in dealing with difficult or problematical issues. Both WBSI and the Connected Education faculties also have their electronic "teachers' lounges." They are vital to increasing the enjoyability and effectiveness of the process of learning to teach online.

"Would I do it again?" asks Kendy Rudy. "Yes," she answers. "All in all, the experience was positive . . . I am teaching the same course this semester without EIES assignments; I find that something has been lost in communication with and between students. Given a choice, I'd keep the EIES system permanently."

Enrico Hsu observes:

> The group dynamics made the class an extremely cohesive learning group. Through constant guidance in an informal manner, I was able to get psycho-

logically close to the students. In contrast to the other section of OS-471 that I taught without the benefit of EIES, "virtual lab" has enabled the students to communicate much more freely and with "rich" content.

Robert Meinke concluded that a totally online course in Introduction to Sociology is not appropriate at Upsala, due to the characteristics of the course (an introductory survey of many topics), of the freshmen students who lacked self-discipline and good reading and writing skills, and of the inadequate equipment situation at Upsala. However, he concludes that:

> While I have taken a strong stand against completely converting introductory social science courses to online courses, I am strongly in favor of using online assignments and discussions as supplements in such courses. They have the ability to stimulate creative in-depth exploration of major themes, and they introduce novelty and excitement to the course.

Would it be a good medium for you? Read the full accounts (in Appendix III) of the faculty members who have taught this way carefully and decide for yourself. If you want a technology that will minimize the time and effort you spend on teaching so that you can spend more time on activities you like better, the answer is no. If you want something that has the potential to increase your effectiveness as a teacher, the answer is yes.

Student Perspectives

Below is the text of a message from a student in the management laboratory, sent after the course was officially over:

> Roxanne, I just completed Enrico's 471 class here on EIES. I felt that I should give you what I feel about the class and what it has done. It was the most stimulating, fascinating, educational and social experience I have ever had! From the subject itself to how it was presented to the activity and enthusiasm of this class, it was beyond words. I feel that the method of how it was presented here, on the system, had more than a great deal to do with it. It also had to do with Enrico's abilities as well as a bunch of very energetic people who were able to excel in his or her own way through the extended class on the system.
>
> A lot of what happened, the massive activity in the conferences, the massive amount of time spent online by each participant, and the new, good and lasting friendships that developed (AND THERE ARE A LOT OF THOSE) will never be given justice in whatever the results of this project are, but they are what was really meaningful in this course. A great deal of learning was accomplished concerning the topic and a lot of other ideas. Learning that would not have been so great and varied as it was (without the system).

I am not the only person who feels this way; its shared by most of the class. . . .

I have never dreaded so much the end of a semester and I hope that the group that formed and its cohesiveness that was so strong will continue afterwards. I don't want to belabor the point, but do want to emphasize what a great thing it was and hope to see it continue for a long time to come because the quality of the educational experience is greatly increased not only for the subject matter, but on a social level as well.

Thanks for giving us this chance.

Essentially, that's what the Virtual Classroom software provides – a chance to participate in a different kind of learning experience, one based on an active learning community working together to explore the subject area of a course. Note that the management laboratory was referred to above as "officially" over. Several months after the grades had been turned in, the class conference was still active, with over a hundred new entries which continued to discuss the issues raised in the course. This type of behavioral indicator of development of a high level of interest in learning validates the responses of students to questionnaire items.

Nor is research and development of the Virtual Classroom over. Hopefully, the readers of this book will feel inspired to try this new option for teaching and learning, and to contribute to its enhancement and to knowledge about its limitations and possibilities.

REFERENCES

Abercrombie, M.L.J. (1979). *Aims and techniques of group teaching* (4th ed.). Guilford, UK: Society for Research into Higher Education.

Alavi, M. (1991, December). *Innovation in education: The role of computing and telecommunications in support of collaborative learning.* Presentation at the Twelfth International Conference on Information Systems, New York, NY.

Anderson, J.R. (1983). *The architecture of cognition.* Cambridge, MA: Harvard University Press.

Attewell, P., & Rule, J. (1984). Computing and organizations: What we know and what we don't know. *Communications of the ACM, 27* (12), 1184–1192.

Bales, R. (1950). *Interaction process analysis.* Reading, MA: Addison Wesley.

Baroudi, J.J., Olson, M.H., & Ives, H. (1986). An empirical study of the impact of user involvement on system usage and information satisfaction. *Communications of the ACM, 29* (3), 232-238.

Beach, L.R. (1974). Self-directed student groups and college learning. *Higher Education, 3,* 187–199.

Benford, S., Burke, E., & Foxley, E. (1992, April 6–8). Courseware to support the teaching of programming. *Proceedings of Developments in the Teaching of Computer Science.* University of Kent at Canterbury, UK.

Bloom, B. S. (1956). *Taxonomy of educational objectives, Handbook 1, cognitive domain.* New York: David Kay.

Blunt, M.J., & Blizzard, P.J. (1973). Development and initial assessment of a teaching-learning programme in anatomy. *British Journal of Medical Education, 7,* 224–250.

Bork, A. (1981). *Learning with computers.* Bedford, MA: Digital Press.

Bork, A. (1985). Advantages of computer based learning. *Journal of Structured Learning, 8.*

Bouton, C., & Garth, R. Y. (1983). *Learning in groups* (New Directions in Teaching and Learning, No. 14). San Francisco: Jossey-Bass.

263

Bridwell, L.S., Sirc, G., & Brooke, R., (1986). Revising and computers: Case studies of student writers. In S. Freedman (Ed.), *The acquisition of written language: Revision and response.* Norwood, NJ: Ablex Publishing Corp.

Carey, J. (1980). Paralanguage in computer-mediated communication. *Proceedings of the Association for Computational Linguistics,* pp. 61–63.

Carroll, J.M., Mack, R.L., Lewis, C.H., Grischkowsky N.L., & Robretson, S.R. (1985). Exploring exploring a word processor. *Human Computer Interaction, 1* (3), 283–307.

Centra, J.A. (1982). *Determining faculty effectiveness.* San Francisco: Jossey Bass.

Chambers, J. A., & Sprecher, J. W. (1980). Computer assisted instruction: Current trends and critical issues. *Communications of the ACM, 23* (6), 332–342.

Clark, R.E., & Salomon, G. (1986). Media in teaching. In M.C. Wittrock (Ed.), *Handbook of research on teaching* (3rd ed.). New York: Macmillan.

Clement, D.E., (1971). Learning and retention in student-led discussion groups. *Journal of Social Psychology, 84,* 279–286.

Collier, K.G. (1966). An experiment in university teaching. *Universities Quarterly, 20,* 336–348.

Collier, K.G. (1980). Peer-group learning in higher education: The development of higher order skills. *Studies in Higher Education, 5* (1), 55–62.

Collins, A. (1982). *Learning to read and write with personal computers.* Cambridge, MA: Bolt, Beranek, and Newman.

Cooley, C. A. (1902). *Human nature and the social order.* New York: Scribner.

Cooley, C. A. (1927). *Life and the student.* New York: Alfred A. Knopf.

Costin, F. (1972). Lecturing versus other methods of teaching: A review of research. *British Journal of Educational Technology, 3,* 4–31.

Culnan, M. J., & Markus, M. L. (1987). Information technologies: Electronic media and intraorganizational communication. *Handbook on organizational communication.* Beverly Hills, CA: Sage.

Daiute, C. (1985). *Writing and computers.* Reading, MA: Addison-Wesley.

Daiute, C., & Taylor, R. (1981). Computers and the improvement of writing. *Proceedings of the ACM.* Baltimore, MD: Association for Computing Machinery.

Davie, L.E. (1987). Facilitation of adult learning through computer conferencing. *Proceeding of the Second Guelph Symposium on Computer Conferencing* (pp. 11–22). Guelph, Ontario, Canada: University of Guelph.

Davie, L. E., & Palmer, P. (1984). Computer teleconferencing for advanced distance education. *Journal of University Continuing Education, 10* (2), 56–66.

Davis, J. A., Dukes, R., & Gamson, W. A. (1981). Assessing interactive modes of sociology instruction. *Teaching Sociology, 3*(3), 313–323.

DeLoughry, T.J. (1988, April 20). Remote instruction using computers found as effective as classroom sessions. *The Chronicle of Higher Education.*

Dewey, J., & Tufts, J.H. (1939). Intelligence in social action. In J. Ratner (Ed.), *Intelligence in the modern world* (pp. 435–466). New York: Random House.

Duranti, A. (1986). Framing discourse in a new medium: Openings in electronic mail. *The Quarterly Newsletter of the Laboratory of Comparative Human Cognition* (University of California at San Diego), *8* (2), 64- 71.

Ehrmann, S. C. (1988). *Technologies for access and quality: An agenda for three conversations* (Working paper). Washington, DC. The Annenberg/CPB Project, Corporation for Public Broadcasting.

Ennis, R. (1962). A concept of critical thinking. *Harvard Education Review, 32*, 81–111.

Ericsson, K. A., & Simon, H. (1984). *Protocol analysis: Verbal reports as data.* Cambridge, MA: MIT Press.

Erskine, C.A., & Tomkin, A. (1963). Evaluation of the effect of the group discussion method in a complex teaching programme. *Journal of Medical Education, 37*, 1036–1042.

Estes, J.E. (1979). Research on the effectiveness of using a computerized simulation in the basic management course. *ABSEL Conference Proceedings* (pp. 225–228). Tulsa, OK: Association for Business Simulation and Experiential Learning.

Farson, R. (1987). *The electronic future of executive education.* Unpublished paper, Western Behavioral Sciences Institute, La Jolla, CA.

Field, B.O. (1973). In D.E. Billing & B.S. Furniss (Eds.), *Aims, methods and assessment in advanced scientific education.* Carmel, IN: Hayden Books (Division of Macmillan).

Foxley, E. (1992, June). Personal interview and demonstration of the Ceilidh system, University of Nottingham.

Geithman, D., & Slowinski, G. (1990). Distance learning, computer-mediated conferencing, and the traditional classroom. In *Management education: Some effectiveness measures. Proceedings of the Northeast Decision Sciences Institute Annual Conference* (pp. 133–135). Saratoga Springs, NY.

Gleason, B.J. (1987). *Instructional management tools on EIES* (Tech. Rep. No.87-12). Newark, NJ: Computerized Conferencing and Communications Center, New Jersey Institute of Technology.

Goldfield, J.D. (1991 Summer). Real Accents! brings foreign language support to networks. *IAT Briefings* (Institute for Academic Technology, Research Triangle Park, NC), p. 20.

Goldschmid, M.L., & Goldschmid, B. (1976). Peer teaching in higher education: A review. *Higher Education, 5*, 9–33.

Goodwin, N.C. (1987). Functionality and usability. *Communications of the ACM, 30* (3), 229–233.

Gould, J.D., Boies, S.J., Levy, S., Richards, J.T., & Schoonard, J. (1987). The 1984 Olympic message system: A test of behavioral principles of system design. *Communications of the ACM, 30* (9), 758–769.

Greenlaw, P.S., & Wyman, R.P., (1973). The teaching effectiveness of games in collegiate business courses. *Simulation & Games, 4* (2), 259–264.

Haggerty, J.J. (1981). Space derived health aids. *Spinoff* (Annual Report, Technology Transfer Division, Office of Space and Terestial Applications, NASA, pp. 88–89). Washington, DC: U.S. Government Printing Office.

Hamilton, L.C. (1980). Grades, class size, and faculty status predict teaching evaluations. *Teaching Sociology, 8* (1), 47–62.

Haile, P., & Richards, A., (1984). *Supporting the distance learner with computer teleconferencing.* Unpublished paper, New York Institute of Technology, Islip, NY.

Hansen, W.J., & Haas, C. (1988). Reading & writing with computers. *Communications of the ACM, 31* (9), 1080–1089.

Harasim, L. (1986). Computer learning networks: Educational applications of computer conferencing. *Journal of Distance Education, 1* (1), 59–70.

Harasim, L. (1987). Teaching & learning on-line: Issues in computer-mediated graduate courses. *Canadian Journal of Educational Communication, 16* (2), 117–135.

Harasim, L. (1989). Online education: A new domain. In R. Mason & T. Kaye (Eds.) *Mindweave: Computers, communications & distance education* (pp. 50–62). Oxford: Pergamon Press.

Harasim, L. (Ed.). (1990). *Online education: Perspectives on a new medium.* New York: Prager/Greenwood.

Harasim, L., & Johnson, E.M. (1986). *Educational applications of computer networks for teacher/trainers in Ontario.* Toronto, Ontario: Ministry of Education.

Heimstra, G. (1982). Teleconferencing, concern for face, & organizational culture. In M. Burgoon (Ed.), *Communication yearbook 6.* Beverly Hills, CA: Sage.

Hiltz, S.R. (1983). Viewing computing systems within a social context. In R.E.A. Mason (ed.), *Information processing '83.* Amsterdam: Elsevier Science Publishers B.V. (North-Holland).

Hiltz, S. R. (1986a). Recent developments in teleconferencing & related technology. *In* A.E. Cawkell (Ed.), *Handbook of information technology & office systems* (pp. 823- 850). Amsterdam: North-Holland.

Hiltz, S. R. (1986b). The virtual classroom: Using computer-mediated communication for university teaching. *Journal of Communication, 36* (2), 95–104.

Hiltz, S. R. (1986c). *Branching capabilities in conferences: A manual and functional specifications* (Tech. Rep. No. 86–1). Newark, NJ: Computerized Conferencing and Communications Center, New Jersey Institute of Technology (Revised 1987).

Hiltz, S. R. (1986d). *The virtual classroom: Building the foundations* (Res. Rep. No. 24). Newark, NJ: Computerized Conferencing & Communications Center, New Jersey Institute of Technology.

Hiltz, S. R. (1988a). *Learning in a virtual classroom* (Vol. 1 of *A Virtual Classroom on EIES,* Rese. Rep. No. 25). Newark NJ: Center for Computerized Conferencing and Communications, NJIT.

Hiltz, S. R. (1988b). *Teaching in a virtual classroom* (Res. Rep. No. 26). Newark, NJ: Center for Computerized Conferencing and Communications, NJIT.

Hiltz, S. R. (1989). Productivity enhancement from computer-mediated communication: A systems contingency approach. *Communications of the ACM, 31* (12), 1438–1455.

Hiltz, S. R., & Johnson, K. (1990). User satisfaction with computer-mediated communication systems. *Management Science, 36* (6), 739–764.

Hiltz, S. R., Johnson, K., Aronovitch, C., & Turoff, M. (1980). *Face to face vs. computerized conferences: A controlled experiment* (Res. Rep. No. 12). Newark, NJ: Computerized Conferencing and Communications Center, NJIT.

Hiltz, S. R., Johnson, K., & Turoff, M. (1986). Experiments in group decision making, 1: Communications process and outcome in face-to-face vs. computerized conferences. *Human Communication Research, 13* (2), 225–252.

Hiltz, S. R., Kerr, E. B., & Johnson, K. (1985). *Determinants of acceptance of computer-mediated communication systems* (Res. Rep. No. 22). Newark, NJ: Computerized Conferencing and Communications Center, NJIT.

Hiltz, S. R., Shapiro, H., & Ringsted, M. (1990). Collaborative teaching in a Virtual Classroom. *Proceedings, Third Guelph Symposium on Computer-Mediated Communication* (pp. 37–55). Guelph, Canada: University of Guelph.

Hiltz, S. R., & Turoff, M. (1978). *The network nation.* Reading, MA: Addison-Wesley.

Hiltz, S. R., & Turoff, M. (1985). Structuring computer-mediated communication systems to avoid information overload. *Communications of the ACM, 28* (7), 680–689.

Hsu, E. (1989). Role-event gaming simulation in management education: A conceptual framework & review. *Simulation & Games, 20* (4), 409–438.

Hsu, E. (1991). *Management games for management education: A case study.* Unpublished doctoral dissertation. Graduate School of Business, Rutgers University, Newark, NJ.

Hsu, E., & Geithman, D. (1988). Experiential learning in management education: "Virtual Lab," management games & group decision support systems. *Proceedings of the Sixth World Productivity Congress,* pp. 507–531.

Hsu, E., & Hiltz, S.R. (1991). Management gaming on a computer-mediated conferencing system: A case of collaborative learning through computer conferencing. *Proceedings of the Twenty Fourth Annual Meeting of the Hawaii International Conference on System Sciences,Vol.IV.* (pp. 367–371). Washington, DC: IEEE Computer Society.

Huber, G. P. (1982). Organizational information systems: Determinants of their performance and behavior. *Management Science, 28* (2), 138–153.

Johansen, R., Vallee, J., & Spangler, K. (1979). *Electronic meetings: Technological alternatives & social choices.* Reading, MA: Addison-Wesley.

Johnson, D. W. (1981, January). Student-student interaction: The neglected variable in education. *Educational Research* (pp. 5–10).

Johnson, D. W., & Johnson, R. T. (1975). *Learning together and alone: Cooperation, competition, and individualization.* Englewood Cliffs, NJ: Prentice-Hall.

Keen, P. (1981). Information systems and organizational change. *Communications of the ACM, 24* (1), 24–33.

Keenan, T. P. (1987). Electronic communication and crime. *Proceedings, the second Guelph symposium on computer conferencing* (pp. 223–226). Guelph, Ontario, Canada: University of Guelph.

Kennedy, M. M. (1991, May). Policy Issues in teacher education. *Kappan,* p. 661.

Keller, F.S., & Sherman, G.S. (1974). *PSI: The Keller plan handbook.* Menlo Park, CA: W.A. Benjamin.

Kerr, E.B., & Hiltz, S.R (1982). *Computer-mediated communication systems: Status and evaluation.* New York: Academic Press.

Kiefer, K., & Smith, C. (1984). Improving students' revising and editing: The Writer's Workbench system at Colorado State University. In W. Wresh (Ed.), *A writer's tool: The computer in composition instruction.* Urbana IL: National Council of Teachers of English.

Kling, R. (1980). Social analyses of computing: Theoretical perspectives in recent empirical research. *Computing Surveys, 12* (1), 61–110.

Kling, R., & Iocono, S. (1984). The control of information systems developments after implementation. *Communications of the ACM, 27* (12), 1218–1226.

Krathwell, D.R., Bloom, B.S., & Masia, B.B. (1984). *Taxonomy of educational objectives: The classification of educational goals, Handbook II: affective domain.* New York: David McKay.

Levinson, P. (1988, Winter). Connected education: The first two years. *Learning Tomorrow,* pp. 205–220.

Malec, M. (1982). A PSI statistics course. *Teaching Sociology, 10* (1), 84–87.

Malone, T. (1981). Toward a theory of intrinsically motivating instruction. *Cognitive Science, 5* (4), 333–369.

Maier, N.R.F., Solem, A.R., & Maier, A.A. (1975). *The role-play technique: A handbook for management and leadership practice.* San Diego, CA: University Associates, Inc.

Markus, M. L. (1983). Power, politics, and MIS implementation. *Communications of the ACM, 26* (6), 430–444.

Mason, R., & Kaye, A. (1989). *Mindweave: Communication, computers and distance education.* Oxford: Pergamon Press.

McCreary, E. K., & Van Duran, J. (1987). Educational applications of computer conferencing. *Canadian Journal of Educational Communication, 16* (2), 107–115.

Mowshowitz, A. (1981). On approaches to the study of social issues in computing. *Communications of the ACM, 24* (3), 146–155.

Nipper, S. (1987). *3rd generation distance learning.* Paper presented at the Second Guelph Symposium on Computer Conferencing, University of Guelph, Ontario, Canada.

Parry, W. (1970). *Forms of intellectual and ethical development in the college years.* New York: Holt, Rinehart and Winston.

Paulhus, D. (1983). Sphere-specific measures of perceived control. *Journal of Personality and Social Psychology, 44* (6), 1253–1265.

Paulhus, D., & Christie, R. (1981). Spheres of Control: An interactionist approach to assessment of perceived control. In H.M. Lefcourt (Ed.), *Research with the locus of control construct* (Vol. 1). New York: Academic Press.

Paulsen, M.F., & Rekkedal, T. (1990). *The electronic college: Selected articles from the EKKO Project.* Bekkestua, Norway: NKI Forlaget.

Quinn, C.N., Mehan, H., Levin, J.A., & Black, S.D. (1983). Real education in non-real time: The use of electronic messaging systems for instruction. *Instructional Science, 11,* 313–327.

Rabinowitz, J.C., & Craik, F.I.M. (1986). Specific enhancement effects associated with word generation. *Journal of Memory & Language, 25,* 226–237.

Rice, R. E. (1980). Computer conferencing. In B. Dervin & M. Voigt (Eds.), *Progress in communication sciences* (Vol. 1, pp. 215–240). Norwood, NJ: Ablex.

Rice, R. E. (1987). Computer-mediated communication and organizational innovation. *Journal of Communication, 37* (4), 65–94.

Rice, R. E., & Case, D. (1983). Electronic message systems in the university: A description of use and utility. *Journal of Communication, 33*, 131–152.

Rice, R.E., & Associates. (1984). *The new media: Communication, research, and technology.* Beverly Hills CA: Sage.

Rice, R.E., & Love, G. (1987). Electronic emotion: Socio-emotional content in a computer-mediated communication network. *Communication Research, 14* (1), 85–108.

Rosenthal, B. (1991). *Computer-mediated discourse in a writing workshop: A case study in higher education.* Unpublished doctoral dissertation, New York University Program in Educational Communication and Technology.

Rotter, J.B. (1966). Generalized expectancies for internal vs. external control of reinforcement. *Psychological Monographs,* 80 (1) (whole issue).

Rudduck, J. (1978). *Learning through small group discussion.* Guildford, UK: Society for Research into Higher Education.

Rushinek, A., & Rushinek, S.F. (1986). What makes users happy? *Communications of the ACM, 29* (7), 594–598.

Schramm, W. (1977). *Big media, little media: Tools and technologies for instruction.* Beverly Hills, CA: Sage.

Shavelson, R.J., Stasz, C., Schlossman, S., Webb, N., Hotta, J. Y., & Goldstein, S. (1986). *Evaluating student outcomes from telecourse instruction: A feasibility study.* Santa Monica, CA: Rand.

Shneiderman, B. (1987). *Designing the user interface: Strategies for effective human-computer-interaction.* Reading, MA: Addison Wesley.

Short, J., Williams, E., & Christie, B. (1976). *The social psychology of telecommunications.* London: Wiley.

Slamecka, N.J. & Graf, P. (1978). The generation effect: Delineation of a phenomenon. *Journal of Experimental Psychology, Human Learning & Memory, 4*, 692–604.

Sproull, L., & Kiesler, S. (1986). Reducing social context cues: Electronic mail in organizational communication. *Management Science, 32* (11), 1492–1512.

Steinfield, C.W. (1986). Computer-mediated communication systems. *Annual Review of Information Science and Technology, 21*, 167–202.

Strassman, P. A. (1985). *Information payoff: The transformation of work in the electronic age.* New York: Macmillan.

Tarter, D. E. (1977). Group incentive techniques. *Teaching Sociology, 10* (1), 117–121.

Turner, J.A. (1984). Computer mediated work: The interplay between technology and structured jobs. *Communications of the ACM, 27* (12), 1210–1217.

Turoff, M., (1972). 'Party line' and 'Discussion' computerized conferencing systems. In S. Winkler (Ed.), *Computer communication- Impacts and implications: Proceedings of the International Conference on Computer Communications* (pp. 161–170). Washington, DC: International Council for Computer Communication.

Uhlig, R.P., Farber, D.J., & Bair, J.H. (1979). *The office of the future: Communication and computers.* Amsterdam: North-Holland.

Weedman, J. (1991). Task and non-task functions of a computer conference used in professional education: A measure of flexibility. *International Journal of Man-Machine Studies, 34*, 303–318.

Wells, R. A. (1990). *Computer-mediated communications for distance learning and training.* Boise, ID: Boise State University.

Welsch, L.A. (1982). Using electronic mail as a teaching tool. *Communications of the ACM, 25* (2), 105–108.

Whipple, W. R. (1987). Collaborative learning: Recognizing it when we see it. *Bulletin of the American Association for Higher Education, 40*(2), 3–7.

Wolfe, J. (1985). The teaching effectiveness of games in collegiate business courses: A 1973–1983 update. *Simulation and Games, 16,* 251–288.

Whyte, W. F. (1980). Social invention for solving human problems. *Footnotes,8,* 1.

Zin, A. M., & Foxley, E. (1991). Automatic program quality assessment system. *Proceedings of the IFIP Conference on Software Quality.* Vidyanagar, India.

Zmud, R.W. (1979). Individual differences and MIS success: A review of the empirical literature. *Management Science, 25*(10), 966–979.

APPENDIX *I*

QUESTIONNAIRES

BASELINE QUESTIONNAIRE FOR STUDENTS
VIRTUAL CLASSROOM PROJECT

COURSE NAME: _____

COURSE NUMBER AND SECTION: _____

INSTRUCTOR: _____

Mode - Mode in which class was presented $X = 1.91$ $SD = 0.84$ $N = 372$
(1) <u>40%</u> Completely Online
(2) <u>28%</u> Partially Online
(3) <u>32%</u> All Offline
SCHOOL - $X = 1.60$ $SD = 0.86$ $N = 332$
I am:
(1) <u>58%</u> An NJIT student
(2) <u>32%</u> Upsala student
(3) <u>4%</u> New School (Connect Ed) student
(4) <u>7%</u> Other _____

SOME BACKGROUND INFORMATION

If you feel that any of these items invade your privacy, you are of course free to decline to answer them.

How important are each of the following reasons for your taking this course and this particular section or mode of delivery of the course? Very Important, Somewhat Important, or Not Important?

	Very Important	Somewhat Important	Not Important	X	SD	N
PROFESSIONAL INTEREST						
I have a professional or job-related interest in the topic	32%	46%	22%	1.89	0.73	331
GENERAL INTEREST						
I have a general interest in the topic	32%	57%	10%	1.78	0.62	329
REQUIRED MAJOR						
Required for my major	47%	74%	100%	1.78	0.83	326
REQUIRED COURSE						
Required for graduation	56%	22%	22%	1.66	0.82	325
INSTRUCTOR'S REPUTATION						
The reputation of the instructor	22%	40%	37%	2.15	0.76	316
NO CHOICE						
No choice- transfer to other sections impossible	5%	14%	82%	2.77	0.52	303

	Very Important	Somewhat Important	Not Important	X	SD	N
CURIOUS						
I was curious about how the technology works	32%	48%	21%	1.89	0.72	326
CONVENIENCE						
More convenient than traditional classes	26%	33%	41%	2.15	0.81	318

EXPECTED GRADE
What grade do you expect to receive in this Course?
55% A 39% B 6% C .3% D $X = 1.51$ $SD = .62$ $N = 321$

EXPECTED DIFFICULTY $X = 3.44$ $SD = .90$ $N = 331$
How easy or difficult do you expect this course to be?

EASY : 1 : 2 : 3 : 4 : 5 : DIFFICULT
            3%   10% 39% 38% 11%
SEX
Your sex: 71% Male 29% Female $X = 1.29$ $SD = 0.46$ $N = 327$

AGE $X = 23.77$ $SD = 6.78$ $N = 320$
Your age at last birthday:
17,18   13%
19-   10%
22–25-   27%
26–34   18%
35 +-   6%

MAJOR
Your major:

NATIONALITY   X = 1.43   SD = .50   N = 250
Nationality:
  (1) 57% USA
  (2) 43% OTHER

ETHNIC GROUP
Ethnic/Racial Background
  14% Black/Afro-American
   7% Hispanic (Mexican, Puerto-Rican, etc.)
  66% White
  12% Asian or Asian-American
   1% Other

ENGLISH   X = 1.19   SD = .39   N = 325
Is English your native or first language?
81% Yes 19% No

TYPING   X = 3.03   SD = .92   N = 331
How would you describe your typing skills?

(1) 4% None
(2) 22% Hunt and peck
(3) 46% Casual (rough draft with errors)
(4) 22% Good (can do 25 w.p.m. error free)
(5) 6% Excellent (can do 40 w.p.m. error free)

ACADEMIC STANDING   X = 2.99   SD = 1.31   N = 321
Academic standing

  16% Freshman
  20% Sophomore
  31% Junior
  21% Senior
  11% Master's candidate
   2% Doctoral candidate
   1% Post-doctoral

PREVIOUS ONLINE   X = 1.15   SD = .47   N = 130
How many online ("virtual classroom") courses have you taken previously?
(1) 90% None. This is my first online course
(2) 5% One
(3) 5% Two or more

IMAGES OF YOURSELF

Please read each of the following and indicate how much you
agree or disagree (1 = Completely DISAGREE: 7 means Completely AGREE).

			DISAGREE				AGREE			
	1	2	3	4	5	6	7	X	SD	N
WORK HARD										
When I get what I want it's usually because I worked haed for it	0%	1%	4%	8%	21%	36%	30%	5.76	1.15	331
GROUP EASY										
I find it easy to play an important part in most group situations	1%	5%	11%	24%	28%	20%	11%	4.75	1.38	329
PREFER LUCK										
I prefer games involving some luck over games requiring pure skill	14%	19%	18%	22%	14%	8%	4%	3.43	1.66	326
POOR SOCIAL CONTROL										
Even when I'm feeling self-confident about most things, I still seem to lack the ability to control social situations	14%	29%	17%	18%	14%	7%	1%	3.15	1.56	324
LEARN ANYTHING										
I can learn almost anything if I set my mind to it.	0%	1%	1%	4%	15%	30%	48%	6.17	1.04	330
MAKING FRIENDS										
I have no trouble making and keeping friends	0%	1%	4%	8%	17%	27%	43%	5.93	1.22	328
POINTLESS										
It's pointless to keep working on something that is too difficult for me	27%	29%	13%	13%	8%	5%	4%	2.80	1.70	328
CONVERSATIONS										
I'm not good at guiding the course of a conversations with several others	22%	25%	17%	15%	12%	6%	2%	2.95	1.61	329
COMPARISONS										
On any sort of exam or competition I like to know how well I do relative to everyone else	8%	5%	7%	13%	16%	27%	24%	4.99	1.86	328
CLOSE RELATIONSHIPS										
I can usually establish a close personal relationship with someone I find attractive	5%	2%	9%	18%	21%	24%	21%	5.07	1.60	327

		DISAGREE					AGREE			
	1	2	3	4	5	6	7	X	SD	N
ABILITY My major accomplishments are entirely due to my hard work and ability	0%	1%	2%	6%	20%	37%	34%	5.92	1.06	328
MAKING PLANS When I make plans I am almost certain to make them work	0%	2%	4%	14%	28%	31%	21%	5.43	1.22	330
STEER INTERVIEWS When being interviewed I can usually steer the interviewer toward the topics I want to talk about and away from those I wish to avoid	3%	7%	15%	29%	23%	15%	6%	4.33	1.43	326
SETTING GOALS I usually don't set goals becasue I have a hard time following through on them	32%	34%	16%	8%	5%	3%	1%	2.34	1.41	328
GETTING HELP If I need help in carrying off a plan of mine, it's usually difficult to get others to help	21%	24%	21%	17%	8%	7%	2%	2.94	1.57	327
COMPETITION Competition discourages excellence	47%	20%	10%	9%	7%	3%	3%	2.32	1.68	329
MEETING PEOPLE If there's someone I want to meet I can usually arrange it	3%	5%	10%	23%	20%	20%	18%	4.86	1.58	329
OTHERS LUCKY Other people get ahead just by being lucky	22%	26%	17%	20%	9%	3%	3%	2.88	1.55	328
POINT OF VIEW I often find it hard to get my point of view across to others	20%	29%	20%	15%	9%	4%	2%	2.84	1.53	330
DISAGREEMENTS In attempting to smooth over a disagreement I usually make it worse	30%	31%	18%	13%	5%	1%	2%	2.45	1.42	327

YOUR PREVIOUS EXPERIENCE WITH COMPUTERS

COMPUTER EXPERIENCE   X = 2.23 SD = .94 N = 331

Which of the following best describes your previous experience with computer systems?

(1) 22% I am a NOVICE; seldom or never use computers
(2) 45% I have OCCASIONALLY used computer terminals and systems before
(3) 22% I have FREQUENTLY used computer systems
(4) 11% Use of computers is central to my PROFESSIONAL work

For each of the following pairs of words, please circle the response that is closest to your CURRENT FEELINGS ABOUT USING COMPUTERS. For instance, for the first pair of words, if you feel computer systems in general are completely "stimulating" to use and not at all "dull," circle "1"; "4" means that you are undecided or neutral or think they are equally likely to be stimulating or dull; "3" means you feel that they are slightly more stimulating than dull, etc.

DULL-1									X	SD	N
Stimulating	1	2	3	4	5	6	7	Dull			
	23%	24%	21%	21%	5%	2%	3%		2.82	1.52	325
DREARY-1											
Fun	1	2	3	4	5	6	7	Dreary			
	22%	27%	23%	15%	8%	2%	3%		2.78	1.49	327
DIFFICULT-1											
Easy	1	2	3	4	5	6	7	Difficult			
	7%	15%	18%	27%	16%	12%	5%		3.82	1.57	327
IMPERSONAL-1											
Personal	1	2	3	4	5	6	7	Impersonal			
	6%	10%	13%	36%	11%	13%	11%		4.20	1.63	324
HELPFUL-1											
Hindering	1	2	3	4	5	6	7	Helpful			
	4%	2%	5%	15%	16%	31%	27%		5.35	1.58	323
UNTHREATENING-1											
Threatening	1	2	3	4	5	6	7	Unthreatening			
	4%	6%	6%	26%	12%	21%	26%		5.02	1.68	325
INEFFICIENT-1											
Efficient	1	2	3	4	5	6	7	Inefficient			
	38%	30%	15%	10%	2%	2%	2%		2.21	1.37	323
OBLIGING-1											
Demanding	1	2	3	4	5	6	7	Obliging			
	12%	12%	13%	40%	11%	8%	4%		3.65	1.54	323
UNRELIABLE-1											
Reliable	1	2	3	4	5	6	7	Unreliable			
	24%	27%	22%	18%	4%	2%	3%		2.70	1.46	326
UNDESIRABLE-1											
Desirable	1	2	3	4	5	6	7	Undesirable			
	25%	26%	16%	23%	3%	3%	4%		2.77	1.57	327

EXPECTATIONS ABOUT THE EIES SYSTEM
[Skip this section if you are not going to use EIES]

Indicate your expectations about how it will be to use this system by circling the number which best indicates where your feelings lie on the scales below.

EASY-1

4%	6%	15%	25%	19%	20%	11%
: 1 :	2 :	3 :	4 :	5 :	6 :	7 :

Hard to learn   Easy to learn

$X = 4.54$ $SD = 1.58$ $N = 246$

FRIENDLY-1

4%	7%	8%	24%	28%	20%	9%
: 1 :	2 :	3 :	4 :	5 :	6 :	7 :

Impersonal   Friendly

$X = 4.60$ $SD = 1.52$ $N = 244$

NOT FRUSTRATING-1

4%	10%	16%	24%	21%	21%	9%
: 1 :	2 :	3 :	4 :	5 :	6 :	7 :

Frustrating   Not frustrating

$X = 4.32$ $SD = 1.59$ $N = 245$

PRODUCTIVE-1

2%	1%	5%	18%	24%	34%	16%
: 1 :	2 :	3 :	4 :	5 :	6 :	7 :

Unproductive   Productive

$X = 5.27$ $SD = 1.29$ $N = 244$

EFFICIENCY-1

Do you expect that use of the System will increase the efficiency of your education (the quantity of work that you can complete in a given time)?

19%	21%	15%	24%	15%	5%	2%
: 1 :	2 :	3 :	4 :	5 :	6 :	7 :

Definitely yes   Unsure   Definitely not

$X = 3.00$ $SD = 1.55$ $N = 245$

QUALITY-1

Do you expect that use of the System will increase the quality of your education?

21%	22%	18%	25%	6%	4%	3%
: 1 :	2 :	3 :	4 :	5 :	6 :	7 :

Definitely yes   Unsure   Definitely not

$X = 5.48$ $SD = 1.74$ $N = 242$

RESENT-1

I resent being required to use EIES for this course.

4%	3%	6%	19%	7%	17%	43%
: 1 :	2 :	3 :	4 :	5 :	6 :	7 :

Definitely yes   Unsure   Definitely not

$X = 2.76$ $SD = 1.46$ $N = 243$

OVERALL-1

Overall, how useful do you expect the System to be for online classes?

23%	27%	20%	19%	6%	3%	2%
: 1 :	2 :	3 :	4 :	5 :	6 :	7 :

Very Useful   Not useful at all

$X = 3.37$ $SD = 1.08$ $N = 237$

EXPECTED TIME   X = 3.37 SD = 1.08 N = 237

While you are part of an online course, how much time in the average week do you foresee yourself using EIES in relation to your coursework?

(1) 4% Less than 30 minutes
(2) 12% 30 minutes to 1 hour
(3) 43% 1 - 3 hours
(4) 29% 4 - 6 hours
(5) 7% 7 - 9 hours
(6) 5% 10 hours or more

EQUIPMENT ACCESS

Please describe your access to a computer terminal or microcomputer at your office or place of work.

WORK ACCESS   X = 3.00 SD = 1.66 N = 264

(1) 28% No terminal
(2) 21% Have my own terminal
(3) 10% Share a terminal, located where I can see it from my desk
(4) 8% Share a terminal, which takes _____ minutes to reach
(5) 33% Not applicable; I do not have an office

HOME ACCESS   X = 1.41 SD = 0.49 N = 267

Do you have a micro or terminal at home (or in your dorm, wherever you live during classes)?
(1) 59% No
(2) 41% Yes

TERMINAL TYPE   X = 2.04 SD = 0.94 N = 200

What kind of terminal do you usually use? (Check all that apply)
42% CRT (video display)
11% Hard copy (printer terminal)
46% Both

MICRO
40% Microcomputer (Brand: _____)
25% With modem
26% With hard copy
34% With disk storage

If you know the name of your communications software (e.g., Smartcom), please list it here: _____

THANK YOU VERY MUCH !!!

POST-COURSE QUESTIONNAIRE FOR STUDENTS
VIRTUAL CLASSROOM PROJECT

COURSE NAME: _____

COURSE NUMBER AND SECTION: _____

INSTRUCTOR: _____

YOUR STUDENT ID: _____

COURSE EFFECTIVENESS

There are three sets of items in this section; we would like you to try to separate them out in your thinking. The first relates to the teaching or presentation style and effectiveness of your instructor; the second, to the course content; and the third, to the outcomes of the course for you. Later in the questionnaire, those who participated in an experimental mode of delivery will make direct comparisons between this course and traditional courses.

For each of the following, please circle a response that corresponds to the following scale:

SA = Strongly Agree
A = Agree
N = Neither agree nor disagree (neutral)
D = Disagree
SD = Strongly Disagree

COURSE CONTENT

	SA	A	N	D	SD	X	SD	N
CONTENT INTERESTING The course content was interesting to me	20%	63%	12%	4%	0%	2.01	0.72	283
CONTENT IMPORTANT Course content is important or valuable	25%	58%	14%	2%	1%	1.96	0.74	283
GOALS CLEAR Course goals were clear to me	16%	59%	19%	6%	1%	2.18	0.80	282
REQUIREMENTS CLEAR Work requirements and grading system were unclear from the beginning	26%	46%	19%	6%	2%	2.11	0.93	283
READINGS POOR The reading assignments are poor	4%	8%	25%	48%	15%	3.63	0.96	283
WRITTEN ASSIGN. POOR The written assignments are poor	2%	4%	28%	49%	17%	3.74	0.87	281

	SA	A	N	D	SD	X	SD	N
LECTURES POOR								
The lecture material is poor	2%	5%	14%	51%	27%	3.95	0.92	279
WORK HARD								
The students had to work hard	18%	45%	29%	7%	1%	2.28	0.88	283
WASTE OF TIME								
This course was a waste of time	2%	4%	14%	32%	49%	4.21	0.96	282

APPROPRIATE LEVEL   X = 3.18   SD = 0.63   N = 280
Is this course taught at an appropriate level?
   1%   8%   68%   21%   3%
:   1   :   2   :   3   :   4   :   5   :
Too easy   Just right   Too difficult

COURSE OVERALL   X = 2.48   SD = 0.97   N = 265
How would you rate this course over-all?
(1)Excellent   (2)Very good   (3)Good   (4)Fair   (5)Poor
   16%   37%   34%   11%   3%

COMMENTS ABOUT THE COURSE CONTENT?
Yes Comment : 16%
No Comment : 84%

CHARACTERISTICS OF THE TEACHING

	SA	A	N	D	SD	X	SD	N
WELL ORGANIZED								
Instructor organized the course well	31%	55%	10%	2%	1%	1.89	0.79	280
GRADING FAIR								
Grading was fair and impartial	29%	50%	18%	2%	1%	1.97	0.80	276
ENJOYS TEACHING								
Instructor seems to enjoy teaching	50%	39%	9%	1%	0%	1.64	0.74	277
LACKS KNOWLEDGE								
Instructor lacks sufficient knowledge about the subject area	2%	4%	5%	29%	59%	4.38	0.95	279
IDEAS ENCOURAGED								
Students were encouraged to express ideas	40%	48%	9%	3%	0%	1.74	0.73	280
PRESENTED CLEARLY								
Instructor presented material clearly and summarized points	27%	55%	14%	3%	1%	1.95	0.79	280

	SA	A	N	D	SD	X	SD	N
OTHER VIEWS								
Instructor discussed points of view other than her/his own	25%	52%	20%	4%	0%	2.02	0.77	279
PERSONAL HELP								
The student was able to get personal help in this course	27%	45%	23%	3%	1%	2.06	0.86	278
INSTRUCTOR BORING								
Instructor presented material in a boring manner	2%	6%	21%	45%	26%	3.85	0.95	277
HELPFUL CRITIQUE								
Instructor critiqued my work in a constructive and helpful way	17%	48%	30%	3%	2%	2.25	0.84	279

TEACHER OVERALL $X = 1.87$ $SD = 0.90$ $N = 279$
Overall, I would rate this teacher as
(1)Excellent   (2)Very good   (3)Good   (4)Fair   (5)Poor
   40%   38%   16%   4%   1%

COMMENTS ABOUT THE INSTRUCTOR OR THE TEACHING?
Yes Comment : 26%
No Comment : 74%

OUTCOMES OF THE COURSE

	SA	A	N	D	SD	X	SD	N
MORE INTERESTED								
I became more interested in the subject	18%	52%	21%	6%	2%	2.22	0.90	283
LEARNED FACTS								
I learned a great deal of factual material	12%	62%	20%	5%	1%	2.20	0.74	283
CONCEPTS								
I gained a good understanding of basic concepts	16%	68%	11%	4%	1%	2.05	0.71	282
CENTRAL ISSUES								
I learned to identify central issues in this field	12%	61%	22%	3%	2%	2.21	0.76	281
COMMUNICATED CLEARLY								
I developed the ability to communicate clearly about this subject	13%	50%	31%	3%	2%	2.30	0.81	283
CRITICAL THINKING								
My skill in critical thinking was increased	12%	50%	32%	5%	2%	2.34	0.82	283

	SA	A	N	D	SD	X	SD	N
ETHICAL ISSUES								
I developed an understanding of ethical issues	8%	39%	42%	8%	4%	2.61	0.87	280
GENERALIZATIONS								
My ability to integrate facts and develop generalizations improved	10%	51%	30%	7%	1%	2.29	0.82	280
COMPLETED READINGS								
I regularly completed the required readings	20%	43%	23%	12%	3%	2.35	1.02	280
DID ADDITIONAL READING								
I was stimulated to do additional reading	7%	23%	42%	23%	5%	2.98	0.97	282
PARTICIPATED								
I participated actively in class discussion	18%	42%	30%	8%	1%	2.32	0.91	279
DISCUSS OUTSIDE								
I was stimulated to discuss related topics outside of class	12%	38%	32%	16%	2%	2.58	0.96	283
WRITTEN AIDED								
The written assignments aided my learning	21%	53%	21%	3%	2%	2.12	0.83	281
COMPLETED WRITTEN								
I regularly completed the written assignments	26%	55%	13%	5%	1%	2.00	0.81	283
THINK FOR SELF								
I was forced to think for myself	24%	60%	13%	1%	1%	1.93	0.69	283
EXPRESSING IDEAS								
I became more confident in expressing my ideas	18%	47%	30%	3%	1%	2.23	0.83	283
NEW FRIENDSHIPS								
I developed new friendships in this class	19%	51%	21%	5%	4%	2.25	0.96	283
VALUE OTHERS VIEWS								
I learned to value other points of view	14%	52%	29%	3%	2%	2.27	0.81	282
DID BEST WORK								
I was motivated to do my best work	19%	51%	25%	4%	1%	2.12	0.84	283
SELF UNDERSTANDING								
I gained a better understanding of myself	10%	39%	43%	5%	4%	2.53	0.87	281
COMPUTER COMPETENCE								
I increased my competence with computers	18%	42%	24%	8%	8%	2.45	1.11	281

	SA	A	N	D	SD	X	SD	N
RELATIONSHIPS I learned to see relationships between important topics and ideas	13%	53%	30%	2%	2%	2.28	0.79	282
CRITICAL ANALYSIS My ability to critically analyze written material was improved	10%	45%	36%	7%	1%	2.46	0.82	283

GENERAL INFORMATION

TOTAL TIME
About how much TOTAL time have you spent each week on this
course? (including "in class" and out, reading and writing, on
and offline)

(1) _1%_ Less than one hour
(2) 11% 1–2 hours
(3) 34% 3–4 hours   N = 275 Mean = 3.6 SD = 0.9
(4) 38% 5–9 hours
(5) 16% Ten hours or more

EASY COURSE
How easy or difficult was this course for you?

	3%		15%		46%		28%		7%	
EASY:	1	:	2	:	3	:	4	:	5	:DIFFICULT

N = 274 Mean = 3.2 SD = 0.9

EXPECTED GRADE
What grade do you expect to receive in this course?
36% A   43% B   16% C   4% D   0% F
N = 273 Mean = 1.9 SD = 0.8

Individual vs. Group Learning

Some courses are essentially a very INDIVIDUAL experience; contact with other
students does not play an important part in your learning. In other courses, communication with other students plays a dominant role. For THIS COURSE, please circle
the number below that seems to be what you experienced.

GROUP EXPERIENCE

	10%		16%		21%		16%		23%		12%
:	1	:	2	:	3	:	4	:	5	:	6

Individual experience   Group experience

N = 266 Mean = 3.6 SD = 1.6

MISLEADING HELP
The help I got from other students was–

6%	26%	36%	17%	11%	5%
: 1	: 2	: 3	: 4	: 5	: 6

Crucially important to me   Useless or misleading

N = 274 Mean = 3.1 SD = 1.2

Students in my class tended to be
STUDENTS COOPERATIVE

1%	6%	16%	29%	34%	15%
: 1	: 2	: 3	: 4	: 5	: 6

Not at all cooperative   Extremely cooperative

N = 273 Mean = 4.3 SD = 1.1

STUDENTS COMPETITIVE

4%	16%	23%	34%	18%	5%
: 1	: 2	: 3	: 4	: 5	: 6

Not at all competative   Extremely competitive

N = 257 Mean = 3.6 SD = 1.2

STUDENT COMMUNICATION
How often did you communicate with other students outside of class, by computer, "face-to-face" or on the telephone?

11%	20%	19%	27%	18%	6%
: 1	: 2	: 3	: 4	: 5	: 6

Never   Constantly

N = 274 Mean = 3.4 SD = 1.4

ATTITUDES TOWARD COMPUTERS

For each of the following pairs of words, please circle the response that represents where you fall on the scale in terms of your CURRENT FEELINGS ABOUT USING COMPUTERS.

DULL

22%	26%	24%	16%	6%	4%	3%
: 1	: 2	: 3	: 4	: 5	: 6	: 7 :

Stimulating   Dull

N = 265 Mean = 2.8 SD = 1.5

DREARY

22%	22%	28%	14%	7%	4%	3%
: 1	: 2	: 3	: 4	: 5	: 6	: 7 :

Fun   Dreary

N = 265 Mean = 2.9 SD = 1.5

DIFFICULT

11%	13%	19%	22%	20%	9%	6%
: 1	: 2	: 3	: 4	: 5	: 6	: 7 :

Easy   Difficult

N = 266 Mean = 3.8 SD = 1.7

IMPERSONAL

9%	11%	19%	28%	15%	9%	10%	
: 1 :	2 :	3 :	4 :	5 :	6 :	7	:

Personal   Impersonal

N = 262   Mean = 3.9   SD = 1.7

HELPFUL

3%	4%	9%	14%	18%	29%	23%	
: 1 :	2 :	3 :	4 :	5 :	6 :	7	:

Hindering   Helpful

N = 265   Mean = 5.2   SD = 1.6

UNTHREATENING

3%	6%	10%	20%	16%	21%	24%	
: 1 :	2 :	3 :	4 :	5 :	6 :	7	:

Threatening   Unthreatening

N = 264   Mean = 5.0   SD = 1.7

INEFFICIENT

28%	27%	19%	17%	3%	2%	3%	
: 1 :	2 :	3 :	4 :	5 :	6 :	7	:

Efficient   Inefficient

N = 263   Mean = 2.6   SD = 1.4

OBLIGING

12%	14%	20%	30%	10%	10%	5%	
: 1 :	2 :	3 :	4 :	5 :	6 :	7	:

Demanding   Obliging

N = 261   Mean = 3.6   SD = 1.6

UNRELIABLE

18%	30%	18%	20%	6%	6%	2%	
: 1 :	2 :	3 :	4 :	5 :	6 :	7	:

Reliable   Unreliable

N = 262   Mean = 2.9   SD = 1.5

UNDESIRABLE

27%	22%	16%	20%	7%	4%	4%	
: 1 :	2 :	3 :	4 :	5 :	6 :	7	:

Desirable   Undesirable

N = 264   Mean = 2.9   SD = 1.7

ATTITUDES TOWARD MEDIA

To what extent do you agree with the following statements?

ENJOY LECTURES
I enjoy listening to lectures.

7%	25%	26%	21%	13%	6%	2%	
: 1 :	2 :	3 :	4 :	5 :	6 :	7	:

Strongly Agree   Strongly Disagree

N = 87   Mean = 3.3   SD = 1.4

LIKE READING
I like to read.

10%	20%	25%	25%	5%	9%	6%
: 1 :	2 :	3 :	4 :	5 :	6 :	7 :

Strongly Agree   Strongly Disagree

N = 87 Mean = 3.4 SD = 1.6

DIFFICULTY WRITING
I have difficulty expressing my ideas in writing.

2%	9%	15%	13%	20%	28%	13%
: 1 :	2 :	3 :	4 :	5 :	6 :	7 :

Strongly Agree   Strongly Disagree

N = 86 Mean = 4.7 SD = 1.6

LIKE DISCUSSION
I like to take part in class discussions.

17%	30%	16%	17%	9%	8%	1%
: 1 :	2 :	3 :	4 :	5 :	6 :	7 :

Strongly Agree   Strongly Disagree

N = 86 Mean = 3.0 SD = 1.6

PARTICIPATION IN THE ONLINE COURSE

If you participated in a traditional course or a course which did not include any online work, skip the rest of the questionnaire.

ACCESS PROBLEM
Is access to a terminal or micro for the online class a problem for you?

7%	15%	19%	20%	39%
: 1 :	2 :	3 :	4 :	5 :

Serious Problem   Not a Problem

N = 176 Mean = 3.7 SD = 1.3

BUSY LINES
How much problem have you had with "busy" lines or no available ports to EIES?

6%	13%	23%	20%	38%
: 1 :	2 :	3 :	4 :	5 :

Serious Problem   Not a Problem

N = 173 Mean = 3.7 SD = 1.3

SLOW RESPONSE
To what extent has the slow response of the EIES system been a problem or barrier for you?

14%	19%	28%	22%	17%
: 1 :	2 :	3 :	4 :	5 :

Serious Problem   Not a Problem

N = 174 Mean = 3.1 SD = 1.3

EXPERIENCES WITH EIES

Indicate your experiences with using this system by circling the number which best indicates where your feelings lie on the scales below.

EASY TO LEARN-2

2%	6%	12%	9%	15%	35%	20%	
: 1 :	2 :	3 :	4 :	5 :	6 :	7	:

Hard to learn   Easy to learn

N = 176   Mean = 5.2   SD = 1.6

FRIENDLY-2

5%	8%	10%	12%	19%	31%	15%	
: 1 :	2 :	3 :	4 :	5 :	6 :	7	:

Impersonal   Friendly

N = 176   Mean = 4.8   SD = 1.7

NOT FRUSTRATING-2

4%	14%	13%	18%	17%	23%	10%	
: 1 :	2 :	3 :	4 :	5 :	6 :	7	:

Frustrating   Not frustrating

N = 176   Mean = 4.4   SD = 1.7

PRODUCTIVE-2

3%	3%	8%	16%	20%	32%	16%	
: 1 :	2 :	3 :	4 :	5 :	6 :	7	:

Unproductive   Productive

N = 176   Mean = 5.1   SD = 1.5

INCREASE EFFICIENCY-2

Did use of the System increase the efficiency of your education (the quantity of work that you can complete in a given time)?

11%	18%	15%	23%	10%	15%	6%	
: 1 :	2 :	3 :	4 :	5 :	6 :	7	:

Definitely yes   Unsure   Definitely not

N = 175   Mean = 3.7   SD = 1.8

INCREASE QUALITY-2

Did use of the System increase the quality of your education?

12%	22%	22%	22%	8%	6%	7%	
: 1 :	2 :	3 :	4 :	5 :	6 :	7	:

Definitely yes   Unsure   Definitely not

N = 175   Mean = 3.4   SD = 1.7

COMPARISON TO TRADITIONAL CLASSROOMS

Please compare online "classes" to your previous experiences with "face to face" college-level courses. To what extent do you agree with the following statements about the comparative process and value of the EIES online course or portion of a course in which you participated? (Circle a number on the scales.)

CONVENIENT
Taking online courses is more convenient.

26%	23%	16%	11%	9%	8%	7%
: 1 :	2 :	3 :	4 :	5 :	6 :	7 :

Strongly Agree   Strongly Disagree

N = 185 Mean = 3.1 SD = 1.9

INHIBITED
I felt more "inhibited" in taking part in the discussion.

4%	9%	13%	29%	10%	21%	15%
: 1 :	2 :	3 :	4 :	5 :	6 :	7 :

Strongly Agree   Strongly Disagree

N = 185 Mean = 4.5 SD = 1.7

LESS WORK
I didn't have to work as hard for online classes.

4%	9%	10%	17%	20%	23%	18%
: 1 :	2 :	3 :	4 :	5 :	6 :	7 :

Strongly Agree   Strongly Disagree

N = 187 Mean = 4.8 SD = 1.7

COMMUNICATED MORE
I communicated more with other students in the class as a result of the computerized conference.

14%	21%	14%	18%	11%	11%	11%
: 1 :	2 :	3 :	4 :	5 :	6 :	7 :

Strongly Agree   Strongly Disagree

N = 185 Mean = 3.7 SD = 1.9

ACCESS PROFESSOR
Having the computerized conferencing system available provided better access to the professor(s).

18%	21%	19%	15%	10%	9%	8%
: 1 :	2 :	3 :	4 :	5 :	6 :	7 :

Strongly Agree   Strongly Disagree

N = 185 Mean = 3.4 SD = 1.9

INCREASED MOTIVATION
The fact that my assignments would be read by the other students increased my motivation to do a thorough job.

16%	25%	14%	20%	6%	11%	8%
: 1 :	2 :	3 :	4 :	5 :	6 :	7 :

Strongly Agree   Strongly Disagree

N = 185 Mean = 3.4 SD = 1.8

STOP PARTICIPATING
When I became very busy with other things, I was more likely to stop participating
in the online class than I would have been to "cut" a weekly face-to-face lecture.

15%	20%	14%	14%	8%	15%	14%
: 1 :	2 :	3 :	4 :	5 :	6 :	7 :

Strongly Agree   Strongly Disagree

N = 183   Mean = 3.8   SD = 2.1

MORE BORING
The online or virtual classroom mode is more boring than traditional classes.

8%	6%	8%	16%	16%	24%	22%
: 1 :	2 :	3 :	4 :	5 :	6 :	7 :

Strongly Agree   Strongly Disagree

N = 183   Mean = 4.8   SD = 1.8

MORE INVOLVED
I felt more "involved" in taking an active part in the course.

17%	22%	18%	19%	13%	6%	6%
: 1 :	2 :	3 :	4 :	5 :	6 :	7 :

Strongly Agree   Strongly Disagree

N = 183   Mean = 3.3   SD = 1.7

COMMENTS USEFUL
I found the comments made by other students to be useful to me.

12%	28%	20%	20%	10%	7%	4%
: 1 :	2 :	3 :	4 :	5 :	6 :	7 :

Strongly Agree   Strongly Disagree

N = 183   Mean = 3.3   SD = 1.6

ASSIGNMENTS USEFUL
I found reading the reviews or assignments of other students to be useful to me.

13%	23%	27%	20%	6%	7%	5%
: 1 :	2 :	3 :	4 :	5 :	6 :	7 :

Strongly Agree   Strongly Disagree

N = 182   Mean = 3.2   SD = 1.6

NOT CHOOSE ANOTHER
I would NOT choose to take another online course.

11%	9%	6%	10%	10%	19%	35%
: 1 :	2 :	3 :	4 :	5 :	6 :	7 :

Strongly Agree   Strongly Disagree

N = 182   Mean = 5.0   SD = 2.1

BETTER LEARNING
I found the course to be a better learning experience than normal face-to-face
courses.

17%	15%	14%	25%	10%	9%	10%
: 1 :	2 :	3 :	4 :	5 :	6 :	7 :

Strongly Agree   Strongly Disagree

N = 183   Mean = 3.6   SD = 1.9

LEARNED MORE
I learned a great deal more because of the use of EIES.

10%	20%	15%	27%	9%	11%	8%
: 1 :	2 :	3 :	4 :	5 :	6 :	7 :

Strongly Agree   Strongly Disagree

N = 182   Mean = 3.7   SD = 1.8

TRADITIONAL MORE
I would have gotten more out of a traditional course.

12%	7%	6%	21%	15%	16%	23%
: 1 :	2 :	3 :	4 :	5 :	6 :	7 :

Strongly Agree   Strongly Disagree

N = 73   Mean = 4.6   SD = 2.0

OVERALL COMMENTS AND SUGGESTIONS

What one or two things about your virtual classroom experience did you like the best?

(1) 34% CONVENIENCE
(2) 16% ENJOY COMPUTERS
(3)   9% COMMUNICATE EASY
(4) 10% CLASS INTEREST
(5)   4% HARD COPY
(6)   1% READ HELPFUL N = 119
(7) 14% SHARE W/OTHERS
(8)   2% CATCH-UP EASY
(9)   2% SAY ANYTHING
(10) 7% SELF-PACED
(11) 1% ACCOMPLISH MORE

What one or two things about your virtual classroom experience were the "worst," the most in need of improvement?

(1) 33% SLOW EIES
(2) 14% NO ACCESS
(3)   4% HATE COMPUTERS
(4)   4% NO HELP
(5)   3% TIME CONSUMING
(6)   3% NEED DOCUMENTATION
(7)   5% HATE SELF-PACED
(8)   4% TOO MUCH WORK N = 103
(9)   3% MORE COORDINATION
(10) 4% TOO HARD
(11) 1% NO CATCH-UP
(12) 1% LESS MATERIAL
(13) 13% BRANCH PROBLEMS
(14) 3% OTHERS COPIED
(15) 2% TIME TESTS
(16) 3% MORE TRAINING
(17) 2% POOR GRAPHICS

Other comments or suggestions for improvements?

(1)   4% REDUCE WORK
(2)   7% EIES RESPONSE
(3)   9% MORE ONLINE
(4) 16% MORE TERMINALS
(5)   2% HELPS INDEPENDENCE
(6)   4% IMPROVES PEER RELATIONSHIPS
(7) 11% HINDERS INDEPENDENCE
(8) 11% NEED FACE-TO-FACE
(9)   4% HARD COPY N = 45
(10) 20% IMPROVE BRANCH
(11) 2% MORE DOCUMENTATION
(12) 4% OTHERS SHOULD READ
(13) 2% IMPROVE SCREENS
(14) 2% STANDARDIZE SOFTWARE

VIRTUAL CLASSROOM SOFTWARE FEATURES

How valuable or useless - and how well designed - do you currently find each of the following features or capabilities of EIES for online classes? (If you have not actually used a feature, please check "Cannot say" and skip to the next feature.) Use the space by each feature for any comments or suggestions.

PEN NAMES   Comments
    10%   25%   21%   6%   7%   31%
:   1   :   2   :   3   :   4   :   5   :   ___
Valuable   Useless   Cannot
                                                          Say

              N = 165   Mean = 2.7   SD = 1.2

    16%   31%   40%   8%   5%
:   1   :   2   :   3   :   4   :   5   :
Well Designed   Poorly Designed
              N = 122   Mean = 2.6   SD = 1.0

BRANCH- RESPONSE
    15%   21%   20%   15%   8%   21%
:   1   :   2   :   3   :   4   :   5   :   ___
Valuable   Useless   Cannot
                                                          Say

              N = 164   Mean = 2.7   SD = 1.2
         12%   18%   32%   18%   20%
:   1   :   2   :   3   :   4   :   5   :
Well Designed   Poorly Designed
              N = 131   Mean = 3.2 S D = 1.3

BRANCH- READ

10%	21%	17%	10%	4%	39%
: 1 :	2 :	3 :	4 :	5 :	
Valuable				Useless	Cannot Say

N = 163 Mean = 2.6 SD = 1.1

12%	23%	37%	19%	10%
: 1 :	2 :	3 :	4 :	5 :
Well Designed			Poorly Designed	

N = 101 Mean = 2.9 SD = 1.1

QUIZ

38%	19%	6%	2%	0%	36%
: 1 :	2 :	3 :	4 :	5 :	
Valuable				Useless	Cannot Say

N = 64 Mean = 1.6 SD = 0.8

44%	27%	20%	7%	2%
: 1 :	2 :	3 :	4 :	5 :
Well Designed			Poorly Designed	

N = 41 Mean = 2.0 SD = 1.1

RUNNING FORTRAN OR PASCAL COMPILERS

6%	6%	13%	5%	0%	70%
: 1 :	2 :	3 :	4 :	5 :	
Valuable				Useless	Cannot Say

N = 63 Mean = 2.5 SD = 1.0

21%	10%	37%	21%	10%
: 1 :	2 :	3 :	4 :	5 :
Well Designed			Poorly Designed	

N = 19 Mean = 2.9 SD = 1.3

GRAPHICS-INPUT Comments

4%	8%	9%	4%	3%	72%
: 1 :	2 :	3 :	4 :	5 :	___
Valuable				Useless	Cannot Say

N = 160 Mean = 2.8 SD = 1.2

8%	26%	38%	15%	13%	
: 1 :	2 :	3 :	4 :	5 :	
Well Designed				Poorly Designed	

N = 47 Mean = 3.0 SD = 1.1

GRAPHICS- DISPLAY

5%	10%	8%	2%	3%	72%
: 1 :	2 :	3 :	4 :	5 :	___
Valuable				Useless	Cannot Say

N = 158 Mean = 2.6 SD = 1.2

16%	24%	28%	18%	14%	
: 1 :	2 :	3 :	4 :	5 :	
Well Designed				Poorly Designed	

N = 50 Mean = 2.9 SD = 1.3

QUESTIONNAIRE FOR STUDENTS WHO DROPPED COURSE
VIRTUAL CLASSROOM PROJECT

Course Name: _____

Course Number and Section: _____

Instructor: _____

Student ID Number: _____

SCHOOL $X = 1.00$ $SD = 0.00$ $N = 9$

I am:

(1) 100% An NJIT Student.

(2)   0% Upsala Student.

(3)   0% New School (Connect-Ed) Student.

(4)   0% Other _____ .

How important were each of the following factors in your decision to drop the course?

Reason	Very Important	Somewhat Important	Not Important	X	SD	N
DHEALTH Health problems or personal problems	22%		78%	2.56	0.88	9
DHARD The course was too hard for me	11%		89%	2.78	0.67	9
DWORK The course was too much work		11%	89%	2.89	0.33	9
DINSTR I did not like the instructor	22%	22%	56%	2.33	0.87	9
DBORING The subject matter was boring or irrelevant	22%		78%	2.56	0.88	9
DDROP I had too many other courses and needed to drop one (or more)	22%		78%	2.56	0.88	9
DPOOR I was doing poorly	11%	11%	78%	2.67	0.71	9
DNOLIKE I did not like the "virtual classroom" approach	22%	11%	67%	2.44	0.88	9
DDEMAND I had too many outside demands (other classes, full-time work)	33%		67%	2.33	1.00	9

DMATCH   X = 2.44 SD = 1.42 N = 9
The course did not match my expectations:
       33%   22%   22%   11%   11%
:   1   :   2   :   3   :   4   :   5
:

     Strongly   Agree   Don't   Disagree   Strongly
      Agree   Know   Disagree

DTRANS   X = 1.56 SD = 0.53 N = 9
I transferred to another   44% Yes
section of the same
course   56% No

DAGAIN X = 3.44 SD = 1.59 N = 9
If I had the opportunity, I would register for another class which used the "Virtual
Classroom" approach:
       11%   22%   22%   0%   44%
:   1   :   2   :   3   :   4   :   5
:

     Strongly   Agree   Don't   Disagree   Strongly
      Agree   Know   Disagree

DMOST   X = 2.62 SD = 1.60 N = 8
(1) 38% CONFLICTED
(2) 12% SIMILAR CLASS
(3) 12% FAMILY PROBLEMS
(4) 25% TOO HARD
(5) 12% DISLIKE INSTRUCTOR

DBEST   X = 2.75 SD = 0.50 N = 4
What did you like best about the virtual classroom approach?
(1) 25% IDEOLOGY OF SYSTEM
(2) 75% CONVENIENCE

DWORST   X = 3.00 SD = 1.41 N = 6
What did you DISLIKE the most about the virtual classroom as it was implemented
in your course?
(1) 17% LESS TERMINALS
(2) 17% SYSTEM TOO HARD
(3) 33% HINDERED DISCUSSION
(4) 17% ASSIGNMENTS HARD
(5) 17% DISLIKE INSTRUCTOR

ANY ADDITIONAL COMMENTS?

THANK YOU VERY MUCH FOR COMPLETING AND
RETURNING THIS QUESTIONNAIRE TO:
(USING THE ENCLOSED POSTAGE PAID ENVELOPE)

Ellen Schreihofer
CCCC @ NJIT
323 King Blvd.
Newark, NJ 07102

APPENDIX I-D
ITEMS COMPRISING COMPOSITE INDEX MEASURES

Table A-1

ITEMS IN THE COMPUTER ATTITUDES INDEX

For each of the following pairs of words, please circle the response that is closest to your CURRENT FEELINGS ABOUT USING COMPUTERS. For instance, for the first pair of words, if you feel computer systems in general are completely "stimulating" to use and not at all "dull," circle "1"; "4" means that you are undecided or neutral or think they are equally likely to be stimulating or dull; "3" means you feel that they are slightly more stimulating than dull, etc.

									X	SD
DULL-1 [R]										
Stimulating	1	2	3	4	5	6	7	Dull		
	23%	24%	21%	21%	5%	2%	3%		2.8	1.5
DREARY-1 [R]										
Fun	1	2	3	4	5	6	7	Dreary		
	22%	27%	23%	15%	8%	2%	3%		2.7	1.5
DIFFICULT-1 [R]										
Easy	1	2	3	4	5	6	7	Difficult		
	7%	15%	18%	27%	16%	12%	5%		3.8	1.6
IMPERSONAL-1 [R]										
Personal	1	2	3	4	5	6	7	Impersonal		
	6%	10%	13%	36%	11%	13%	11%		4.2	1.6
HELPFUL-1										
Hindering	1	2	3	4	5	6	7	Helpful		
	4%	2%	5%	15%	16%	31%	27%		5.4	1.6
UNTHREATENING-1										
Threatening	1	2	3	4	5	6	7	Unthreatening		
	4%	6%	6%	26%	12%	21%	26%		5.0	1.7
INEFFICIENT-1 [R]										
Efficient	1	2	3	4	5	6	7	Inefficient		
	38%	30%	15%	10%	2%	2%	2%		2.2	1.4
OBLIGING-1										
Demanding	1	2	3	4	5	6	7	Obliging		
	12%	12%	13%	40%	11%	8%	4%		3.6	1.5
UNDESIRABLE-1 [R]										
Desirable	1	2	3	4	5	6	7	Undesirable		
	25%	26%	16%	23%	3%	3%	4%		2.8	1.6

Notes: [R] indicates item was reversed for scoring
       Range = 7 (least favorable) to 70 (most favorable)
       Alpha = .82

Table A-2
Items Comprising the "EIES Expectations" Index

Indicate your expectations about how it will be to use this system by circling the number which best indicates where your feelings lie on the scales below.

EASY-1

4%	6%	14%	25%	19%	20%	11%
: 1 :	2 :	3 :	4 :	5 :	6 :	7 :

Hard to learn   Easy to learn

(Mean = 4.5, Std Dev = 1.6)

FRIENDLY-1

4%	7%	8%	24%	28%	20%	9%
: 1 :	2 :	3 :	4 :	5 :	6 :	7 :

Impersonal   Friendly

(Mean = 4.6, Std Dev = 1.5)

NOT FRUSTRATING-1

4%	10%	16%	24%	21%	21%	9%
: 1 :	2 :	3 :	4 :	5 :	6 :	7 :

Frustrating   Not frustrating

(Mean = 4.3, Std Dev = 1.6)

PRODUCTIVE-1

2%	1%	5%	18%	24%	34%	16%
: 1 :	2 :	3 :	4 :	5 :	6 :	7 :

Unproductive   Productive

(Mean = 5.3 Std Dev = 1.3)

EFFICIENCY-1 [R]
Do you expect that use of the System will increase the efficiency of your education (the quantity of work that you can complete in a given time)?

19%	21%	14%	24%	15%	5%	2%
: 1 :	2 :	3 :	4 :	5 :	6 :	7 :

Definitely yes   Unsure   Definitely not

(Mean = 3.2 Std Dev = 1.6)

QUALITY-1 [R]
Do you expect that use of the System will increase the quality of your education?

21%	22%	18%	25%	6%	4%	3%
: 1 :	2 :	3 :	4 :	5 :	6 :	7 :

Definitely yes   Unsure   Definitely not

(Mean = 3.0 Std Dev = 1.6)

RESENT-1
I resent being required to use EIES for this course.

4%	3%	6%	19%	7%	17%	43%
: 1 :	2 :	3 :	4 :	5 :	6 :	7 :

Definitely yes   Unsure   Definitely not

(Mean = 5.5 Std Dev = 1.7)

OVERALL-1 [R]
Overall, how useful do you expect the System to be for online classes?

23%	27%	20%	19%	6%	3%	2%
: 1 :	2 :	3 :	4 :	5 :	6 :	7 :

Very Useful   Not useful at all

(Mean = 2.8 Std Dev = 1.5)

EXPECTED TIME

While you are part of an online course, how much time in the average week do you foresee yourself using EIES in relation to your coursework?
(1) 4% Less than 30 minutes
(2) 12% 30 minutes to 1 hour
(3) 43% 1 - 3 hours
(4) 29% 4 - 6 hours
(5) 7% 7 - 9 hours
(6) 5% 10 hours or more
Notes: Range = 9 (worst expectations) to 62 (highest)
          Cronbach's Alpha = .82

Table A-3
ITEMS INCLUDED IN THE COURSE RATING INDEX

WASTE OF TIME (R)
This course was a waste of time   SA   A   N   D   SD
COURSE OVERALL
How would you rate this course over-all?
(1)Excellent   (2)Very good   (3)Good   (4)Fair   (5)Poor
MORE INTERESTED
I became more interested in the subject   SA   A   N   D   SD
LEARNED FACTS
I learned a great deal of factual material   SA   A   N   D   SD
CONCEPTS
I gained a good understanding of basic concepts   SA   A   N   D   SD
CENTRAL ISSUES
I learned to identify central issues in this field   SA   A   N   D   SD
COMMUNICATED CLEARLY
I developed the ability to communicate clearly
about this subject   SA   A   N   D   SD

(R) INDICATES ITEM WAS REVERSED FOR SCORING

RANGE = 7 (BEST) TO 35 (WORST)

ALPHA = .88

Table A 4
THE INSTRUCTOR RATING INDEX

WELL ORGANIZED
Instructor organized the course well   SA   A   N   D   SD
GRADING FAIR
Grading was fair and impartial   SA   A   N   D   SD
ENJOYS TEACHING
Instructor seems to enjoy teaching   SA   A   N   D   SD
LACKS KNOWLEDGE (R)
Instructor lacks sufficient knowledge
about this subject area   SA   A   N   D   SD
IDEAS ENCOURAGED
Students were encouraged to express ideas   SA   A   N   D   SD
PRESENTED CLEARLY
Instructor presented material clearly
and summarized main points   SA   A   N   D   SD
OTHER VIEWS
Instructor discussed points of view
other than her/his own   SA   A   N   D   SD
PERSONAL HELP
The student was able to get personal
help in this course   SA   A   N   D   SD
INSTRUCTOR BORING (R)
Instructor presented material in
a boring manner   SA   A   N   D   SD
HELPFUL CRITIQUE
Instructor critiqued my work in
a constructive and helpful way   SA   A   N   D   SD
TEACHER OVERALL
Overall, I would rate this teacher as
(1)Excellent   (2)Very good   (3)Good   (4)Fair   (5)Poor

(R) indicates item scoring was reversed for the scale

Range = 11 (best) to 55 (worst)
Alpha = .88

Table A-5
Components of the INTEREST and SYNTHESIS Indexes

Index of Increased INTEREST in the Subject

MORE INTERESTED [R]
I became more interested in the subject   SA   A   N   D   SD
DID ADDITIONAL READING [R]
I was stimulated to do additional reading   SA   A   N   D   SD
DISCUSS OUTSIDE [R]
I was stimulated to discuss related topics
outside of class   SA   A   N   D   SD

[R] indicates response values reversed for index scoring
Range = 3 (least interest stimulated) to 15
Alpha = .66

Items Included in the Synthesis Index

CENTRAL ISSUES [R]
I learned to identify central issues in this field   SA   A   N   D   SD
GENERALIZATIONS [R]
My ability to integrate facts and develop
generalizations improved   SA   A   N   D   SD
RELATIONSHIPS [R]
I learned to see relationships between important
topics and ideas   SA   A   N   D   SD

Range = 3 (low synthesis) to 15
Alpha = .80

Table A-6
ITEMS COMPRISING THE "COLLABORATION" INDEX

| I developed new friendships in this class [R] | SA | A | N | D | SD |
| I learned to value other points of view [R] | SA | A | N | D | SD |

Individual vs. Group Learning

Some courses are essentially a very INDIVIDUAL experience; contact with other students does not play an important part in your learning. In other courses, communication with other students plays a dominant role. For THIS COURSE, please circle the number below that seems to be what you experienced.

1	2	3	4	5	6
Individual					Group
experience					experience

The help I got from other students was – [R]

1	2	3	4	5	6
Crucially important					Useless or
to me					misleading

Students in my class tended to be

1	2	3	4	5	6
Not at all					Extremely
cooperative					cooperative

How often did you communicate with other students outside of class, by computer, "face-to-face" or on the telephone?

| 1 | 2 | 3 | 4 | 5 | 6 |
| Never | | | | | Constantly |

Items marked R reversed for scoring
Range = 6 (least collaboration) to 34 (most collaboration)
Alpha = .74

APPENDIX *II*

INTERVIEWS WITH STUDENTS

GUIDE FOR PERSONAL INTERVIEW WITH STUDENTS

Interviewee _____ Date _____

Interviewer _____

Introduction: Hello, my name is XX and I am working as (job title) in the Virtual Classroom project.

What I would like to do is ask you some questions that will give us a deeper insight into your own personal experiences and reactions to the online course you participated in than we are able to get from the standard questionnaire. [If still online . . .]. Then I would like to watch you for a little while while you sign online, and tell me what you are thinking as you interact with the system and the class. We will share a summary of the comments by all the students in your class whom we interview with your instructor, but we will not identify any of the comments as coming from any particular student, OK?

1. Initial recruitment and feelings

How did you first hear about the virtual classroom project or the experimental online section in which you participated?

What were your initial feelings or reactions . . . what attracted you, what didn't sound good about this approach?

2. How about the initial training session . . . after it was over, did you feel that you would be able to sign online and find your class conference, or

was there something that was not clear about what the procedure would be?

3. Where did you go to use the microcomputer equipment you needed to participate each week?

Were there any problems with the availability of facilities or with the lab assistant's ability to help you get online?? (probe)

Did you have any sort of regular schedule each week when you would sign online to participate, or how was it that you decided when to log on?

4. What were your initial feelings or impressions about the online class during the training and the first week? Can you remember what you particularly liked, or what you didn't like or found confusing? (probe . . . anything else?)

5. What were your reactions to reading the comments or contributions by the other students . . . to what extent did you find this interesting or helpful, and to what extent did you feel this was a waste of time? Why?

Did you feel that you were part of a group or class working together, or did you feel that you were pretty much alone in learning the material?

(If felt part of group). Did you or the instructor do anything in particular that helped you to be able to work and socialize with other students in the online class?

6. How about the lecture-type material presented by the instructor . . . did you find it easier to understand the material in writing, or do you think you would have learned it better if you had listened to it in spoken form? Why?

7. Did you ever look at or join any of the public conferences on EIES, besides your class conference?

If yes . . . which ones, and what did you think of them?

If no . . . why not?

Did you ever exchange messages with anybody online who was not in your class or connected to the project?

If yes . . . how did this happen?

How did you feel about this experience of communicating with "strangers"?

8. How would you describe your relationship to your instructor online? Do you feel MORE or LESS able to communicate and relate to your teacher? Why?

Q 9 varies depending on whether interview is with current student or fall student

9. [This question for fall students—look first at their open-ended questions]

On the questionnaire you completed, you said that the things you liked best were [read quote]. Could you expand on that?

You also said that the things you liked least about the virtual classroom approach were [read quote]. Looking back, do you have anything to add to that?

[This question version for current students]

Have you developed any particular routines or tricks of the trade that are making EIES more valuable to you than it was at first?

At this point in your online course, what do you like best about the Virtual Classroom approach . . . that is, what is good about it compared to a course given in the traditional classroom? [probe . . . anything else?]

What do you currently like least, or feel are the greatest problems or shortcomings about this mode of course delivery?

10. What advice would you give a student who is thinking of signing up for an online course?

How about your instructor . . . what advice would you give about how they could be more effective if they try teaching this course online again?

11. Is there anything else you would like to tell us about your experiences . . . anything that was especially funny, or memorable, or valuable, or unpleasant about your experience?

****

Selected, slightly edited interview transcripts follow.

Interview 1
Face-to-Face Interview with a Positive Math 305 Student
Roxanne Hiltz, March 26, 1987

Q- How did you first hear about the project?

R- The reason I took it was it was the only section I could get into. It said "taught via computer" and I did not know what that meant. It fit in my schedule and I had to take something. I had never heard about it before – did not know what it was about until we got to class the first day. I was real intrigued by it. I like computers a lot. I've had a lot of fun with EIES.

Q- What's fun about it?

A- I don't want to sound bad about the course, but the fun part I've had is in the "Murder 1" conference. That was fun checking it out everyday, seeing what the group responses were. And the same with the statistics class. Before we started going to +quiz and +branch, everything was a conference comment. You could see what people said, like what they liked and what they didn't like . . . They were putting jokes in there . . .

I was trying to think how to describe it when you sent me that message. It's DIFFERENT. It's nice to have a class taught a different way than everyone sitting in front of the teacher. And the teacher goes on and writes, and you write it down . . . and you take the test and hand your homework in . . . I do think I miss it though, because she seems like she'd be GREAT teaching in front of a class. I've heard other people who have taken it with her there in the class, they say she is a great teacher, doesn't bore you or overwhelm you with work. She's kind and friendly and everything.

Q- Does any of her personality come through online?

R- Yes. she'll put a message in and say, "Have a great week," or "Hope your spring break is real nice." Especially, if you have a message or a problem, she'll write back, and say, "Hi there, how have you been? You have a problem with this. . . . " It's really almost like talking on the phone. I try to send messages back the same way, real casual. It's not a strict teacher–student kind of thing. Because of her, you feel a lot closer, because it's so easy just to pop a question. She'll answer the next day, or whenever you come online.

Q- You still feel you have a relationship, though you hardly ever see her?

R- Yes. Also, I won't use the guy's name, but the first class, there was this jerk in the back, I said thank God we will not meet in this class with him anymore. In a way it's good, I can avoid him . . .

Q- In the beginning it was all comments, trying to get the students comfortable with the system and with each other. You're saying you were a bit disappointed when it got down to business?

R- In a way, because you miss participating in a class. But I do like the idea, I really do. Like the fact that some people could take the class from say, Chicago or California . . .

Q- The initial training session . . . basically, for your class, we did not have the right space for it.

R- Yeah, there was a lot of doubling up. I was lucky, I got there early and got a terminal. There was a guy who stood next to me, and I see him all the time now. We go over the assignments, or we yell across the Center, "Hey, did you get the homework?" So I run over there and get on the system and get it printed out . . .

Q- That's interesting, that you do talk occasionally to other students in the class.

R- Um-humm. And of course you run into them every once in awhile in 306. It's good for me because it's my first semester here. It's almost as easy as meeting somebody in [a regular] class. You say, "Hey, I had a problem with number 2, I'll trade with you for number 1." For the first half of the semester I was having a problem doing all of it myself, and there's always some people to trade with.

Q- I'm glad to hear that students still have relationships and work on things together. . . . You normally go to 306, you don't have a micro-computer?

R- I have one at home but I don't have a modem.

Q- How often do you go?

R- I normally go every day. Except Wednesday, I don't have classes then, and it's a long drive. But I go every day about 10am, quarter after 10. Print out whatever is on there.

Q- About how long are your sessions?

R- Half hour. But that's because I don't sit there and read off the computer. I think you'd go blind after awhile! I have it printed out and then take it home. Then work out problems and come back in the day it's due or the day before. I usually go through it once, read the people's comments and things . . . I just read them once and don't take them home. Then I figure out the lessons and whatever and print them out. Then when I come in, I just have to log on and put the assignments in. So I'm not on as much as somebody who just sits there online and reads it all. But it's really better, because for the final or something, what are they going to do, read them all again?

Q- Has there been any problem with having enough printers in 306?

R- There's only one that works. The AT&T doesn't have a tractor feed, and it jams. You just have to time it right, and get there when someone isn't on it.

Q- Are there any other routines or ways of using the system that you have developed that work well for you?

R- Not really, because that's really all that I do.

Q- How do you find the workload compared to other courses?

R- It's a lot easier, but that's because my other courses, it's really wild. This other course, 90% of my time is that course, I have to study it all the time, fight my way through it.
It's like two and a half hours a week I spend online, then at home, I have to read over the stuff and work on the problems. I use a marker on the printouts, and go through the book the same way. The total time is about five hours a week. But before a quiz it's more. Though in essence it's an open book quiz, because you have a time limit, if you don't know where to find it, it would take more than half an hour to do it.

Q- Are there any topics in the course where you found it really hard to understand from the combination of what's online and what's in the book?

R- Yeah, at the beginning, with the different kinds of probability theory, subjective, a priori, all those . . .

Q- So, it wasn't the mathematical part, it was the theoretical or philosoph-ical part?

R- Um-humm. I'm not very good at philosophy. The math part, you have what she teaches online and the book and between the two you can figure it out.

Q- What are your general reactions to reading comments by other students?

R- They're entertaining. Some of those people have some witty comments. That makes the class more interesting. If you find that there are a lot of comments, then you get online just to see them. I've joined in there and provided a little wit here and there. It adds levity, you know, if everything is all bare bones and cut and dry, you're not interested, you don't want to study that much, you only care about your grade. This way, it adds interest to it.

Q- Do you feel more or less free to say something witty in a conference than you would in a class?

R- Probably more free. Because, I may seem gregarious, but I'm pretty shy. It's easier from here. Because it seems like one-on-one.

Q- Do you learn things from the comments of others, or is it more the sociable interest?

R- I think it's more the sociable, in the comments. But we don't have the comments now, we have the branches.

Q- How did you get into the Murder 1 experiments . . . how and when and where did you find other things online?

R- When you first get online, they have an EIES headline. It turned out that I was spending a LOT of time at it. There are other things on there, but I'm going to stay away from them the rest of the semester.

Q- Do you now exchange messages with anybody you met in Murder 1? Or communicate with anybody on the system who's not in your class?

R- Now, I don't. At the end of Murder 1, we were trying to find out where we were all from. One guy's in California, Jill's in Texas, somebody in Woodbridge. We all said, wouldn't it be great if we could get together? But aside from class, I haven't gotten together with anybody else on EIES.

I'm wondering- will I still have that number after this semester?

Interviewer—Yes, everybody is given the option of keeping their number, but it drops to a class two account, which gives poor response during busy hours.

R- Yeah, I'd be curious to. You run into people and you find out they are on EIES, And you say, "All right, I'll send you a message." Like, what are you doing on Friday? That would happen in any class.

Q- You mentioned about quiz and branch. Would you talk about your feelings about those procedures?

R- Pluses—it's a lot harder to cheat. You can't look at conference comments and see what everybody else did. Especially when we did a couple that were actual problems, you wouldn't have to study if they were regular comments. I can see the reason for them. And I like the idea with Branch that you can find out what other people's answers are once you put your answer in. I do know people who have abused it.

Q- How do you abuse it?

R- You do it with somebody else. And find out the answers. I've seen that done. But it's better that you do it alone. As far as I'm concerned, I'm here to learn. Some people are just after grades. There's one guy in a couple of my classes who cheats left and right.

Q- He cheats in all classes? And found a way to do it this way too?

R- Right. If you want to cheat, you can. You find out who those people are. And when they ask, you say, "Oh, no, I didn't do the homework either," you don't give it to them. Because you don't get anything back from them. If it's a two way street, I don't consider that cheating. I'm not going to say names, but there is one person who does not reciprocate, and no one is helping him. No one talks to him in class.

Q- This is in the online class?

R- Both.

Q- In the beginning, the things that you mentioned that were good were that it fit around your schedule, and it's different and therefore interesting. Anything else you can think of as an advantage?

R- Related to the fact that when I signed up for it was listed as Wednesday and Friday, but since it's my only class on Wednesday, I don't have to come to school on Wednesday, and I can take it whenever . . . I can take the quiz anytime before Thursday. I find it very flexible that way. I can come in between classes and do it. So you can "front load" it all in the beginning of the week, or wait till the end if something else has come up. That's what's good about it.

Q- What about the greatest problems or shortcomings?

R- That immediate answer to a problem which you will get in a class. Where you raise your hand in class and the teacher answers. A lot of times, even if Rose is on, I send the question and sign off, because it might be 10 or 15 minutes until she answers. So I'll get it the next day. Aside from that, I don't see any problems with it.

Q- What kind of advice would you give a student who sees this on a schedule?

R- I'd say take it, especially if you have not had any computer experience. Anybody in their right mind knows that somebody who has not had any computer experience will be passed by in jobs by somebody who does.

Q- What you saying is, take it, because besides learning statistics, you are going to learn something about computers?

R- That's one reason. The other is the flexibility. You can learn as much as if she were teaching it face to face.

Q- Do you have any questions for me about the project?

R- Are there plans to have other courses? I think there are 2 or 3 now?

Q- Right now we don't necessarily have funding for next year. We hope to get enough hardware at NJIT so that regularly, there might be say half a dozen courses that have online sections.

R- I'd like to take other courses. There are obviously things it would be hard to apply to- say a mechanics course on structures – but English

Interviewer – Yes, we had an English course online. And CIS seems to work well.

R- Yes, that would. But unfortunately, I took 213 already. I'd like to take another course.

[end of interview chat and thanks edited out]

Interview 2
TELEPHONE INTERVIEW WITH NEGATIVE
MATH 305 STUDENT
George Baldwin, 7/2/87

Q: Do you remember what it was like when you first came into the program? That is, when they told you it was to be offered "online" how did you feel?

A: I didn't like it!

Q: Did it come as a surprise to you?

A: Yes

Q: Did they offer you an alternative?

A: Yes, a night class. And that didn't fit my schedule.

Q: So, did you feel that they were not being straightforward with you about how the class was to be offered?

A: Well, it wasn't in the registration material, if that's what you mean. Maybe it was, but I just missed it.

Q: They gave you a training session. How did you feel about the training conference?

A: Just fine. There were plenty of people to help.

Q: Where did you usually use the computer to get online?

A: At my home. I have a computer at home.

Q: Then would you say that it was convenient for you to do your work?

A: Once I got a modem, yeah!

Q: Did they explain to you how to plug the modem into your computer?

A: I already knew how to do that. I usually signed on when I got home at night.

A: Since you were signing on from home, there weren't any lab assistants available to you. Did you have any problems in not having help?

A: I could usually hack my way around!

Q: Did you have a regular schedule that you followed each week in signing on for class?

A: No. . . . That was one of my biggest problems . . . I know you're going to ask that. Personally, I usually try not to take self-study classes. And that's pretty much what that is. I don't feel that I have the self discipline for it. I don't have enough time in my day as it is. To sit down and make myself do something like that. . . . .Self study takes a certain kind of person to do that. And I'm not that kind of person.

Q: The first week that you signed on to the system . . . can you remember what your first impressions of the system were?

A: It didn't bother me to take a class online like that. I am not scared of computers. I just don't like self study. I don't have complaints about the class.

Q: When you did go online with the other students, how did you feel about the comments and contributions of the other class members? Were they of any use to you, or did you find them to be just a waste of time?

A: I usually just blew off the other class members comments and went straight to the professors lectures. I wouldn't say that the other students comments were a waste of my time, I just didn't read them!

Q: Did you feel like you were part of a group, or were you pretty much alone in learning the material?

A: Pretty much alone . . . but I feel that way about my other classes as well. I have two other friends that I sometimes study with, but that's about it.

Q: Did the instructor do anything that you found helpful in doing your work?

A: She was very helpful. She gave us her home phone number and we were able to call her at the office . . . voice or online.

Q: Did you ever ask her for help online?

A: No, usually I went to see her at her office.

Q: How did you feel about the lecture material presented by your instructor? That is, did you like getting the lectures in written form online or would you have preferred a real-time voice lecture?

A: I would have rather had it in a regular lecture type classroom. I don't really LIKE sitting in a classroom, but I find it easier for me. It works better. If you have a question you can just stop and ask right then and there.

Q: While you were doing your online class, did you ever join any other public conferences?

A: No.

Q: Why?

A: I worked full time and went to school full time. Busy. It's kinda tough. I'd usually go to work . . . then to school,.. then to work and then back to the house to study at 11 at night, and I didn't want to sit down and read some other stuff.

Q: How about private messages? Did you private message any of the other people in your class?

A: Yes.

Q: How often, and why?

A: Sometimes to ask them a question about something-or-another. Some of the time with the T A . . . who was there to help. I send her messages sometimes.

Q: How about people outside of the class? Did you ever send them private messages?

A: No, I didn't know anyone outside of the class. I really don't think that I used the system as well as I could have. But I think that's because I didn't have any time.

Q: The relationship that you had with your teacher—did you feel more or less able to communicate with the professor through the computer?

A: Less

Q: You mentioned that you liked to go to her office and talk with her..

A: Yes, more personal.

Q: You wrote on your questionnaire that you felt that the EIES system was impersonal. That's one of the things I'd like to talk about. Could you tell me why you thought it was impersonal?

A: Because you had a computer in front of you . . . instead of a person. Like I said before, if I have a question in class I can just stick my hand up. You can't do that on a computer. You just have that text in front of you. You know how it is . . . sometimes you can sidetrack the professor. Get'em to bull shit for a while . . . you can't do that on a computer.

Q: What was the best thing about the EIES system?

A: I could sit down and do my work at any time.

Q: And the worst thing?

A: That it was self study. If it came down to taking another self-study class like that again, I'd really have to think long and hard about it. I usually try not to.

Q: If you had a friend or another student who asked you for your advice about taking an online class, what would you tell them?

A: I'd tell them what it was like, then say, "It's up to you as to whether you can do it or not." It's self-study.

Q: If you were talking with a professor who was thinking about teaching an online class, what advice would you give the prof?

A: I'd tell 'em that you have to make yourself available. You really do. Personal interaction.

Q: Not just online?

A: Yeah. You don't have to have millions of office hours, but you gotta

make yourself a little bit more available. Just in case there is a problem
. . . you just can't settle it over a computer.

*****

[Note: Besides regular office hours, the instructor made herself available
in the Lab for 2 hours every Thursday, specifically to help online
students with any difficulties. This student shows no recognition of
these opportunities.]

Interview 3
INTERVIEW WITH MODERATELY POSITIVE
CC140Y STUDENT
Roxanne Hiltz, April 10, 1987

Note: the student responded to a message requesting volunteers for
interviews. She was one of the better students in the course.

Key: I or Q = Remark or question from Roxanne Hiltz, Interviewer

R = response from student

Q- How did you first hear about the experimental means of delivery for
   this course?
R- In the class, the first day. I had no idea before then.
Q- What were your impressions that first day?
R- "Oh, No!" (laughs . . .) "What are we getting into . . . this is something
   new!"
Q- Did you consider transferring to another section at that point?
R- No, not me. (Q- why not?) R- Because I knew that every new thing, in
   the beginning it's hard, but then you get used to it.
Q- So, to you it was sort of a challenge?
R- Yes.
Q- Do you have any thoughts about those first couple of sessions, any
   ways they should have been done better?
R- The handouts were very good. I used them later on. In the first session,
   I was really confused, I did not know what was going on. It was pretty
   crowded; hard to listen and hard to know what was going on. I paid
   attention but it did not help too much. I think it would be better in a
   classroom. Put it on the board and go over the handouts.
Q- One idea would be to start in the lab; do a very brief demo, saying "here

is the system you are going to use;" move to a classroom and explain it on the board, referring to the handouts . . . .

R- Yes, and then go back to the lab afterwards. Some people may not have used the handouts.

Interviewer- Maybe that is why they had so much trouble . . .

R- I think it is better if the teacher himself give the lecture. Show about the conference, where to put messages..

Q- Try to compare this to courses you have had in the traditional classroom . . . what do you like, what don't you like, what problems you have had . . .

R- What's good is that you don't have to be in class. But that's a problem, too. I'll say, ' I have time, till Wednesday,' then once you start to read everything you find out you have to read it at least twice. You sometimes don't do your homework really well, because it is a last-moment exercise before you know it." If you have class every 2 days, you know you have to be prepared. So, it's good and bad . . . you have the time, but you have to know how to make good use of it.

Another problem is, sometimes you don't feel comfortable asking the teacher questions through the computer. In class, you can raise your hand, or you can ask questions after class. It is not as comfortable to ask a question online, so you don't ask.

Probe- What makes you feel less comfortable?

R- Maybe he will take off credits or something. Sometimes it is too late to put a question in (the assignment is already due). It's more personal when you see the teacher.

Q- Do you ever work at all with other students in the class?

R- Not really working, but sometimes people ask questions.

Q- How could things be improved so that there is more communication with the teacher and the other students?

R- With the teacher, the communication was good. It was just the part about asking questions about the material. The idea of quizzes— probably nobody will like it, but I think it was a good idea. It will force you to sit down an do your homework. You have to do it on time, which is very good. He should start this from the beginning. What has happened is, now I got my new assignments, and so many things were put at the last moment. He should put more in the beginning, to divide it better so all the pressure does not come at the end.

How to improve . . . hmm . . . it's cute idea to use it; I like it. Maybe a few more examples would help. Maybe he should direct, "This student and this student, you have to do this assignment together, through the computer."

Q- OK . . . one of the things we wanted to do was somehow getting the students doing something together online.

R- From the beginning to the end, this could be done, but the partners could be changed for different assignments.

Q- How would you feel about being assigned a partner?

R- No problem. Like (name) and I, we write each other messages all the time about questions. But nobody else asks me questions other than (X). So, you could change partners, and sometimes have a group assignment. Then, you do have to depend on your partner; and if he doesn't do his part in the end . . .

Q- Yes, that is one problem, assigning grades when the partners do not work equally. That's a good idea, though.

Q- Do you think that the freshman or sophomore level is good for this sort of course delivery, or should it be only for upper level courses?

R- If you want to study, you study; it does not matter if you are a Freshman or a Junior or a Senior. It's a challenge.

Q- Is there anything else you particularly liked about this mode of delivery, other than not having to go to class?

R- Yes, I like having the complete lecture. You can get it and then read it three days later; or you can go in the middle of the night. It was easier for me.

Q- Some of the students have not been very active in the class at all. Have any of them said anything to you about why this is?

R- Probably because they don't have the time. They postpone it until the last minute, and then the last minute it is too late to do everything.

Interview 4
TELEPHONE INTERVIEW WITH NEGATIVE
CC140 STUDENT
George Baldwin, 6/30/87

In the follow-up questionnaire, this student indicated that she did not like the EIES classroom approach. By her own admission she also did not do well with her final grade. She DID like the instructor. Text of the interview follows.

Q- Do you have time to talk with me about your experiences with your online EIES computer class?

A- I have time, but I didn't do well in the class!

Q- Oh, that's okay. I just want to find out about your experience with the class.

A- Oh, okay!

Q- Great. Do you remember what it was like the first time you used the terminal to go to class?

A- I thought it was interesting.

Q- You weren't intimidated by the machine or the computer at all?

A- Oh, no. Because before I had taken Stats I had had computers.

Q- Then you had used computers before. How did you feel about the course being taught online – could you give me your impressions about how you felt when you heard that the course would be offered online?

A- I didn't understand it at first. I thought that, it, well, I didn't really know what it meant. I didn't know what "online" meant until I got there.

Q- They gave you some training before you went online. Do you remember what the training was like and how you felt about it?

A- Well, there were two training sessions and they were 2 hours each and they went over all the commands and how to hook up to EIES and the phone numbers.

Q- Did you feel confident in signing on, and getting into your class conference?

A- Well, it took me about a week more before I could sign on and get on by myself. They had people there to help me in the beginning, but then I started picking up on my own.

Q- Where did you go to get online? That is, where did you use a computer for signing onto your class conference?

A- At my college – at Upsala.

Q- You didn't have any problems of access to a computer?

A- Well, no. Sometimes they were busy, but I usually didn't have to wait too long. . . . about 5 minutes.

Q- Did you have problems in getting help from a lab assistant?

A- No. They were the ones who helped me get online in the beginning and then I picked it up. And they helped me print it out.

Q- How often do you recall signing on each week?

A- My course was only 6 weeks: In the beginning I didn't sign on at all because I was sick. Then I started going three times a week. Same as my other classes.

Q- Oh, then you had a regular time for signing on?

A- Yes. About 10:00. It fit into my other classes.

Q- If you had a computer at home, would you have signed on from there or still gone to school?

A- I probably would have blown off the one at school . . . after I had learned to sign on at the lab. . . . maybe getting my assignments at school, but doing my work at home.

Q- Can you remember the first week you signed on? Can you remember what you particularly liked or disliked about the EIES system?

A- Well, I thought it was pretty easy to understand. I mean, the computer told you everything to do! The only thing that I had trouble with was like trying to get to the scratchpad . . . because like in the beginning you had to hit break and all that.

Q- Did you have problems with the scratchpad editor?
A- No, not at all.
Q- When other students made entries, and you read them . . . how did you find their comments: useful, interesting, or a waste of time?
A- Well, most of the students who made comments were the ones who really understood the class and they were about the lectures. And they were pretty helpful, especially when the homework could be checked.
Q- Did you make very many comments yourself?
A- No.
A- You had to send conferences to your teacher, but I didn't say much.
Q- Well tell me: Did you feel that you were a part of a class, or did you feel alone in your studies?
A- Well, we had a buddy system, and this other girl and I went together. I felt by myself, or with her.
Q- About the instructor. Was the instructor there to help you?
A- Yes.
Q- Your instructor presented lecture material online. Did you find it easier to understand it in writing, or would you have preferred to have had it in a verbal type lecture?
A- I liked it better in writing.
Q- Better than in a spoken form? Why was that?
A- Because I always find that when someone gives me something written I find it easier to comprehend it. Sometimes when people talk your mind wanders and you don't get it. But when it's written, its all there for you. When people talk they don't keep repeating themselves. This way I could just read it over and understand it.
Q- Do you think you keep good notes in class?
A- Sometimes, but like I say my mind wanders and you just try to pick it up but it's pretty hard. But otherwise I take decent notes.
Q- While you were on EIES, did you try any of the public conferences besides the one for your class?
A- Well, my girlfriend was in a French class and she connected with someone from NJIT and they conversed back and forth. And I used to read some of her stuff about what they would say to each other.
Q- Why did you not join any of the other conferences? Were you short on time, or did you just not know about the public conferences?
A- I guess I just didn't know about them. The only conferences I read were the ones with my class.
Q- Did your teacher, or any instructors ever mention to you about the other public conferences?
A- Some lady did mention that you could get messages or conferences somewhere around the third week.
Q- Did you ever exchange messages with someone not in your class?
A- I never exchanged messages with someone not in my class, but I did

with people in my class. Like when I got sick, I left messages for that girl I used to go with. She got it okay!

Q- Could you describe your relationship with your instructor for me? Were you able to communicate well with him?

A- Well, I did find it hard if I had a problem, because I was sick.

Q- I see . . . is that because you didn't have a terminal at home, or

A- Right. But he said he was always in his office, and everything.

Q- At this point, could you tell me about what you liked about the EIES Virtual classroom approach? What do you think was the best aspect of it?

A- I liked that I was independent and that I could go whenever I wanted to. And I liked how the conferences were written down and I could get my notes. It also helps if you miss a day or two. Because the computer always has your assignments there for you.

Q- What did you like the least about it?

A- There wasn't anything that I didn't really like about it. I thought it was very well organized.

Q- If another student came up to you and said they were thinking about signing up for an online course, what kind of advice would you give that student?

A- Not to get sick! Unless they have a computer at home.

Q- I am thinking about teaching a course online. Speaking to me as a teacher, what advice would you give me about teaching an online course?

A- Well, the teacher that I had was very good. He left messages about what time he would be available for students, if you had any questions or problems. And in his lectures he would put the pages and the chapters. And you could read them along with his lectures if you didn't understand it.

Interview 5
INTERVIEW WITH SATISFIED OSS VC STUDENT
Roxanne Hiltz, March 29, 1987

Q- I want you to think back to when you first heard about how this course was going to be delivered . . . what were your impressions?

R- It was the first day of class. I liked it. I thought it was cool. I just like working with the computer. It seemed different . . . fun. It's turned out pretty good so far.

Q- What is it that it about it that is fun?

R- It lets up some of the class time. You're not pressured to have something done right away – you can do it whenever you want . You can be more free on the computer. Some kids are hesitant to speak up in class. You can put in your thoughts.. people read it. Sometimes they care, sometimes they don't. If they don't, they can just skip on by it. It's also good because there is easy access whenever you want. I have a modem at home. I can go on at 3 o'clock in the morning. That's usually when I do most of my work.

P- Do you do it all at home, or do you sometimes use the computers here?

R- I never use the school system. I heard a lot of kids have problems in the library. They leave messages like, "sorry, I can't read what I'm writing." I bought a modem specially for the class. I saw that it would be kind of useless to come down every day to use the school system. It works much better from home.

P- Anything else that you like about it?

R- I don't know. Dr. Hsu makes all the students participate. For instance, we have two businesses competing against each other, and separate conferences to compete. The more work you do and the better your profits, the better your grade. So that's pretty good. If you do the work, you get the grade. He does not base it so much on book learning. I can't learn it from a book. You learn it as you go along, you get ideas from everybody else, not what one author thinks.

P- Picking up on that–to what extent do you think it is either boring or interesting to read comments from the other students?

R- Dr. Hsu really doesn't say all that much. He leaves it almost entirely up to the kids. I think it's good. I'm learning so many things. We're not held tight to OS471. I've learned a lot, like people ask about jobs, and just general information giving. For instance, we have a chapter on informal and formal businesses, and he'll say, "What's your opinion?" Then you can read other people's opinions and let that help you form your opinion. You can go back and change your opinion if you want, which is good.

Q- Do you send private messages to anybody?

R- Yeah, I have a few people I send messages to. (gives names) (some are on staff).

P- So sometimes it's about the course, and sometimes it's not?

R- Yeah, sometimes it's just goofing around.

Q- Have you gotten involved in anything else going on on EIES?

R- Not really. I've played around a little. Nothing seemed to concern me to much. I was looking at Interests; I saw other people had them listed, but I couldn't figure it out. And the games. The reviews and surveys I haven't figured out how to work yet. But i got time.

Interviewer–Survey, you should really stay out of . . . if you want to set up an online survey, it's pretty complicated.

Q- What about your relationship with Dr. Hsu? Does he seem the same online, or different online?

R- He's pretty much the same online. I think he's a really good teacher. I would recommend him highly. I think that course is much better with the online part. I think you'd be bored to death sitting there learning about business every time. The application is great. I'm glad that I have it. I'd take it again . . . I've already recommended it to my friends. I think it's just so much better. And Dr. Hsu, he's great. He's got a great personality, not a real strict or stingy type guy. For the most part he wants your opinion on things, and he'll conform to your opinion. In fact, he asked us how we want him to grade our tests. He leaves things up to us. He has a good sense of humor too.

Q- What about disadvantages? Do you think you're missing anything or are there things that annoy you about using the system?

R- Definitely disadvantages. Some people are lazy. I just can't afford to be lazy because that's what the teacher is grading you on. But online you don't have to log on if you don't want to. You're only hurting yourself. . . . No, you're hurting the others, too, because they aren't getting your opinion on things. I guess some of them are restricted to school use, and the computers here are down half the time anyway. You don't have to worry about keeping records because you can always call everything back up. I don't see too many disadvantages really. I've never had a problem with it.

Q- Have you used branching?

R- Yes

Q- What was your reaction to that?

R- I'm not crazy about it. It's kind of a hassle to put in, and then search through the branches. I see why he does it. But once you're in it, you see everything anyway, so what's the difference? You could just put it on the regular conference. It's for organization type purposes I guess. For instance, our resumes are all in a branch. I never went back once I put mine in, personally. So I don't see too great an advantage of it, except for organization.

Q- Have you developed some sort of routine; ways of attacking the system once you sign on?

R- Yeah, I always do the same thing. I always want to see who's online, in case any of my friends are online. Then, if there are any messages, I'll read them. Then I'll either answer the messages if there were any left for me; then I'll go to conference choice. I always do conference 1732 first; then the other one for the company. I read all the responses. I save everything to disk, so I just usually scroll it up. Then I'll go back and write comments. Then I goof around after that, and log off.

Q- How much time do you spend?

R- I sign on every day. I usually spend about an hour; it depends how much other work I have. Sometimes as little as half an hour; sometimes two or three hours. Sometimes I sign on several times a day. I spend a lot of time online. I love it.

Q- More than you spend on other courses?

R- Yeah. This is my favorite course. I don't mind putting in the hours, the time just flies by.

Q- Suppose we were doing a brochure for prospective students. Are there any warnings we should give them? What kind of advice would you give them?

R- If you do it from home, make sure you contact the telephone company first because you can run up a big phone bill if you don't get special services from them. I called about a week after I got my first phone bill. Now it just costs about $4.00 a month.

P- We did mention this the first class.. but you think we should be stronger about this.

R- Yeah. I was running up 20 to 30 hours a month. (tape ran out here and fumble-fingers interviewer took awhile to get new one in)

Q- If you were going to add something to what's available, can you think of any features that you would like to have available?

R- Not now. I'll have to think about that. That's a tough one. I've never used any other system.

Q- Anything you would like to anonymously tell Dr. Hsu?

R- He has a group read a chapter and put their outline on the system. I think it's a waste of time because no one is reading the chapters. Nobody asks questions in class because nobody's reading the chapters. When it came time for the midterm, we were all complaining. Plus his two points for every right answer and two points off for every wrong one – it's different. That didn't go over too well. I like the way he presents his material. Sometimes he puts a comment in and says you have until that night to do it – who has free time like that? I'm not too crazy about that. But I guess he has to do it that way and it's our fault for not getting it on.

Q- Can you think of anything else that was especially memorable, or funny?

R- On the system. Sure, when we were all first trying to learn it, sending messages to each other, some of them were going to the wrong people. Someone in class got an anonymous message This guy Stacey got a message from "an admirer," and it was anonymous. And no one wanted to claim it.

P- I see. The man's name was Stacy; so it could be a woman's name? Somebody sent it to him and looked again – and oops!

R- Yes. he left a note on the conference saying, thanks, to whoever sent him the message, and he hopes he gets another one. No one has since written a message. Then the teacher, Dr. Hsu, put on a question, "what's your opinion on anonymous messages?" That was pretty funny. And his making it an assignment, that was good. He does that a lot, asking your personal opinion on everything. That was pretty funny.

Q- Do you have anything you want to know about the project or the system?

R- What's coming now? I know there's going to be a new EIES?

Q- (interviewer explains two new systems and prototypes) We hope eventually to put up a utility and to offer a number of courses this way.

R- So you wouldn't have to come to class at all? I think that would really be something to try to see how it works. I would do that.

Interviewer – Most of the courses online now are totally online.

R- Oh, are they? I didn't know that.

Interviewer – They come to their training, and then don't meet again until the final exam.

R- Yeah, we tried to coax our teacher to give us an online midterm. He wouldn't go for that. We asked if we could have a virtual midterm, and he said, "How would you like a virtual grade?"

Interviewer – The problem is that it is possible to cheat.

R- He mentioned that you were thinking of having a time limit and you couldn't log off until it's done. that's a pretty good solution. Of course it's still possible to cheat, unless you make it explicitly an open-book, open-notes exam. (Interviewer explains that 213 and NJIT statistics course are totally online this semester).

R- Too bad I had 213 already.

Q- Anything else you can think of?

R- Yeah, what courses are you going to be putting online?

Interviewer – I don't know. Right now we don't have a mainframe to regularly run on.

R- What about keeping our account? Interviewer explains . . .

R- That's good.

(More irrelevant chat about future plans)

Interviewer – Thanks a lot for stopping by.

Interview 6
TELEPHONE INTERVIEW WITH A NEGATIVE CIS STUDENT
Starr Roxanne Hiltz, August 2, 1987

Q: How did you first hear about the virtual classroom project or the Online CIS 213 course?

R: I read about it in the registration material, and I decided I did not want to take it. Being a [non-CIS] major and going to school at night, I worked full time during the day, and I didn't know whether I would be able to dedicate enough time to it. What happened was, when I went to register, I registered for another course. And the registrar said there was a course open on Wednesday night, so I registered for it. The night the course was starting, that's when I found out it was the virtual classroom.

Q: I see, so you really got into it by accident . . .

R: He saw two CIS 213's, and he put me in the one that was open.

Q: What were your initial feelings at that point, when you got to the training and discovered what you were in?

R: I had a lot of apprehension. I mentioned it to the instructor, BJ, that I was kind of worried. I was ready to dedicate the time that I could to it, but I was still worried, because I thought there was a little extra that was needed. I think BJ mentioned that if there was any way he could help, he would do his best to assist. So I said, OK, how bad can it be? And besides, I really needed to take the course, and I wanted to take the course, and so I decided to stick with it. I was a little nervous. I really didn't want to take a virtual classroom course.

Q: Where did you go to use a microcomputer? Did you have equipment at home, or go to the Lab, or what?

R: That was the other problem. I felt that I was at a disadvantage because I did not have a personal computer. I really didn't have access to a computer except at work, and I had to compete against everyone else. There were like four for a department of 30 people, each running their own LOTUS or whatever; I had to fit myself between there. So I was forced to work after hours, 7–8 o'clock at night. Even that was a problem, because then I had to battle against the guys that were cleaning and waxing. I was at the point where I was getting frustrated because I was not able to work on it when I wanted to. The days when I really wanted to work on it were Saturdays and Sundays., I do a lot of my homework then. And the Institute was not open. I guess it was open, if you made an appointment or something you could get in for a few hours.

Q: So it would have been much easier for you if you could have gone somewhere on weekends.

R: Either that, or I was even looking for a good way to lease a personal computer. I went to a couple of places after the semester had started, and prices were just outrageous. To rent a computer for a month, it was like $400.00.

Q: Yes, that really is outrageous, they don't sell for a whole lot more than that!

R: I was really tight for money at that time. Under the circumstances, I just had to do the best I could.

Q: So, you work full time, and you would normally go in about one night a week?

R: That's about all I had. That's exactly what it worked out to be. I was able to dedicate one full night a week. That was like five or six hours a week. On the initial questionnaire, it asked about how much time you would spend, and I felt I was going to need at least two to three hours a day. If I had my own computer . . . but I didn't, I wasn't able to dedicate that much time. I think I did get a D in that course. I was hoping for something better, but under the circumstances, I think that a D was probably the most appropriate grade. I wish I had done better and I think I would have been able to.

Q: That long session one night a week, did you do it from work or did you go into NJIT?

R: From work, and I tried to get into NJIT a few times. When I did that, it was only to try to clean up the bugs on a program. It was more desperation, get-it-done kind of work, and I really was not picking up a whole lot of information . . .

Q: When you were out there, fighting for a computer at work, did you feel that you were part of a group or class, or did you feel really all alone out there.

R: That's a good question. I always knew that I was part of a group, but I also felt alone because I did not communicate like I really wanted to. There were some of the students who were on, sending messages two or three times a day. Those are the ones who communicated with each other. I even tried to do it, but with once a week, I didn't get a whole lot of practice with sending messages. For instance, I sent a few to [name], but it was difficult, because he had already progressed to a point where he could send messages all the time. I could send a regular message, but I didn't know about how to to the talking online . . . the ones who were doing that were the ones who were on two or three times a day. I couldn't devote that much time to it, and as a result, I didn't have that much communication. And as a result of that, I was more of an individual rather than part of a group.

Q: Did you read the comments by other students in the conference, or did you tend to skip over them?

R: My downfall was in trying to minimize reading of the comments during the time I had to devote to it. I didn't read them on the screen, I printed them out and took them home. Then things would happen. I work long hours, I live alone and have to cook dinner . . . I did look at a few of them, but my downfall was that I tried to do everything as fast as I could in order to maximize what I could finish during that one night. I tried to bring the paperwork home, but you bring home a book and often it does not happen . . . I read maybe 60% of it. There were things that I would look for, like the lectures. Then I would make my own little notes on the print of the lectures.

Q: On the lectures, do you find it easier or harder to understand the material in writing, as compared to hearing it?

R: That was easy. They were clear and well put together . . . Sometimes I had some trouble associating the material in the lecture with what was in the book. If you didn't do that, and then tried to walk in and take the quiz.. it became more and more difficult.

Q: Did you ever send messages to BJ, or didn't you have time to do that?

R: I sent a few, but not nearly as much as I really wanted to. I think BJ noticed that right off the bat, he even mentioned that I was getting kind of quiet. I did send messages to him, things like whether I could get more time. We talked, but I don't think I got to be as close to him as I wanted to.

Q: Thinking about the relationship you had with BJ online, and the relationship you've had with professors whom you have seen one night a week, did you feel less able or more able to communicate with BJ? Did you feel closer or further away?

R: Definitely closer, but I wish I could have gotten as close as some of the other students seemed to be getting. That was one of the problems . . . looking at some of the comments other students were making, it was like, Wow! Look at the questions he's asking, and look at the comments he's getting back! Why am I not having thoughts like that?

Q: Well, because you were not there every day, right?

R: Exactly.

Q: If a student saw a course like this at registration and asked for your advice, what kind of advice would you give?

R: It would depend on the individual. I could not make a recommendation to a person I don't know. I could recommend it to someone who I know does have the time, and will dedicate the time and the effort, and who· has the the equipment available at home to do it. I considered that probably the key to being successful in the class. Especially if the person needed the course, and would otherwise have to wait another semester; then I would recommend it.

Q: But only if they have the equipment, and if they are willing to work harder?

R: Well, I don't know if you have to work harder, but if you don't have the computer at home, you work 9 or 10 hours a day, then you have to go home and cook dinner . . . somebody like that, somebody in exactly the same circumstances that I had, I would have to think very, very hard about it. You want to get the most you can out of a course, and I don't think I did. I don't think it was BJ's fault, it was not having the right equipment to work with.

Q: What about BJ? What advice would you like to pass on to him if he were ever to do this again?

R: There were a couple of things . . . I don't know if I conveyed them in the questionnaire, when I filled it out it was like the night before the final, and I just wanted to get it done and study for the final. I wanted to do

more "dinky" programs. I think we did two big programs that were
assigned to us. I would have loved to have seen a tiny little program
due every week, along with a couple of big ones. The practice would
have been good, I would have become more familiar with it.

Int: Well, I really appreciate your taking the time to talk to me. I wish
things had worked out better for you.

R: Believe it or not, I just bought another book on Pascal programming. I
still want to learn. I'm still trying to pick it up, on my own. I felt bad
when the course ended, and I really didn't pick up as much as I wanted
to.

Interview 7
Telephone Interview with Positive CIS213 Student
Interviewer : Roxanne Hiltz- July 1987

I- Hi! (name). This is Roxanne.

R- OK.

I- I am recording this. I will be anonymously using some quotes. What I
found while going through the data from the survey is that they are
kind of dry. So I'd like to ask you some questions so that I can get more
of a feeling for what you really experienced. OK?

R- OK.

I- I want you first to think all the way back to last January when you first
heard about the VC project for CIS213 online – What you heard, what
your reactions were and why you decided to take it.

R- OK. Lets see – I guess it was over the December vacation that I got it
in the mail and I saw that they were offering CIS213 – (this is for me
you know since I already knew Pascal) – I saw it was online and that I
had a modem and everything, so I said "Easy A" – That's really why I
wanted to take it. I knew pretty much about modems and all that stuff,
and I said it should be pretty easy. You know you got to keep grades.

I- Okay. So you had a modem and microcomputer right at home and
access wasn't any problem for you?

R- Yeah! It was at school – I was on campus.

I- You were on campus. So it was like in your dorm room?

R- Yeah!

I- Did you have any technical difficulties at any time?

R- Technical difficulties. . . . No. I didn't have any kind of difficulties.

I- When you actually got started, what were your feelings at that point ?
What did you initially like? Dislike? Did you still think it was an easy
"A" or were there some other things happening or what?

R- No. I still thought it was an easy "A". I thought the system was. . . .

pretty good. . . . . I don't know – I couldn't tell you how now – It could be better. It just seems it was pretty easy to get around – I didn't have any real problems – No major problems.

I- Did you have some sort of regular schedule each week when you were signed online, or how and when did you decide to participate or take part?

R- It was like whenever I had spare time.

R- You know I didn't log on just for the course – like when I wanted to download and once it was up I'd dump it in my buffer like 2 in the morning . . . or whenever I had the chance and I'd print it out next day.

I- So your normal thing was to download and then print and read it at your leisure?

R- Yeah! I'd read it first. But just to have a hard copy, you know for review and all that, it was a lot easier than going thru . . . you know . . .

I- The comments that other students made – to what extent did you find that it was interesting or helpful or engaging to see some things from them – or to what extent did you think that what the other students said was a waste of time?

R- I'm not sure I understand you . . . . You said that some people said – "it was a waste of time"?

I- No! Some of the comments were entered by the instructor and some of the material was students making contributions, making comments or asking questions. Did you like to read the other students comments, or skip over them, or what was your reaction to things done by other students?

R- No, I thought, you know, it was helpful to have everybody partici- pate – I didn't skip over – I read everything – just to see – you know, compare yourself to the rest of the class and know how they are doing and what they know and what they don't know and all that.

I- When you were out there at the end of your modem, did you feel that you were part of a class or a group that was working together, or did you feel you were kind of all alone?

R- No. . . . Nah! I felt that I was computing a little bit. No! I thought I was in a classroom, you know.

I- Do you think that (instructor's name) did anything that was helpful to the class to become like a class that worked together, or on the other hand that he hindered that?

R- Did (instructor's name) ?

I- Is there anything that he did that helped the class to feel like a real group, or that got in the way of students feeling like it was a real class?

R- The Instructor tried to get everyone involved. He posted comments to encourage participation.

I- What about lecture type material? Comparing reading it to listening to it in a classroom. What do you see are the advantages/disadvantages?

R- May not want to be in class at the scheduled time – So it is better online. In addition, the lecture was only outlining major points covered. Advantages to both offline and online. For me it was easier in online lecture. The instructor made up the lecture personally, not as if he were copying it out of a book. Made it easy.

I- What about other people on EIES. Did you ever get involved in conferences or messages with people outside your class?

R- Yes, I joined a few public and private conferences and made friends that I still have now.

I- Wow! That is interesting. Are they friends in New Jersey?

R- Some people in my class and others – I even have my own conference now. Turbo Pascal conference.

I- Oh! I didn't know that. So you went from student to conference moderator. How would you describe your relationship with (instructor's name) as an instructor? Did you feel more able or less able to relate to him as compared to teachers in a regular classroom?

R- Little more able to relate.

I- Why?

R- Because he doesn't see you – all he knows is what you type. He can't be prejudiced against you based on the way you look.

I- So you are saying he was more objective in this medium in reacting to the work you did and not to other things?

R- Yes! It's more fair this way. You're being judged really on your work, not on your personality.

I- Do you think you learned more/less or the same as you would have if you took this course in a regular classroom?

R- More for me – learned the system – I already knew Pascal. Most people who take this course already know a little about computers.

I- So you're saying that you didn't necessarily learn more course material, but that you learned other things about other uses of computers?

R- Yes. If people aren't enthusiastic about computers – I don't know if they would learn more about it. They'd probably do less till they got the hang of it.

I- Why do you think they would probably do less?

R- Well! Most people are intimidated about it, wouldn't understand it – It's kinda like a hassle when you are first learning it, especially for those people who have not used computers since they were young like I did. So I got the hang of it quickly.

I- So, what you are saying is that the hardware/software didn't get in your way – it was like transparent to you.

R- For somebody else it might get in the way a little bit – added disadvantage to their learning.

I- Yes. Besides the fact that people who aren't familiar with computers would be slowed down while they got over the hurdle – Can you think of other problems or shortcomings in trying to use a Virtual Classroom approach to deliver courses?

R- For me? No! I didn't have any problems.

I- What if a student came up to you and said, I saw this thing – you took it – should I take it or not? What kind of advice would you give? What kinds of questions would you ask, to think about in trying to decide if the student should do this or a regular course?

R- I'd say definitely do it.

I- For everybody or just certain kinds of students?

R- Uhhh . . . I'd probably say for everybody – I'm not saying they'd get as good a grade – I'm just saying, do it for the experience and for fun.

I- Tell me about that. What was especially fun about it or more memorable – what made it different and fun?

R- I don't know – Just a change – Seems like more fun.

I- Do you think it was fun because it was the first time you did it – I mean if you took another course, would that be fun too, or would it not be as much fun?

R- I don't know – I've used a lot of computer systems, and for me it is just more convenient/interesting.

I- Okay. Is there anything else you can think about? It's been a little while but what could have been done differently or better? What should people know about in order to understand what it's like to take a course this way?

R- No! Not really.

I- Okay. Thank you. Goodnight.

APPENDIX *III*

COURSE REPORTS

The following is an outline of the topics which instructors were requested to include in their case histories of experiences teaching online.

1. Description of the topics covered in the course; with a kind of syllabus-outline of what was covered week by week.
2. Description of the materials and activities you provided for your online class (type, length, frequency) (or class segment) How did this differ from ftf class materials, activities, and scheduling, and why?
3. Description of what worked well in terms of students seeming to learn and to participate, and what the major problems were . . . things that did not go over well.
   You might include here problems with procrastination (uneven and delayed participation); with software or hardware inadequacies; with getting students to actually actively ask questions or discuss issues. Try to also include a section on any "group" or "collaborative" learning activities; how these worked and how they did not.
4. Reporting and if possible (if you have easy access to a stat pack) analysis with t-tests of any differences between comparable grades.
5. How do you, as a faculty member, feel liberated and/or constrained by the fundamentals and/or particulars of EIES? What sorts of teaching strategies would you try next time, and, conversely, what kinds of teaching seem so constrained or distorted by CC as not to be worth the effort?

All instructors completed these reports. The complete set is included in the final technical report on the project. Selected course reports follow, edited to delete sections of least general interest.

Complete online course materials ("electures," assignments, questions for discussion) are available on diskette from NJIT for anyone who wishes a copy.

VIRTUAL CLASSROOM REPORT
RESULTS OF TEACHING CIS 213 ONLINE
FOR A SECOND TIME
INSTRUCTOR: BJ GLEASON

In this report, I will compare the experiences I had while teaching Introduction to Computer Science for the virtual classroom over a period of two semesters.

The class offered was CIS 213, Introduction to Computer Science. This is a core course, required for majors and non-majors alike, as well as graduate students entering the Master's program. The course covers many topics in Computer Science, as well as programming, in the FORTRAN and Pascal Computer languages. Provisions were developed to allow these programs to be done online.

The first semester that I taught was the hardest. The first major stumbling block was the lectures to present to the students. To obtain the lectures, I recorded my face-to-face class, and then transcribed it. It was a lot of work. I would even sometimes cut the online lecture short to get it to the students on time.

The second problem was gauging the students reaction to the material presented. The students would read the material, and very few would ask questions. In a face-to-face class, there were more questions asked, and I could judge the class on a whole to see if the material was getting through to them. This is very difficult to do online, since this form of contact is completely lost. In response to this, I developed a +QUIZ facility to give the students a quiz each week. I could then tell via the quiz results if the material was being understood.

In short, the first semester was long and tiring. But many of the problems faced were organizational. Once these problems were solved, the second semester would flow easier.

During the first semester, I had 9 students. During the second semester, I started with 22 and ended up with 15. While this is only a slight increase in number, it does add to the work load.

My first problem from the first semester was solved. I still had the lectures, and now I even had more time to refine them, and to add in the section that I had originally cut out.

In the first semester, some of the students complained that the course was too easy. The root of this, I found out, was that many of the students taking this course could read a lecture faster than I could say it. So a 2 hour lecture online only took about an hour to read. So to pad this out, without going ahead of the offline classes, I decided to add supplementary materials to the class lectures. The materials were newspaper and magazine articles dealing with computer science. I obtained these and added them in for the students to read, but not to be tested on. The reaction to this was very good. I gave an assignment to the students for each of them to enter an article in the class conference. Many of them entered more than just one. A few even entered extra articles in the conference much later. I found this to be very encouraging. The students were sharing ideas with each other in a way that I never saw in my offline class.

Perhaps the main reason for this, is that when a student enters a comment for the entire class to read, it is not like my standing in front of them to read it. You don't quite get the feeling that you are talking in front of a crowd, but rather just entering a comment into the computer.

Gauging student reaction was done much the same, using the quiz facility. I found, even with the added materials, and the supplemental lectures, that the students were still able to keep up without much effort.

A problem which became clearer in the second semester was talking to the students via private messages. Due to the increase in the number of students, the assignments and quizzes, I found I was writing a lot more private messages to the students than in the previous semester.

To cut down on this problem, I developed a number of programs that would easily let me send one line messages to my students. They were automatically addressed and sent, cutting down on my time. I also developed a program to automatically grade the quizzes, and send the results back to the students. This drastically reduced the amount of time spent online correcting and mailing grades to the students.

In summary, I found the second semester to be easier than the first. The mind numbing task of transcribing my lectures was gone, but an increased number of students added to the amount of online time required to answer all the messages the students were sending. The further development of the support programs also eased the burdens on the instructor and the students. By reviewing what had gone wrong (and right) during the first semester, programs and techniques were developed and corrected. On the whole, I felt that the second semester of CIS 213 was a much smoother and more pleasant experience for the students and teacher.

INTRODUCTORY SOCIOLOGY WITH EIES
Robert J. Meinke

MY PREPARATION

When I was asked to teach this Introductory Sociology course online, I had previous, but limited, experience using the EIES system. For several years our Sociology/Anthropology/Social Work Department at Upsala College had been using it for departmental communication and, in addition, I had briefly participated as a student in an online course given through EIES.

In the summer of 1986, I began the preparation of my course lectures and assignments and soon discovered that there were many things about the system with which I was unfamiliar; in fact, even my facility in using those procedures with which I had previously worked was limited. To complicate things even more I had been provided with a new microcomputer for teaching this course, one which was entirely unfamiliar to me, required much experimentation, and produced much confusion. Therefore, the first month or so was absorbed in coping with the mechanics of computing and the EIES system and often resulted in great frustration.

COURSE CONTENT

The first question that arose in my mind when faced with adapting my Introductory Sociology course for online was, could the students cover the same amount of material that they usually did? It seemed to me that probably they could not. Certain constraints existed online that were not present in the traditional introductory course; even more, perhaps, than would be present in an advanced upper level course.

The reason was this: Introductory Sociology courses are survey courses; they cover an extraordinarily broad range of diverse topics. Most chapters in the text are fairly discrete and self-standing. While there are broad theoretical perspectives that more or less link the topics together, only some of the topics are related to each other in a step-by-step logical interrelationship. Further, each chapter summarizes the principal sociological findings about its topic and requires the student to master a great deal of detail.

In the normal classroom situation, it is possible through a mix of lecturing and quick oral review of the chapter content to reinforce this broad range of material and to quickly detect areas of confusion. Computer conferencing, on the other hand, seemed to limit my ability as instructor to cover these extensive and detailed amounts of material quickly, if at all. Especially did this seem to be true when the conference members would be mostly young freshmen and sophomores inexperienced in this mode of communication and frequently lacking in basic college study skills. A new chapter a week had to be the usual pace, and this meant that about 12 to 13 chapters must be covered in a semester. Conference discussions and responses, being asynchronous, seemed more adapted to very intensive, creative analyses of a few broad issues rather than an extensive, detailed coverage of many.

Why? In the first place, in a face-to-face class, lecturing can serve several purposes: to present a more in-depth discussion of an important topic than the text does; to discuss the same material as the text but from a different and, perhaps, more meaningful angle; and finally, and especially, to provide an alternative mode of communication, an auditory one in contrast to the written word. This latter purpose is vitally important with freshman and sophomore students, who today are frequently very unskilled in comprehension reading. While lectures in a computer conference are certainly able to serve the first two purposes, they are totally unable to handle the third.

Secondly, it seemed to me that computer lectures would best serve these inexperienced students by being fairly short, a page or two at most; otherwise, fatigue and overload would likely occur. Also, the number of them submitted each week should be carefully limited and emphasize only the most important points. Unfortunately, the result of this policy would be to heavily depend on the students themselves to master most of the detailed material from the text, something that most of them are not very good at doing.

Thirdly, if lectures must be short and limited, then the majority of the online time would be mostly used for assignments and discussions. Here again, however, the emphasis would be on intensive rather than extensive coverage in a course where extensive coverage is essential. Of course, assignments whether on or offline are always intensive. Most are usually designed to force the student to apply some specific concept or area of knowledge to life situations or to think through the logical implications of an idea. On the other hand, discussions in an offline class can be very flexible, quickly shifting from one topic to another, quickly leaving behind what is well understood, and then again becoming very intensive on a particular area. This flexibility is very important but depends on the condition that the group is gathered together in one place and time and allowed to interact spontaneously. Online discussions are not like this. People enter their comments at different times creating significant time gaps in the dialogue. This has the advantage of encouraging more considered and thoughtful responses and discussion, and, at best, leads to in-depth exploration and creative interactive thinking. To do this, however, requires lots of time, and in a course where a new chapter is introduced weekly, the discussions must be limited in number and truncated to make room for those of the next week.

Fourthly, in each face-to-face class hour it may be possible for the discussion to explore several different topics, not in depth, but sufficiently for some students to gain reinforcement and better comprehension. While it is certainly possible online to carry on several simultaneous discussions with different themes (especially with a branching capability), this seemed to me to require a level of thinking and conferencing skills far beyond what could be reasonably expected of beginners. So, again, this meant that at least in the early weeks of the course the amount of discussion in any one week would have to be limited to one or two themes. My later experience confirmed this impression.

Thus, I tended to see a basic conflict between the need to cover a constantly changing, extensive content and the use of a communication mode that encouraged in-depth, exploratory discussion. It would certainly be possible, and in many courses highly desirable, to emphasize this latter capability. This would definitely be true if the course were intended to aim at the exploration of one basic theme as many advanced sociology courses do, but I was teaching a course in which mastery of a broad, detailed, and specific content was expected no matter where it was taught or by whom. As a compromise I decided to structure the course by entering into the conference each week the following items: a set of learning objectives (which would also be the basis of the exams), one or two minilectures, one or two assignments, one or two discussion questions and an objective quiz.

SELECTION OF STUDENTS FOR THE ONLINE COURSE

Any assessment of the online course must take into consideration the characteristics of the students. It is possible that the way the students were recruited influenced their characteristics and, therefore, the course outcome. Unlike the regular offline course, there was great concern up to the last minute as to whether there would be enough students registered for this course to run. On the one hand, the Dean normally required that courses have a student body of at least 7 or 8, and on the other, the purposes of the experiment required enough students to make a meaningful comparison with the regular offline class, which already had 19. Registration was almost complete, and we had not met these expectancies. Definite attempts had already been made to publicize the course with the faculty and student body. A detailed course description had been submitted with the early registration materials. Later, posters had been prepared and placed around the campus by the administrative assistant of the project. However, the preregistration results indicated that little interest had developed. As the registration period drew to a close, an unusually vigorous attempt was made by some advisors to encourage students to sign up. The result was a final register of 16, but, I suspect, it contained only a few who chose the course out of tremendous interest, and a large number who needed a last minute course or were attracted by the fact that there would be no face-to-face class attendance. It also included one high school student who had been given special permission to register.

This experience demonstrates the tremendous importance of publicity when preparing to give an online course. Afterwards we realized that many of the Upsala faculty had had no, or at best, a very minimal awareness of the proposed experiment, even though materials describing the course had been distributed. Thus, most of them had made no attempt to suggest the course to their advisees.

THE TRAINING OF STUDENTS IN EIES

This course was designed so that the only formal face-to-face contact with the instructor or with other students was to occur at the first meeting, the mid-term exam and the final exam.

The first class meeting was intended to acquaint the students with the nature of the course, its requirements and the EIES system. At this meeting, a number of Xeroxed items were handed out: a course syllabus, copies of two articles to be used in later assignments; and an instruction sheet for mastering the basic EIES skills of sending private messages and conference comments.

After a brief initial question and answer period, the class adjourned to the computer lab for hands-on instruction. Because of the very limited number of terminals yet in working order, three or more students gathered around each terminal with one actually operating the equipment. Professor Hiltz announced each step by step procedure, and two of her assistants from NJIT and myself moved from group to group assisting those who needed help. As soon as the first student had entered the directory and successfully sent messages, the others had their turns at following the same procedures.

The results of the training session were mixed. Some students, the most adventurous and aggressive, followed the steps quickly and for the most part effectively. However, the general atmosphere tended to be noisy and chaotic which made it difficult to hear the instructions and keep everyone moving together. Some of the first students rushed ahead without waiting for the next instruction, confusing many of those watching. It was obvious, even in this first training session, that some students wanted to hurry off as soon as possible and not take the trouble to master the details. The result was that the students, when they were later on their own, needed a great deal of help from the lab assistants and took some time to become adjusted. (Note: only 1.25 hours was available for this training; this was not long enough.)

STUDENT INTERACTION WITH THE HARDWARE/SOFTWARE

Two of the most important factors in the success of an online course are the ease with which the students have access to terminal facilities and the degree to which the software meets their communication needs. In the Introductory Sociology course these factors were fairly adequately covered, but far from optimally.

a) Hardware: Terminal Facilities. All of the students, except initially two, were dependent on the use of the Upsala computer labs. When the course began, some of the equipment had still not been installed and some had not been delivered. The available terminals represented a variety of different manufacturers, each requiring a different set of procedures for establishing communication with EIES. Both students and lab assistants, especially in the early part of the semester, often ran into frustrating problems in attempting to get online. Some terminals were more popular than others because of their ease of operation. Students, naturally, became attached to the terminal which gave them least trouble and with which they were most familiar. But because of limited equipment and heavy usage, students were not always able to get their preferred machines. Also machine malfunctioning was frequent enough to be irritating.

Another problem centered on the printers. All terminals did not have a workable printer attached. Breakdowns in operation often occurred and were extremely frustrating; then I would receive complaints that an important lecture or assignment could not be printed out.

Lab assistants were naturally uneven in their skills and technical knowledge. Some were very expert and able to aid students in solving machine problems and even EIES difficulties. Others were not sufficiently familiar with the EIES system to be of much help.

The lab's time schedule seemed to be adequate, roughly 10–9 on Monday–Thursday; half day on Friday and Saturday. The closing on Sunday did not seem to bother most students; very few were ever active on weekends or even Fridays. The lab hours were usually maintained, but I did receive several strident complaints from one student who had a pattern of going to the computer room first thing in morning and sometimes found that the lab assistant did not arrive on time.

b) Software: The EIES System. The EIES system proved to be an excellent medium for this course. After some initial confusion and additional advice, all the students did master the basic procedures required.

The system with its diversity of available options did provide flexibility in teaching.

The one most annoying difficulty with EIES was its slowness. This definitely frustrated students and interfered with creativity. Like failures of equipment, the seeming interminable waiting distracted from the learning goals and made concentration difficult for both the students and myself. While this course was in session, so were many other courses using the lab; this combined with the normal EIES load made for many long waits. These delays were magnified during the most busy daytime hours, especially during midday. Unfortunately, those were also the most popular hours for students. Since many students avoided coming back on campus at night and few had home computers, many did not avail themselves of the night hours when access was often easier. I, myself, found it so frustrating to go online during the day that I soon established a pattern of waking about three or four o'clock in the morning to gain easy access.

One final comment on EIES. I was surprised how few students explored on their own initiative the variety of non-course opportunities available on EIES, (the public conferences, etc.). Also how few made any attempt to talk to their fellow classmates in other than required ways. One girl did attempt on several occasions to ask the others questions like "Did you find this assignment difficult?" or "Did you have trouble finding the index?" She never received a response. I must take partial responsibility for this lack; I realize that the instructor must continually search for ways to get the students to interact. However, one of the difficulties with teaching such a course for the first time is that one becomes focused on the mechanics of the course and keeping it going. And, of course, students experience the same difficulty.

CHAPTER OBJECTIVES

Both the chapter learning objectives and the quizzes were primarily designed to encourage students to master the wide range of detail contained in each text chapter. Their purpose was to ensure extensive learning, while that of the minilectures, assignments, and discussions was to focus more intensively on specific issues.

The list of objectives was entered into the conference at the same time that the chapter was assigned for reading and study. Students were encouraged to make printouts of them. Each set of objectives consisted of ten to twenty items that the students were expected to be able to discuss after they had mastered the chapter and minilecture material. Students were informed that their exam questions would be drawn directly from these objective lists and they were. Because the lists were so extensive, they stressed many significant areas that we did not have time to discuss online, and, therefore, which the students had to master on their own.

QUIZZES

Each quiz consisted of 20 objective questions: true or false, multiple choice, or fill-in items. They were purposely very detailed to encourage a thorough study of the text.

After receiving the students' answers and grading them, I then had to develop a simple, reasonably quick procedure by which to communicate the grades and provide comments on the answers. I wanted to avoid using excessive time sending a private message to each student. Fortunately the EIES system allowed students to choose a pen name which only they and myself knew. By entering a conference comment using these pen names, I was able to communicate everyone's grade with anonymity. (Note: Gradebook was not available the first semester).

The problem of commenting on the quizzes still remained. In a regular class the quiz can be given simultaneously to all students and can be immediately reviewed with the correct answers and, if necessary, with explanations. With the online class this was impossible. Students took the quiz at different times; some did not meet the deadline or, if they did, it was only at the last minute. Consequently it took me some time to collect all the answers and grade them. Almost a week could pass between the time that the first students took the quiz and the time that all their grades were submitted. Feedback was delayed and its teaching effectiveness greatly weakened.

I soon discovered that providing written explanations of each answer demanded much more time than was practical, considering all the other work involved in keeping up with the conference. I, therefore, decided to provide explanations of only those questions which a large number of students answered incorrectly. Looking back, I question whether the effort to provide these explanations was worth the trouble. I suspect that most students looked primarily for their grades and gave the explanations only a fleeting glance; while this is often their inclination in offline classes too, there they are a captive audience, and it is more likely that some of the discussion of answers will be absorbed.

In retrospect, I am still unhappy over the degree of control available for encouraging and insuring mastery of the wide range of material contained in each chapter. While I have the same problem in regular classes, the lack of face-to-face contact intensifies it in computer conferencing courses.

MINILECTURES

The minilectures seemed to be successful; the points made in them were usually reinforced with appropriate assignments. The still unresolved question was how many and how long these should be. I quickly found that I needed to write more in some chapters than others depending on how many complex ideas there were that required special attention. It may well be that even more minilectures would have been preferable. One student did complain about the lack of more lecture discussions. She had difficulty absorbing the material from the text; she eventually dropped out.

ASSIGNMENTS

Overall the assignments were successfully completed and served their purpose. They were designed to force the students to apply course ideas and concepts to their everyday life and personal experiences. I found that most students liked to talk about themselves and were less sensitive about exposing their private worlds in writing than they usually were orally in the regular classes. In general, they also wrote more.

There remained the question as to where the instructor's responses to assignments should be sent: to the conference where everyone could read them or to the student as a private message? I used both methods, especially the private message mode when the response drew upon very personal experiences and information. However, in general, I prefer the public conference response because it utilizes one of the unique advantages of conferencing; it allows students to see the quality of other people's work in comparison to their own. This opportunity is seldom provided in the normal classroom. Even more useful might be a public publication of grades so that students could learn what a good grade requires, but I was reluctant to go that far. My responses to assignment answers usually took the form of a private message to each student containing the grade and a personalized commentary.

Looking back, I feel that much more could be gleaned from their assignment answers. It would seem that if these were placed in the conference where everyone could read them, then they might elicit commentary from the other members and stimulate online discussions. Unfortunately, with this class I was never able to get this kind of activity started.

DISCUSSIONS

One of the teaching goals of the online course was to encourage interactive discussion among students. Unfortunately I was never able to achieve this goal. Although students were frequently encouraged to respond and react to the each other's comments, they did only to a minor extent. When discussion questions were introduced, most students did contribute an opinion but real dialogue did not ensue. Even when occasionally a student directly asked the others for help or clarification, there was no response; they relied upon me as coordinator to handle such requests.

Several factors contributed to this lack of interaction. 1) Students brought to the conference their previous behavior patterns. Even in the regular classes our students are generally reluctant to dialogue and contribute. 2) Both the students and myself tended to focus our attention on that with which we were most uncomfortable, the mechanics and procedures of computer conferencing. Just getting the comments in and keeping up with the flow received priority. In the early days of the course I found that I was often distracted by these formal demands and sometimes didn't respond rapidly enough to student contributions, thus weakening the momentum. 3) We all suffered at times from overstimulation. The seemingly endless flow of comments, assignments, lectures and instructions coming in in a rather unorganized stream, confused and distracted. The use of branching would have avoided this condition, but I was reluctant to introduce branching immediately and did so only in the last month of the course.

Branching should be introduced quite early. I did not choose to do so in this situation for two reasons. First, the students were having a hard enough time getting used to the system and mastering the simple tasks of sending private messages and conference comments; I simply didn't want to add to their discomfort. Second, I knew that the branching program was still in the process of development. It had an extraordinarily slow response time, and students were already frustrated with system delays. By the time that I did introduce it, the program had been greatly improved; yet even then many technical problems remained. Students had lots of trouble getting it to work; I had lengthy discussions with the programmer before things were finally smoothed out; one of the better students, somewhat annoyed, challenged me to explain the advantage of using it. By the end of the course, however, the branching program was working well but too late to our meet our needs.

EXAMS

The two exams, a midterm and a final, were given face-to-face. The midterm results were extremely disappointing and disturbing. Of the thirteen students who took the exam, eight earned a D or an F. (On the other hand, two earned a solid A; one was a full-time employed, adult night student, and the other, the high school student.) These poor results created a very serious situation. We had an obligation to the students taking this online course to see that they had a success chance equal to those taking a regular offline course. I, therefore, arranged two unscheduled face-to-face review sessions and permitted those who attended to retake the mid-term. Six used this opportunity although two of them still only earned a D and an F on the retake.

Also one other change was made. Since the exam questions were based on the chapter objectives, I decided that I should increase the emphasis on them and begin to occasionally ask some student to answer an exam-like question in the conference. This, I hoped, would provide an example of what I expected on exam answers; however, looking at the final exam grades, there is no evidence that this made any major difference.

CONTROL OF STUDENT PARTICIPATION

Student participation did not in general meet the requirements that had been set at the beginning of the course. I had expected that students would come on line at least three times a week and would keep up with the assignment schedule. Soon it was obvious that for many this was not happening. In order to monitor their activity level, I began to maintain a weekly summary of the number of times that each did come on line. The EIES system makes available on request a list of conference members and the comment identification number of the last comment that each had read. I made a copy of this list every morning and marked any student who had read additional comments since the previous day as having come on line. It was then apparent that many were averaging only two times a week or less, not three.

I immediately put pressure on those students with both conference and private messages. Sometimes I telephoned. By the middle of the course, however, the pattern that each student had established did not change greatly no matter how much I complained. This attitude, of course, is not unique but a typical one of some students in any course, but in this type of course without face-to- face contact it was especially easy to be absent.

Besides a low level of conference participation, the amount of time most students spent on line was not impressive. Nevertheless, several of these students complained about the amount of time required for the course. One young man, a fairly good student, insisted that the course required more time than he could afford and much more that other classes; yet his record of time online did not reflect this. Several others felt that the number of assignments was too demanding. In reality I know that most students spent less time on this course than they did in almost any other class. My assessment of this contradiction is that either those students had not taken other courses that were very demanding (six of the failures were freshmen) or that their attitude reflected their frustration with a mode of communication that was often extremely slow and demanded an unusual degree of self-discipline on their part. However, it should also be noted that several students were very conscientious about participation.

THE INDEX

About half way through the course the need for an index of chapter objectives and assignments became apparent. Many students never mastered the search capabilities of EIES and were frequently asking me in private messages about where to find those items which for some reason they had missed or had to review and make copies. This I provided as a + READ request and kept adding to it as additional items were assigned. By the end of the course I had mixed feelings about the index. It did meet a legitimate need for a listing of important materials, but it also encouraged some students to depend only on it exclusively and more or less ignore all other conference comments not directly relevant to a graded assignment. There already had existed a tendency by some to quickly skip over any conference comments, whether by myself or by others, that were not directly related to them individually; the index only made it easier to do so. The demand for an index also reflected the growing trend among some students to fall behind in assignments and start turning in items very late. Without the index they had trouble locating the original assignments that they were missing. In some courses I would not have accepted these late items, but again, a concern that the students in this course have an equal opportunity to succeed encouraged leniency. This lateness problem grew as the semester moved to completion, and the demands of other courses increased. It was obvious that under pressure neglect of the online course was easier than neglect of a face-to-face course.

PRIVATE MESSAGES

While I had no direct access to them, my impression was that there was very little intercommunication between the students themselves through the use of private messages. There was, however, considerable communication between individual students and me. Most of their queries to me concerned the operation of EIES, questions about assignments and exams, and explanations regarding nonparticipation or absences. On only two or three occasions did anyone ask for a clarification of course content material. This dearth of content related questions was not unique to this course, but is typical of many regular courses as well. How to stimulate students to think and ask questions remains a major instructional challenge.

My private messages to students mostly contained suggestions for improving assignments, clarification of EIES procedures, encouragement and praise and additional unsolicited explanations of content where I saw weakness in comprehension. Almost all of these private messages were important, but without a pattern of interstudent communication, they tended to reinforce the traditional instructor–student relationship, not a student–student one.

MY ASSESSMENT OF THE COURSE

As an educational experience, this course was not equivalent to the regular face-to-face Introductory Sociology. Several factors, many of which have been touched upon in the previous discussion, are responsible for this assessment.

1) As I originally had anticipated, considerably less content material was covered than in the regular course. Normally two or three additional chapters would have been required and discussed. I don't believe that this outcome could have been substantially improved. With inexperienced students a large amount of course time must be used for EIES training and problem solving. Further, because of the very nature of computer conferencing, the communication interaction among conference members is not simultaneous; a considerable time lag develops while everyone submits comments, and even more is required if the members are allowed to respond to each other's initial comments. As a result, the number of discussions must be limited. If not, those of one week will overlap and interfere with those of the next week. This is especially important since in this course most weeks must begin with an entirely new topic.

2) Not only was there less content, but less enrichment and elaboration of the content. The amount of lecture material was reduced and also the opportunity for detailed review. In addition, the complex, subtle signals one gets from students in face-to-face oral interaction were missing; this made it very difficult to determine what parts of the chapter students really understood and what needed further explanation.

Consequently, I don't think online courses are best used for introductory courses in the social sciences for, as I explained previously, these are built upon a brief sampling of a variety of topics in rapid succession and with much factual detail. Online courses are much more adaptable to advanced courses where the aim is intensive exploration and creative indepth thinking about a single content area, i.e., sociology courses like Social Change or Complex Organizations.

3) Message and comment overload combined with inexperience in the use of of the system by both the students and myself frequently led to a feeling of confusion and discomfort. There was so much to cope with at the same time. There is no question that if branching had been easier to use and introduced very early, a much more orderly environment would have emerged. The conference would certainly have appeared more structured and controllable to everyone.

4) The conditions mentioned in point 3 also led to an overemphasis on

those course elements which are directly graded and specifically required, i.e., the assignments. By the end of the course student attention focused on getting the assignments completed and in. This concern for completing the formal requirements deemphasized anything that didn't directly contribute to them, especially spontaneous discussion.

5) The way that students were recruited was not typical of the way it is usually done for the regular course. Most of the students were acquired in the final hours of registration in an attempt to ensure that this experimental course would run. Many, I think, came with no particular interest in the course and an unrealistic idea of how much work the course would entail. The idea that there were no formal classes to attend on a weekly basis may have given a false impression. The result was an unusually high dropout rate and very disappointing mid-term grades.

6) Most of the students were freshmen and first semester sophomores. Many were very inexperienced in college and had not developed good study habits. This is not an unusual condition in the Introductory Sociology course, but it had especially serious consequences in an online conferencing course. Online courses emphasize those very skills in which many of our students are most lacking, reading and writing. Reading and comprehending a textbook is very difficult for many, and the online course intensifies this difficulty by requiring even more reading. Further, it eliminates the very means by which many students actually do their learning, through the spoken word. For this reason alone I believe that online courses are most adaptable to advanced courses where students are experienced and more likely to come with better developed study skills.

7) For the same reasons mentioned in point 6, many of the students were lacking in self-discipline. This also is a quality that is developed with more experience in college. Many who lack this are eliminated in the first year or so. This is another reason that I feel that online techniques are less adaptable to freshman level courses. Students must be capable of managing their own time, of establishing and maintaining a routine schedule of computer usage and of coming to the lab just as they would to an offline class.

After having taken a rather critical assessment of the course, I would like to emphasize some very positive elements. Online courses do encourage students to write better responses to their assignments. The fact that other students will read what they have written often stimulates more effort. I also found that students seem to feel more at ease about revealing personal experiences. The options that EIES provides of sending anonymous or peonage responses encourages the more shy person to express him or herself more openly.

The fact that they must write also forces them to get practice in writing. As mentioned before many contemporary students have had little writing experience; colleges like Upsala must provide remedial training. Online courses help to reinforce these skills.

They also allow students to see what other students produce. In most courses this opportunity is not available. Seeing other people's work may help students to develop a more realistic evaluation of their own performance.

Finally, I found that designing and coordinating this course forced me, as the instructor, to rethink my own approach to the introductory course in a disciplined manner. I was forced to rearticulate my goals and consider the means that I had been using. The result is that I have altered aspects of the regular offline courses, especially demanding more written assignments and taking more care to clearly convey the course objectives.

While I have taken a strong stand against completely converting introductory social science courses to online courses, I am strongly in favor of using online assignments and discussions as supplements in such courses. They have the ability to stimulate creative in-depth exploration of major themes, and they introduce novelty and excitement to the course.

WHAT SHOULD BE DONE DIFFERENTLY?

1) Much more publicity should be given before registration. The advantages of the course should be sold to both the students and the advising faculty. Hopefully this would encourage the enrollment of really interested students. The publicity, however, should also be realistic, clearly emphasizing the discipline and work that will be demanded. Participation should be limited to students who have taken the basic introduction to computers. Of course, the most desirable requirement, but unrealistic at the present time, would be that students must have their own terminal; this would encourage more regular and spontaneous participation.

2) A more efficient training program should be developed. Rather than large group training, a number of smaller group training sessions should be arranged. Students should also be required to immediately study sections of the EIES manual and be tested on comprehension. The quicker that students master the basic techniques, the more quickly the course can proceed.

3) Now that the minilectures and assignments have been established, more time should be devoted to developing techniques that encourage student interaction.

4) Instructors should be given many opportunities for using online assignments in regular courses before organizing totally online ones. The more experience they have the better the outcome is likely to be.

5) Branching should be introduced as early in the course as possible. It

is the only way to maintain a sense of order and encourage creative interaction.

6) More opportunities should be given students to practice writing answers to questions based on the course objectives so that they would know what was expected of them on examinations.

7) Whatever is necessary to provide labs with adequate working equipment and knowledgeable lab assistants should be carefully done. This is very important. Students should not be distracted by inadequate and faulty equipment nor by technical problems.

MY STORY: VIRTUAL LAB FOR
OS 471 MANAGEMENT PRACTICE
L. ENRICO HSU

Description of the Topics Covered in the Course

OS 471 is an overview of management practice for students who are NOT majoring in business or business-related fields. A 3-credit course has to cover all practical aspects of management. The selected textbook (David R. Hampton Management, 3rd edition, McGraw-Hill, Inc.) closely reflects the content of the course. The syllabus is as follows:

Session	Topics	Reading Assignment
1	Orientation and introduction	
2	EIES training	
3	Organization Design and Organization Structure	Ch. 7 & 8
4	Coordination	Ch. 9
5	Groups in action	Ch. 10
6	Motivation	Ch. 11
7	Leadership	Ch. 12
8	Communication	Ch. 13
9	Controls	Ch. 16
10–11	Production and operations management	Ch. 17
12	Review of materials covered	
13	Mid-term exam	
14–16	Management information system	
17	Mission and objectives	Ch. 4
18–19	Strategy and policy	Ch. 5
20–21	Decision making	Ch. 6
22	Conflict, change and development	Ch 14

23	Human resources management	Ch. 15
24	Managers and managing	Ch. 1
25	Perspectives on management	Ch. 2
26–27	Organizations, environment & social responsibility	Ch. 3
28	General review of topics covered	
29	Final exam	

All the course materials were covered in face-to-face sessions. In parallel with the course topics, a series of practical activities were planned for the students to perform. Through students' own efforts, a simulated company was organized and operated. The following is the list of planned activities:

Item	Description
1	Ad hoc committee for organization
2	Resume writing
3	Interview and appointment of functional managers
4	Interviews and selection of departmental staff
5	Departmental organization meeting
6	Position description and performance standards
7	Departmental planning meeting
8	New product planning meeting
9	Production planning meeting
10	Product coordination team formation
11	Production crisis meeting
12	Cost improvement program
13	Major crisis management
14	MIS proposal
15	MIS design review
16	Record management meeting
17	Performance review
18	Strategic planning for the next fiscal period

Obviously, class sessions did not contain enough hours to conduct these meetings and discussions. Neither was it possible to schedule additional hours for the purpose. The bulk of communication was, therefore, conducted through EIES. A conference was set up for the main body of discussions, assignments, reports, minutes of meeting, proposals, etc. Messaging facility is used extensively for behind-the-scene deliberations and negotiations. Membership directory is maintained not only to display regular identification information, but also to show the positional title within the simulated company.

Materials and Activities Provided by the Instructor – The materials distributed through the online conference were the following:

- Assignments: reading assignments, writing assignments (resume, etc);(see above)
- Instructions or Standard Operating Procedure: Either for using EIES or for performing company functions;
- Analysis: Budget analysis, break-even point calculation, MIS needs survey, MIS functional specifications, form design, etc.;
- Announcements: Public notices, meeting announcements, schedule changes, exam coverages, etc.;
- Pep talks: For the tasks well done.

It is to be emphasized here that no lecture was delivered online. That is the major point of departure from the general practice of *Virtual Classroom*. The rationale behind this practice was that the textbook chosen was easy to read and did not require repetitive entry of course materials. On the contrary, the communications as enumerated above were creative in nature and specific for the class in question. Furthermore, each item involved some work to be done. Thus "virtual lab" was a more descriptive connotation.

What Worked Well?

The EIES system made it possible to organize various groups (company, departments, sections and study groups) and the group dynamics made the class an extremely cohesive learning group. Through constant guidance in an informal manner, I was able to get psychologically close to the students.

In contrast with the other section of OS-471 that I taught without the benefit of EIES system, "virtual lab" has enabled the students to communicate much more freely and with "rich" content (expression of satisfaction, pleasure, and desire to continue their involvement). Statistics might shed some light to my assertion: during the semester, the class entered 403 comment items (9,865 lines) an equivalent of a book of 150 pages. Moreover, four comments of mine elicited dozens and dozens of responses, using the *branch* facility which is an enhancement to EIES specifically designed for the Virtual Classroom project. In addition, an unknown number of lines of messages were exchanged among the members for behind the scene consultations and deliberations.

The fact that the president of the simulated company was an old hand in EIES (Ed Kietlinski began using EIES in 1984; he was also the president of Microcomputer User Group) must have helped the operation of the simulated company on EIES.

The availability and operation of Virtual Classroom Project Laboratory (Weston Hall 306) with a number of microcomputers and printers directly connected to EIES system facilitated the operation of our virtual lab tremendously. In fact, Heidi Harting, a system programmer who makes her office inside the laboratory, has told me many times that my students frequent the laboratory most regularly.

Comments on the Grades

While the lab work has a great impact on the acquisition of practical skills, the accomplishment was NOT reflected in the grades given to the two sections of students because 50% of the grade was based on the written exams taken from book materials that were covered in face-to-face sessions for both sections. The other 50% of the grade represented "efforts" in performing tasks in the simulated company. Therefore, I did not expect any differences in grades between two classes. I did not want to penalize the section without virtual lab for producing less written materials since the volume of output was constrained by the clumsiness of telephone communications among the students, manual typing, Xeroxing and distribution of various documents.

Comments on Group Learning

The very nature of virtual lab and its intrinsic objective is group learning. The most important accomplishment of group learning was the acquired skills in group communications and group decision making. I regard the frequency of revisions of conference comments as one indicator of the positive results of learning. I assume that the assignments submitted to the conference were modified to reflect some improvement through the examples of other people's work. I counted 31 such revisions which is a significant number.

Room for Improvement

Any such innovative experiment has room for improvement. In fact, some students made meaningful suggestions for improvement which are immediately implementable:

- Instead of one, two simulated companies could operate in competition with each other;
- Two competing companies should run their own conferences;
- Instructor should interfere when students waste too much time and efforts on some topics irrelevant to management practice, such as detailed design of product;
- Instructor should also simulate the environment and let the two companies react to environmental changes.

SECOND TIME AROUND OF VIRTUAL LAB
FOR OS 471 MANAGEMENT PRACTICE
Enrico Hsu

1. Description of the topics covered in the course

The topics and syllabus remained essentially the same as the first semester. However, the conduct of the course (I am speaking of two sections I taught) underwent a significant change, both in the conduct of face-to-face meetings and in the virtual lab portion of the course.

2. Changes in the conduct of face-to-face meetings

Students were divided into six study groups consisting of 5 to 6 students each. Groups were assigned a number of chapters of the text book, on a rotation basis, and were required to prepare the chapter outline to be posted in the EIES conference prior to verbal presentation in the class. Further coordination within the group as to who does what during the presentation is entirely up to the group. Groups have informal leaders responsible for internal coordination. As expected, the group which presents the material mastered the materials thoroughly. The rest of class is advised to read the materials in advance so that they can participate in discussion. Success in this area is limited. Without a strong incentive (10% of the final grade), students habitually defer reading of materials assigned to other groups until much later. Presentations were evaluated by the students in the audience. Instructor makes comments on the students' presentation, adds supplemental remarks on the course materials, elicits discussions relative to the subjects just presented. The basic ideas behind these changes were: to encourage students to read the text at least partially during the semester rather than at the very end, to make class presentation more varied, to encourage group learning, and to afford students the experience of running informal groups for a specific type of coordination.

3. Changes in simulated business operations

Instead of one organization (as in Fall 1986), two competing organizations were simulated. Approximately 40% of class time was devoted to running company or department meetings for the purpose of laying down some ground rules of communication, or making task assignments, knowing that the communication will continue through electronic media.

4. Changes in the use of EIES

Instead of one conference (Fall 1986), three conferences were set up:

- General conference for the whole class: A general conference is set up for all the class members with the instructor as the moderator. The instructor uses this conference to make announcements of general nature, e.g. course syllabus, class schedules, lab activity schedule, exam scope and schedule, grading policy, reading assignments, etc., and to conduct discussions/debates on many chosen subjects. Most recent examples are: formal vs.. informal organization, your preferred leadership styles. Students use this conference to enter the outlines of the course materials they are assigned to present, and to communicate with any or all members of the class on subjects of public interest.
- Two other conferences were set up for the two simulated companies with the respective presidents as the moderators. Students belonging to one conference have no access to the other conference. Students use these private conferences to conduct their simulated company business. Assignments or comments of a general nature are: resume and job application, negotiations for specific job assignment, job description of the acquired position, departmental budget preparation, functional specifications of an information system. Other comments pertain to their specific job assignments, such as sales forecasting, product design, product specification, product costing, marketing research, marketing plan, etc. When the companies are operated smoothly, the instructor introduces some environmental disturbances, such as market change, new

government regulations, foreign competition, etc. Then these two companies will learn to cope with the environmental disturbance and conduct business communications (meetings, conversations, memos, letters, announcements, etc.) in the conferences. Aside from their official capacities, colleagues in these simulated companies also develop informal relationships. In summary, these conferences are the forum to practice their interpersonal roles within different types of organizations (business organization and study groups).

5. Student Reaction to the Changes

Students' reactions to the newer way of conducting the course were extremely favorable. Below are some excerpts from their comments. (References are made to the actual comment No. of the general Conference 1732; students were told that these conference comments might be quoted in a report). They generally express enjoyment, approval, and intense interest in the online laboratory activities, though with some exceptions.

Eric : "Well, I just wanted to say that I enjoy it. I don't think the virtual classroom is the way of the future, but it is an experience worth having." (C1732CC69, 2/16/87)

Steve: "This is great. I enjoy this system. To fully appreciate this system you must have a hook-up from home. Sit back, put the radio on, have a beer and attend class. I'm sure glad this is the '80s." (C1732CC91, 2/23/87)

Paul: "This class is really cool and so far everything is going well as far as I am concerned."

Tana: " . . . since we are using EIES for virtual lab. This is definitely related to progress." (C1732CC240, 4/2/87)

Paul: "In this course we have really stopped beating the material from the books into our heads and started applying the knowledge that we have already obtained. Everything we learn now is put into effect almost immediately, not like those silly math formulas that just reside in the back of our memory banks." (C1732CC242, 4/2/87)

Evan: "We are learning about management in a practical way by doing. And in our class we are learning management as our companies grow."

Mark: "Tyron Edwards says, 'The great end of education is to discipline rather than to furnish the mind; to train it to use its powers, rather than fill it with the accumulation of others.' This is what I believe you have been saying to us all semester." (C1732CC249, 4/4/87)

Eric: " Dr. Enrico has particularly stressed one point this semester: There are no absolute answers to any questions of management. That is why we have the lab. In it, we can practice the principles involved in effective management . . . Not to memorize them, but to familiarize ourselves with them so that we might have some prior experience when we need to call on this knowledge in our futures . . . Another famous quote from Dr. Hsu: 'We are here to have fun!'" (C1732CC294, 4/6/87)

Grace: "Of course our class is not typical! I've told quite a few people about our 'virtual experiment'; I detected a spark of envy in the eyes of those people . . . exciting and "an ongoing, happening" class situation." (C1732CC357, 4/16/87)

Robert: "I think that our class is very interesting and innovative, it is the first virtual class that I have taken and I have enjoyed using the EIES system very much. It has made the course fun and easy, and I would recommend other people who are thinking of taking OS 471 to get involved in your EIES experiment. The EIES system has helped me develop better communication skills, not to mention first hand experience in management problems, through our company. I believe that you should continue using the virtual class because it's indeed a unique experience." (C1732CC360, 4/16/87)

Steven: "The EIES system has made this a very exciting class . . . I enjoy working with the computer and feel I have gained a valuable tool." (C1732CC361, 4/16/87)

Bill: "The nicest thing about this class is that there is an emphasis on learning and not so much on cramming in a bunch of facts you're going to forget anyway. Thank you, Prof. Hsu for running your class differently than the normal boring class I expected." (C1732CC387, 4/26/87)

Tana: "This class is a requirement and I can see why. I hope to be in a management position someday; not at the bottom. Now I understand the concepts and "skills" involved in being a good manager. By using EIES and setting up fictitious businesses, I put what we learned into practice. Now it's not just facts but skills. . . . Thanks, Enrico, for helping us learn what is important and not just a list of concepts that we were never given the opportunity to practice. This course would not have been the same without EIES. It would have been boring and I would have dreaded going to class. Instead, especially with the part of the class on EIES, I looked forward to doing the work. I spent most of my breaks in the virtual lab classroom working on the system." (C1732 CC394, 4/28/87)

Jorge: "Enrico, I can honestly say that I have learned much in your class through the use of the EIES system, I have worked on problems facing our company, communicated to people in our company through the use of EIES. . . . " (C1732 CC396, 4/28/87)

Eric: "I agree with you in respect to EIES and this course. It definitely made a major difference. It's an experience everyone should have." (C1732 CC399, 4/28/87)

Sharon: "I agree with most of my fellow classmates about this system EIES. It has made the class more interesting." (C1732CC420, 4/29/87).

Lance: "Throughout the semester I have noted that all the comments concerning the EIES system have been positive ... I have learned to appreciate EIES with the help of my classmates who have made it very interesting. . . . The class has been rewarding because of EIES, which has allowed everyone to express their ideas and opinions openly." (C1732 CC409, 4/30/87)

6. Motivation for Students to Do More Work

It is easy to conclude that students have spent considerably more time on this particular section of OS471 with Virtual Lab than the traditional sections, simply by counting the number of lines of comments students entered in the conferences. What motivated students to do so? I believe that the motivation is two-fold: genuine interest as expressed in the previous section, and a heavy percentage of the course grade assigned to the EIES work. In the beginning of the semester, it was announced that 50% of the grade would be assigned to the EIES related work. When I discovered that exams, quizzes and projects in other courses caused a decrease of activity in EIES work, I aannounced to the class that another 15% of the final grade was being transferred from the final exam to EIES work. Sure enough, EIES work became active again throughout the rest of semester. This is consistent with the general belief that "grade" is a prime motivator for most practically minded students.

7. Debate and Controversies Stimulate Communication

It was observed that debate and controversies will hold students' attention and stimulate them to make comments. Debate on "formal vs.. informal organization" was very popular with students, who not only express their opinions, but also cite their personal examples. Arguments about the usefulness of "sales persons" were pretty hot, because those students who had sales jobs couldn't stand insulting comments on sales persons.

8. How Would I Do It Differently in the Future?

The main objective of the experiment is to identify effective ways of training future managers in acquiring management skills. To achieve this end, attention is directed to making the learning more interesting (for example, two colleges running competing business organizations; incorporation of management games) and effortless; and to adopting a better system as a learning tool. A better system is defined as a system closer to business reality, by simulating the business roles in a realistic way. When roles of business executives are played out, the moves, plays, communications and behavior in general are monitored through virtual lab. Comments and guidance by experienced instructors will help future managers to distinguish essentials from trivia, and to evaluate consequences of alternative moves. The late Norman R. Maier, in the Preface of the book *The Role-Play Technique* (1975), states: "As with any skill, book learning and demonstrations are needed, but they never will replace practice. The best kind of practice is performing under competent supervision. The greatest need in all training programs that involve the ability to relate to other people is the opportunity to practice without being hurt or without hurting anyone else."

ANTHROPOLOGY WITH "EIES": AN EXPERIMENT WITH USING ONLINE UNITS
Kendy MacColl Rudy, Ph.D
Upsala College

For the past several years Upsala College has been one of the colleges working with the EIES network and experimenting with various forms of online teaching. In the fall semester of 1986 three unit assignments within the junior-level course Anthropology 350 Indians of North America were presented to the class using the EIES network.

I have used EIES both personally and professionally for the past six years. In addition, I have used computer-assisted instruction software and computer simulations of social change in other classes from time to time. This was the first time I have served as moderator of a conference, and the first time I had a chance to incorporate the class assignments into networking.

All in all, the experience was positive. At times it was a rocky ride; unanticipated difficulties arose in training and developing appropriate assignments, students reacted differently to the assignments, and the class ultimately divided on using the computer. I am teaching the same course this semester without EIES assignments; I find that something has been lost in communication with and between students. Given a choice, I'd keep the EIES assignments permanently.

TRAINING STUDENTS [AND TEACHER]

Seventeen students enrolled in the Indians course; since this is classed as a Writing Intensive Course, the cap is set at 20. Students were informed in the initial class meeting of the nature of the EIES assignments, which were also indicated prominently on the syllabus for the course. A class meeting to train students to use EIES was scheduled for the second week of class. Each student was given an account and a folder containing basic instructions about EIES. Bob Meinke had written a simple, one-page instruction sheet for the first training session; with suitable modifications [such as identifying me as the instructor and giving the correct conference number] I used Bob 's format as a training guide.

The training session was scheduled during a regular class period. We met in the usual classroom and went as a group to the Microcomputer Laboratory. Somehow, on the way, three students decided to evaporate [more on these later]. By the time the students got to the Lab, accounts were ready for them and "codes" had been established in the system for them. I had already written a "welcome" message into the conference so that when a student learned to enter the conference there was a message waiting. Two NJIT project assistants and Roxanne Hiltz introduced the students to the system, starting with the directory. The assignments for the introduction to the system were: to establish directory information for yourself; to send a message to someone else in the class; to send a message to me; and to enter the conference. Students were given 1 week to complete the assignment.

Students were asked to work in pairs, one at the keyboard and one with the instruction sheet. Student reaction was mixed. Some students plodded through the instructions, did a minimum job on the communications, and left. Several students got stuck and had a mental block about touching the keyboard and had to be led through the processes step by step. Two students whizzed through the instruction and began to send messages to anyone they could find; one of them immediately found the public conference list and is hooked for life. One student became so upset that he could not continue to try to work with the system and was cajoled into making a private appointment with me for personal instruction. (He later became a system addict.)

The initial training session helped about 11 of the 17 students. Later individual meetings were necessary to work with the last 6, either because they skipped the training session or because they needed personal attention and coaching in order to get over their gut reaction to using the system. From talking to the other instructors I don't think this is an unusual percentage; time needs to be budgeted at the beginning to deal with fear and confusion.

THE EIES ASSIGNMENTS

1. Bibliography, communication, and facts: the arctic and subarctic The first unit of the Indians course is a brief survey of white–Indian contact, a discussion of the archaeological evidence for the entrance of Homo sapiens into the New World, and case studies in cultures of the arctic, subarctic and northwest coast. Throughout the unit the policies of Canada and the United States towards native peoples–Eskimo, Indian, Aleut and Metis–are presented. The class assignment was to create a bibliography about the modern situation of native peoples of the arctic and subarctic.[1] For the first task, each student chose a geographic area or specific people; they then went to the library and located as current an article as possible about "their" people. Initially, all they had to do was list the reference.

The second task was to help other students when, in the course of looking for "your" article, an article appropriate for another student was found. Students were asked to send messages to each other under these circumstances. Three such messages were sent.

The third task was to explain the situation reflected in the article to the class, in no more than two paragraphs. I was looking for informal writing styles, with each student somewhat knowledgeable about "their" problem. What I got was a foretaste of things to come. Three students, whom I shall call Rapid Rachel, Responsible Rene, and Dutiful Doris entered their material and asked each other questions. Constant Complaint Charles, Enthusiastic Edgar and Modify Morris [who is never satisfied with his own answers and modifies them over and over and over] followed. Then there was a gap; I reminded the class that the assignment was part of their grade, and got two more answers. Several students did not enter their responses by the date specified and received a "0".

After the deadline for EIES comments we held an in-class debate on the nature of today's problems in the arctic and subarctic, an assignment I

---

[1]None of the writing or bibliography assignments for the course, whether online or in class, could have been so smoothly accomplished without the cooperation of the reference staff of the Upsala library. I gave them a copy of the assignments for the course at the beginning of the semester; their tactful help to the students reduced the library time and gave more time for the online work for the students.

have used before. This class was much better informed than previous classes, and was more comfortable challenging each other's data. I kept a tally of who was active in the debate. Those who had done the EIES assignment talked; those who had not sat quietly. The one exception was a student who works full-time as a night nurse and attends school full time in the day; she was obviously informed, but told me privately that the only time she could get to the microcomputer lab to enter her comments was identical to the only time she could sleep and she was just too tired to come to the college just for computer access. I arranged for her to have access to a dumb terminal in a departmental office (later when the Upsala library EIES access was established she used those terminals) and she became one of the more reliable participants.

2. Cooperative learning; study questions on line

The second EIES assignment was related to preparing to take the second unit test. In each class I teach, one week before the test I distribute a set of questions about the material covered in the readings, lectures, class discussions and films. These questions reflect the major points from the unit and form the basis for the unit exams. Usually there are between 25 and 40 questions for a unit, ranging from definitions to know to asking students to draw a conclusion from some material and defend it. The study questions are harder than the test, because the test is limited to an hour or so and consists of a subset of the questions. In many classes students form study groups, divide up the questions, and study together. In this second assignment I wanted to see if the study group concept could be used online. Instead of printing out the study questions and distributing them to the class one week before the test, I entered the questions as messages in the conference at the beginning of the unit; each student got four questions.[2] [I did give a full set of questions to the blind student in the class.] In both the conference comment and in class I asked the students to prepare responses to their four questions as we came to the appropriate material in the unit, and to put the answers in the conference. Other students could then [in theory] comment back. I checked into the conference regularly during the unit, and noted that very few answers were entered until the exam date became imminent.

Since so few students had taken the time to enter their conference questions by one week before the test date I announced in class that those whose questions were not answered by 3:30 PM the day before the test

---

[2]The brighter students of course figured out that if they printed the conference they got a complete set of the questions, if not the complete set of answers.

would be counted as not having done the assignment. There was a burst of activity. I had been concerned, however, because during this second unit of the class three students completely stopped attending, didn't sign on to EIES, and did not respond to personal letters sent to their boxes.[3] Since sections of the study sheet had been assigned to them, it was clear that some parts of the course should not, in fairness, be on the test.

The night before the test, at 9:30, I received an angry group phone call from Rapid Rachel, Dutiful Doris , Constant Complaint Charles and Modify Morris. They were livid. A student "Rip-off Richard" [the one who had piggy-backed on the first assignment], had not put any answers into the conference. Just before the microlab closed, he and two other nonresponders from the class came to the microlab and printed out copies of everyone else's answers. When challenged, he said he didn't have time to study his questions and only wanted to prepare for the exam. Rachel, Doris, Charles, and Morris felt cheated and used; they demanded retribution, or at any rate, the removal of any questions assigned to Richard and his friends from the test because they had relied on a fellow student to prepare and had been let down, and now had to do "other peoples questions overnight." (I did modify the exam to the extent of giving people a choice of question to answer.) When I got to the class the next day the entire seating arrangement had been changed. No one was sitting anywhere near Richard and his two friends. There was a general growling in their direction before the test. In fact, the seating arrangements never reverted to the original pattern after this.

From a teacher's perspective there had been an unexpected consequence of the assignment. In work and in "real life", when a group works together and someone doesn't do their assignment, the group report suffers and the group as a whole is criticized. In most academic assignments, which are based on individual study and preparation, when members of a class do not prepare the only one irritated is the instructor. For the first time, the students in the Indians course saw the cost to a group; they didn't like it. One of the students commented to me that since we were studying social control among small scale societies and had determined that ostracism is one way of dealing with those who violate the norms, they had decided to apply an Indian remedy to Rip-off Richard.

I had given the class the opportunity to vote on whether they wanted the third study sheet online; not surprisingly, they said no. However, Rachel, Doris, Charles, and Morris came to me after class and asked if there was any way they could have a "closed" conference for just them to work on the study sheet; I told them that the only way would be through

---

[3]It later transpired that one had dropped the course, one was hospitalized, and one was just avoiding the possibility of work.

private messages sent to themselves as a set. In the end, they reverted to a pencil-and-conversation study group.

3. The Hopi–Navajo land dispute; a successful debate

The last online assignment concerned one of the most distressing problems between modern Indian tribes, a dispute between the Hopi and Navajo tribes over the "joint use area"; there are no villains, just a situation in which everyone loses somehow. The class had studied both traditional and modern Hopi and Navajo. Some class material about the Land Dispute was distributed, and students were asked to go to the library and read as much as they could find about the situation. They were then to put the references they found into the conference, and were to take a position about the questions raised. They could take the Hopi side, the Navajo side, represent the interests of Peabody Coal Company, or address a legal question, but they had to justify their position in the online comment. At this point in the semester most of the nonparticipants had dropped from the class by one route or another; even Rip-off Richard entered a position on this question.

The similarity between this assignment and the first assignment is clear. Students did a much better job on this assignment than in the first one. The in-class debate went extraordinarily well. On the basis of their conference comments, students identified those who had developed a similar position and were given part of a class period to caucus and come up with major points. Since it turned out that there were four positions [Hopi, Navajo, Federal responsibility, and a "plague on both your houses"] the classroom was rearranged in a square, and the debate began. I wish I had recorded it; students referred to each others conference comments ("How can you say that when you are contradicting what you wrote?), challenged the articles ("But that article was in local newspaper and MINE is in a professional journal") and were able to present a lot of data in a short time. We ran well over the class schedule into lunch and no-one noticed.

WOULD I DO IT AGAIN?

Yes.

The parts that worked well were repeating similar assignments so students got used to particular types of work on the network. I need to give some more thought to cooperative assignments; this has been discussed at some length in our project meetings, and is something I am still working on. Parts of the experience that still need work are improving access to computers, since none of the students own terminals, and improving the response time of the software.

One interesting result of this semester was to note that students are like themselves, only more so, when on line. The chatty ones write long responses, the worriers modify their messages, the dutiful ones do what is required reliably but without brilliance, and the irresponsible are conspicuous by their absence.

A second observation of online teaching is that any flaw in the normal class situation gets magnified. The students who skip classes and don't do work on time skipped EIES instruction sessions and were late or never in submitting responses. Where an assignment needed more thought on the part of an instructor it shows in the student struggles. In the case of the Indians course, both the students and the instructor had to face both the positive and negative group dynamics even more clearly than a solely face-to-face class.

PEER WRITING GROUPS IN THE VIRTUAL CLASSROOM
Mary Swigonski, Ph.D.
Upsala College

The following is a set of reflections on my experience with the use of EIES as one component in a freshman writing seminar centered around the topic of friendship. My initial response to the possibility of including the use of EIES as an element within this course was one of nearly unbounded enthusiasm. Over the previous several years I had developed soothing of an addiction to the use of computers for word processing. The opportunity to share with students that discovery and the enhancements it can provide to one's writing seemed too good to pass up! Even more wonderfully, the possibilities that EIES held for peer review and collaborative writing seemed truly delightful. This was to be an opportunity designed in heaven!

To give you a sense of how this undertaking evolved, I have included the course description and objectives as they were presented to the students who enrolled in the course. These are followed by a few comments about some of the objectives and the focal topics that provided the developmental trajectory of the course. Then I have highlighted some of the writing assignments, discussing how the use of EIES was incorporated into these projects. And, finally I have included some comments along the theme of "if I had to do it over . . . "

COURSE DESCRIPTION:

Friendship plays an important role in each of our lives, as a source of laughter and tears, of inspiration and frustration, of love and loneliness. Poetry, short stories, essays, social science theory and research, and children's fiction will be explored to discover some of the fantasies, feelings and facts that other authors have sought to convey about friendship. Examination of these works will provide a beginning point for our own writing in this area.

This semester an experimental component is included within this course. In addition to traditional teaching/learning methods, interactive computerized conferencing will be incorporated into class activities. Students will be expected to use this computer system and its word processing capability in the writing of their assignments and to supplement classroom activity.

OBJECTIVES:

This is primarily a writing course. You will be expected to write regularly and to write often. My hope for each of us is that by the end of the semester we will grow to appreciate more deeply the beauty and power of our language; that we will learn to play more skillfully with words and ideas. Adrienne Rich, a poet, suggests that the adept use of language is one of the most powerful tools available to human beings. She says that writing is a process of "Re-vision" through which we can change our lives and the world in which we live!

Through active participation in this course, you will increase your knowledge and/or skill in the following areas:

- the meaning of friendship, and select concepts associated with it;
- the use of resources housed in the Upsala library;
- precision in critically reading and analyzing ideas, one's own and those of other authors;
- the effective communication of your thoughts and ideas through written presentation;
- the ability to work collegially, within a small group context, to develop, organize and prepare thoughts and ideas for presentation to a larger audience;
- the use of computers as a tool for preparing and disseminating ideas.

These objectives can be organized in three layers. The primary level focuses on developing the students skill in writing in general and in writing about friendship in particular. In order to do that the secondary layer of objectives comes into being, that the students also develop greater skill in critical thinking, and that they learn to work collaboratively. For this experimental version of the course a third layer of objectives was introduced, that the students develop skill in the use of word processing and of an interactive computer system.

The course was organized around the following topics:

– Introduction and Overview
– What is Friendship
– Friendship and Self Perceptions
– Friendship and Gender Differences
– Emotions, Ethics, and Friends
– Marriage, Divorce, and Friendship
– Beyond Friendship (how and why friendships end)

I intended that the class would use EIES to facilitate both word processing and collaborative learning. To accomplish that the class was divided into three "working groups" with six or seven students in each group. These groups were each given a conference space, and all assignments were to be written there. Each assignment was to be "peer reviewed" by all others in the conference, with the comments typed into that area. The entire class also had a conference in which discussions on friendship-related issues were to occur.

TRAINING:

During the first class meeting, the experimental component of the course (the intended use of computers), was explained to the students, and they were given an opportunity to transfer into another section if they so desired (no one did). Once the fundamentals of the course were laid out, an in-class discussion was held about the EIES system, introducing messages, conferences, and the role they would play in our class. The students were provided with the EIES manual, and an EIES survival sheet, and were then taken to the college microcomputer lab, for a hands on demonstration of the EIES system. Working in pairs, all students were shown how to "sign on" to the system, how to input information into their directory and how to send a message. In a subsequent demonstration they were shown how to use the conference area, and were introduced to basic text editing commands.

ASSIGNMENTS:

The students first assignment was to write a brief description of themselves in their directory, and to send a brief message to their instructor. This proved more harrowing then it sounds, and was only accomplished by some after much effort on the part of the students, and significant handholding by the computer room assistants! Once this was accomplished, subsequent assignments were of two general characters. One set was longer writing assignments to be included in the work conferences. These were to be peer reviewed by the other students in that conference, and then revised by the original author to incorporate the suggestions of their colleagues. The second set of assignments was shorter discussion questions that were included in the larger class conference. Each student was to check into the class conference on a weekly basis and contribute to the discussions in progress there.

One example of the type of assignment, and the peer review questions applied to it, is shown below. This topic followed the conclusion of the section on friendship and gender differences.

In your "work" conference, write about 50 lines (more or less) on the following topic: Men and women form different types of friendships. a) explain what some of these differences are; b) and what some of the causes of these differences might be; then c) suggest some things that might improve the quality of friendships for both men and women.

PEER REVIEW QUESTIONS

In order to complete their peer review, students were expected to complete the following questions about each others drafts.
1) Does the essay fulfill the assignment?
2) Write a sentence or two that summarizes the main point of the essay.
3) Note any weak spots in the organization.
4) Give a suggestion to improve the introduction.
5) Give a suggestion to improve the conclusion.
6) Are there any paragraphs that need particular improvement?
7) Can you offer any suggestions to improve vocabulary or grammar?

Discussion writing assignments posed in the full class conference included the following topics:
- What is friendship?
- Why do friendships occur? Why do we need friends?
- Why do people become friends?
- What does friendship mean to you? How do you think attitudes toward friendship change with age?
- "We learn much about ourselves in our relationships with friends, learning that comes partly from who they are, how they respond to us, what we see reflected in their eyes. Friends become for us a mirror on the self ... " What have you learned about yourself through your friends?

- How have your friends helped you to learn who you are, or who you can be?
- Are your friends similar to you or different from you?
- Do you have different types of friends — people whom you like, but who may not especially like each other?
- Describe your ideal spouse.
- Can friends introduce sexuality into their relationship and still remain friends? (This was everyone's favorite discussion topic!)

FUTURE SUGGESTIONS:

Several problems are now apparent with this plan. The work conferences, with six or seven students in each conference, were too large and unwieldy. It is now apparent to me that peer review works most effectively with groups of three (or at most four) students. When the group size expands beyond four, the simple volume of work required of the students (to read and comment on five or more papers, and then to read the comments of five students on their own paper) becomes excessively cumbersome.

Student procrastination is also a significant issue that is magnified with the size of the group. Students cannot comment on papers that have not yet been written, and they similarly cannot incorporate peer comments that do not exist! In face-to-face situations eye-to-eye contact is a wonderful motivator, inducing both guilt and action. Electronic connections (or disconnections) enabled students in work groups to simply avoid each other and the guilt until the last possible moment, which was often too late for meaningful peer contributions to be made.

Large groups size also exacerbated other peer review issues, particularly the politeness syndrome: if I'm nice to everybody, then they will be nice to me; if I say something critical, then they won't like me; if I say something critical, then they will criticize me! In order for collaborative learning to be effective, future implementations of this sort of project will need to intentionally overcome the politeness syndrome early on in the semester.

Also, students use of EIES seemed to be impeded by their unfamiliarity with typing in general and editing commands in particular. Future projects might profit from the incorporation of assignments that specifically attend to the development of this knowledge and skill so that the technology is experienced by the students as enabling and not a disability. In particular, students need to be encouraged to spend more time online so that they can overcome the initial frustration of mastering a novel experience. One way that this might be accomplished is to begin with a series of very short writing assignments and gradually increase the length as students develop facility with the technology.

VIRTUAL CLASSROOM REPORT
"STATISTICS FOR TECHNOLOGY" ON EIES
AN OVERVIEW FOR TWO SEMESTERS
INSTRUCTOR: ROSE ANN DIOS

In this report I will discuss the experience of teaching a technically oriented statistics course on EIES. I had received a year's training in preparation for this project, since I had not been familiar with computerized conferencing prior to Fall 1985. It was in the fall of 1985 that I had the opportunity to engage in the exchange of messages, participate in public and private conferences, and observe the delivery of a course on the subject of artificial intelligence given electronically at the New School in New York. I experienced the excitement and intellectual stimulation of witnessing clever, philosophical debates on the issues surrounding the question of existence of life and the attempt to understand boundaries of life and death. It was truly a learning experience for me and I felt challenged to attempt the delivery of a course on a subject whose traditional mode of presentation was completely at the opposite end of the spectrum: a heavily mathematical course treating essential topics in probability and statistics, and the applications of these theories to technological problems.

It had always seemed to me that a critical component of this course should be the treatment of the philosophical foundations of probability and statistics, as well as a discussion of the relevance of these theories to current decision making, particularly on highly controversial issues (such as nuclear power, strategic defense, etc.). And so I embarked upon the course by devoting the first week to an historical and philosophical discussion of the theories of probability and statistics with an emphasis on applications to decision theory and risk analysis. The students were surprised—some pleasantly, others not. They had expected the course to deal solely with the mathematical treatment of these concepts. More surprises were forthcoming since one of my goals was to make the course an exciting learning experience.

Initial training on EIES for the students

In the fall semester, the course was scheduled to meet on Monday night from 6:15 to 9:20 PM. The first class night was entirely devoted to acquainting the students with EIES and trying to communicate as much information as possible on the different features of the system without overwhelming them. Students were provided with a manual and other helpful documents and were asked to log on. Once on the system, they received some private and group messages extending welcome, and were asked to practice sending messages to each other and the instructor. They were then led to the course conference and there they found awaiting them an eighteen page discussion of the philosophy of probability and statistics culminating in an assignment that included three opinion-oriented questions. Realizing that it would have been better to allow a week without course material for practising the use of the system, this material was presented during the second week during the spring semester course.

Teaching assistants and other project personnel were available during this training session of three hours but students still felt uncomfortable with the system and requested additional training time. A second training session was scheduled for the following week, which was particularly useful to those students who registered late for the course and had missed the first class meeting. After the second training the consensus was positive and students felt further encouraged by knowing that teaching assistants would staff the Virtual Classroom laboratory during regular hours and would be available for both help with the system tutorial assistance with the course content during designated times. In addition, the instructor held regular office hours during this week and would visit the laboratory on Monday evenings.

Course assignments, quizzes, tests, exams

It was announced to the students that lecture material would be entered into the course conference weekly (or biweekly depending upon student feedback, and performance on homework assignments, quizzes and tests), with the exception of midterm exam week during which an online test would be administered. They were expected to sign on at least weekly in order to receive the lecture, submit homework and take quizzes and tests as scheduled. The course required the submission of twelve homework assignments as well as the completion of eight online quizzes in the form of individual response branches, and four online tests using the + quiz feature.

Homework assignments were due sometime between seven and fourteen days after they were announced and the students were asked to enter their solutions to the given problem as a conference comment, thus sharing them with the rest of the class. Each student received a different homework problem or set of problems with the goal of maximizing the diversity of examples and simultaneously encouraging individual work. But some students were very upset because they felt that the problems they had received were far more difficult than those of their peers, and realistically it was impossible to maintain the same level of difficulty throughout the entire problem set. Moreover, from a pedagogical perspective, a variety of difficulty is preferred. This issue was remedied by the use of response branches allowing for the entire class to answer a given question prior to viewing the solutions presented by others. These questions were classified as quizzes but possessed the same point value as the homework assignments. The 12 homework assignments and 8 quizzes constituted 25% of the course grade.

Fifty percent of the grade was determined by performance on the four tests given electronically. Students were asked to sign on for the test sometime over a designated 2-week period and they were given 60 minutes to complete the test. When the related software was being developed some problems arose with the taking of online tests. Students were cut off from EIES because they sometimes did not enter any material onto the system for over 20 minutes (the standard time-out value) during which time they were solving the test problem on paper. Also, since the system was designed to prevent signing on to the test a second time, students had no recourse but to contact the instructor and submit their test on paper through interoffice mail. The online test software was then changed to eliminate these problems. Many students, however, had been struggling with other problems related to the use of EIES and then fell into the pattern of submitting all work through either interoffice or external mail. The instructor accepted all work submitted in this fashion because it also became necessary to mail out some of the lectures that were heavily dependent upon diagrams and complex formulas including symbols not available on screen. The Personal TEIES software that would facilitate the delivery of such lectures electronically was still in the process of development.

Fall Semester: Some Problems and Some Benefits

Some of the other problems experienced by students were related to the initial due date of assignments. Since the course was originally scheduled to meet on Monday evenings, initially assignments, quizzes, and tests were due by Monday midnight. Although students were allowed to submit their work anytime during the week, they regularly came to the Virtual Classroom laboratory on Monday evenings with the intention of entering their work and receiving the material and assignment for the following week. Since user density is so high on Mondays, the response time of the overloaded system was very frustrating to those students experiencing a time pressure, especially if they were using the branch software, which is slow even when the EIES system is under moderate use. I addressed this problem by changing the due date of assignments from Monday to

Wednesday, but many of the students continued to come on Mondays because they had classes (or other unalterable commitments) on the other evenings of the week. Most of the class held full-time jobs during the day. The instructor continued to visit the Virtual Classroom laboratory on Mondays to offer assistance since this time was most suitable to the majority of the class. Students would frequently submit their work in person at the laboratory.

Another problem that became evident was that of inappropriate exchange of information on quizzes and tests. The instructor was able to identify those students who had indeed mastered the material by their performance on the face-to-face final examination. It was very clear that one of the students who had received high scores on the online tests did not understand certain critical concepts of the material. The final examination, which constituted the final 25% of the course grade, had the effect of appropriately adjusting the final grade.

Messages were sometimes sent by students requesting information or assistance with material to the instructor, but most often the request was for a face-to-face appointment and/or telephone conversation, and arranging a time to meet in the laboratory. Students would meet with each other in the laboratory and exchange solutions to difficult problems and other important information and would often schedule the meeting time through the exchange of private messages. A strong sense of comraderie was present at these meetings, and the instructor and students agreed that the course mode of delivery was in many ways responsible for the sense of teamwork present.

There are two special cases that warrant mentioning since they really capture some of the benefits of the Virtual Classroom. First, a student who registered for the course in the fourth week of the semester because of a preceding hospitalization was able to make up all of the lost time in two weeks because he had complete access to all of the lecture material and homework assignments. This student received the highest grade in the class for the final examination! Secondly, another student became a parent for the first time in the middle of the semester. Because of complications, he missed five weeks of the course but was also able to, upon his return, make up lost work and quizzes to complete the course with a grade of "B". Both of these students felt that their success was possible because of the unique mode of delivery.

A Comparison of the Control and Experimental Groups

Both classes did very well on the final exam and many students received an "A" or "B" for the final grade. But the online students communicated the feeling that the course had been more valuable to them when discussing it with the instructor.

What kinds of material are learned particularly well or relatively poorly in the Virtual Classroom? Some insight into this question may be gained by a detailed comparison of scores on quizzes that tested different kinds of knowledge or skills. Four examples are presented below.

Test and Quiz Problem 1: 'Descriptive Statistics'

Testing for: speed; memory; concepts of central tendency and dispersion and their attributes.

Skills: Integration and data trends; ability to unify and compactify

	FTF	VC
Mean Scores:	82%	91%
	(21 students)	(9 students)

Test and Quiz Problem 2: 'Hypergeometric Distribution'

Testing for: categorization; concepts of 'universe and subset identification';

Skills: Creation of new universe in each segment of experimental process; diversity in dealing with alternative assumptions.

	FTF	VC
Mean Scores:	78%	84%

Test and Quiz Problem 3: 'Binomial Distribution'

Testing for: Recognition of homogeneity in sequential experiments; identification of appropriate assumptions; uniformity of definitions and constraints.

Skills: Using characteristics of 'consistency' in repetitive and sequential experimentation; recognition of constrained environments and working within necessary constraints; dealing with restrictive experiments and their mathematical models.

	FTF	VC
Mean Scores:	94%	100%

Test and Quiz Problem 4: 'Derivation of a Theoretical Probability Distribution'

Testing for: ability to generalize about probability functions using classical theory and algebra of sets.

Skills: quantification of a qualitative process; creation of mathematical model via abstract elements (equations, variables); identification of mathematical relationships; ability to fuse abstract processes and inject a creative unity for a variety of experimental frameworks.

	FTF	VC
Mean Scores:	76%	72%

It was noted that on the first 3 problems that focused upon DATA ANALYSIS AND SAMPLING METHODS (WITH & WITHOUT REPLACEMENT) and dependent upon the ability to IDENTIFY DATA TRENDS, CATEGORIZE DATA VARIABLES, & UNDERSTAND SEQUENTIAL EXPERIMENTATION, THE VC STUDENTS PERFORMED BETTER THAN FTF (no significant difference but always with VC scoring higher).

On the 4th problem which required the students to IDENTIFY AND CREATE APPROPRIATE PROBABILITY FUNCTIONS dependent upon the ability to FUSE ABSTRACT PROCESSES AND INJECT CREATIVE APPROACH TO THE GIVEN EXPERIMENTAL FRAMEWORK, the FTF STUDENTS PERFORMED BETTER THAN VC (but with no significant differences).

When the instructor checked for INCORRECT PROBLEM SOLUTION DUE TO COMPUTATIONAL ERRORS (i.e., solutions to problems that were correct except for a single error in addition, subtraction, etc.) on the Math 305 tests/quizzes, it resulted that

12% of FTF class had computational errors.

4% of VC class had computational errors.

The VC students had significantly less computational errors than FTF. This may be due to rechecking their work as they type solutions into EIES from paper.

Students seem to perform best in the VC mode when dealing with laboratory–type problems and have more trouble with theoretical subjects and topics.

The 4th problem in Math 305 (in which students scored lower in VC mode) was on material sent to the students through the mail because the graphics package was still under development. Most of the theoretical material dealing with multiple diagrams and complex equations was mailed to the students . . . and they seemed to have some trouble with the abstract concepts connected to it.

The Spring Semester Online Class

There was a great boost in enrollment for the spring-term online class: 27 students registered for the course and 25 completed the course, with a large number of A's and B's given as the final grades. The course ran very smoothly in the spring since most of the major problems had been identified and remedied during the fall semester. We were able to implement some additional software into the course process: the use of *selection* branches; and the use of the graphics package, Personal TEIES.

Selection branches allowed students to choose their own homework problems with the condition that those who signed on first had the greater choice option. Students felt that this was very beneficial because it once again allowed for a greater variety in the review of homework problems. It also made the assignment of final course projects more efficient and allowed students to choose those projects (or questions) most relevant to their unique undergraduate course of study.

The Personal TEIES package allowed the instructor to create some basic diagrams and equations for the lecture material. The primary setback was that most students had to use Personal TEIES in the laboratory since their home machines often lacked the necessary memory size to employ the package.

Conclusions

There is no question that the electronic delivery of a mathematical course is a challenging experience to both the instructor and the students. But it is a goal well worth achieving. Both the instructor and many of the students in the project felt that the pluses outweighed the minuses. Many students felt a strong sense of accomplishment for their mastery of the skills of computerized conferencing and statistics.

APPENDIX IV

ACTIVE MEMBERS OF THE ADVISORY BOARD FOR THE VIRTUAL CLASSROOM PROJECT

[The notation *E indicates service on the evaluation panel]

Martin Elton, Professor of Communication [*E], The Interactive Telecommunications Project, New York University

Nicholas Johnson, former FCC Commissioner; Professor, University of Iowa

Charles Kadushin, Professor of Sociology [*E], The Graduate School and University Center, City University of New York

Paul Levinson, Professor of Communication, Farleigh Dickinson University; and Director, Connected Education, Inc.

Bert Moldow, Staff Consultant, IBM Systems Research Institute

Ronald Rice, Associate Professor of Communications [*E], Rutgers University

Ben Shneiderman, Professor of Computer Science, University of Maryland, College Park

Fred Weingarten [*E], Program Manager, Communication and Information Technologies Program, Office of Technology Assessment, U.S. Congress.

EX OFFICIO

Arnold Allentuch, Associate Vice President for Research, NJIT

Steve Ehrmann [*E], Program Manager, The Annenberg/CPB Program

Starr Roxanne Hiltz, Project Director, Professor of Computer and Information Science, New Jersey Institute of Technology

H. Edwin Titus, Vice President for Academic Affairs, Upsala College

375

AUTHOR INDEX

SUBJECT INDEX